… it is impossible, within patriarchy, to suppress a market economy. And it is impossible, in a market system, to not devastate the planet. It is up to women, now, to reclaim the voice of humanity ….

— (d'Eaubonne ([1990] 1997, p. 4)

Corporate Social Responsibility and Environmental Affairs in the British Press

An ecofeminist criticism of neoliberalism, this book uses economic growth, CSR and the press coverage of environmental affairs as a case study. The author argues that CSR is part of a wheel of neoliberalism that continually perpetuates inequality and the exploitation of women and Nature. Using an ecofeminist sense-making analysis of media coverage of food waste, global warming, plastic, economic growth and CSR, the author shows how the press discourse in writing is always similar and serves to preserve the status quo with CSR being just a smokescreen that saved capitalism and just one cog in the wheel of neoliberalism. While available research offers perspectives from business and public relations studies, looking at how CSR is implemented and how it contributes towards the reputation of businesses, this book explores how the media enforce CSR discourse while at the same time arguing for environmental preservation.

The book presents a combination of quantitative and qualitative methods to explain how and why CSR is being pushed forward by the news media, and how the media preserves the status quo by creating moral panic on environmental issues while at the same time pushing for CSR discourse and economic growth, which only contributes towards environmental degradation. The original research presented in the book looks at how the media write about economic growth, plastics, food waste, CSR and global warming. This interdisciplinary study draws on ecofeminist theory and media feminist theory to provide a novel analysis of CSR, making the case that enforcing CSR as a way to do business damages the environment and that the media enforce a neoliberal discourse of promoting both economic growth and environmentalism, which does not go together.

Examining the UK media as a case study, a detailed methodological account is provided so that the study can be repeated and compared elsewhere. The book is aimed at academics and researchers in business and media studies, as well as those in women's studies. It will also be relevant to scholars in business management and marketing.

Martina Topić is a Reader at Leeds Business School, Leeds Beckett University, UK. She is an editor of the 'Culture, Media and Film' section of the *Cogent Arts and Humanities* Open Access journal (Taylor and Francis), editor-in-chief of *Corporate Communications: An International Journal* and editor-in-chief of the book series *Women, Economy and the Labour Relations*.

Routledge New Directions in PR & Communication Research
Edited by Kevin Moloney

Current academic thinking about public relations (PR) and related communication is a lively, expanding marketplace of ideas and many scholars believe that it's time for its radical approach to be deepened. Routledge New Directions in PR & Communication Research is the forum of choice for this new thinking. Its key strength is its remit, publishing critical and challenging responses to continuities and fractures in contemporary PR thinking and practice, tracking its spread into new geographies and political economies. It questions its contested role in market-orientated, capitalist, liberal democracies around the world, and examines its invasion of all media spaces, old, new, and as yet unenvisaged.

The New Directions series has already published and commissioned diverse original work on topics such as:

- PR's influence on Israeli and Palestinian nation-building
- PR's origins in the history of ideas
- a Jungian approach to PR ethics and professionalism
- global perspectives on PR professional practice
- PR as an everyday language for everyone
- PR as emotional labor
- PR as communication in conflicted societies, and
- PR's relationships to cooperation, justice, and paradox.

We actively invite new contributions and offer academics a welcoming place for the publication of their analyses of a universal, persuasive mindset that lives comfortably in old and new media around the world.

Corporate Social Responsibility and Environmental Affairs in the British Press
An Ecofeminist Critique of Neoliberalism
Martina Topić

For more information about this series, please visit: www.routledge.com/ Routledge-New-Directions-in-PR–Communication-Research/book-series/ RNDPRCR

Corporate Social Responsibility and Environmental Affairs in the British Press

An Ecofeminist Critique of Neoliberalism

Martina Topić

LONDON AND NEW YORK

First published 2022
by Routledge
2 Park Square, Milton Park, Abingdon, Oxon OX14 4RN

and by Routledge
605 Third Avenue, New York, NY 10158

Routledge is an imprint of the Taylor & Francis Group, an informa business

© 2022 Martina Topić

The right of Martina Topić to be identified as author of this work
has been asserted by her in accordance with sections 77 and 78 of
the Copyright, Designs and Patents Act 1988.

All rights reserved. No part of this book may be reprinted or
reproduced or utilised in any form or by any electronic, mechanical,
or other means, now known or hereafter invented, including
photocopying and recording, or in any information storage or
retrieval system, without permission in writing from the publishers.

Trademark notice: Product or corporate names may be trademarks
or registered trademarks, and are used only for identification and
explanation without intent to infringe.

British Library Cataloguing-in-Publication Data
A catalogue record for this book is available from the British Library

Library of Congress Cataloging-in-Publication Data
A catalog record has been requested for this book

ISBN: 978-0-367-55011-0 (hbk)
ISBN: 978-0-367-55020-2 (pbk)
ISBN: 978-1-003-09159-2 (ebk)

DOI: 10.4324/9781003091592

Typeset in Times New Roman
by codeMantra

Contents

List of illustrations		ix
About the author		xi
Acknowledgements		xiii

1 Introduction and personal reflection   1

2 Ecofeminism: theory, issues and advocacy   17
Ecofeminism as an anti-capitalist movement 20
*Ecofeminism and the relationship with nature, science
  and technology 32*
Ecofeminism, hierarchy and masculinities 37
*Ecofeminism vs deep ecology debate and the criticism
  of ecofeminism 44*
The approach of the book 48

**3 Corporate social responsibility: an ecofeminist reading
of the concept**   53
CSR literature: definitions, ambiguities and saving capitalism 60
Shareholder vs stakeholder orientation to CSR 66
CSR and the media 80
CSR and women 91

4 The press coverage of economic growth and CSR   99
Economic growth 99
The coverage of economic growth 105
The coverage of CSR 116

viii *Contents*

**5 The press coverage of environmental affairs: global warming,
plastic and the food waste** 122
Global warming 122
The coverage of global warming 127
Plastic pollution 141
The coverage of plastic 144
Food waste 156

6 The wheel of neoliberalism and the responsibility of the press 161

References 173
Index 219

Illustrations

Figures

4.1	Global Carbon Footprint on 17 January 2021	104
6.1	The Wheel of Neoliberalism	162

Tables

1.1	Selection of Articles (*Daily Mail* and *The Guardian*)	11
2.1	Plumwood's Dualisms	34
4.1	Coverage of Economic Growth in *Daily Mail* ($N = 99$)	106
4.2	Coverage of Economic Growth in *The Guardian* ($N = 352$)	106
4.3	CSR Coverage Overall ($N = 110$)	116
4.4	CSR Coverage in *The Guardian* ($N = 23$)	117
5.1	Coverage of Global Warming in *Daily Mail* ($N = 112$)	127
5.2	Coverage of Global Warming in *The Guardian* ($N = 313$)	127
5.3	Coverage of Plastic in *Daily Mail* ($N = 268$)	145
5.4	Coverage of Plastic in *The Guardian* ($N = 426$)	145
5.5	Coverage of Food Waste in *Daily Mail* ($N = 56$)	158
5.6	Coverage of Food Waste in *The Guardian*	158

About the author

Dr Martina Topić is a Reader at Leeds Business School, Leeds Beckett University, UK. Martina worked as a journalist in print media in Croatia, Slovenia and Italy prior to joining academia. In academia, Martina first worked at the University of Zagreb (Faculty of Political Science) as a research assistant (2007–2013). At Leeds Beckett University, she was first appointed as a graduate teaching assistant (2014–2016), then lecturer in public relations (2016–2017), senior lecturer in public relations (2017–2021), and since September 2021, she works as a Reader.

She has worked as a researcher on many research projects, including UNESCO Media Development Indicators (2008–2009), FP7 Identities and Modernities in Europe (2009–2012), Public Service Employment (July 2017–October 2017), yellow sticker shopping project (2017–2018), sustainability and consumer views (2018–2019) and COMPETE IN project (2017–2021). She was project lead for the British Academy project on Women in Advertising Industry, HEFCE project on Women in British Journalism and HEFCE projects on Women in Public Relations and Marketing and research-based teaching and student satisfaction. She currently leads the EUPRERA project on Women in Public Relations, HEFCE-funded project "The Environmental Costs of Vanity? Mirrors, Beauty Industry and the Impact of Patriarchy on the Environment" and she is a research lead for the #WECAN project (Women Empowered through Coaching and Networking), funded by the European Social Fund and Department for Work and Pensions.

She is a member of the editorial board of several academic journals including *Sociology* (British Sociological Association) and *The Qualitative Report* (Nova Southeastern University). She is an editor of the section "Culture, Media and Film" of *Cogent Arts & Humanities*, an open-access journal (Taylor & Francis), editor-in-chief of *Corporate Communications: An International Journal* (Emerald) and editor-in-chief of the book series *Women, Economy and the Labour Relations* (Emerald). She is a member of the British Sociological Association, EUPRERA, ECREA, the Conference of Socialist Economists and the British Academy of Management.

Her research interests include organisational studies, journalism practice and women's studies, with particular emphasis on ecofeminism and

xii *About the author*

environmental affairs. She has co-authored a monograph on the Croatian media system and edited four books on cultural diplomacy (Peter Lang), religion (Cambridge Scholars Publishing, Lexington) and sustainability affairs (Emerald). Currently, she is working on a monograph on women in communications industries in England and two edited books, *Women in the Media* (Intellect) and *Women and Leadership in Public Relations* (Routledge).

Acknowledgements

I knew about ecofeminism vaguely for many years, but it never got my attention until I read about it in an issue of *Womankind* magazine. After I read a short article in *Womankind*, I never stopped exploring this wonderful stream of feminism and the rest is history. Therefore, I would like to thank Ms Antonia Case, the editor-in-chief of *Womankind* magazine and her editorial collective for writing about ecofeminism and for all the weekends I have been spending with *Womankind* for years now. You are a testament that good, engaged and socially responsible journalism is possible and this research monograph is for you!

Besides, I would like to thank Dr Kevin Maloney, an editor of the Routledge series at the time when I was submitting the proposal for this book, for his enthusiastic support of the book and fantastic facilitation of the review process. A special thanks also to my Routledge editor, Mr Guy Loft for pleasant and effective collaboration, and friendly support throughout this journey. Needless to say, a massive thanks to my Christian, for so many evenings and weekends in my home office when he sat with me and kept me company.

Finally, the book is not meant to aggravate anyone and I express gratitude to all scholars who wrote on this issue before, many of whom are quoted in this book. I am also grateful to *The Guardian* for platforming environmental activists and this research should be taken in the spirit it is intended, as constructive criticism. This book aims to offer a different perspective and provide a criticism of neoliberalism, which I believe the news media perpetuate. The main aim of the book is to contribute to the debate and point to shortcomings of the neoliberal system and the role of the press in fostering and perpetuating neoliberalism. I am aware I might be labelled as too radical or called "lefty looney", but it is my hope that, if nothing else and if humanity still exists, someone in the future might read the book and say, she was right.

1 Introduction and personal reflection

The idea for this book did not start from a large project or a PhD thesis, but from a combination of various researches I've done since 2014. I first became aware of the corporate social responsibility concept when I accepted a job at Leeds Beckett University in 2014. I embarked on a second PhD and the original topic was in the field of cultural diplomacy and cultural imperialism following my first edited book (Topić & Rodin, 2012). On starting a job, I soon realised that universities are privatised and capitalist to the point that objectives, metrics and KPIs are the new divine in a marketised and liberalised higher education system such as the British one, and I was advised (in good faith) to change my PhD topic to fit more into School's research agenda as this could then be useful for School's REF policy. As a large part of the research agenda in Leeds Business School is centred on studying corporate social responsibility (CSR), I was advised to consider a topic around this area. Since I came from a journalistic professional background with experience in media research (including a first PhD tackling the role of the press in national movements), this naturally led towards a thesis studying CSR and the media, and I researched the coverage of the sugar debate and the supermarket industry in the British press (2010–2015) using an agenda-setting theory of the media. I argued that there are an anti-business hostility and bias in media writing and sourcing of stories on sugar and supermarkets where the press promotes a CSR agenda and actively advocates for the sugar agenda and pressurises supermarkets to subscribe to this agenda and engage in what I saw as undermining their own business model and refraining from selling and making a profit (Topić, 2020; Topić & Tench, 2018). I instantly found myself in cognitive dissonance because, from one side, I agreed with Milton Friedman and his view that corporations are not responsible for the well-being of society but only obliged to work for profit (Friedman, 1962, 1970). On the other side, I consider myself a socialist only to find myself supporting one of the most prominent capitalist names in the world of business and economic theory.

In the same way as with CSR, I found myself doing liberal feminist studies of looking at the glass ceiling and pay gap (Topić & Tench, 2018; Tench et al., 2017) and once again I felt discomfort for only tackling stuff I find

DOI: 10.4324/9781003091592-1

2 Introduction

fundamentally capitalist. Then I started looking at how women communicate where I initially did not find differences between men and women (Tench et al., 2017), but this did not grasp under the surface either. So I went back to the comfort zone of media research and looked at women in the media, which resulted in a programme of projects I was leading, studying lived experiences of women, the office culture and leadership in journalism, public relations and advertising industries. Throughout these explorations, I embraced a Difference Approach (Tannen, 1995, 1990, 1986; West & Zimmerman, 1983; Vukoičić, 2013; Merchant, 2012; Yule, 2006; Maltz & Borker, 1982) and Bourdieu's (2007) habitus theory, and I started to develop the concept of blokishness and cultural masculinities in these industries (Topić & Tench, 2018; Topić, 2020a, 2020b, 2020c, 2021), thus tackling more structural issues with the equality and the fact women work in a masculine organisational culture and face expectations they cannot always meet (see also Mills, 2014, 2017; Gallagher, 2002; Ross, 2001; North, 2009a, 2009b, 2016a, 2016b; Lobo et al., 2017; Alvesson, 2013, 1998; Acker, 1990, 2006, 2009; Bourdieu, 2007; Bourdieu & Wacquant, 1992; Topić & Tench, 2018; Topić, 2020a, 2020b, 2020c, 2021). The Difference Approach is thus something that derived from my initial work on differences between men and women because while initially I just looked at the European Communications Monitor data and argued that women non-stereotypically show a preference towards what is normally considered as a masculine form of communication, which effectively refuted the Difference Approach (Tench et al., 2017), further research took me towards embracing it by discontinuing looking at large data and engaging in qualitative research, talking to women and studying cultural masculinities in organisations (Topić & Tench, 2018; Topić, 2020a, 2020b, 2020c, 2021). This research programme using the Difference Approach is relevant for this book because the Difference Approach has a link to ecofeminism in a sense that authors working in this field argue women and men are different and do things differently, yet organisations and societies, in general, seem to work in a masculine way (Nicolotti Squires, 2016; Mills, 2017, 2014; Topić & Tench, 2018; Topić, 2020a, 2020b, 2020c, 2021).

The works on women in journalism are particularly relevant because women have merged into the masculine culture of newspapers (Gallagher, 2002; Mills, 2014, 2017; Topić & Tench, 2018; Ross, 2001; North, 2009a, 2009b, 2016a, 2016b; Topić & Bruegmann, 2021), and this opens up a question whether we can expect any meaningful change in journalism practice if both men and women embrace masculinity. In journalism, this means hard news reporting and newsrooms remaining places for blokes, which impedes women from taking a stance different from the one of men (Gallagher, 2002; Mills, 2014; Ross, 2001; North, 2009a, 2009b, 2016a, 2016b; Topić & Tench, 2018; Topić & Bruegmann, 2021), and this has relevance for women because women have historically been more inclined to embrace environmentalism (Mallory, 2006; Brownhill & Turner, 2019; Goldstein, 2006; Leahy, 2003; McStay & Dunlap, 1983; Poole & Harmon Zeigter, 1985; Shapiro

Introduction 3

& Mahajan, 1986; Steger & Witt, 1989; Diani, 1989; Schahn & Holzer, 1990; Blaikie, 1992; Franklin & Rudig, 1992; Stern et al., 1993; McAllister, 1994; Hampel et al., 1996; Tranter, 1996; Godfrey, 2005; Shiva, 1989; Brownhill, 2010; Godfrey, 2008; Holy, 2007; Mann, 2011; Stoddart & Tindall, 2011; Giacomini, 2014; Kirk, 1998; McMahon, 1997; Salleh, 1984; Topić, 2020d; Topić et al., 2021); however, as they work in a masculine environment the question is to what extent can we expect women to drive change when journalism remains one of the bastions of masculinity.

Ecofeminism encompasses, in my view, elements of both radical and socialist feminism (as I have argued in some of my works, Topić, 2020b; Topić et al., 2021), and nevertheless, there is a branch of ecofeminism called socialist ecofeminism. This approach is particularly suitable for analysing the CSR discourse and the media agenda on CSR-related topics because ecofeminism is fundamentally an anti-capitalist theory but the one, unlike for ecosocialist theory, that links capitalism with patriarchy and argues that the oppression of women and Nature are interlinked and,

> the late 20th century crises – social and environmental – are inevitable because of "masculine" values and behaviours. The keystone of this destructive patriarchalism is identified in the everyday notion that men represent the sphere of "humanity and culture", while women, indigenes, children, animals, plants, and so on, are part of "nature" [...] Ecofeminists focus on the dominant Eurocentric industrial capitalist patriarchal formation and its material impacts.
>
> Salleh (2001a, p. 109, emphasis in original; see also Salleh, 2000;
> Waldron, 2003; Sydee & Beder, 2001)

In the case of CSR, an ecofeminist approach helps in understanding why CSR seems to be such a stalemate and the debate does not move forward from describing the phenomenon and making claims that CSR helps. Ecofeminism made me ask myself, *CSR helps but to whom and to do what precisely?* Thus, through the reading of the ecofeminist critique of capitalism, I concluded that CSR must be studied in the context of capitalism because corporations are capitalist enterprises and we have to examine the concept of CSR within a capitalist framework. What is more, journalism also needs to be examined in the context of capitalism because media organisations are also nowadays profitable capitalist enterprises and are prone to influence from owners and other corporations because of advertising income (Sandoval, 2013; Mosco, 2009; Herman & Chomsky, 1988; Garnham, 1998). Ecofeminist theory links capitalism with patriarchy (saed, 2017; Brownhill & Turner, 2020; Sydee & Beder, 2001; Delveaux, 2001), thus proving a rounded up concept for the analysis.

When it comes to CSR, while the mainstream literature on CSR would have one believe that Milton Friedman (1962, 1970)[1] alone is a capitalist who wanted to protect corporations by indeed arguing it is not the responsibility

4   *Introduction*

of business to look after society,[2] I am arguing that mainstream scholarship is preserving the capitalist status quo and further contributing towards marketisation and liberalisation of the economy, which then leads to environmental degradation by supporting CSR initiatives that serve as a smokescreen to the fact corporations still enforce consumerism that damages the environment and perpetuates inequality of women, working classes and indigenous population through mass exploitation, over-production and creating the need that simply isn't there through corporate advertising and marketing. Nevertheless, by being forced to spend on CSR, companies further run for profit to make up for money lost in these initiatives, which does not serve society as the environment is constantly degraded and humanity is faced with climate change. It would be, of course, naïve to think corporations would not run after profit had they not had to donate to CSR due to pressures from various NGO actors and the public on social media (through the influence of mainstream media that sets the agenda); however, my thesis is that CSR can only exist in the context of capitalism where companies work for profit and then donate part of it, with which CSR becomes a fundamental part of what I call the wheel of neoliberalism and I am arguing that CSR has saved capitalism as it emerged at the time of unease and criticism of corporations (Cutrone, n.d.; Waterhouse, 2017; Pillay, 2015; Nunn, 2014; Gamble, 1989; Jessop, 2003; Gareau, 2013).

Sandoval (2013) argued that

> it is unlikely that corporations will voluntarily refrain from irresponsible behaviour if this undermines their profit interests. This, therefore, points at the limits of voluntary CSR. The idea of voluntary corporate self-regulation is deeply flawed; it strengthens rather than limits corporate power, it depoliticises the quest for a responsible economy, and it ideologically mask how corporate interests, competition and power structures are related to irresponsible conduct.
>
> p. 51

In addition to that, Banerjee (2014) argued that "the limits arise from both the structure of the modern corporation and the political economy in which it is embedded. The current structure and purpose of corporations is designed to deliver shareholder value, which limits a corporation's ability to pursue social goals" (p. 3).

In my view, the problem is fundamentally in the capitalist and neoliberal system and the corporate/capitalist media that promote capitalist policies, and the issue of blokishness and masculinity in newsrooms play a role in this process. Media play a fundamental role in enforcing CSR discourse and while at the outset they appear to campaign for environmentalism, I am arguing that this is not the case. I am arguing that media serve in preserving the status quo of capitalism through coverage that can be defined as an attempt to create better capitalism that allegedly cares for people and the

Introduction   5

environment and where economic growth can somehow go hand in hand with environmental protection and businesses can solve social problems. I am arguing that this is impossible and that CSR is just one part of the capitalist policies, which are pervasive in society and perpetuated by media coverage and this is visible in the coverage of CSR-related initiatives such as environmental coverage. Nevertheless, I am arguing that while women generally show more interest in engaging in environmental affairs (Mallory, 2006; Brownhill & Turner, 2019; Goldstein, 2006; Leahy, 2003; McStay & Dunlap, 1983; Poole & Harmon Zeigter, 1985; Shapiro & Mahajan, 1986; Steger & Witt, 1989; Diani, 1989; Schahn & Holzer, 1990; Blaikie, 1992; Franklin & Rudig, 1992; Stern et al., 1993; McAllister, 1994; Hampel et al., 1996; Tranter, 1996; Godfrey, 2005; Shiva, 1989; Brownhill, 2010; Godfrey, 2008; Holy, 2007; Mann, 2011; Stoddart & Tindall, 2011; Giacomini, 2014; Kirk, 1998; McMahon, 1997; Salleh, 1984; Topić, 2020d; Topić et al., 2021), in the case of media, this activism is largely lacking due to blokishness and the lack of women in business sections, and journalism and the media generally remain a domain for men and masculine practice. Therefore, by capitalism and news media being inherently masculine where even women who succeed have to merge to blokish culture, no change is in sight unless the gender dynamic and expectations in the journalism profession change. To that end, I am arguing that while we do not need the CSR concept because it only perpetuates capitalism and hides the real problem of consumerism and environmental degradation, we do need socially responsible media because media have a different role in society and should not be driven by profit and interests of owners, editors, or journalists. In a nutshell, I am rejecting the CSR concept while concurrently endorsing the media social responsibility concept, both of which will be elaborated on in the book.

I am focusing on analysing media coverage of CSR and environmental affairs. I am looking at who writes about environmental affairs and in what way and also who and how writes about CSR and economic growth in media to show the interconnectedness of neoliberal policies of economic growth, the introduction of CSR and the view that environment and Nature can be managed, with liberal media and their coverage of these affairs. In other words, this book is first and foremost about neoliberalism and CSR being just one cog on a larger wheel of neoliberalism with media coverage consistently showing the same line of argumentation embedded in neoliberalism, thus spanning across all debates, CSR, economic growth and environmental affairs. In even more words, the media are looking for environmental solutions by preserving capitalism and capitalist status quo, and while at the outset it appears they are anti-business, in reality, the criticism is only visible in the so-called dirty industries such as fossil fuels and coal but there is no meaningful criticism of capitalism and consumption as drivers of environmental degradation, with which they ultimately keep the capitalist system intact and CSR is there to keep companies in line as a useful smokescreen to avoid protests and discontent unseen since the 1970s and 1980s, which

6 *Introduction*

is when CSR got operationalised by neoliberal politicians such as Ronald Reagan and Margaret Thatcher (Pillay, 2015). In the same way, as Thatcher thought businesses could solve social problems by asking them to help with youth unemployment (Moon, 2004, 2005), the media perpetuate this discourse by pushing companies to give more to societies, ultimately endorsing the politics of economic growth and draining of resources.

Thus, this book looks at how media report on CSR, economic growth and environmental affairs and makes sense of news media coverage on these issues and how media perpetuate capitalism. I am also looking at coverage of CSR as a concept and of three main elements of the environmental debate, which constitutes CSR policies. CSR originates from environmentalism and charitable giving where companies have historically given to causes to show goodwill and they also implemented policies to protect the environment. While there was a period of the shift towards stakeholder orientation of looking into how companies treat communities, suppliers, employees and everyone who could be seen as a stakeholder, recently, the CSR policies again shifted more strongly towards environmentalism, thus raising the question of whether CSR is indeed just a greenwash and whether companies only mirror the zeitgeist with their policies (Topić et al., 2020a). Therefore, I am looking at the coverage of CSR, economic growth, food waste, global warming and plastic.

By media, I am focusing on the press as the form of media that still sets the public agenda and influences public debates and attitudes (McCombs, 2014, 2005, 2004, 2003; McCombs & Stroud, 2014; McCombs et al., 2011; Tan & Weaver, 2013).[3] In that, I am arguing that the press, which I see as patriarchal and fundamentally masculine (Topić & Bruegmann, 2021; Mills, 2014, 2017; Gallagher, 2002; Ross, 2001; North, 2009a, 2009b, 2016a, 2016b; Lobo et al., 2017; Alvesson, 2013, 1998; Acker, 1990, 2006, 2009; Bourdieu, 2007; Bourdieu & Wacquant, 1992) perpetuates status quo by supporting CSR concept while also supporting both business growth and environmental initiatives, which does not go together (Salleh, 2000, 1994; Shiva, 1999; d'Eaubonne, [1990] 1997; Georgescu-Roegen, 1971; Meadows et al., 1972, 2004; Ehrlich & Holdren, 1971; Cleveland, 1984; Douthwaite, 1999; Mishan, 1967). Thus, a status quo remains and the UK is facing a prospect of public encountering fatigue with environmental affairs due to incessant and repetitive coverage of issues that do not lead towards a sustainable solution.

Since ecofeminist theory argues that capitalism goes hand in hand with masculinity and patriarchy, the link emerges with the way media operate, and I am arguing that media's support of CSR and anti-business coverage is a smokescreen for preserving the capitalist status quo because the media also support economic growth and have a managerial approach to environmental affairs. In order to explore these issues, I embarked on a comprehensive analysis of the press coverage of five topics, economic growth, CSR, global warming, plastic and food waste. All these topics are relevant because, as already emphasised, economic growth is often seen

Introduction 7

as incompatible with environmental protection (Salleh, 2000, 1994; Shiva, 1999; d'Eaubonne, [1990] 1997; Georgescu-Roegen, 1971; Meadows et al., 1972, 2004; Ehrlich & Holdren, 1971; Cleveland, 1984; Douthwaite, 1999; Mishan, 1967), whereas remaining topics cover the CSR coverage. Media do not write so much about CSR as CSR, which is why the sample is low in two selected newspapers; however, they do extensively cover environmental policies that constitute CSR and nationally there is an overview of how media write about CSR. In this case, plastic, food waste and global warming are hot topics that the public, policymakers and the media debate, and these policies are often debated in environmental studies as constitutive of the environmental problem.

Therefore, in this book, I am critically analysing the existing understanding of the CSR concept from an ecofeminist point of view and as part of a larger wheel of neoliberalism where CSR presents just one cog in the wheel. I am also arguing that the CSR concept in itself is irresponsible and I am supporting Friedman's view that businesses only have responsibilities to comply with laws and satisfy their shareholders; however, I am not doing this from a capitalist or pro-market perspective. I am arguing that it is the job of the Government to regulate working rights, the rights of suppliers, environmental protection and other elements that proponents of CSR currently support; however, my argument is that CSR actually serves as an extension of marketisation and liberalisation that has been happening in the UK for a while now. I am also arguing that the reason for the prominence of CSR lies in the national media. I see the issue of CSR and environmental protection as sensationalised without actually offering any meaningful solution. Nevertheless, I argue that it is the liberal media that enforce this incomprehensible discourse of promoting the economic growth, CSR and sustainability initiatives, but ultimately these do not work together and only lead towards further liberalisation of the market where corporations self-regulate with pressures from the public and the media, thus public and the media effectively taking the role of policing corporations while the market further liberalises and the UK further sinks towards a corporation-led country with a week state regulation.

Promotion of economic growth and trade policies is something that ecofeminists see as fundamentally masculine (Salleh, 2000, 1994; Shiva, 1999; d'Eaubonne, [1990] 1997) and thus I am exploring whether this applies to the British press and if so, what is the role of women in promoting these (masculine) policies. In that, I am arguing that the masculinisation of women in journalism has further exacerbated the problem with environmental affairs as it is hard for mainstream women to succeed in journalism, and thus potentially engage with environmental activism. In other words, numerous studies have shown that women are more likely to support environmentalism (Mallory, 2006; Brownhill & Turner, 2019; Goldstein, 2006; Leahy, 2003; McStay & Dunlap, 1983; Poole & Harmon Zeigter, 1985; Shapiro & Mahajan, 1986; Steger & Witt, 1989; Diani, 1989; Schahn & Holzer,

8 *Introduction*

1990; Blaikie, 1992; Franklin & Rudig, 1992; Stern et al., 1993; McAllister, 1994; Holy, 2007; Hampel et al., 1996; Tranter, 1996; Godfrey, 2005; Shiva, 1989; Brownhill, 2010; Godfrey, 2008; Mann, 2011; Stoddart & Tindall, 2011; Giacomini, 2014; Kirk, 1998; McMahon, 1997; Salleh, 1984; Topić, 2020d; Topić et al., 2021); however, the question that led me to do this research is whether all masculinisation of women in journalism has led to a situation that women journalists act like men and engage in hard news reporting and sensationalising while not offering any meaningful solution to the problem. Also, are women journalists promoting economic growth and CSR, and thus engaging in creating the so-called better capitalism?

Therefore, I am analysing the CSR concept using the ecofeminist understanding of Earth being a victim of a patriarchal and masculinist way of exploitation, and I am extending this argument to argue that the rise of mass media, press in particular, continually perpetuates this inequality. Ecofeminism argues that the attitudes that lead to environmental degradation and women's oppression are grounded by the social construction of patriarchy where both women and Nature are dominated as property (Adams, 2007; Holy, 2007; Besthorn & Pearson McMillen, 2002; Warren, 2000). The earth is "being violated and degraded resulting in damage that is often irreparable, yet only a small proportion of humans have engaged their consciousness with this crisis" (Spretnak, 1990, p. 2). I am following an anti-essentialist view of ecofeminism – that is, I do not assume that women are inherently connected to Nature nor that all men seek to destroy Nature; instead, I recognise that women's lived realities place women's issues and sustainability as inextricably intertwined (Puleo, 2017; Dimitropolous, 2018; Topić et al., 2021). As ecofeminist theory postulates, women do not have enough power to change things and are thus not responsible for environmental degradation (the exception being a small number of successful elite women) and not less importantly, in some cultures women are blamed for diseases, get thrown out of communities out of fear they will spread the disease and women (generally) face job losses when they are no longer economically useful or in time of crisis. For example, during the COVID-19 crisis, researchers reported soon after the introduction of national lockdowns that women are losing jobs disproportionately, and for example, women in academia immediately started to fall behind men in the number of academic papers they were able to write due to the burden of caring and housework (Frederickson, 2020; Zimmer, 2020).

First findings on media and CSR reporting highlighted that the media assign meaning to CSR and contribute to the enforcement of CSR as debate drivers. For example, Buhr and Grafström (2006) analysed the *Financial Times* coverage of CSR between 1988 and 2003 and found that the newspapers attempted to contribute to "shaping the meaning of a new management concept" (p. 1). The analysis showed how the concept of CSR evolved from a concept related to the creation of jobs and charitable contributions, which would belong to Friedman's (1962, 1970) understanding of CSR to

Introduction 9

the responsibility that companies have towards society. The debate on CSR already started during the 1990s when CSR was first associated with marketing and demands to run only ethical advertising campaigns; however, towards the end of the 1990s the concept got associated with ethics and this trend continued after the turn of the millennium when debates intensified putting the business under pressure to be ethical and consider environmental and social issues in their businesses (Buhr & Grafström, 2006). Corporate scandals contributed to both an increase and negative tone of future coverage. For example, in the period of 2006/2007, major news media in Britain reported their own CSR while at the same time expressing pressure on British companies to perform better in terms of their social commitment; however, CSR still remained driven by internal rather than external factors (Gulyas, 2009). In other words, it was media organisations themselves that enforced CSR, and not the external factors that forced them to do so. This can also be because of a desire for higher financial performance as results from Zyglidopoulos, Georgiadis, Carroll and Siegel (2011) confirmed. It has been acknowledged, however, that the media set an agenda on business and this is because people learn about companies from the media, with which media become drivers of corporate reputation (Carroll & McCombs, 2003; Staw & Epstein, 2000). Tench, Bowd and Jones, on the other hand, argued that media see organisations that enforce CSR through five characteristics, or "conformist, cynic, realist, optimist, and strategic idealist" (Tench et al., 2007, p. 355).[4] Among media professionals, it seems they see CSR mostly through obligation, or something that companies have to do. But a majority of practising journalists agreed that CSR should include donations and community development (ibid). These findings were confirmed in a study by Grafström and Windell (2011) that showed financial newspapers see CSR as soft regulation and as something that should go beyond the law; and human resources where CSR is seen as a tool to ensure better working conditions and as a means to promote the employer to their employees. This immediately brings a question of whether CSR is then indeed a tool of further liberalisation of the market where companies will start self-legislating and the market will become independent from the Government.

The reason for this focus of the book lies in the fact that the majority of studies do not question whether the concept of CSR was a good idea or why is it a responsibility of the business to self-restrict instead of the Government that collects taxes. Is this way of businesses self-regulating another way of further imposing an open market, liberal ideology? While media coverage of CSR has been the subject of the analysis (Buhr & Grafström, 2006; Christensen et al., 2007; Gulyas, 2009; Grayson, 2009; Grafström & Windell, 2011; Zyglidopoulos et al., 2011), no works are offering an ecofeminist analysis of this debate, specifically looking at capitalism and patriarchy and their interplay in CSR and the news media within a neoliberal context and thus CSR as just a small part of neoliberalism and as a policy that preserves the status quo.

10   *Introduction*

The media analysed are two newspapers, *The Guardian* (often considered as centre-left albeit I am arguing that *The Guardian* is neoliberal while nominally supportive of environmental policies) and *Daily Mail* (often considered centre-right and in my view neoliberal expressing hostility towards environmentalist movement). *The Guardian* is a broadsheet and seen as a quality newspaper, whereas *Daily Mail* is often labelled as the tabloid; however, this is not true because *Daily Mail* does not have a red top on the cover page and the journalism the newspaper produces is different and more detailed than what tabloids produce albeit the coverage is often sensationalist. The reason these two newspapers have been selected lies in their diametrically opposite ideologies where *Daily Mail* supports right-wing initiatives such as focusing on immigration and Brexit, whereas *The Guardian* traditionally supports more left-wing and liberal initiatives such as equality and diversity and the relationship with the EU. In terms of circulation, and if tabloids are put aside, *Daily Mail* and *The Guardian* have high readership and popularity on their respective sides of the political spectrum. According to the data from the Press Gazette from November 2020, *Daily Mail* is the most read newspaper in the country,[5] whereas *The Guardian* is the most read newspaper on the left albeit its readership is a fraction of the readership of *Daily Mail* (990,106 vs 111,953 respectively) (Press Gazette, 2020a). Equally, *Guardian's Observer* has a readership of 152,129 whereas *Mail on Sunday* has 870,745 (ibid). Both regular edition and Sunday editions were included in this analysis, which was deemed relevant as these two editions, in each newspaper, have different editors. While *The Guardian* and *The Observer* follow similar editorial policy, *Daily Mail* has been known to conflict with *Mail on Sunday*. For example, during the Brexit referendum, the editor of *Mail on Sunday* supported remaining in the EU whereas *Daily Mail* was one of the strongest advocates of Brexit (*Mail on Sunday* Editorial, 2016; Tobitt, 2018; The Guardian Staff and Agencies, 2016).

Articles were selected using the Lexis Nexis database. Keywords were used to select articles, namely economic growth, global warming, plastic, food waste and corporate social responsibility. The CSR was analysed twice, on a national level analysing all national and regional press, and then separately in *Daily Mail* and *The Guardian*. The articles were analysed in a period of 12 months, thus providing a good overview of the media agenda and the coverage on these issues.[6] The dates selected for the analysis were from 25 February 2019 to 25 February 2020, which is a period preceding coronavirus pandemic, which would skew the data as it is logical that the media will write about the economic impact of extensive worldwide lockdowns. Therefore, a period preceding the pandemic provided a good ground on the media agenda at the time when there is no obtrusion from a major crisis such as a pandemic. In February 2020, it was already known that something is happening and there are reports on potential impact if pandemic escalates, which then provides a good overview of media coverage of environmental affairs and economic growth at the time of no crisis as well as at the beginning of an unfolding crisis.

Articles that were removed were duplicates, as well as articles that appeared in searches because of a keyword but had nothing to do with the researched topic. For example, articles that discuss personal growth appeared in a search for economic growth. Equally, some articles discuss toxic waste instead of food waste and so on. In addition to that, many articles that the press publishes were written by activists, politicians, academics and experts and these were all removed from the sample as they present an opinion, and even though the fact newspapers published this type of opinion shows editorial policy, these articles still cannot be considered as media writing of the problem, nor would it possible to discuss how journalists write about these issues if authors are not journalists. Nevertheless, not all articles had a note emphasising that the article was written by an external person, for example when someone famous such as the environmental activist Greta Thunberg or the British MP Caroline Lucas were authors. Therefore, all articles were checked to identify potential external authors and when found, these articles were removed. Equally, a careful check was made on the gender of the journalist. For example, BAME names were checked by googling journalists to check their gender because this is not always clear due to diversity of names and cultural conventions, and also journalists with names that have historically belonged to men but were often used by women (Chris, Alex, etc.) were also checked. Only journalists' names who could be labelled as unconditionally male or female were included without googling journalists to check for gender (Mark for men, Fiona for women, etc.). The number of articles on issues selected for the analysis immediately revealed a major interest of the press on environmental affairs as well as economic growth. Table 1.1 shows the number of articles that appeared in searches as well as the number of articles selected for each topic that was subjected to the analysis.

In addition to the analysis in Table 1.1, and due to the low number of CSR articles in the two analysed newspapers, CSR coverage was also analysed in totality by looking at CSR coverage in all national and regional newspapers, which resulted in a total of 110 analysed articles (459 results overall).

Table 1.1 Selection of Articles (*Daily Mail* and *The Guardian*)

Topic	Number of Articles from the Search (Daily Mail)	Number of Selected Articles (Daily Mail)	Number of Articles from the Search (The Guardian)	Number of Selected Articles (The Guardian)
Economic growth	114	99	905	352
Corporate social responsibility	2	2	25	23
Food waste	69	56	180	109
Global warming	145	112	581	313
Plastic	918	268	1,892	426
Total national newspapers	1,248	537	3,553	1,223

12 *Introduction*

Therefore, in total, 1,248 articles from *Daily Mail*, 3,553 articles from *The Guardian* and 459 articles from all national and regional press were analysed to establish their suitability for the analysis. Of that, a total of 537 articles from *Daily Mail*, 1,223 articles from *The Guardian* and 110 articles from the national and regional press were selected for the analysis. This brings a total of analysed articles to 1,870 articles altogether. A sample of this size enables a meaningful discussion on the role of the media in CSR and environmental affairs and the media social responsibility problem, and this sample also enables a discussion on the role of women in the media coverage of what was historically known as a feminine area of interest and passion (environmentalism).

The articles were first compiled as explained above and then subjected to rigorous reading and analysis. After initial analysis tackling who writes on issues and to what extent, the writing is then analysed using an ecofeminist analysis. Ecofeminist analysis is conceptualised as a sense-making analysis exploring how media write and whether the media could be seen as neoliberal. For example, on CSR, do they take a critical stance or a supportive stance and on economic growth, whether the media support economic growth. With three environmental topics (global warming, food waste and plastic) the analysis concentrated on exploring *whether writing shows hierarchy in which Nature exists to serve the interests of humanity, to what extent women write more supportively of environmental affairs than men* (as per ecofeminist studies that have been showing for decades that women are more inclined to support environmental activism due to their social experiences and realities) and also *to what extent media express support for capitalism through environmental reporting* (either by directly arguing that capitalism is the desirable system or through calling for changes in policies that fit into neoliberal support for economic growth, CSR and environmentalism or by writing in a way that preserves capitalism). In other words, the media's view of capitalism is explored through a dual analysis of the media coverage of economic growth as one of the founding postulates of capitalism but also through environmental coverage and the coverage of CSR to explore in-depth to what extent media propose solutions that are meant to preserve capitalism or fix it rather than criticise the regime and to illustrate how neoliberalism works where, as already emphasised, I am arguing that the CSR is a smokescreen and just a part of neoliberalist policies that promote capitalism, over-consumption and a domineering view of Nature.

The method used for the analysis of newspaper coverage is thus a sense-making method of news writing using concepts identified in ecofeminist theory. This means I have first conducted a content analysis of media coverage of economic growth, CSR and environmental affairs and I analysed tones of articles by looking at whether the coverage is positive, negative and neutral. The latter is common in works analysing media coverage of CSR (Deephouse, 2000; McCombs & Ghanem, 2001). After that, I conducted an ecofeminist sense-making reading of media coverage of these complex issues

Introduction 13

and read them by trying to make sense of whether media enforce hierarchy and neoliberal policies. In the findings chapters, this sense-making analysis reads as an analysis of narrative using ecofeminist concepts and I am providing a narrative and sense-making analysis of media coverage embedded in literature which has extensively been reviewed in the first two chapters, as well as a case study literature on food waste, plastic, global warming and economic growth which is reviewed in findings chapters.

In a nutshell, my view is that everything needs to be analysed in the context of neoliberalism and that includes women's position, CSR concept as such as well as media coverage of CSR and environmental affairs. However, even more importantly, I am a constructionist and my view of the media is that we cannot observe what media and journalists do impartially, as the postulate of positivism proposes, but that we need to see the world (and this includes media too) as a construct of humans. The constructionist approach means that researchers have to

> make sense of the subjective and socially constructed meanings expressed by those who take part in research about the phenomenon being studied. Social constructionism indicates that meanings are dependent on human cognition – people's interpretation of the events that occur around them.
>
> Saunders et al. (2012, p. 546)

In the case of media, if journalists and editors are considered responsible for media content and if this media content is considered to have an impact on audiences, then it is possible to see both journalists/editors and the public as co-creators of everyday reality. The constructionist approach is common in media studies because it enables meaningful analysis of the media content and the way media construct realities. For example, using the social constructionist approach, Boero (2007) explored how the media define obesity as a social problem and a problem of individuals at the same time. According to her findings, the media are framing obesity as an epidemic, with which they are creating chaos and fear (ibid). In research on framing, constructionism has a prominent role. Gamson offered a constructionist understanding of framing where he treats media discourse and public opinion "as two parallel systems of constructing meaning" (Gamson & Modigliani, 1989, p. 1). Gamson and Modigliani (1989) furthermore argued that policy issues should be seen as "a symbolic contest over which interpretation will prevail" (ibid, p. 2), and this symbolic contest then forms a cultural system that "has logic of its own" (ibid). Gamson and Modigliani (1989) also saw this cultural system through cognitive lenses arguing that besides cultural level psychological level that enables the construction of meaning must also be considered. Ecofeminism is also a constructionist approach because ecofeminists are analysing the way societies are constructed and embedded in patriarchy, which is also a social construct. Wilson (2010)

14   *Introduction*

defined ecofeminism as a typical left-wing critical academic approach that belongs to the same group of approaches such as postmodernism, constructionist social anthropology, critical socialist scholarship, deep ecology and neo-Marxism.

Finally, something needs to be said about the writing style of the book. Susan Griffin in *Woman and Nature* uses two writing styles, passive and first-person writing (Griffin, 2015) following observation from Julia Stanley who made an argument that using passive in analytical writing is a masculine practice where this type of writing hides who did or said something with which the structures of power are shown as stable and unquestionable. At the time of writing, Griffin (2015) was worried about how would this be received but then decided it would give the book a dramatic tone (ibid); however, nowadays she writes in the first person only. She also correctly argued that men are not inherently antagonisers but it is the thinking that founds masculine domination that has an antagonistic view of everything different, and one does not have to be a man to hold that view (ibid). It is indeed inherently against the ecofeminist worldview to write in the "objective" way because this distanced view from the research an individual conducts is seen as masculine and patriarchal. In other words, it is men who are taught since an early age to be distanced, reserved and hide emotions (Salleh, 1993, 1984; Griffin, 2020; Gilligan, 1993) and it is also men who started the modern science, at some points in history, also at the expense of burning women healers as witches and by writing so-called intellectual documents that argued women are inferior to men (Gaard, 2011; Griffin, 2020, 2015; Marjanić, 2020; Milardović, 2016; Holm & Jokalla, 2008; Holy, 2007; d'Eaubonne & Michel, 1997). Therefore, ecofeminists believe that with so-called objectivity in writing, authors hide their connection with the topic of research and since ecofeminism insists, among many things, on personal responsibility on each individual, writing in the third person is often seen as cowardice and an attempt to show alleged superiority (Holy, 2007). While it is mainstream in some disciplines or in some journals to write in a third person under the claim that texts are not scientific or scholarly enough if written in the first person, ecofeminists often see this view as a patriarchal and masculine way of talking and writing. Many women throughout history, and up to the present day, accepted this practice either because they feared they will not be taken seriously or simply because some journals refuse to publish papers written in the first person (myself included). Nevertheless, it was quite common in history, and this still happens today, that women use masculine versions of their names to conceal their feminine identity (e.g. signing work as Alex rather than Alexandra) or they used pseudonyms when writing fiction.

In this book, I am embracing an ecofeminist approach and when referring to my work, I am writing in the first person. However, I also write general information and an analysis of the work of others in a neutral style as per usual standards of writing literature reviews and presenting the work of others, which can be seen as masculine, but it also provides a dramatic

Introduction 15

connotation as argued by Griffin (2015) and it re-enforces arguments more strongly. In the same way, I have chosen to write the term Nature with capital letters when referring to Nature as a whole ecosystem encompassing not only humanity but everyone who exists in the ecosystem in living or any other form.

In the subsequent part of the book, I am first analysing ecofeminist theory outlining the main arguments of ecofeminism. In that, I focus on main arguments on the interplay between the oppression of women and Nature, and I also engage (albeit less extensively) with outlining arguments from different streams of ecofeminism and criticism of ecofeminism. After that, I am critically analysing CSR literature using ecofeminist thinking and arguments as well as the argument from critical CSR scholarship. Finally, I present and analyse media data on the news coverage of economic growth and environmental affairs in two daily newspapers, *Daily Mail* and *The Guardian* as well as a general analysis of CSR coverage in both national and regional press.

Notes

1 The term social responsibility (SR) gained prominence in academic debates during the 1960s when American economist Milton Friedman criticised proponents of the social responsibility concept. According to his opinion, social responsibility advocates were trying to dominate the system without an armed revolution (Friedman, 1962, 1970). Friedman believed corporations have to pay taxes and report to shareholders, while proponents of social responsibility initially advocated the protection of the environment, as part of Corporate Social Responsibility (CSR). Since then, the concept of CSR turned into a stakeholder approach, where corporations are expected to consider the interests of all stakeholders, and not just shareholders as Friedman argued. In other words, the stakeholder approach argues that corporations must think of the interests of customers, suppliers and employees, to be seen as socially responsible (Freeman, 1984, 2010).

2 The majority of works published on the issue of corporate social responsibility (or social responsibility of business) only mentions Friedman's understanding of the business ethics presented in chapter VIII (Monopoly and the Social Responsibility of Business and Labor, pp. 119–137) of his famous book *Capitalism and Freedom* (see e.g. Branco & Rodrigues, 2007; Falck & Heblich, 2007; Golob & Bartlett, 2007; Blowfield & Frynas, 2005; Bowie, 1991). By doing that, his thoughts are taken out of context because one cannot understand Friedman's strong opposition to imposing philanthropy or any similar form of obligation on businesses if a whole view is not taken into account, and if his view on liberalism as a doctrine and the notion of freedom that is central to liberalism is not considered. A notable exception when it comes to analysing Friedman is Bowie (2012) who also recognised misunderstanding of his work albeit not when it comes to defending liberalism as a doctrine. Bowie (2012) emphasised that Friedman's influence on debates on CSR should not be neglected and that "academic defenders of corporate social responsibility and business leaders that practice it needs either to refute Friedman or accommodate him" (p. 2). This is indeed the truth, and there is a lack of academic literature seriously considering Friedman or offering criticism of CSR as a concept, and asking why is it the role of business to help society by going beyond laws? There is even less work on the role of the

16 *Introduction*

media and on the gender problem, and it seems as if the whole field is taken for granted, with very little critical research on CSR. The shareholder/stockholder approach (shareholder hereafter) has been advocated by Milton Friedman (1962) who positioned himself as a defender of liberalism, and this defence of liberalism and opposition to what he perceived as socialism is at the centre of his understanding of business ethics. While much of Friedman's work is concentrated on the notion of philanthropy, which is where CSR originates, the definition has moved forward and thus today CSR goes that far to include interests of anyone considered a stakeholder whereas philanthropy is seen in a cynical view and considered as PR or greenwash.

3 The existing research shows that the power of the press did not decrease with the growth of social media, and increased diversity in media outlets which now include blogs, news websites, etc. (Cushion et al., 2018; Tan & Weaver, 2013; Meraz, 2011, 2009, 2008; McCombs, 2004, 2014; Hamilton, 2004; Dearing & Rogers, 1996; Breed, 1955; Manheim & Albritton, 1984; Winter & Eyal, 1981; Weiss, 1974). While some authors debate the future of journalism and the death of the press, this is far from happening. As correctly argued by Cushion and associates (2018) press still has an agenda-setting potential, not just because people still read the press (albeit in an online form; for more details on changes that journalism as a profession is going through, see Franklin, 2014) but also because the press content is still discussed in TV shows, and journalists from the press are invited to speak about the so-called mood of the press. Nevertheless, the press still plays an agenda-setting role for broadcasters that report on debates from the press (Lewis & Cushion, 2017).

4 In other words, organisation is conformist if it is involved in CSR "because everyone else is", and they see CSR as a cost that needs to be paid off. Cynic organisations are those that perceive companies that have CSR as self-promoting themselves, and CSR is seen as "a cost, a management fad and something to be endured". Realist companies are those that see CSR as a concept that includes self-interest, but they are ok with the concept because they also see it as something that has a "potential to transform business, social, economic and other practices for the better". However, these companies also think that CSR should not be imposed, but that the change will come with time. Optimists are companies that "focus on the positive benefits of CSR for themselves, their communities and their businesses", and tend not to see negative aspects of the concept. Finally, strategic idealists are companies that "seek to maximise the positive benefits and minimise the negative effects of CSR", and these companies do this by developing long-term strategies (Tench et al., 2014, p. 356).

5 In the previous years, the tabloid *The Sun* was the most read newspaper in the country; however, as of beginning of 2020, *The Sun* no longer provides data on ABC circulation. *The Telegraph* and the *Times* have also decided the same (Press Gazette, 2020a).

6 Winter and Eyal (1981) argued that a period between four and six weeks is the optimal effect span for the transfer of the single issue to the public agenda (cited from Kim et al., 2010). On the other hand, Stone and McCombs (1981) argued that at least four months must be analysed for a multiple issue to make an impact (quoted from Kim et al., 2010).

2 Ecofeminism

Theory, issues and advocacy

Ecofeminism is a feminist movement "and current of analysis that attempts to link feminist struggles with ecological struggles" (Sandiland, 1999, p. xvi), and as such ecofeminism focuses on the duality of oppression of women and Nature (Mallory, 2012) by the ideology of hegemonic masculinity and patriarchy, both of which are also linked to capitalism (von Werlhof, 2007; Merchant, 1992; Stoddart & Tindall, 2011; Radford Ruether, 2012; Henderson, 1997; Maclaran & Stevens, 2018; Gaard, 1997; Ling, 2014; Warren, n.d.; Đurđević & Marjanić, 2020). With this, ecofeminism becomes a movement that combines elements of radical feminism (focus on patriarchy and the domination of women and Nature) and socialist feminism (opposition to capitalism) (Topić, 2020d). Even though it is often said there are as many ecofeminisms as ecofeminists, the common definition of ecofeminism is an anti-hierarchical and anti-capitalist movement that works on a global scale as evidence on a wide range of activism across the globe have demonstrated so far (Griffin, 2020; Fakier & Cock, 2018; Holy, 2007; Shiva & Bandyopadhyay, 1986; Jain, 1984; Bandyopadhyay, 1999; Moore, 2011; Mishra et al., 2021; Green Belt Movement, n.d.).

In other words, as opposed to other feminisms that are either overly dogmatic or overly white and Western to apply to everyone, ecofeminism indeed can be (and has been) used in a variety of contexts. Therefore, as already emphasised, ecofeminism encompasses elements of radical feminism (which sees women as inherently different than men and predominantly because of the gendered socialisation process and thus focuses on criticising patriarchy) and socialist feminism (due to its focus on capitalism and hierarchy as well as focus on class differences and the difference between the Global North and the Global South and the accompanying oppression) (Topić, 2020d). The fundamental view of ecofeminism is that the reason for oppression lies in the dichotomy of culture vs Nature where men are associated with culture and women with Nature, which then ends up in oppression of both women and Nature. The idea developed from the view that humans separated themselves from Nature and belong to the culture, which is seen as an anti-thesis to Nature (Holy, 2007), and this is also why ecofeminists did not join other ecological movements but ended up forming their own.

DOI: 10.4324/9781003091592-2

18 *Ecofeminism*

It is relevant to point out that Nature refers to the whole universe and the whole material world and forces that co-exist in Nature (this includes everything and everyone whether alive or not) whereas environment refers to the natural environment, which includes air, soil, water, climate and alive creatures, and this term also sometimes includes cultural heritage created by humans. Ecofeminists speak of Nature and its protection albeit environmentalism is sometimes used when describing ecological and environmental movements. For example, when we say that women are more likely to engage with environmentalism, we use this term because it captures women who subscribe to, for example, the liberal feminist doctrine that places emphasis on individuals and argues that environmental protection needs to be regulated (Merchant, 2020). The term ecofeminism, however, encompasses women who support interconnectedness between humans and Nature in its totality.

Ecofeminists advocate for the rearrangement of production and reproduction among men and women as well as Nature (Salleh, 1991). d'Eaubonne believed that a planet "placed in the feminine will flourish for all" (d'Eaubonne, 1994, p. 194) and she also believed that there is a strong connection between the domination of Nature and women, and that "active engagement in the liberation *of* nature (from the manipulative control of modern society's instrumental rationalism) as the key to woman's autonomy and control of her destiny" (Gersdorf, 2006, p. 212, emphasis in the original). This view was directly opposite to the view of Simone de Beauvoir who suggested that women should be freed from Nature so that women can become autonomous and self-defined, which has been a cannon for many feminists and remain so until the present day (d'Eaubonne, 1994; Gersdorf, 2006) (most notably, this view is prominent among many liberal feminists). Rosemary Ruether (1975) summarised what ecofeminism stands for and this definition is as current today as it was back in the 1970s when the movement was formed:

> Women must see that there can be no liberation for them and no solution to the ecological crisis within a society whose fundamental model of relationships continues to be one of domination. They must unite the demands of the women's movement with those of the ecological movement to envision a radical reshaping of the basic socioeconomic relations and the underlying values of this [modern industrial] society.
>
> p. 204

While the term ecofeminism, has been formally coined during the 1970s, ecological activism has been present in feminism even earlier with Rachel Carlson (1962) warning during the 1960s that Americans need to start looking after the environment or "all man's assaults upon the environment (including) the contamination of air, earth, rivers and sea with dangerous and even lethal materials (will undoubtedly) shatter or alter the very materials – upon which the shape of the future depends" (cited from Kamble, 2012, p. 1). Ecofeminist fundamental claim is that the oppression of Nature and women is intertwined and based on a similar premise of the domination of men. Nevertheless, ecofeminists see women at the centre of the environmental struggle and many works demonstrated that women have been actively campaigning for the environment decades before the current environmental debate started (Mallory, 2006; Brownhill & Turner, 2019; Goldstein, 2006; Leahy, 2003; Salleh, 1989; McStay & Dunlap, 1983; Poole & Harmon Zeigter, 1985; Shapiro & Mahajan, 1986; Steger & Witt, 1989; Diani, 1989; Schahn & Holzer, 1990; Blaikie, 1992; Franklin & Rudig, 1992; Stern et al., 1993; McAllister, 1994; Hampel et al., 1996; Tranter, 1996; Godfrey, 2005; Holy, 2007; Shiva, 1989; Brownhill, 2010; Godfrey, 2008; Mann, 2011; Stoddart & Tindall, 2011; Giacomini, 2014; Kirk, 1998; McMahon, 1997; Salleh, 1984; Topić, 2020d; Topić et al., 2021). However, this is not to say that all women have a connection with Nature and actively seek to protect it nor that all men actively seek to destroy it. Many women show negligence or even hostile attitudes towards Nature and the environment, while many men support environmental protection and actively campaign for it. What is central for an ecofeminist inquiry is that women are dominated in the same way as Nature, which makes environmental degradation a woman's issue (Puleo, 2017).

While the approach of ecofeminism can be seen as a utopia because the movement opposes all -isms, namely sexism, racism and speciesism, and it is continually in conflict with all major ideologies (e.g. liberalism, conservativism, fascism, nationalism) and it opposes capitalism and patriarchy (Đurđević, 2020; Marjanić, 2020; see also saed, 2017; Brownhill & Turner, 2020), Klein (2014) correctly argued that no civil or any other movement has become a crisis and came to the public agenda until someone made that happen, and this includes, for example, abolitionism, racism, apartheid and sexism. In the same way, feminists have created a crisis on women's rights with, for example, the Suffragette movement fighting for the right to vote, and in the same way, ecofeminists could create a crisis on the environmental degradation, sexism and speciesism if they continue to work against these problems and raising their voices. Some women, around the world, have already done so. For example, in India, the globally known Chipko movement was started by women to stop the destruction of forests (Shiva & Bandyopadhyay, 1986; Jain, 1984; Bandyopadhyay, 1999; Moore, 2011; Mishra et al., 2021). In Kenya, the Green Belt Movement encompassed 50,000 women who fought against the destruction of the environment and planted millions of trees as well as founded a training centre to educate people on ecological agriculture (Green Belt Movement, n.d.). Wangari Maathai won a Nobel Peace Prize and she was the first person to win this prize coming from an ecological movement (Holy, 2007).

20 *Ecofeminism*

Ecofeminism as an anti-capitalist movement

Ecofeminism can also be defined as "the recognition and struggle against capitalists' racist colonization and exploitation of (that is, extraction of profit from) nature and women" (Brownhill & Turner, 2020, p. 1). Brownhill and Turner (2020) argue that ecofeminism is an anti-capitalist theory that concerns itself with various forms of oppression while not minimising any form of oppression as less relevant, thus being a movement that tackles both socialist issues of class inequality but also patriarchal oppression and domination of women. For example, this means that ecofeminism is equally concerned with the struggle of women in Nigeria who were shouting "Fish, not oil" when they were faced with environmental degradation, but it is also concerned with living realities of those women,

> whose livelihoods are tied more immediately to the built environments of city streets and white-and-blue-collar workplaces, a loud "No!" to sexual harassment and assault on the job is equally workers' gender struggle for agency and control over the ecologies they inhabit (e.g. #MeToo).
>
> ibid (p. 3)

What is relevant for ecofeminism is a rejection of exploitation founded on market competition (Besthorn & Pearson McMillen, 2002), which leads to questioning the focus of liberal economies on economic growth and further exploitation of resources.

An ecofeminist view is that the economic growth and excessive consumption fuel exploitation of resources and degradation of Nature, which then also fuels inequalities. Thus, scholars also expressed criticism of the exploitation of resources from an anti-capitalist point of view; however, the focus of ecofeminism is always embedded and tackles the isms, namely racism, sexism and speciesism. Salleh (2000) argued that the global economic system is aggressive and contributes towards deepening tensions between class, race, gender and interests of species because one-fifth of the world controls four-fifths of all resources. The patriarchal and masculine system resulted in free trade policies, competition in exporting and this has an immense impact on the environment. Shiva (1996) also argued that trade agreements present the third wave of globalisation and bear little difference to colonialisation. Shiva (1996) argues that globalisation is not a collaboration of cultures but an imposition of certain cultures over other and equally globalisation can be seen as a predatory view of certain classes and races over others, with trade agreements further contributing towards domination, exploitation and ecological destruction. Price and Nunn (2016), for example, analysed the EU's relationship with countries in African, Pacific and Caribbean groups since the 1960s and argued that various agreements the EU made were paternalistic and characterised by "a broadly Keynesian approach to managed development" (p. 457) and this is because all agreements provided for "non-reciprocal trade, preferential access for ACP goods to the EU market, commodity stabilisation measures to offset market volatility and development aid based initially on grants" (ibid). Price and Nunn (2016) also argue that many of these contracts, especially the ones negotiated and re-negotiated during the 1990s were "WTO compliant and in line with broader neoliberal agenda" (p. 457). Thus, Price and Nunn (2016) argue that the neoliberal agenda is introduced under the guise of being pro-poor and committed to sustainable development.

A commonly noted observation is that if the whole world was living in the same way as the "developed world", three planets would be needed to accommodate the consumption (Salleh, 2000). However, Salleh (2000) also argues that many environmentalists work under capitalist assumptions and are trying to make amends to the existing system without considering advocacy for more efficient economic growth and development or abandoning economic growth strategy altogether. Salleh (2000) argues that this is a problem in the Global North, which is neoliberal in practice regardless of their nominal philosophy and she sees this view as inward-looking because it does not consider the impact of neoliberalism on the planet and other species, or the fact the wealth is controlled and the world pretty much run by one-fifth of the population that controls four-fifths of resources. In the same way, a part of the global population is leading the planet into neoliberal capitalist policies destructive of the planet without others having much influence. For example, the Copenhagen Climate Conference of the Parties in 2009 depicted an obese Justitia, Western Goddess of Justice as sitting on the back of an emaciated Black man, thus signalling exploitation of the Global South by the Global North. The image of Justitia was captioned with the following wording, "I am sitting on the back of a man – he is sinking under the burden – I will do everything to help him – except to step down from his back" (Sandberg & Sandberg, 2010, p. 8, see also Griffin, 2020). As argued by Gills and Morgan (2019), the planet is deeply interconnected and actions of some parts of the world have far-reaching consequences to the rest of the world, but this is not how the neoliberal system operates.

Salleh (2000) thus argues that many on both liberal and socialist sides in the Global North believe that the rest of the world strives towards living the way the so-called developed countries do, and she sees this as a class, race, gender and species bias because, for example, "each day whole species lines become extinct under the pressure of consumerist resourcing" (p. 28), and are thus arguing that the North somehow needs to help the South while the resources are continually being drained because of excessive consumption of the North, as with an example of Justitia above (Sandberg & Sandberg, 2010). Nevertheless, because of managerial hierarchies and the continuous extraction of resources and manufacturing products, labour is needed, which contributes towards inequality and is a class and a gender issue because manual labour is provided by the working classes who earn a mere fraction of the profits made. In addition to that, women also bear the brunt

22 *Ecofeminism*

of production and keeping the capitalist system intact with domestic labour in the North and also food farming in the South (Salleh, 2000, 1994). For example, UNDP (2020) report stated that

> across all regions, women are paid less than men, with the gender pay gap estimated at 23 per cent globally. Gender equality and the empowerment of women and girls continue to be held back owing to the persistence of historical and structural unequal power relations between women and men, poverty and inequalities and disadvantages in access to resources and opportunities that limit women's and girl's capabilities.
>
> n.p.

The same report also stated that women are paid 70 cents for every dollar a man makes, pointing towards the conclusion that women are exploited in capitalism despite data showing that in the majority of countries women make up more than half of the total country population (World Bank, 2019). International Labour Organisation (ILO) continually warns about pay inequality and in 2020, the organisation also warned that the impact of the global pandemic will affect women more than men due to already existent inequality in the work market (ILO, 2020). Salleh (2000, 1994) thus calls the capitalist system predatory and inherently unequal, which means that reaching equality becomes impossible when the system is based on exploitation and inequality. D'Eaubonne ([1990] 1997) argued that

> capital, now in the imperialist stage, will only disappear with an ecological solution of production (and of consumption) which will constitute the only possible elimination of the outdated structures of dominance, aggressiveness, competitiveness, and absolutism in order to replace them with those of cooperation and equality between individuals (thus between sexes), and of the species with the environment.
>
> p. 2

In terms of class, this also means that the Global North relies on the cheap workforce from the Global South and there is economic colonisation in place through free trade and technology transfers. As Shiva (1989) argued, neoliberal Governments re-direct resources to corporations and take them from the poor, and the resources are then subsidised by heavily promoted global junk food culture. Shiva (1989) also argued that poor economies are labelled poor through the bias in the Global North because,

> perceived poverty may not be real material poverty: subsistence economies which satisfy basic needs through self provisioning are not poor in the sense of being deprived ... millets are nutritionally far superior to processed foods, houses built with local materials are ... better adapted to the local climate.
>
> p. 10

Latouche (1993) provided a sociological analysis of this culturally conditioned bias and argued that if humanity was after universalism we would be inviting experts from the "primitive" regions of the world "to draw up a list of the 'lacks' from which we, the people of the developed countries, suffer: loneliness, depression stress, neuroses, insecurity, violence, crime rates, and so on" (p. 201, emphasis in the original). Gaard (2015) thus argued that "climate change and the first world consumption are produced by masculinist ideology, and will not be solved by masculinist techno-science approaches" (p. 4)

In addition to that, it can be argued that economic growth in masculine patriarchy or a male-oriented economy,

> only adds burden to women's lives. Money that might sustain women breadwinners goes instead into armaments, six-digit executive salaries, and a paper whirlwind of speculation. Under capitalist patriarchy, it is men in government, business, unions, academia, and international agencies who hold most decision-making positions, and who set priorities that are comfortable for them. The presence of a few female executives in the corporate hierarchy will have little impact as long as masculinist priorities remain unchallenged.
>
> Salleh (1994, p. 110)

With this ecofeminism is closely linked not just to mainstream feminisms that advocates for the equality of women but also to the Difference Approach in feminism, which argues that women and men do things differently and also organisational studies, which have been arguing for decades that organisations work under masculine patterns.[1] For example, organisational researchers stipulated that men monopolise higher positions while women remain in lower positions, which is a direct result of the gendered division of labour (Alvesson, 1998). Alvesson (2013) argued that many technical jobs are masculine and carry a masculine meaning because it is based on masculine characteristics such as aggression in business approach, persistence, toughness and determination. Thus, organisations work under understanding that comes more naturally to men than women (Alvesson, 1998), which also means that organisations have gendered expectations of their employees such as being gender-neutral, bodiless and not emotional (Acker, 1990, 2009) and this has historically benefited men (Saval, 2015). What is more, societies still expect women to care for children and the elderly, which impedes their progress in careers as many women cannot have a work-first attitude and put in long hours to succeed (ibid).[2] For example, in the advertising industry in the UK, masculine work culture dictates long working hours and this includes attending social events with clients after work, because of which many women leave the industry as they find it impossible to combine career and home life (Crewe and Wang, 2018; McLeod et al., 2011; Gill, 2014; Clare, 2013; Jarvis and Pratt, 2006; Grabher, 2004).

However, one of the major issues for women in capitalist societies is that inequality is so ingrained in daily life that many women fail to notice it,

24 *Ecofeminism*

which further prevents them from acting to change something. For example, in my research into women's experiences in advertising, journalism and public relations in England it appeared that women themselves outline masculine characteristics as desirable for leaders, thus showing they've been socialised into what is known as masculine habitus (Bourdieu, 2007; Topić, 2020b, 2020c; Topić, 2020e; Topić, 2021; Topić & Bruegmann, 2021). In all three industries, blokishness is a norm and women are expected to embrace masculine behaviour and communication to fit in and succeed. The majority of women cannot do this and thus fail to progress and feel ostracised and discriminated whereas only the minority which shows preference towards the masculine way of thinking, communicating and behaving manages to succeed. This is often linked with the early socialisation where women who spent lots of time with boys developed tomboy attitudes and thus easily fit into the organisational world, which still works according to masculine patterns (Bourdieu, 2007; Topić, 2020b, 2020c; Topić, 2020e; Topić, 2021; Topić & Bruegmann, 2021). Nevertheless, ecofeminism strives towards the celebration of differences between men and women and calls for embracing a "feminine" caring approach towards Nature (Salleh, 1991). With this, ecofeminism is also close to radical feminism where MacKinnon (1989) for example, argued that differences are used as a reason for discrimination of women rather than discrimination being naturally, logically or biologically justified by differences. As argued by Eisler (1987b) unequal gender relations are culturally produced and socially conditioned. Thus, ecofeminism stands between radical feminism (that argues that men and women are different and calls for celebrating these differences) and socialist feminism (because ecofeminism is fundamentally anti-capitalist and anti-hierarchical) (Topić, 2020d); however, ecofeminism also proposes these two doctrines and aligns them to ecological criticism and argues, as explained earlier, that a fundamental plight for women's equality can only be made in conjunction with a plight for the end of abuse of Nature.

However, not all ecofeminist positions are the same and there are substantial differences between approaches. Different authors emphasise different versions of ecofeminism. For example, Kamble (2012) argued that ecofeminism is one of four main branches of feminism, along with liberal,[3] radical[4] and socialist feminism (Kamble, 2012) and the movement grew in influence during the 1980s and the 1990s among women from environmental, anti-nuclear and lesbian organisations (Lorentzen & Eaton, 2002) following the coining of the term by a French philosopher Francoise d'Eaubonne in 1974 and further developments by Ynestra King in 1976. On the other hand, Warren (1996) argued that the term ecofeminism encompasses a variety of approaches such as socialist ecofeminism, cultural ecofeminism, radical ecofeminism, ecowomanism (Warren, 1996; Geiger, 2006a, 2006b), but what is central to ecofeminism is that while it encompasses a diversity of views it fundamentally focuses on the relationship between women and Earth and the link with a patriarchal society that explains this relationship (Merchant, 1992; Geiger Zeman & Zeman, 2010).

Ecofeminism 25

In other words, some authors distinguish between essentialist ecofeminism that speaks of biological differences between men and women and sees women as biologically closer to Nature (Daly, 1978; Griffin, 1978; Collard & Contrucci, 1988; Mies, 1986; Griffin, 1990; Eisler, 1990; Razak, 1990; Spretnak, 1990), whereas constructionist ecofeminism argues that gender is socially constructed and thus women's connection to Nature is socially constructed too (Merchant, 1990; Braidotti et al., 1995; MacCormack, 1980; Seager, 1993; Plumwood, 1993; Warren, 1994). Therefore, the constructionist perspective also supports a view that "women's and men's relationship with nature needs to be understood as rooted in their material reality" and this would then also include class, caste, race and gender (Agarwal, 1992, p. 126; Leahy, 2003). Nevertheless, while there are lots of studies that show that women are more likely to express environmental concerns (Mallory, 2006; Brownhill & Turner, 2019; Goldstein, 2006; Leahy, 2003; McStay & Dunlap, 1983; Poole & Harmon Zeigter, 1985; Shapiro & Mahajan, 1986; Steger & Witt, 1989; Diani, 1989; Schahn & Holzer, 1990; Blaikie, 1992; Franklin & Rudig, 1992; Stern et al., 1993; McAllister, 1994; Hampel et al., 1996; Tranter, 1996; Godfrey, 2005; Shiva, 1989; Brownhill, 2010; Godfrey, 2008; Holy, 2007; Mann, 2011; Stoddart & Tindall, 2011; Giacomini, 2014; Kirk, 1998; McMahon, 1997; Salleh, 1984; Topić, 2020d; Topić et al., 2021), there are also studies that show that other characteristics such as class, age and education are more important in influencing environmental support (Van Liere & Dunlap, 1980; McStay & Dunlap, 1983; Diani, 1989; Franklin & Rudig, 1992; McAllister, 1994). Inevitably, since many eco-friendly products are more expensive, environmentalism and consequentially ecofeminism became a class issue (Plumwood, 1993; Sturgeon, 1997; Twine, 2001a).

There are some streams of ecofeminism that see women as closer to Nature because of women's bodies and distinctive experiences such as ovulation, menstruation, pregnancy, childbirth, breast-feeding; however, there is also the oppression argument, which believes that "women's separate social reality, resulting from a sexual division of labour and associated oppression, has led women to develop a special insight and connection with nature" (Archambault, 1993, p. 19). The biological argument has been heavily criticised. For example, Roach (1991) pointed out that men also have bodily functions that can be seen as close to Nature such as eating, sleeping, eliminating waste, getting sick, dying and also ejaculation of semen which serves as a reproduction of life. Also, the question is whether women who do not have children are then less close to Nature since they do not go through childbirth and breastfeeding. Nevertheless, the body argument has also been criticised because it overlooks the fact some women have been complicit in environmental degradation and have embraced the masculine view of dominating Nature, thus leading to an argument that some women have ambivalent views of the environment (Kaur, 2012) albeit there is evidence that women have historically been at the forefront of environmental protection and that environmentalism is indeed a woman's issue (Mallory, 2006;

26   *Ecofeminism*

Brownhill & Turner, 2019; Goldstein, 2006; Leahy, 2003; McStay & Dunlap, 1983; Poole & Harmon Zeigter, 1985; Shapiro & Mahajan, 1986; Steger & Witt, 1989; Diani, 1989; Schahn & Holzer, 1990; Blaikie, 1992; Franklin & Rudig, 1992; Stern et al., 1993; McAllister, 1994; Hampel et al., 1996; Tranter, 1996; Godfrey, 2005; Shiva, 1989; Brownhill, 2010; Godfrey, 2008; Mann, 2011; Stoddart & Tindall, 2011; Giacomini, 2014; Kirk, 1998; McMahon, 1997; Salleh, 1984; Topić, 2020d; Topić et al., 2021).

However, claiming that women are biologically connected to Nature can indeed be seen as re-enforcing the patriarchal ideology of domination (Archambault, 1993; Twine, 2001a). Dobson (1990) argues that women cannot all fall under the same category and Archambault (1993) correctly argues that "a number of women exhibit what might be regarded as 'masculine' traits while a number of men exhibit what might be considered 'female' characteristics" (p. 20, emphasis in the original). Research has been showing for a long time that women who embrace masculine characteristics succeed better in the organisational (man's) world. For example, in journalism scholarship, this is known as bloke-ification or a situation in which only women who act like blokes and merge into blokish culture succeed in journalism. These women become one of the boys and engage with masculine banter and they embrace the masculine understanding of what constitutes news and how news writing works (Gallagher, 2002; Mills, 2014, 2017; Ross, 2001; North, 2009a, 2009b, 2016a, 2016b; Lobo et al., 2017; Topić & Tench, 2018; Topić & Bruegmann, 2021). When asked what constitutes a good editor or a good leader, across communications industries, women show a tendency to outline masculine characteristics, thus showing they merged into a masculine habitus (Bourdieu, 2007). In public relations, for example, women mention being asked to change the personal appearance and also being called "comms girls" and public relations as a profession seen as fluffy, not being taken seriously even when they do manage to join the board, and they generally face exclusions from important business decisions and confinement to lower and technical positions (Topić, 2021, 2020e; Van Slyke, 1983; Cline et al., 1986; Miller, 1988; Lance Toth, 1988; Dozier, 1988; Singh and Smyth, 1988; Broom, 1982; Scrimger, 1985; Pratt, 1986; Theus, 1985; Topić et al., 2019; Topić 2020e; Lee et al., 2018; Dubrowski et al., 2019; Aldoory and Toth, 2002; Grunig, 1999). In advertising, women equally reported exclusion, boys clubs and sexism and sexual harassment (Topić, 2020b, 2020c, 2020e; Broyles & Grow, 2008; Gill, 2014; Gregory, 2009; Grow & Deng, 2015; McDowell, 1997; McLeod et al., 2011; Mortimer, 2016; Stein, 2017; Thompson-Whiteside et al., 2020; Weisberg & Robbs, 1997).

Therefore, a generalisation is not welcome because then one might include both desirable and undesirable characteristics such as, for example, subservience, which is a negative characteristic associated with women (Archambault, 1993). However, some authors correctly emphasise that ecofeminism is not an uncritical celebration of Mother Nature or women's goodness or goddess status. This type of criticism is seen by some authors as reversed sexism or "feminism of uncritical reversal" (Plumwood, 1993, p. 31) because this critique,

> confronts itself to the very reality of women being active contributors to environmental destruction in some contexts [...] However, examining the ways in which gender and nature have been associated historically and reinforced culturally has much explanatory power and [...] it can provide the basis for an integrated liberatory ethics and politics.
>
> Alloun (2015, p. 152)

Some authors also warned that it is politically dangerous to speak of women's caring nature because these are socially constructed as feminine but also private, and thus "revaluing care in the way many ecofeminists seem to do results in an affirmation of gender roles that are rooted in the patriarchal dualisms that all feminisms [...] must aim persistently to resist and disrupt" (MacGregor, 2004, p. 58). Besides, authors also warned that we should not be "replicating production-reproduction binary" because this could limit "ecofeminist analysis to relations reified by patriarchy – of reproducing the patriarchal equation of nature, women, and the nature of women's role in reproduction" (Rudy, 2006, p. 107). In other words, just as "master's tools will never dismantle the master's house", in the same way "embracing the master's equation of women's labor as reproductive and grounded in biology only serves to rearange the furniture and applicances such that the kitchen and bedroom are moved closer to the front door" (ibid, p. 108, emphasis in the original).

Some also argued that celebrating women's difference is the new biologism, thus accusing ecofeminists of essentialism (Eisenstein, 1983) and bringing ecofeminism along with some version of Darwinism. During the 1980s, the charge of essentialism was used by liberal and some left-leaning feminists to undermine ecofeminism for writing about the difference between women and men and celebrating these differences (Salleh, 1991). Salleh (1991) thus asked why are Marxists not charged with essentialism for "describing specifics and commonalities in the condition of working-class people in Britain, say, and the Philippines?" (p. 169). Salleh (1991) argued that ecofeminism draws from the Woman/Nature theme of oppression so similar that is helps in unpacking the,

> complex and over-determined positioning of women along with nature in mythology and language; in the gendered division of labour, where women's work traditionally mediates nature and culture; and in the impact of women's reproductive experience, as this, in turn, is shaped by myth, language, and a social division of labour.
>
> p. 170

28 *Ecofeminism*

This means that when it comes to the majority of cultures, women have no voice or they have very little influence because they are treated in the same way as Nature; however,

> when ecological feminists take up the question of human embeddedness in nature, anti-essentialists start to see flashing lights. Marx himself explored the human metabolism with nature (albeit in a typically instrumental way to nature's disadvantage), yet this project did not lead him to abandon the constitutive role of history/ideology. On the other hand, women whose inquiry revives this aspect of the master narrative, are pulled up short by their socialist and other sisters for wielding 'the floating signifier', essentialism.
>
> Salleh (1991, p. 171, emphasis in the original)

A useful depiction of differences between various types of ecofeminism has been provided by Warren (1987) who argued that ecofeminism is based on four claims, that there is a connection between the oppression of women and Nature, to understand this oppression we need to understand the nature of these connections, feminism must include ecological concerns and ecological solutions must include feminist concerns. While ecofeminism can mean different things to different ecofeminists, these four postulates are what guides the ecofeminist theory and what seems to be in common to all ecofeminists (see also Birkeland, 1995). The difference between different ecofeminisms is in the emphasis they place on how we are to change the current system of oppression (Warren, n.d.). For example, social and socialist ecofeminism uses "materialist methods to analyse class and capitalist economic systems, whereas cultural ecofeminist often employs spiritual or associative, poetic modes to explore oppression on a personal as well as on a larger social level" (Carlassare, 1994, p. 221; Geiger, 2002). Socialist ecofeminism is constructionist whereas cultural ecofeminism is often called essentialist because it considers biological characteristics between men and women, which are seen as essentialist because they fail to consider social, historical and cultural context, which is variable and rooted in the patriarchal and capitalist socialisation process. As such, socialist ecofeminism sees inequality rooted in capitalist patriarchy and seeks replacement of this regime by a non-hierarchical social organisation that will not be domineering towards Nature or humans, and often socialist ecofeminists see socialist regimes as more likely to provide the possibility for dismantling capitalist patriarchy due to lack of consumerism and competitiveness in its economic models (Topić, 2020d). Merchant (1990) argued that the constructionist position of socialist ecofeminism is desirable in deconstructing and dismantling capitalism; however, she also argues that socialism in its new form could solve the problem of inequality and domination because a revolutionary social change and dismantling of capitalism and patriarchy can save the planet and liberate humanity. Socialist ecofeminists reject biological arguments because biology has been used by patriarchal structures to oppress women by reducing them to biology and thus denying opportunities and limit personal development and aspirations. Nevertheless, socialist ecofeminists agree that women and men are often different but they see this as a social construct (Sydee & Beder, 2001).

Salleh (1984) argued that women are treated as other, and this otherness comes also from the gendered socialisation process where children are socially and psychologically conditioned by the patriarchal culture and the process can be seen as confusing and deforming because it follows a similar pattern across different cultures, "women, nurturant and expressive, men, competitive and instrumental" (p. 10). This means that girls are allowed to freely express their feelings while boys are discouraged from doing so but they are not discouraged from showing aggression because this "benefits the warrior/bread-winner role" (ibid). In the same way, girls learn to be supportive and caring, and with this women are in a way producing a surplus value and this keeps patriarchy going because "the wheels of social change" keep going (ibid). This is because men are historically taught to be strong and manly, not cry and show feelings, and not stand in the way of development. As argued by Griffin (2020), no society can survive without empathy and thus by assigning empathy only to women whileactively teaching men not to be "weak", this is then continued by giving power to men. The latter ensures that empathy has no place on corporate boards or in decision-making situations; however, it is the lack of empathy towards Nature that is now threatening the survival of humanity despite masculine advances in industrialisation and technology that created economic supremacy of the West. Men certainly possess empathetic feelings as much as women; however, through societal pressure they learn not to show them not to be seen as weak. Salleh (1984) also argued that women's need for gratification is not met during the aggressive socialisation process but because of this imposition of caring nature women are more likely to notice environmental problems. This process is also known as sexual identities or sex roles, and this means that the socialisation process has a biological but, even more importantly, social connotation. Therefore, children gain a sense of their sex and sex roles in the first years of their lives; for example, children know they are either a boy or a girl in the first three years of life (18 months to 3 years). However, even more, relevant are social differences that children start to learn very early and these differences involve hierarchy that goes against girls during the socialisation process. Galić (2020), along the lines of MacKinnon (1989) outlines that social differences are justified with biological differences and seen as natural, and this then leads towards traditional and patriarchal role assignment. The latter also includes stereotyped expectations on what constitutes appropriate behaviour for boys and girls, and these roles later translate into a woman's role being less recognised and valued and this leads towards the symbolic relationship between women and Nature. Puleo (2017) also argued that socialisation has an influence on woman's oppression and particularly

30   *Ecofeminism*

in regard to Nature. Puleo (2017) correctly observed that women historically did not have an access to weapons and were traditionally responsible for caring for children and the elderly as well as maintaining households, which enabled women to develop subjectivity founded on personal connections, caring and closeness with others. However, this also resulted in the fact that women are more likely to engage with environmental activism (Mallory, 2006; Brownhill & Turner, 2019; Goldstein, 2006; Leahy, 2003; Salleh, 1989; McStay & Dunlap, 1983; Poole & Harmon Zeigter, 1985; Shapiro & Maha-jan, 1986; Steger & Witt, 1989; Diani, 1989; Schahn & Holzer, 1990; Blaikie, 1992; Franklin & Rudig, 1992; Stern et al., 1993; Holy, 2007; McAllister, 1994; Hampel et al., 1996; Tranter, 1996; Godfrey, 2005; Shiva, 1989; Brown-hill, 2010; Godfrey, 2008; Mann, 2011; Stoddart & Tindall, 2011; Giacomini, 2014; Kirk, 1998; McMahon, 1997; Salleh, 1984; Topić, 2020d; Topić et al., 2021). In my own research of eco-villages, the majority of founders of these sustainable communities are either women or a combination of a woman and a man, and eco-villages founded and led by women are less likely to have a strict hierarchy, pry into private lives of members and enforce puritan rules, as well as less likely to be religious but more likely to be secular and socialist (Topić, 2020d), thus showing women's inclination towards collec-tivism, solidarity but also women's disinclination towards militarisation and religiousness, both of which are seen as masculine. Nevertheless, military and religious institutions are seen as masculine and patriarchal institutions founded on the premise of inequality (Kirk, 1998; Reardon, 1985; Omolade, 1989; Enloe, 1993; Salleh, 2005).

Merchant (1992) argued that her socialist ecofeminist position means that she believes in "partnership ethic that treats humans (including male and female partners) as equals in personal, household and political relations and humans as equal partners with (rather than controlled by or dominant over) nonhuman nature" (p. 18). This approach advocates refraining from de-structive behaviour that contributes towards natural disasters and showing compassion towards all living life and Nature, and this includes people of different races sexualities, cultures as well as all animal life. The approach "avoids gendering nature as a nurturing mother or a goddess and avoids the ecocentric dilemma that humans are only one of many equal parts of an ecological web and therefore morally equal to a bacterium or a mosquito" (ibid, p. 19) while, at the same time, appreciating Nature and all living life (human and nonhuman). Clarke (2001) also argued that the materialist ap-proach to ecofeminism shares,

> a conception of labour and exploitation that goes beyond traditional concerns of the left with wage labour and the extraction of surplus-value. They adopt the ecofeminist view that the existing economic order must be understood as a continuation not only of the history of capitalism but also of the history of patriarchy.
>
> p. 87

Ecofeminism 31

According to Salleh (2001b), materialist and dialectical thinking that ecofeminism fosters means having a view that "humans are embedded in the ground of nature and history" and this also means that "ontology and epistemology are inseparable" while applying also "praxis or historical judgement" (p. 444).[5] Socialist ecofeminists thus predominantly research capitalist patriarchy and argue for a socialist system that would restructure the domination of women and Nature (Merchant, 2020).

Salleh (2010) argued that dismantling capitalism to achieve environmental protection will not suffice because "hegemonic masculinity and the diminishment of nature and women still have to be unravelled" (Canavan et al., 2010, p. 187). Thus, Salleh argues for embodied materialism, which would incorporate Marxism and its view of capitalism as an obstacle towards environmental protection and improvement in labour rights, but also ecofeminist concerns of masculine hegemony. This approach is also known as material ecofeminism or socialist ecofeminism. In Salleh's view, the embodied materialism,

> reaches out to re-ground Left thought and action by re-membering our human origin as nature, and - embodiment joins the human condition to its natural condition, making politics deeply and consistently material. This is a message for idealists and postmoderns. – Embodiment joins theory to praxis, making politics historically sensitive and accountable. This is a message for realists and positivists. – Embodiment join the experience and knowledge of workers, mothers, peasants, gatherers, making Left politics whole. This is a message for all movement activists.
> Cited from Canavan et al. (2010, pp. 189–190; see also Salleh, 2003)

In other words, Salleh (2005) argued that many women during the 1960s discovered "the sex/gender blind character of politics in the labour, peace and environmental movements" and even though these women highlighted how capitalist patriarchal relations work, they were sometimes silenced because the movement was "masculinist in both internal structure and functioning" (p. 10). This then resulted in an uprising of feminists and a slogan "the personal is political"; however, when trying to form women's groups these women were accused of separatism even though some men told them to do feminism elsewhere so as not to disrupt the main message of the Left (Salleh, 2005). Salleh (2013) also argued that "the psychology of masculinity is actively rewarded by the capitalist system, thereby keeping that economy intact" (ibid, p. 11). This then leads to a conclusion that socialists need to embrace the critique of patriarchy as well as capitalism because these two go hand in hand, and this is also how socialist ecofeminism emerged.

Vandana Shiva, in her speeches in Orlando and Seoul, argued that there are two conflicting views of the land, "terra madre" and "terra nullius" where terra nullius is uninhabited land that has not yet been recognised as ownership by a human coloniser. Such land is, according to this view,

32   *Ecofeminism*

"emptied by the hyper-wealthy who ignore already existing living economies of the poor", such as for example the fact that only "2% of Nigerian land is used by women to produce 50% of the country's food" (no author a, 2005, p. 145). This inevitably leads to a conclusion that ecofeminism is an anti-capitalist approach to studying women, with which ecofeminism is close to socialist feminism and this is also a reason why there is a stream of ecofeminism called socialist ecofeminism. In other words, ecofeminism's position is that capitalism is at the heart of the social and environmental crisis and the essential characteristic of capitalism is also patriarchy (saed, 2017; Brownhill & Turner, 2020). Thus, "the material and discursive institutions of patriarchal capitalism require the systematic domination and exploitation of both women and nature" (Sydee & Beder, 2001, p. 1, see also Delveaux, 2001). Nevertheless, ecofeminists postulate that "capital relies on the perpetual division of the 99 per cent through racism, sexism, xenophobia, and other divisions, such as clinically-stratified wage gaps" (Brownhill & Turner, 2020, p. 4). Thus, the capitalist regime relies on labour and domination of Nature, both of which are turned into a corporate commodity and assigned a value; however, this is only possible because capitalism relies also on the "hierarchy of labor power", which is tied together with a "male deal" between capitalists and those dispossessed men who are enticed, impressed, acculturated, or employed to channel use and intrinsic values from (waged and unwaged) labor and nature" (Brownhill & Turner, 2020, p. 4). As such, ecofeminism is a critique of "an irrational male-produced social order" (Salleh, 1984, p. 8).

Ecofeminism and the relationship with nature, science and technology

Ecofeminism is particularly concerned with our relationship with Nature and this is a central theme in all ecofeminist research. Thus, Cross (2018) argued that "in order to protect the earth from irreparable ecological destruction we need to change the relationship we have with the natural world from one which is hierarchical and fragmented to one which is ecologically responsive" (p. 29). According to Cross (2018) our current relationship with Nature is hierarchical and fragmented because it is "rooted in a culture where science and technology are posited as the epitome of reason in contract with pre-modernity, which was centred around nature, myth and religion" (p. 29).

These opposites or dualisms are the predominant ideology and the way societies operate and it leads to a culture of separation (Plumwood, 1991, 1996; Carlassare, 1994). The dualism has roots in Western patriarchal ideology and several dualisms explain the current world, such as "culture/nature, reason/emotion, subject/object, science/art, public/private, hard/soft [and] mind/body [...] These basic dualisms are gendered and hierarchical, in that the latter side of each pair has been associated with the feminine

Ecofeminism   33

and devalued in the culture" (Birkeland, 1995, n.p.). Therefore, culture (seen as order) has always been associated with male whereas Nature has been associated with the female (seen as chaos) and the female component also includes "women as a case, slaves, indigenous people, non-white races and animals" (ibid). As Nancy White famously said: "My mother used to say that the black woman is the white man's mule and the white woman is his dog" (cited from Hill Collins, 1990, p. 160). These groups, associated with the feminine, have then been seen as existing to satisfy "(elite, white) Man's purpose and needs" with domination and control of these groups being seen as natural (ibid; see also Emel, 1995). Nevertheless, some ecofeminists argue that "within patriarchy, the feminisation of nature and the naturalisation (and animalisation) of women has been crucial to the historically successful subordinations of both" (Warren, 1990, p. 133). Thus, many ecofeminists look at issues such as class, age, race and lived experiences because there is a recognition that the domination of women and Nature is deeply rooted in historical and cultural practices (Warren, 1990; Alloun 2015; Mayer, 2006; Iovino, 2013). For example, some ecofeminists traced oppression and patriarchal subordination of women and Nature back to Eurasia 4500 B.C. (Lahar, 1991) and the pre-modern times were described as matrilineal, agrarian and peaceful times (Warren, n.d.; Holy, 2007; Bahofen, 1990). Eisler (1987) argues that women in this period had prominent roles and Nature, expressed in feminine terms, was cherished and respected. The situation changed when Indo-European warriors took power and enforced patriarchy onto the world and changed the social system based on collaboration to the one of domination (ibid). Therefore, some ecofeminists argue that there is also a conceptual connection (and not just the historical one), and this means that structure of dominations were formed with the rise of patriarchy to dominate women and Nature and construct them in a male-biased way. These conceptualisations then led to the construction of dualism with men being assigned what became seen as superior quality. According to Eisler (1987), the problem is not in men but in the way masculine identity is conceptualised and defined because patriarchy equates masculine identity with domination and conquering and this then includes, Nature, women and those perceived as others (e.g. all races other than the white one).

Plumwood (1993) outlined a list of dualisms that shape the world, and this classification provides a useful overview of how the world works because the first category is always assigned a masculine meaning whereas the second one is always assigned feminine meaning (Table 2.1), thus showing that what is inherent to the masculine is always seen as first and relevant whereas the feminine is often associated with second or other, and thus less relevant and subject to domination.

Ecofeminists thus argue that the ecological devastation peeked with the rise of modernity when the growth of science and scientific reasoning was led by a "masculine way of thinking of the world" (Bordo, 1986, p. 441). This way of thinking, grounded in Cartesian dualistic objectivism, placed

34   *Ecofeminism*

Table 2.1 Plumwood's Dualisms

Culture	Nature
Reason	Nature
Male	Female
Mind	Body (nature)
Master	Slave
Reason	Matter (nature)
Rationality	Animality (nature)
Reason	Emotion (nature)
Mind, spirit	Nature
Freedom	Necessity (nature)
Universal	Particular
Human	Nature (non-human)
Civilised	Primitive (nature)
Production	Reproduction (nature)
Public	Private
Subject	Object
Self	Other

Source: adapted from Plumwood (1993, p. 43).

an instrumental role on Nature in which humanity denies a connection with Nature, and instead seeks to dominate it (Singer, 2002). Nevertheless, this view means that humans have the right to exploit Nature because humans are at the centre of the universe (Godfrey, 2008), which is an anthropocentric view endorsed by Descartes and has contributed towards creating a dichotomy of us vs them or humanity vs Nature where Nature has ended up as "other". Descartes was not alone in endorsing these views. Many highly esteemed intellectuals were involved in witch hunts, for example, thus engaging in an irrational and hateful practice of accusing women (most of whom were healers using plants to heal the sick) as witches to impose the modern science, which is supposedly based on rationality (Holy, 2007). At the same time, the war of modern science against natural remedies presents a continuation of the "us vs them" narrative. However, while masculine patriarchy oppresses and denigrates the feminine and Nature, ecofeminism celebrates both and attempts to turn oppression into empowerment (Eckersley, 1992). Thus, ecofeminism celebrates historically undervalued feminine characteristics such as "care, love, friendship, trust, and appropriate reciprocity" (Warren, 1990, p. 141). In the same way, ecofeminism celebrates Nature. Nevertheless, ecofeminism argues that "women and men act in fundamentally different ways" albeit there is a distinction that gender differences come from "learned social arrangements rather than to innate biological instincts" (Scharff, 1995, p. 165).

With the rise of modernity and dualism, masculine domination over Nature had a rise in scientific experimentation and particularly with experiments on animals, which was leading to the development of the "masculine" rationalist paradigm (Singer, 2002, p. 198). Bordo (1986) argued that Cartesian masculinity was a direct influencer on the crystallising of the masculine way of thinking which underpins scientific thought, and this resulted in masculine consciousness, which entirely removed feminine consciousness. This was also a period of the rise of capitalism, the division between public and the private sphere where men worked and led social progress while women had to stay at home, and this then also led to a dualism between reason and emotion with the reason being needed for the progress while emotion was to remain confined to the home (Donovan, 1990). Thus, both women and Nature were seen as passive and treated unequally and dominated, and this exploitation is commonly done by capitalists (Giacomini et al., 2018). In the same way, women were often seen as wild and untamed, which draws a parallel with Nature with men being seen as those who have to tame women and subordinate them, and in the same way, they subordinated Nature through the exploitation of natural resources and animal life (Shiva, 1989; Ćorić, 2014).

Equally, a process of geoengineering has been introduced with a belief that Nature can be controlled through technological intervention. In other words, this process is a deliberate intervention into Earth's processes to attempt to reverse climate change, such as Carbon Dioxide Removal (removing carbon dioxide from the atmosphere), iron fertilisation of oceans (to increase the production of algae blooms, which has also been on the downfall) and Solar Radiation Management (to reflect sun's rays back into space to reduce temperatures) (Sikka, 2017; Hulme, 2014; Preston, 2012). Buck et al. (2014) therefore argued that most of the demographic pushing for this agenda is male and the control these processes seek to achieve is "anthropocentric and oriented towards and instrumentalist view of nature" and the technology designed to achieve changes in Nature are aligned with "masculine temperament of abstraction, objectivity, precision and calculation" (p. 653). Scholars also noted that women are largely missing in research teams proposing and designing policies to engineer changes to climate change and that women will be adversely affected if something goes wrong (Bronson, 2009; Buck et al., 2014; Sikka, 2017), which is already the case with natural disasters where women have been more impacted, according to some studies (Banford & Froude, 2015).

Bronson (2009) also argued that the media discourse on geoengineering is largely sexualised and masculinist and the discourse goes in line with the Western enlightenment approach of "controlling the earth", which is fundamentally patriarchal. Therefore, some authors also started to speak of cyber/ecofeminism "as a challenge to the dualistic tendency to perceive ecological concerns as the opposite to technology or the cyber revolution" (Kailo, 2003, p. 1). However, ecofeminists also argue that modern science was "set out to virtually extinguish ('substitute') not only life, death, and the creation of life as we know it but also humanity, women, and mothers; the earth, plants, and animals; and matter itself" (von Werlhof, 2007, p. 25). As such, many ecofeminists see technology as masculine and as something that possibly benefits middle-class men who designed these technologies but

36 *Ecofeminism*

it can hardly be said this benefited women and workers, e.g. those in sweat-shops whose health is being hurt because of their work in factories (Salleh, 1993). Also, Salleh (1991) argued that the underlying premise of ecofeminism is that there is an equation mark between the abuse of women and Nature, and this can be linked with the rise of technology founded on masculine principles. For example, "in the harvesting of female bodies through *in vitro* fertilization and surrogacy experimentation; and equally, in the fact women, an 'invisible' resource put in seventy per cent of global 'labour' time" (p. 171, emphases in the original). Thus, Nature is adjusted to humanity, which violates the natural unity and natural processes, and creates subjects and objects where human is a man, and Nature is a woman, and since man is active in dominating nature, Nature has to return in giving birth and putting up with domination (Cifrić, 1990, pp. 78–79). This view is central to both ecofeminism and social ecology and the process of domination results in hierarchical subordination of women and Nature by men (Buzov, 2020). However, this position is criticised by some economists too. For example, Gills and Morgan (2020) also expressed criticism of technology as a saviour of the environment. They argued that "it is continually assumed that the economic 'costs' are limited to some lost growth within continued growth and that innovation and technological change ('progress') will be sources of solutions to any given environmental problem" (ibid, p. 6). This then also leads to the notion that we have to have faith in,

> market mechanisms and the logic of capitalism in the form of an expansionary capital accumulation system. By default it leads to a deemphasis of the positive or even necessary role for prohibitions, large scale state intervention, government planning, and regulation, in halting and reversing material expansion. Moreover, it entirely ignores radical social change organized 'from below' (substituting for this the green consumer).
>
> ibid[6]

Some ecofeminists argue that modernity has reached its end and that it has done nothing to improve the lives of humans but destroyed it (von Werlhof, 2013). Therefore, modernity has been criticised as being the bastion of patriarchy and capitalism. This process is by some feminists seen as a capitalist patriarchal world in which women and their contribution have been systematically unrecognised because of women's housewife-isation which is unpaid and unvalued labour because it does not directly contribute to the accumulation of capital (von Werlhof, 2013; Mies, 1986). A large part of this masculine culture derives from the focus on wars and the rise of militarism. Ecofeminists are therefore critical of the military as the most masculine and patriarchal institution where "militarized masculinity" has been constructed (Enloe, 1993, p. 52), and this particularly involves the link between violence and sexuality that comes up in military practice where

Ecofeminism 37

they see "rape as a weapon of war, and pornography and sexual servicing as an integral part of military culture. At root, the military organizations are sexist and racist institutions" (Kirk, 1998, p. 4, see also Reardon, 1985; Omolade, 1989). Salleh (2005) argued that women's analysis of the patriarchal structure highlighted the military as part of the problem for the oppression of women, but women's voices were silenced also because the movement itself was internally masculine.

Ecofeminism, hierarchy and masculinities

While ecofeminism celebrates women and speaks of their differences, ecofeminists also recognise that there are "women male dealers" such as Margaret Thatcher, Theresa May, Marine Le Pen, Hillary Clinton, Condoleezza Rice and other women in power who have embraced masculine characteristics and many of whom have ended up,

> being even more 'tough' than their male counterparts just to prove that they are not 'soft', emotional women, and are able to 'get the job done', that is to advance enclosures, open markets, and call on the armed force of the state, even to torture and cage children, in order to stop anyone who opposes the goals of profitable enterprise.
> Brownhill and Turner (2020, p. 5, emphasis in the original)

This is linked to already mentioned bloke-ification developed in journalism (Gallagher, 2002; Mills, 2014; Ross, 2001; North, 2009a, 2009b, 2016a, 2016b; Topić & Tench, 2018; Topić & Bruegmann, 2021) and also public relations (Topić, 2021, 2020e; Van Slyke, 1983; Cline et al., 1986; Miller, 1988; Lance Toth, 1988; Dozier, 1988; Singh and Smyth, 1988; Broom, 1982; Scrimger, 1985; Pratt, 1986; Theus, 1985; Topić et al., 2019, 2020; Lee et al., 2018; Dubrowski et al., 2019; Aldoory and Toth, 2002; Grunig, 1999) and advertising (Topić, 2020b, 2020c, 2020e; Broyles & Grow, 2008; Gill, 2014; Gregory, 2009; Grow & Deng, 2015; McDowell, 1997; McLeod et al., 2011; Mortimer, 2016; Stein, 2017; Thompson-Whiteside et al., 2020; Weisberg & Robbs, 1997) where women have also been able to advance if demonstrating what is commonly understood as a masculine style of behaviour, communication and leadership.

According to ecofeminist reasoning, patriarchy is embedded within masculine thinking because it "uses psychological tools, which can be seen as having masculine characteristics, such as a certain kind of rationality to entrench man's position as not only outside of but also as controllers of nature" (Cross, 2018, p. 29). However, material ecofeminist theory also adds that the focus of the analysis should not be on means of production and ownership, as with classical Marxist works, but that we need to focus on the "psychosexual domination of men over women and therefore over nature. That is the treatment of both women and nature as resources, and limitless

38 *Ecofeminism*

commons to be exploited and as sources of externalities to be poisoned and discarded" (Sydee & Beder, 2001, p. 10). Therefore, Salleh (2017) and Mellor (1992) argue that psychosexual schism between men and women is at the centre of the division of labour and domination and as such, serves as a precondition for capitalism. Salleh (2011) also argues that "psychological denial protects a structural hierarchy of wealth, power, and bonding opportunities between men. But near the lower rungs of this narrow ladder of rewards stand youth, indigenous peoples, and housewives – the 'others' of neoliberalism and its hegemonic masculinity" (p. 46).

As a result of this capitalist-patriarchal social system, masculine domination and masculine way of thinking "suppressed and subdued any connection humans have with the natural or the feminine" (Cross, 2018, p. 29) and this resulted in a division to masculine vs feminine and human vs Nature (Plumwood, 1991) as well with the division of labour and the private vs public sphere (Donovan, 1990). In this hierarchical and fragmented system embedded in dualisms, Kantian ethical and moral theories provide a masculine identity centred in rationality because the reason is equalised with masculinity and thus men use reason as a tool to dominate both women and Nature, which resulted in women being aligned to Nature and men as separate and opposite to Nature (Cross, 2018). Adams (2007) argued that the oppression of women and Nature are connected and is one of the main causes of environmental destruction. This is particularly the case for the Western world where the domination of women and Nature is grounded in patriarchy and hierarchy that relies on established values and duality (Warren, 1990; Godfrey, 2008). Salleh (2017, 2000) argues that the culprit can be found in Eurocentric capitalist patriarchal culture while Merchant (1990) argues that the "logic of science and capitalism, and intertwining of economics and rationalism has greatly contributed to the domination of women and nature, particularly during European colonial expansion" (see also Gaard, 1993).

What is more, ecofeminism (and socialist ecofeminism, in particular) argued that Marxist or socialist feminism alone cannot resolve the oppression of women because the founding postulate of Marxist feminism is centred on means of production and work and thus this stream of feminism argues that "maintenance and reproduction of the working class remains a necessary condition for the reproduction of capital" (Marx, 1976, p. 718). However, ecofeminists correctly argue that what is neglected is work done by women and Marxist feminism takes this notion and explores it through the analysis of social reproduction and housework. Therefore, "Marxist feminist analysis has demonstrated how women's unpaid care work that reproduces the working class acts as a subsidy for capital by externalizing the cost of social reproduction" (Fakier & Cock, 2018, p. 44). Since this work is unpaid, Marxist feminists have concentrated on critiquing this situation because external work for capitalists could not be effective without women's work at home since this work creates social bonds and keeps households and communities going (Fraser, 2014). Therefore,

> capitalist commodification of the conditions of life means that markets, money and wages mediate biological processes under modernist and developmentalist conditions at least as much as men and women mediate different aspects of biological processes for women, but that which is "biological" is wildly diverse.
>
> Rudy (2006, p. 107, emphasis in the original)

However, Marxist feminism insufficiently grasps masculine domination and the link between patriarchy and capitalism, which is why socialist ecofeminism is needed. But it needs to be emphasised that socialism alone does not resolve the problem of women's inequality either, because it is often centred on the masculine way of thinking, which a priori excludes women. For example, socialist ecology "suggests greater attention to the natural sciences but with a socialist approach" (no author b, 2011, p. 4); however, this approach again concentrates on building sciences that will not be based on bourgeois ideologies and objectives, again focusing only on capitalism and the doctrine according to which natural sciences are focused on working towards exploiting nature for capital but ignoring the reality of women being healers using herbs, which was destroyed through witch hunts when men were developing modern medicine, thus natural sciences being fundamentally based in the masculine domination (Gaard, 2011; Griffin, 2020, 2015; Marjanić, 2020; Milardović, 2016; Holm & Jokalla, 2008; d'Eaubonne & Michel, 1997; no author b, 2011). Historically, when someone questions industrialisation or technological development (both of which are associated with masculinity and patriarchy), they are labelled as sentimental or childish, and most of all, irrelevant. As some ecofeminists argue, since early childhood we are taught rationality in approach and led to believe that the only way to observe the world is scientific objectivity, and this means that, for example, every destroyed tree can be replaced with any other tree since trees are observed in groups and are seen to represent the same type of trees (ibid). Ecofeminism posits that without understanding that we are a part of all life on the planet, with which we are interconnected, humanity will continue making decisions that are jeopardising our future on Earth (Griffin, 2020).

von Werlhof (2007) also argued that the Left "exists, thinks, and feels *within* capitalist logic" and is "deeply entrenched in patriarchy" (p. 23, emphasis in the original). While it can be argued that capital has always been hostile to women and exploited them in numerous ways, this is also the case with patriarchal ideology. However, while patriarchy has existed longer than capitalism (i.e. it has existed for about 5,000–7,000 years), some on the Left incorrectly assumed that patriarchy is a historical remnant that would

40   *Ecofeminism*

eventually disappear with progress (von Werlhof, 2007). It is enough to look at the main characteristics of patriarchy to conclude that patriarchy is alive despite all progress that has been made, for example in science and technology. Patriarchy stands for,

> war as a means to plunder and conquer; systematic domination (the state system); the categorical submission of women; class divisions; systems of exploitation of humanity and nature; ideologies of male 'productivity' and religions of male 'creation'; alchemical practices that are supposed to 'prove' them; and dependence on the real productivity and creative forces of other – a thoroughly 'parasitic civilization'.
>
> von Werlhof (2007, p. 23, emphasis in the original)

These elements of patriarchy are instantly intertwined with capitalism and the desire for profit and domination of workers and women; however, capitalism can be seen as "patriarchy's latest expression" or as the "utopian project of modern patriarchy" (ibid, p. 24).

Ecofeminists therefore oppose separating humanity from Nature and the view that humans can and should control Nature but call for interconnectedness with Nature and developing new relationships based on ecological responses (Donovan, 1990). In other words, Salleh argued that humans should be "nature in embodied form" (Canavan et al., 2010, p. 184);, instead "capitalist patriarchal economies rest heavily on a profound human alienation from nature, one that is generated in the exploitation of people's labour and resources" (ibid). Connell (1987) also argued that hegemonic masculinity does not stop on men dominating women but also extends itself to the domination of "subordinated" masculinities such as gay masculinity. Embodiment is of particular importance to ecofeminism theory because it enables looking at the mastery of Nature and nature-associated people, and how domination works because both people associated with nature, and women in particular, and Nature are dominated through patriarchal ideology (Twine, 2001a). Birkeland (1995) therefore argued that

> in a power-based society, or 'patriarchy', many people feel they can only ensure the provision of personal needs (such as sex, love and belonging) through material accumulation and the display of wealth. Until we face the problem of hyper-masculine identification in the self and the culture, I suspect that there will be no fundamental social change. Were the masculine identity delinked from power, and the feminine identity delinked from submission and self-sacrifice, the basis of personal relationships could begin to change from dominance to reciprocity.
>
> p. 4

Connell (1987) emphasised femininity as "defined around compliance with this subordination to patriarchy. Other types of femininity are organised

Ecofeminism 41

around strategies of resistance or non-compliance" (Connell, 1987, p. 183, cited from Leahy, 2003, p. 109). Leahy (2003) argues that emphasised femininity is centred on a view that women are closer to Nature and that the denigration of Nature is therefore a feminine concern, but one that was never meant to carry any social power (Bloch, 1978; Merchant, 1990; Plumwood, 1993; Seager, 1993).

In other words, emphasised femininity postulates a view that women should defer social power to men and these men might define their economic interests in a way that opposes environmentalism. Therefore, marriage and kinship also have a role because women are intertwined with men in their daily lives and there is a link with social class or a situation in which some may want to be more active in environmental protection but simply cannot afford it. For example, in a quantitative study on shopping behaviour, we conducted in the UK (Topić et al., 2021) on a large sample of the UK population, it appeared that women who come from a lower socioeconomic status had a significantly more negative view of discounted food (e.g. yellow-sticker food from UK supermarkets[7]), reduced-price shopping habits and were more likely to waste food and not plan their shopping sustainably. The reason for this view was an emotional reaction to not being able to have agency in deciding whether to buy discounted food due to their socioeconomic status but being forced to purchase it, rather than being necessarily anti-environmental. However, the study has also shown that women from lower socioeconomic status are less likely to see environmental movements as credible because they do not perceive people who participate in these organisations to have the same food purchasing options as they do. Thus, women from the lower socioeconomic background are less likely to identify as environmentalists and values associated with environmentalism, and some even expressed hostility towards these values because of the lack of perceived power and agency and a sense of resentment was visible in not having a choice on what food to buy (ibid).

Leahy (2003) argues that some working-class people see the environmental movement as a middle-class movement that pushes for one particular agenda without consideration of an effect on working-classes while some middle-class people see the environmental movement as a threat to capitalist enterprises from which they profit, and thus those part of middle classes who advocate for environmental protection are sometimes seen as traitors of their class. It is indeed true that the environmental movement has always had links with anti-consumerism (Roszak, 1992). As Hugo Blanco (a former peasant leader in Peru) wrote,

> At first sight, environmentalists or conservationists are nice, slightly crazy guys whose main purpose in life is to prevent the disappearance of blue whales or pandas. The common people have more important things to think about, for instance how to get their daily bread ....
> Blanco (1991, cited from Martínez-Alier, 1997, p. 97)

42   *Ecofeminism*

This is also linked to the notion of hegemonic masculinity where excessive competition is seen as a masculine trait and a masculine ideal (Connell, 1987; Macpherson, 1962). Some authors argued that this distinction is a result of different identities and a sense of self among men and women. Gilligan (1993) argued that women identify relationally whereas men identify through separation and individuation, which means that for men separation from mother is a sign of masculinity while women define their development through attachment to others. As a result, "male gender identity is threatened by separation and males tend to have difficulty with relationships, while females tend to have problems with individuation" (Gilligan, 1993, p. 8, see also Salleh, 1993, 1984). This then leads towards women leaning more towards "an ethic of responsibility, which relies on the concept of equity, the recognition of differences in need" (Gilligan, 1993, p. 164), and this then leads to developing compassion and care. On the other hand, men tend towards an "ethic of rights", which is based on equal respect and fairness (Gilligan, 1993, pp. 164–165). Ecofeminists are wary of ethics because of its emphasis to care about human animals only rather than all life on the planet and as such, the ethical ideas are centred on rights and justice (Yudina & Fennell, 2013). Ecofeminism, in contrast, emphasises empathy, "which connects us to the rest of the natural world and allows us to become aware of the interests and needs of individual beings" (ibid, p. 57). Therefore, some ecofeminists explore the connection between meat-eating and the oppression of women because animals are also oppressed and dominated (Gaard, 2002; Govedić & Marjanić, 2008; Holy, 2008) and used for meat-eating, which also contributes to environmental degradation (Marjanić, 2020, 2008; Milardović, 2016; Holm & Jokalla, 2008).

Vegetarian ecofeminists called for vegetarianism or veganism because people need to stop their own acts of oppression if inequality is to be eradicated within humanity (Houde & Bullis, 1999). The refusal to eat meat then presents an embodied response that shows our feelings for others, and this is done through concrete action (Kheel, 2009). This form of ecofeminism also uses the notion of "personal is political", which derives from radical feminism to examine dietary choices (Gaard, 2002). However, this can also be extended to capture ecology because personal is always "ecological, communal and political economic in character" (Rudy, 2006, p. 109). Some ecofeminists noted that people are the only living creatures on the planet that consume milk from other animals and that continues to consume milk even in the adult age, which results in the oppression of animals and fits into speciesism that ecofeminism also tackles. In an ecofeminist view, women are attached to the domestic sphere where they prepare food to serve men while animals are food, thus both women and animals serving the institution of food which is dominated by men (Adams, 1991; Gruen, 1993). Meat, in particular, represents the objectification of animals because animals that preceded the food on the plate are objectified and invisible and the treatment of animals, which face violence, corresponds with the violence women face too (Adams, 2017, 1991; Radulović, 2020). Nevertheless, a patriarchal criticism of veganism is often directed towards men vegans who are seen as weak even though being conformist is a sign of weakness in all other contexts, which means that men who refuse to conform to patriarchal norms and eating meat are not weak by the definition of conformism (Didulica, 2020). Thus, women are more likely to eat fruit and vegetables while men are supposed to eat meat, both of these views being socially and patriarchally constructed (Adams, 2010). This culture of violence against animals (Adams, 2017, 2010, 1991) is projected to women who were historically prevented from speaking about their own oppression through social norms and imposed expected roles (Stepanović, 2020). For example, Suffragettes were judged negatively for fighting for their voting rights because aggression was seen as inappropriate for women, and this is still the case because women are forged into caregivers during the socialisation process. However, while women managed to eventually start speaking against their oppression, animals never had a voice. Therefore, Adams (2010) argues that eating meat is to animals what is homophobia to gay people, white racism to people from diverse origin, and misogyny to women. However, there is surprisingly little work on the meat industry in ecofeminist theory. In other words, while many ecofeminists tackle veganism and vegetarianism, not much work has been done on media silence on the environmental impact of the meat industry. Media often write on emissions and pollutions, but it is difficult to find articles that specifically show data on the impact of the meat and dairy industry (or cattle breeding), which is higher than transport industry, the latter often being quoted by the media (Marjanić, 2020, 2019, 2017, 2008; Milardović, 2016; Holm & Jokalla, 2008).[8]

While ecofeminists do not question that science liberates and helps, they also point out that scientific and technological development has also contributed towards global warming and the destruction of the planet. This is particularly connected with the West and its developments that contribute more towards pollution and global warming due to excessive consumerism, than the Global South which is suffering consequences of global warming more (Holy, 2007; Hösle, 1996; Salleh, 2000, 1994; Sandberg & Sandberg, 2010; Griffin, 2020). Therefore, Griffin (2020) asked whether it is finally the time to re-examine these processes and impacts on the environment as well as whether it is the time to examine values and the way of life people lead, especially if looking from the perspective of the Global South. These issues are fundamentally linked to science and the so-called objectivity because scientific research has for a long time contributed towards perspectives that Western people are somehow superior to non-Western people, which historically justified exploitation. For example, theories on race, size of sculls and brains were used to justify slavery because people were seen as inferior because of which some authors argued that Nature is again being used by humans only this time to justify political inequality (Condorcet, 2012). This is closely linked to objectivity in which humans learn to distance themselves

44 *Ecofeminism*

from the natural environment through patriarchal masculine dogma. For example, subjective feelings and empathy are dismissed as irrelevant and sensitive and thus many colonisers or members of corporations who take land from indigenous people to foster their private interests are taught to push these feelings aside to the point many do not even consider it. Gender is naturally connected to this behaviour because women are seen as overly sensitive and emotional and this behaviour has historically been dismissed as weak and incompatible with the development and growth of humanity, because of which men still control most of the world's resource and hold power globally.

Ecofeminism vs deep ecology debate and the criticism of ecofeminism

Criticism of ecofeminism came from some streams of feminism, as already mentioned earlier in this chapter, but the most hostile criticism came from the deep ecology, an approach that advocates "the cultivation of conscious-ness: of being aware of our surroundings and of those beings that are around us as well. Part of this consciousness is clearly intuitive for it involves appre-ciating the 'actuality of rocks, wolves, trees and rivers ...'" (Booth, 2000, p. 5). According to Hallen (1999), deep ecology essentially does not consider feminist theory and when they do consider some works on women, they have often taken into consideration opinions of male authors and they also tend to conflate with just one version of ecofeminism. Besides, deep ecol-ogy postulates a gender-neutral approach, which often leads to gender bias and omission of specific issues women face in the contemporary world and also since the introduction of patriarchy, which happened some 5,000–7,000 years ago (von Werlhof, 2007) consequences of which are still felt today. Nevertheless, deep ecology also looks at population pressures but without looking at the fact that women very often have no power over controlling their own reproductive processes. Gaard (2015) argued that women's fertil-ity in the South is not a problem but over-consumption in the North and its contribution of greenhouse gases, which totals to 80% of the world's emis-sions. She argues that

> reducing third world population becomes increasingly important when first-world overconsumers realize that the severe climate change out-comes already heading for the world's most marginalized communities will create a refugee crisis and urgent migrations of poor people. Since the growing population of the Two-Thirds World will be hardest hit by climate change effects and will seek asylum in One-Thirds nations – a migration perceived as a threat to the disproportionate wealth (i.e. "security") of the North – the spectre of climate refugees has inspired arguments for increased militarization as protection against migration.
> Gaard (2015, p. 16)[9]

D'Eaubonne ([1990] 1997) also argued that women were first prevented from controlling their bodies through abortion bans, which increased the population because the manpower was needed, but then when the situation for capitalism changed, in the industrialised societies, their bodies got controlled through unemployment, which is why contraception suddenly got introduced. As such, ecofeminists labelled deep ecology as a white, middle class and masculine ideology because deep ecologists omit specific issues with the domination of women, Nature and also diverse races and different classes (see also Hallen, 1987; Warren, 1987; Slicer, 1995; Plumwood, 1993; Salleh, 1984, 1992, 1993). Nevertheless, many ecofeminists (both cultural and socialist as two opposing ends of ecofeminism) have been critical of the views of the father of deep ecology, Arne Naess, who claimed that total equality is impossible because some form of exploitation will always have to happen (Salleh, 1993). Salleh (1993) argued that women's unfavourable reduction to reproductive labour and a labour resource is not considered in the deep ecology approach and, nevertheless, serves as a way of subsuming women's energies,

> most often by means of the institution of the family, is homologous to exploitative class relations under the capitalist system. The family is integrally connected with and makes industrial production possible by "reproducing" the labour force, in the several senses of that word. However, as productivism intensifies with new technologies and the promise of ever-greater profits, labour becomes increasingly removed from the satisfaction of basic needs. As a result, under the guise of "development", a new dimension is added to the women's role constellation – that of conspicuous consumer.
>
> Salleh (1993, p. 15, emphasis in the original)

In this sense, deep ecology fails to understand that women have not been consulted about the system and in the same way the environment is being damaged by the development, women are also being violated by "men's systematic appropriation of their energies and time" (ibid). Salleh (2013) argues that women face dual oppression and while the behaviour is a social construct that often comes from the socialisation process, there is also a biological component of women bodies and violence women have experienced for thousands of years despite being a majority in any class or any ethnic group.

Deep ecology has been founded by Arne Naess, and this approach emphasises that people are a part of the planet Earth, which has a much wider ecological framework and only unity with Nature can humans fulfil themselves and their duties. Deep ecology believes that all living creatures are equal and that humans are not more relevant than other living creatures, as humans are inhabitants of the same biological community as are others (Holy, 2007). Naes (1989), thus formulated eight principles of the deep ecology, which are centred on valuing all life on the planet (human and

46 *Ecofeminism*

non-human) and appreciating the richness and diversity of life on Earth as beneficial for both humans and non-humans. In this view, humans do not have the right to use resources other than to satisfy their basic needs and the human influence on the non-human world is unnecessarily high, thus economic, technological and ideological structures need to change living conditions and ensure that non-human life on the planet can also grow and not just human population. Ideological change means that the change should happen so that humans would start appreciating the quality of life and not the high standard of life, and those who subscribe to these principles must adhere to them and actively encourage change.

Deep ecology is different from other ecological movements because it does not advocate for technological developments to resolve the climate crisis but ask questions about our way of life. The latter view is a similarity between deep ecology and ecofeminism because ecofeminism also questions consumerism as our way of life and thus criticises capitalism as inherently incompatible with environmental protection. In the same way, both movements encompass people regardless of their race and origin and open question on racism and indigenous population, for example. The main difference between the two approaches is that ecofeminists do not blame the anthropocentric view of the world (as deep ecologists) but an androcentric, patriarchal worldview that assumes domination and oppression (Holy, 2007). While some deep ecologists express criticism of ecofeminism, some deep ecologists accepted ecofeminist criticism according to which deep ecology uses patriarchal language and worldview; however, these deep ecologists also mention that women have been influenced by patriarchy due to its long existence and think in patriarchal way (Zimmerman, 1990), thus challenging ecofeminist view of women's difference; however, as some works have shown, the majority of women are indeed inclined to engage with environmental protection (Mallory, 2006; Brownhill & Turner, 2019; Goldstein, 2006; Leahy, 2003; McStay & Dunlap, 1983; Poole & Harmon Zeigter, 1985; Shapiro & Mahajan, 1986; Steger & Witt, 1989; Diani, 1989; Schahn & Holzer, 1990; Blaikie, 1992; Franklin & Rudig, 1992; Stern et al., 1993; McAllister, 1994; Hampel et al., 1996; Tranter, 1996; Godfrey, 2005; Shiva, 1989; Brownhill, 2010; Godfrey, 2008; Holy, 2007; Mann, 2011; Stoddart & Tindall, 2011; Giacomini, 2014; Kirk, 1998; McMahon, 1997; Salleh, 1984; Topić, 2020d; Topić et al., 2021) and do have different characteristics than men due to socialisation process; however, it is those who fit into the patriarchal way of thinking and doing things that succeed in the current world (Gallagher, 2002; Mills, 2014; Ross, 2001; North, 2009a, 2009b, 2016a, 2016b; Topić & Tench, 2018; Topić & Bruegmann, 2021).

Another important difference is that deep ecologists often think the population needs reducing because of the shortage of resources whereas ecofeminists oppose the population argument by arguing the problem is in our behaviour and consumption and that deep ecology ignores class, race and gender and accompanying inequalities as a reason for the population

Ecofeminism 47

growth (Holy, 2007). Some of the harshest critics of ecofeminism from the deep ecology camp argue that women are highly responsible for environmental degradation. For example, Fox (1995) argued that women are high spenders of the beauty industry that destroys the environment and are complicit in animal abuse because animals are used to test beauty products. However, what is missing here is the fact fashion has been imposed on women as part of patriarchal domination because women were historically expected to look appealingly, thus this issue is a complex and fiercely debated in feminist scholarship (Parkins, 2006; Mellicker, 2016; Wolf, 1991; Faludi, 1991; Scott, 2006; Topić & Polić, 2020).[10]

Also, ecofeminism has been accused of essentialism; however, when critics write about this they usually refer to concepts from cultural ecofeminism or radical feminism, albeit they do not always articulate this, with which they attempt to undermine ecofeminism as a whole. Salleh (2010) argued there is nothing essentialist about ecofeminism, as "that charge has often been tossed off before any effort is made to understand what our epistemological claims actually are. And sometimes, the prosecutor has only a very hazy idea of what essentialism itself actually means" (cited from Canavan et al., 2010, p. 190). Salleh argued that there are everyday essentialisms that are present and unquestioned such as liberal feminism, Marxism and patriarchy. For example, it would also be essentialist to say that both men and women are complicit in environmental degradation, and this is used on an everyday basis. Salleh is also particularly concerned with criticism for looking at "men vs women" dichotomy which some feminists criticised as heterosexist imperialism and homophobia albeit ecofeminists, and Salleh in particular, consider sexualities to be a continuum and not binary (cited from Canavan et al., 2010); however, *ecofeminists look at "man vs woman dichotomy" or "masculine vs feminine" dichotomy because this is how societies are still constructed.* It can be argued that, for example, transgender men and women also fall under the feminine paradigm in patriarchy and are subjected to similar discrimination as women. In the same way, gay men will often suffer from discrimination for failing to meet the macho requirement, which is centred on heterosexuality. This is why it is central to look at masculinities and femininities and to particularly focus on the position of women. In other words, women and everyone associated with them suffer from patriarchal discrimination and thus without solving the problem of patriarchy it is unlikely that equality will be achieved. However, patriarchy is closely linked with capitalism, and thus dismantling these two intertwined systems are the road to equality in the view of ecofeminism.

What is also an issue is that many ecological movements have patriarchal and masculine structures and thus apply aggressive methods in environmental campaigning, which are failing in achieving large public support. For example, an organisation Earth First! used aggressive methods of campaigning until Judi Bari joined and insisted on non-violent action to stop the devastation of redwood forests in California by cutting down trees. Instead

48 *Ecofeminism*

of aggressively fighting, Bari insisted that activists guard the trees against destruction, which increased public support for the campaign. This change led to an internal conflict where some members of the organisations sided with Bari in advocating a human approach to protecting Nature and agreed to tackle sexism in the way actions are being organised; however, the old members abandoned the movement arguing the movement is not a leftist social movement but a movement to preserve Nature only (Holy, 2007).[11] Richard Twine (2001b) also correctly argued that ecofeminism is not forgetful of the critique of capitalism unlike other ecological movements, which advocate for environmental protection but ignore that the root of environmental degradation is in excessive consumption, which is inherent to capitalism. What is more, ecofeminism criticises not just capitalism and inequality that emerges from this system but also three major isms, racism, sexism and speciesism which leads to degradation and devastation of Nature. Since ecofeminism is a synthesis of ecologism and feminism, Holy (2007) thus argues that ecofeminism is a meta feminism, but certainly not a loosely connected mix of ecology and feminism.

The approach of the book

In this book, I am using socialist ecofeminism as a framework. This form of ecofeminism is particularly relevant for analysing CSR because it shows how CSR functions as part of capitalism in which news media endorse CSR and economic growth while also supporting environmental initiatives, with which news media perpetuate the same discourse that corporation does, i.e. they support environmentalism using a liberal doctrine of regulating environmental protection, but even more importantly, the news media support capitalism either directly through looking for ways to create the "better capitalism" or by simply calling for initiatives that do not challenge the status quo or make a meaningful contribution to the debate. However, due to the enormous coverage of environmental affairs, there is a real danger of environmental fatigue among members of the British public, which can result in an environmental catastrophe.

One could ask why would it be the role of the media to foster environmental protection since media are supposed to be impartial? There are two answers to that question, (a) the media have already taken a stance with their editorial policies and official positions (analysed in the findings chapters) and with that, they have voluntarily given up the defence of media impartiality and (b) media impartiality is a dogma of some scholars and practitioners but it is not the only view on this issue. Some authors and practitioners argue that media have a different role due to their mass reach and that the media are the fourth pillar of democracy (including also executive power, legislative power and judiciary), with which one can argue that media have a responsibility towards societies, which is not linked with the usual CSR concept. Therefore, an approach called media social responsibility argues that media do have certain responsibilities for society, which is discussed in the next chapter and which is also one of my arguments.

In other words, media affect attitudes and views on a mass scale, which has been demonstrated in decades of scholarship (McCombs & Shaw, 1972; McCombs, 2004, 2005, 2014; McCombs et al., 2011; Shaw, 1979; Manheim & Albritton, 1984; Terkildsen & Schnell, 1997; Kim et al., 2002; Shuck & de Vreese, 2006; Boomgaarden & Vliegenthart, 2007; Picard, 2014; McCombs & Stroud, 2014; Figenschou et al., 2015; Topić, 2020a). With that, their role becomes more important than the role of the Government or any policy institution because it is media that still have the power to set the agenda and put issues before the public, call for action (as they do with environmental affairs nowadays) and affect people's behaviour. Therefore, the media's role in society is different than the one of corporations or the general public and some scholars argue, and this is my position too, that media have a unique social responsibility. This is discussed in the next chapter, within a wider CSR debate. However, before discussing media social responsibility, a concept of CSR is critically discussed using an ecofeminist lens. In other words, before we can move on to analysing media coverage of CSR, economic growth and environmental affairs, it is relevant to analyse and deconstruct the CSR concept, which I see as a smokescreen to preserve the status quo and, in a way, save capitalism.

Notes

1 The Difference Approach, for example, postulates that women and men have different interests and do things differently (Rakow & Nastasia, 2009; Maltz & Borker, 1982; Yule, 2006) and this is, in large part, a result of the socialisation process (Bourdieu, 2007). For example, in the communications field, Tannen (1995, 1990, 1986) argued that women have a supportive communication style centred on building relationships whereas men often have a dominating communication style marked with interruptions and dominating conversations. These differences are also transferred to leadership styles where women are seen as more supportive leaders but because they do not always show toughness they face stigma and career barriers despite male masculine style not achieving higher results than a feminine leadership style (Merchant, 2012; Vukoičić, 2013; West & Zimmerman, 1983; Tannen, 1990; Christopher, 2008; de la Rey, 2005; van der Boon, 2003; Growe & Montgomery, 2000; Crawford, 1995; Stanford et al., 1995; Alimo Metcalfe, 1995; Anderson et al., 2006; Morgan, 2004; Chemers et al., 2000).

2 This leads back to Acker's (1990) argument on the inequality regime and gendered organisations because if workers are conceptualised as men and men have minimum responsibility in procreation then enables men to work long hours and socialise with clients whereas women fall behind. Thus, "the persons at the top of most organisations are likely to be white men; they are very privileged and have great class power compared with most other people in the organisation" (Acker, 2009, p. 3).

3 Liberal feminism follows reform environmentalism and this means changing human relationship with nature through laws and regulations (Merchant, 2020) but it does not discuss deeper connection with nature. Liberal feminism, generally,

50 *Ecofeminism*

sees people as individuals and all people as reasonable creatures working towards meeting their interests and goals. As such, liberal feminism does not seek to undermine capitalism because it sees this regime as fundamental towards progress of humanity. Liberal feminists claim that women are no different than men and that both are reasonable and rational creatures (Merchant, 2020), with which they are opposed to radical feminism (and some branches of ecofeminism) that sees women as inherently different and celebrates these differences (Holy, 2007). According to liberal feminists, environmental problems came about as a result of too fast development and because of a failure to regulate environmental protection; thus, environmental problems could be resolved with science and legislation (Merchant, 2020). Liberals place an emphasis on personal freedom and living a life of one's own choosing (Stanford Encyclopedia of Philosophy, 2020). This means that liberal feminism asks for women to be treated the same as men, and there are two camps: egalitarian liberal feminism asks for more to be done to improve personal and political autonomy of women, while classical liberal feminism asks argues that feminism needs to oppose women being treated different than men (ibid). According to liberal feminists,

> all women and men should be considered full individuals, capable of making rational decisions; a special focus should be placed upon opportunities for women to increase social and political participation only because women have not been treated as full individuals for a long time, and only until this advantage for women is overcome.
>
> Rakow and Nastasia (2009, p. 254)

4 Radical feminism looks at patriarchy and liberation of women, and this is followed in radical ecofeminism where radical ecofeminists research environmental problems within the critique of patriarchy. This is then followed up by proposals for liberating women and nature (Merchant, 2020). According to radical feminists, human nature is founded in biology which determines sex whereas society determined gender and gender differences. Radical feminists celebrate women's differences such as giving birth, breastfeeding, menstruation etc. and believe that the societies under value women's distinctiveness just like they under value nature. As opposed to this view, radical feminists celebrate women's distinctiveness as a source of woman's power (Merchant, 2020). Radical feminism argues that patriarchy has resulted with a historical oppression of women by men and advocate replacing the current system with the new system because the system needs a fundamental change rather than a reform. Radical feminism also argues that women and men are different and celebrates women's distinctiveness and contributions they make to societies (Daly, 1973). Millett (1969) set out a definition of patriarchy that stands for today's world as it did back in the 1960s when she was writing. According to this definition, patriarchy is a social system in which all men dominate women and older men dominate younger men, and this is often visible in differences in upbringing, expected roles between girls and boys when growing up and this later translates into expected roles for men and women (Eichenbaum & Orbach, 1999; Van Zoonen, 2004; Tench et al., 2017; Tench & Topić, 2017).

5 However, other forms of ecofeminism (which are often criticised for essentialism) are (the most criticised) cultural ecofeminism, which focuses on a critique of patriarchy but then moves to an extreme direction by focusing on spirituality and ancient rituals such as goddess worship, moon, animals and the female reproductive system, which also leads to anti-science and anti-technology views (Merchant, 1992). Nevertheless, liberal ecofeminism (which derives from liberal feminism) is criticised by ecofeminists because it does not give adequate respect

to nature but maintain oppressive and patriarchal views of nature as subordinated to humans (Warren, n.d.).

6 Morgan (2019) also asked whether we will work in the 21st century capitalism given all advances in technology and automation.

7 The yellow-sticker shopping is a British term for buying food which is near expiry date and reduced by British supermarkets which normally have a special shelve for this food. For more on views and attitudes on this type of shopping see Kelsey et al. (2019).

8 It is indeed surprising that ecofeminists are not more concerned with meat consumption other than a few vegan/vegetarian ecofeminists. For example, some data shows that livestock industries are contributing towards global warming higher than transport industry, for example (Steinfeld et al., 2006; Friend, 2019). According to Bajželj et al. (2014) further expansion of agriculture is undesirable because agriculture is the main contributor towards climate change and pollution and the biggest contributor towards the loss of biodiversity. Ripple et al. (2014) also had a similar conclusion about global emissions. According to the Food and Agriculture Organization of the United Nations,

> with emissions estimated at 7.1 gigatonnes CO2-eq per annum, representing 14.5 percent of human-induced GHG emissions, the livestock sector plays an important role in climate change. Beef and cattle milk production account for the majority of emissions, respectively contributing 41 and 20 percent of the sector's emissions. While pig meat and poultry meat and eggs contribute respectively 9 percent and 8 percent to the sector's emissions. The strong projected growth of this production will result in higher emission shares and volumes over time. Feed production and processing, and enteric fermentation from ruminants are the two main sources of emissions, representing 45 and 39 percent of sector emissions, respectively. Manure storage and processing represent 10 percent. The remainder is attributable to the processing and transportation of animal products. Included in feed production, the expansion of pasture and feed crops into forests accounts for about 9 percent of the sector's emissions. Cutting across categories, the consumption of fossil fuel along the sector supply chains accounts for about 20 percent of sector emissions.
>
> Gerber et al. (2013, p. xii)

9 Population is also often discussed in liberal economics. For example, Linking economic growth with the population is a common area of research for liberal economics who are measuring growth in population on demand for capital, investment opportunities and savings. For example, Keynes (1937) analysed economic growth in the period between 1860–1913 and argued this has happened because of investment demand and this was because of population growth and the technological changes. In Keynes' view, this growth in investment demand increased the productivity of labour and the standard of life. Hence,

> according to Keynes, the only remaining possibilities for restoring the full employment level of income were a lowering of the interest rate (to encourage capital intensity and investment demand) or to reduce savings and increase consumption through greater equality of income distribution.
>
> Cited from Tarascio (1971, p. 434)

Keynes (1937) was generally interested in achieving full employment and thus looked at what can be done to achieve this. His ideas were of a mixed economy where the economic system drives consumption to drive living standards; however, at the time of crisis, the government is expected to intervene while in times

52   *Ecofeminism*

of stability economies are business-led (Jahan et al., 2014). Nevertheless, foreign trade is seen as a large catalyst of economic growth and classical as well as Keynesian economists often calculate how to achieve economic growth to foster employment. The difference is in the fact Keynes believed in government intervention to help when a recession happens whereas classical economists believed in cyclical nature of the economy and advocated against the government intervention and a full free-market policy (Niehans, 1987; Grampp, 1965). Economic growth, in a nutshell, means increasing production of goods and services, as well as increases in capital goods, labour force, human capital and technology. An estimate used to calculate economic growth is GDP, for example (Investopedia, 2021).

10 For example, some feminists historically criticised the fashion industry because they saw it as a bastion of patriarchy, which created a prejudice that women are only interested in fashion. This resulted with the hostility of many feminists towards the fashion industry and this includes socialist feminism, which saw the industry as extremely capitalist and engaged in exploitative capitalist practice such as producing garments in the sweatshops based in the Global South along with enforcing racist prejudices on beauty by focusing on white, thin and tall women for far too long (Parkins, 2006; Mellicker, 2016). Wolf (1991) argued that the "beauty myth" places social value on women's personal appearance, which is defined with thinness and youthfulness. This focus on appearance is seen as oppressive because of its focus on unhealthy beauty routines that do not provide anything meaningful to women (Wolf, 1991; Faludi, 1991). Some authors also argued that women were also pushed towards interest in fashion as a response of the male-dominated advertising industry to the threat of the second wave feminism (Tyner & Ogle, 2009). However, some feminist authors defend fashion industry by arguing that even though fashion was imposed on women it has been so for too long that now forms part of women's identity and many women remain interested in fashion, and these feminists also emphasise a historical contribution of the fashion industry to women's empowerment (Parkins, 2006; Scott, 2006).

11 Judi Bari later got disabled through a bomb that was placed under her car and the case remains unresolved (Judi Bari official website, n.d.).

3 Corporate social responsibility

An ecofeminist reading of the concept

In this chapter, I am conducting an ecofeminist reading of the CSR concept. In other words, I am arguing that CSR is a capitalist concept meant to preserve a status quo and this is visible in the way this concept is conceptualised and analysed. In that, I am discussing the hierarchical nature of CSR where people working in corporations decide what is good for the society in what can be seen as asymmetrical communication. According to Grunig and Hunt (1984) and the well-known model of organisational communication they developed, an asymmetrical model of communication means organisations are trying to persuade consumers to entice behavioural change for the organisational benefit. While earlier communication was centred on manipulation and deceit, for example the press agentry model of 19th-century communication, this model intends to improve the message to increase sales or improve reputation management, and the persuasiveness of messages comes from the public feedback. In the same way, it seems that companies take information from consumers and then react with changes to their CSR policies. For example, in a study we conducted in 2020 on plastic, industry professionals working in sustainability departments told us that they changed their CSR policies and returned more to sustainability policies because of consumer activism, which prompted changes in supermarket policies and this then came down to packaging companies who had to change the packaging, thus showing that CSR implementation was driven by consumers and not a genuine will of companies to do good. Therefore, we argued that companies are mirroring the *zeitgeist* in their CSR policy design as they shifted to environmental policies when consumers engaged with environmentalism (Topić et al., 2020a). As Sandoval (2013, p. 51) argued,

> it is unlikely that corporations will voluntarily refrain from irresponsible behaviour if this undermines their profit interests. This, therefore, points at the limits of voluntary CSR. The idea of voluntary corporate self-regulation is deeply flawed; it strengthens rather than limits corporate power, it depoliticises the quest for a responsible economy, and it ideologically masks how corporate interests, competition and power structures are related to irresponsible conduct.

DOI: 10.4324/9781003091592-3

54 *Corporate social responsibility*

Gan (2006) analysed philanthropy among 40 Fortune 500 companies and also argued that corporations give to charitable causes for reputation reasons because of external pressures (media attention and lawsuits, in particular) and not for altruistic reasons. These examples show a public relations practice of asymmetrical communication where consumers express concerns and companies then change policies to persuasively show their willingness to listen and help. This in itself presents a hierarchy between organisations and the public as someone in organisational management decides on which consumer feedback to listen to.

Stakeholder management has become an increasingly important issue because of changes in consumer behaviour and different expectations that came as a result of a generational change. For example, Diers-Lawson (2020) argues that crises are common because many crises come as reputation issues and emerge on social media, which is a shift from how crises worked in the past. This can explain the increased focus on CSR, as CSR can be managed on social media and used for reputation management and PR activities. A question can be asked: why is it someone in some corporation that needs to decide what society needs? How does this process work? What is more, the UK is still a class society where one's background persistently influences their life opportunities (Social Mobility Commission, 2019, 2020a; Johnson & Kossyh, 2008) and thus the question is who decides on which type of consumer feedback, views and needs. As already mentioned in the previous chapter, environmentalism has a class tension because many working-class people see it as a middle-class movement they cannot afford to join (Leahy, 2003).

Nevertheless, the concept and the CSR practice, in general, imply that companies' role is to do good for the society and give something back whereas I argue that this is not true and that the whole CSR discourse is a smokescreen to distract attention that companies are fundamentally capitalist enterprises, and investing into CSR goes hand in hand with increasing economic growth and consumerism, which causes environmental damage (Salleh, 2000, 1994; Shiva, 1999; d'Eaubonne, 1997; Georgescu-Roegen, 1971; Meadows et al., 1972, 2004; Ehrlich & Holdren, 1971; Cleveland et al., 1984: Trentmann, 2016; Wright & Nyberg, 2015; Krstić & Krstić, 2017; Coghlan, 2009; Corrigan, 1997; Douthwaite, 1999; Mishan, 1967; Ewen & Ewen, 1992; Calder, 1990; Krstić, 2018; Krstić et al., 2018; Fleming & Jones, 2013; Ireland & Pillay, 2008; Sheehy, 2014). In other words, the majority of large companies in the UK now have sustainability managers or CSR managers and teams of employees working on introducing and enforcing CSR and sustainability policies, which (a) increases costs for companies and (b) CSR policies are, in the majority of cases, used as a public relations tool to appeal to consumers who have become more active in voicing their concerns to companies about sustainability. This critical view is also present in other works that criticise the public relations profession and CSR, such as Chomsky (2002) and critical NGOs who see public relations as a profession that

Corporate social responsibility   55

uses persuasion to influence the media and shift public attention from what really matters (for a discussion see Fawkes, 2007).[1] For example, Frankental (2001) expressed criticism of CSR as a PR invention, arguing that CSR only exists if it brings rewards from the market. Evidence for this, according to him, can be found in the fact that

> if CSR was not just an invention of PR then it would have certain characteristics: a commonly understood definition (within and across companies); a common set of benchmarks to measure the attainment of corporate social responsibility; established processes in place to achieve these benchmarks; a system of internal auditing; a system of external verification by accredited bodies.
>
> Frankental (2001, p. 20)

In other words, CSR policies would not change as often as they do and all companies would have the same policy and procedure as with, for example, some equality policies.

Critiques of CSR as a concept also say that the practice of green marketing (which in the majority of cases they see as greenwashing) stems from a belief that "a company can and should align its profit-seeking self-interests with the general interests of society and the environment. Yet, underneath the language of "sustainable business", the discourse and tools of evaluation remain eerily similar to neo-liberal capitalist thought" (Alves, 2009, p. 2, emphasis in the original). Therefore, Alves (2009) argued that corporations have embraced CSR mostly because of branding and public relations. However, some NGOs have backed the CSR approach to try to achieve their campaigning results by partnering with businesses, but businesses are guided by economic interests and a concern for the environment remains, and what is particularly concerning is that the media's use of the term green is causing saturation and potentially leads to a risk of the public backlashing against the term green (Alves, 2009). Alves (2009) argued that CSR,

> has emerged as the conflicted, paradigmatic compromise between the public demand for sustainable goods and services and investors' demand for business competitiveness (i.e. maximum profits). The former has gained prominence due to environmentalists' and scientists' dire warnings about our impact on the planet's health and the latter is propelled by the global dominance of neo-liberal capitalism.
>
> p. 3

Nevertheless, some authors have argued that capitalism needs a new manifesto that will continue capitalist development and growth but in a more environmentally sustainable and generally more just way (Böhm et al., 2012; Newell & Paterson, 2010), thus proving that the CSR concept is used in a capitalist context to prove to people that companies work for the benefit

56 *Corporate social responsibility*

of the society while generating a profit and using CSR to increase financial performance.

Nevertheless, the rise of CSR can be linked with the rise of debates on sustainable development, which was firstly largely promoted with the Brundtland Report by the World Commission on Environment and Development in 1987 and this report was then further promoted at UNCED Earth Summit in Rio de Janeiro in 1992. However, some authors argue that the main outcome of this summit was institutionalising neoliberal approaches to sustainability (Böhm et al., 2012; Chatterjee & Finger, 1994; Bernstein, 2002; Bruno & Kerliner, 2002). In other words, the outcome of the summit were two fundamental assumptions:

> 1) that free trade regimes and high economic growth rates are not only compatible with, but are important preconditions for, environmental sustainability, and, 2) that market-based tools are the most appropriate instruments to apply in efforts to achieve that goal.
>
> Bernstein (2002, p. 101)

Authors argue that the Kyoto Protocol of 1997 for tackling climate change is part of this neoliberal agenda (Böhm et al., 2012) and this is especially the case since the proposal for the Kyoto Protocol is based on a premise that countries need to create profit to invest into the decarbonising global economy (Newell & Paterson, 2010). Gills and Morgan (2019) argued that all international agreements, such as Kyoto Protocol, have been a "successful failure" with success being getting so many countries to sign up for one agreement, which is not an easy task. However, emissions and pollution increased instead of decreased, or "according to the Tyndall Centre, emissions have increased from an annual GtCO2 of less than 25 in 2000 to more than 35 GtCO2 every year 2012–2018" (Gills & Morgan, 2019, p. 8).

In addition to this, some authors argued that neoliberal and market-driven initiatives are not addressing a problem such as climate change, and have a negative social, environmental and economic impact while benefiting the elite in developed countries and exploiting the underprivileged (Lohmann, 2006, 2008a, 2008b, 2009a, 2009b, 2010; Whiteman et al., 2010). As already emphasised in the previous chapter, this issue is also recognised in ecofeminism where scholars noted that the Global North is neoliberal and inward-looking because no consideration is made towards the impact of consumerism and consumption in the Global North on the rest of the world, planet or species (Salleh, 2000; Griffin, 2020; Sandberg & Sandberg, 2010). Nevertheless, there is no agreement in the Global North on reducing or abandoning the economic growth and even scholars and activists are still polarised about the issue where some argue that constant economic growth leads towards increased consumption and creates waste and pollution which are overwhelming the biosphere and the environment (Georgescu-Roegen, 1971; Meadows et al., 1972, 2004; d'Eaubonne, [1990] 1997;

Corporate social responsibility 57

Ehrlich & Holdren, 1971; Cleveland et al., 1984; Douthwaite, 1999; Mishan, 1967) while others argue that economic growth can go together with environmental protection because an increase in income will make people pay attention to environmental affairs more and this will also be addressed also with the growth of the information society (Shafik and Bandyopadhyay, 1992; Panayotou, 1993; Grossman & Krueger, 1991, 1994; Selden & Song, 1994). What is more, organisations such as OECD have been seen as neoliberal due to its politics of neoliberal globalisation and the competitiveness on which its political economy is based (Nunn, 2015). Thus, the OECD mission states that the organisation works to "ensure the stability of the international monetary system …(by) keeping track of the global economy and the economies of member countries; lending to countries with balance of payments difficulties, and giving practical help to members" (cited from Nunn, 2015, p. 72) and the situation is similar with the IMF which has a policy stating that the mission is to "ensure the stability of the international monetary system … (by) keeping track of the global economy and the economies of member countries; lending to countries with balance of payments difficulties…" (ibid). In other words, all major international organisations have a neoliberal agenda and perpetuate capitalism and a market economy, which does not lead to sustainable solutions or environmental protection.

This leads to Marx's argument on how capitalism works. In other words, Marx and Engels (1975) argued a long time ago that capitalism constantly pushes for economic development and this often goes beyond the limits of controllable growth, which is why major crises tend to occur. These crises include global economic crashes (e.g. 2008) and environmental crises and this results from "capitalism's persistent tendency to deplete natural resources and generate externalities, i.e. environmental costs that are 'dumped' onto nature and society without being accounted for within the capitalist processes of valuation, production and exchange" (Böhm et al., 2012, p. 3). However, these crises so far did not endanger capitalism to a large extent and the system always re-invents itself with new accumulations and legitimations that are being introduced (Moore, 2010; Marx & Engels, 1964; Marx, 1976, 1981). Therefore, CSR can also be seen as part of capitalism's new re-invention. However, as argued by Magdoff and Foster (2010), the capitalist system based on constant expansion and search for new materials, cheaper, labour, new markets and new ways of making a profit, will have to come up against the reality of resources being drained out[2] (see also, Meadows et al., 1972, 2004).

When it comes to CSR, because of the fundamentally bad image of the corporate world created by the mainstream media and the fact corporations are created to make a profit with the industrialisation, CSR policies did not entirely bring expected results anyway, thus again bringing up the question whether we need CSR. Even when companies have strong CSR policies they still face protests. For example, communicating CSR has proven to be a problematic issue and companies "have seen mixed results from the positive

58 *Corporate social responsibility*

to negative and simply ambivalent; quite often it is believed that the media perceive CSR to be nothing more than a "greenwash" or "PR fig leaf"" (Siegle, 2004 in Tench et al., 2007, p. 349, emphasis in the original; see also Tixier, 2003). Thus, even when corporations communicate CSR they face what some authors called "catch 22" (Morsing et al., 2008), which means that if they communicate too much they face the risk of being accused of only doing CSR for marketing purposes, whereas if they do not communicate consumers are not aware that something is being done at all. Nevertheless, it has been proven that communicating too much CSR brings criticism (Tixier, 2003, p. 79; see also Ashforth & Gibbs, 1990; Brown & Dacin, 1997; Morsing & Schultz, 2006; Nielsen & Thomsen, 2007, 2009; Morsing et al., 2008; Vidaver Cohen & Simcic Bronn, 2013). Because of this, CSR Communication is slowly becoming a separate field of CSR with studies trying to explain how to properly communicate CSR without being exposed to criticism and accusations of using CSR as PR (Tench et al., 2014; Mazzei, 2014; Theofilou & Watson, 2014; Rademacher & Remus, 2014; Karunamoorthy et al., 2013; Morsing et al., 2008; Birth & Illia, 2008; Golob & Bartlett, 2007; Nielsen & Thomsen, 2007; Branco, 2006; Dawkins, 2005).

What is relevant is that CSR originally started through policies of donating for causes (e.g. charities) and some authors argue that some form of CSR has existed for centuries (Chaffee, 2017). However, it was during the 1970s that popular discontent arose against business also because of recession and inflation, which led to increased talks on CSR (Latapí Agudelo et al., 2019), and during the 1980s CSR got operationalised. However, this operationalisation came as a result of the Reagan and Thatcher administrations, both keen on reducing the pressure on corporations. Reagan and Thatcher saw the growth and strengthening of economies as an imperative for maintaining the free market environment and minimum state intervention (Pillay, 2015). Thatcherism as a politics was predominantly oriented towards the weakening of working classes, adoption of monetarism, public expenditure cuts, privatisation, attacks on the position of organised labour and opening the economy towards international collaboration, thus replacing Keynesian style of the economy centred on sheltering labour markets and prices[3] (Nunn, 2014; Gamble, 1989; Jessop, 2003). Thus, Reaganomics and Thatcherism became symbols of neoliberalism[4] and CSR operationalisation was born in this context and from two neoliberal politicians.

The opening of markets in the situation of social discontent led to the situation that corporations were facing public hostility, especially from various interest groups to fulfil the social role, so scholars started to look at business ethics and various concepts of CSR (Carroll, 2008; Wankel, 2008). As argued by Latapí Agudelo et al. (2019) there were different societal concerns during the 1980s and this included sustainable development accompanied by corporate behaviour, and,

> some of the initiatives that happened at the time were the creation of the European Commission's Environment Directorate-General (1981), the

Corporate social responsibility   59

establishment of the World Commission on Environment and Development chaired by the Norwegian Prime Minister Gro Harlem Brundtland (1983), the Chernobyl nuclear disaster (1986), the publication of the report Our Common Future presented by the Brundtland Commission which provided a definition of sustainable development (1987), the United Nations (UN) adoption of the Montreal Protocol (1987), and the creation of the Intergovernmental Panel on Climate Change (IPCC) (1988).

n.p.

Therefore, environmental protection and corporate conduct came to the public agenda through increased awareness of environmental concerns and sustainable development, which was then linked with corporate behaviour. Carroll (2008) argued that the major societal concerns about corporate conduct during the 1980s were "environmental pollution, employment discrimination, consumer abuses, employee health and safety, quality of work life, deterioration of urban life, and questionable/abusiveness practices of multinational corporations" (p. 36). This, according to Carroll (2008), prompted scholars to look into business ethics and stakeholder management instead, for example, the role of capitalism in environmental degradation. However, this is the period when CSR implementation and scholarship started to rise, which includes the stakeholder approach. This was further exacerbated during the 1990s when the concept of CSR gained international recognition, with prominent documents and events influencing this change, such as,

the creation of the European Environment Agency (1990), the UN summit on the Environment and Development held in Rio de Janeiro which led to the Rio Declaration on Environment and Development, the adoption of Agenda 21 and the United Nations Framework Convention on Climate Change (UNFCCC) (1992), and the adoption of the Kyoto Protocol (1997).

Latapí Agudelo et al. (2019, n.p.)

As already emphasised, the Kyoto Protocol of 1997 is seen as neoliberal (Böhm et al., 2012) and based on the premise of continuous profit generation to invest into the environment (Newell & Paterson, 2010), which is negatively received in environmentalist circles who argue that neoliberal and market-driven initiatives harm society and the environment and benefit the elite only (Lohmann, 2006, 2008a, 2008b, 2009a, 2009b, 2010; Whiteman et al., 2010). It can be, therefore, argued that many proponents of the CSR concept see themselves as committed to social justice and trying to protect society and the environment; however, in practice, this does not work because companies are fundamentally capitalist enterprises who compete in the market and focus on increasing the profit and satisfying shareholders, and CSR emerged as a response to the sustainable campaigning and increased awareness about the damage to the environment. On top of this,

60   *Corporate social responsibility*

the fact something is wrong with the CSR concept is visible in the ambiguity of the concept and the lack of agreement among academics on what constitutes CSR. However, a review of the literature shows that the language used by academics when analysing CSR policies and arguing they are beneficial is the language of capitalism, which has so far not proven to be committed to equality and social justice or environmental protection (Meadows et al., 1972, 2004; Salleh, 2000, 1994).

CSR literature: definitions, ambiguities and saving capitalism

CSR has been largely debated in the past decades not just within academia but also among politicians, business people and the business press. Some authors argue that CSR has become "a 'buzz' word" due to numerous definitions and endless academic debates (Levashova, 2014; Tench et al., 2007, 2014; Ocler, 2006; Tench, 2014). This has happened because companies "are faced with greater demands for detailed information regarding the social and environmental impacts of their business activities", and "the growth of CSR dialogue indicates that companies are increasingly accepting that dialogue needs to go beyond the dissemination of information and that they cannot simply address the concerns of stakeholders through providing information they define as being important" (Burchell & Cook, 2006, pp. 154 & 167; see also Crane & Glozer, 2016). Some of the questions surrounding CSR can be summarised to,

> Should companies give away hard-earned profits? Is philanthropy just a way to create goodwill? Are corporations trying to assuage guilt for questionable business practices by supporting causes that cover their sins? Are corporate monies going toward social problems that should be addressed by the government or other institutions, or even individuals/ shareholders rather than the company itself? Is corporate philanthropy ethical, or even legal?
>
> Hatfield Edwards (2015, p. 1)

Besides, there is a growing interest in CSR because of media scandals created around the irresponsible behaviour of certain companies, and that has contributed to the lack of trust in businesses (May & Zorn, 2003; Tench et al., 2007; Pomering & Johnson, 2009; Gulyas, 2009).

It is enough to think of corporations such as Enron, WorldCom and Tyco to understand why CSR entered a debate[5]; however, the question remains as to why CSR in particular and what does it aim to achieve.

While at the outset it appears as if businesses are trying to do good for societies, the question emerges what is the definition of a business or a corporation and what is its role in society. One of the first to define CSR was Howard Bowen (1953) who argued that "the obligations of businessman to pursue those policies, to make those decisions, or to follow those lines of

Corporate social responsibility 61

action which are desirable in terms of the objectives and values of our society" (p. 6). Proponents of CSR would thus say that businesses have a responsibility towards society; however, opponents such as Friedman (1962, 1970) would argue that businesses are responsible towards shareholders and their ultimate motive is to generate profit. Generating profit as a mission seems rather incompatible with a sudden will to do good and help societies, which normally belongs to the realm of charities and non-governmental organisations. Thus, the CSR approach suggests (albeit not directly) that corporations need to function as a form of corporate NGO. In other words, corporate scandals and misconduct led to heated debates on what constitutes CSR, and some authors called for more research on how discourses surrounding CSR are constructed, by arguing it is important to "understand who constructed the narratives, and why they did so: what are they seeking to achieve, and how? In whose interests is CSR being promoted, and whose responsibility is it to implement its goals?" (Dobers & Springett, 2010, p. 65; see also Hui, 2017).

Multinational corporations (MNCs) are, for example, the subject of criticism from critical NGOs because of "financial scandals, human rights violations, or environmental degradation" (Inauen & Schoeneborn, 2014, p. 284), and data shows that consumers prefer socially responsible companies (Smith & Acorn, 1991; Creyer, 1997; Murray & Vogel, 1997; Brown & Dacin, 1997; Nelson, 2004; Ellen et al., 2006; Yoon et al., 2006; Pedersen, 2015; Singh & Misra, 2021; Kolcava et al., 2021), thus naturally leading some authors to accuse companies of greenwashing and using CSR as PR. In a nutshell, critical journalists, consumer groups and NGOs are pushing companies to give more to societies (Brown & Dacin, 1997; Freeman & McVea, 2001; Dawkins, 2004; Buhr & Grafström, 2006; Tench et al., 2007; Krishnamurthy et al., 2007; Inauen & Schoeneborn, 2014; Ihlen, 2008; Jones et al., 2009; Grayson, 2009; Johansen & Nielsen, 2011; Grafström & Windell, 2011). Besides, there is a growing body of research on greenwashing where authors have said that this practice has reached epidemiological proportions because numerous products were falsely promoted as environmentally friendly, for example (Lyon & Montgomery, 2015). However, the fact CSR emerged as a result of criticism from critical journalists and NGOs immediately opens a question on the sincerity of CSR policies and corporate intentions.

Regardless of research arguing that corporate social responsibility helps with reputation and consequentially the way business is run, certain authors still argued that CSR as a concept has "unclear boundaries and debatable legitimacy" (Lantos, 2001, p. 595) because even though there are many different definitions of CSR no agreement has been made as to how to define this term. This is because CSR can mean different things and the meaning changes as to how one defines it. Campbell (2007) stated that social responsibility should be defined as a type of behaviour that cares for the local environment, or as a type of behaviour that is considered acceptable in a community where a company is working. In this view, many people

62 *Corporate social responsibility*

understand social responsibility in many ways, but essentially this means that companies,

> ... must not knowingly do anything that could harm their stakeholders – notably, their investors, employees, customers, suppliers, or the local community within which they operate. Secondly, if corporations do cause harm to their stakeholders, they must then rectify it whenever the harm is discovered and brought to their attention.
>
> Campbell (2007, p. 951)

On the other hand, other authors are arguing that discussions on CSR have been polarised because "corporations are often portrayed as saviours and benefactors which can contribute positively to social development by generating economic opportunities and lifting people out of poverty" and "corporations are also portrayed as sinners and adversaries, who by virtue of their profit-maximizing raison d'être are incapable of generating social good" (Dhanesh, 2014, p. 158, emphasis in the original). As a way of overcoming problems with defining CSR, some authors proposed a dual model that will assess companies on a responsible/irresponsible scale. Jones, Bowd and Tench (2009) proposed a CSR-CSI model (Corporate Social Responsibility – Corporate Social Irresponsibility) to overcome difficulties in understanding CSR. In that, they argued that "CSI is a term better suited to describing the workings of the 'old' shareholder business model [...] and that CSR is more applicable to the workings of the new and emerging stakeholder business model" (Jones et al., 2009, p. 301). However, the question why is it irresponsible for companies to work for profit when companies themselves are capitalist enterprises who compete in the market and try to create a surplus and what is being achieved when companies enforce CSR and to what purpose remains. This again brings about an argument that companies should not be companies but corporate NGOs if they have responsibilities towards societies and it opens up a question of whether CSR is, in reality, saving capitalism (especially given the context in which it got operationalised).

It is enough to read academic works about corporate reputation to immediately establish the language and mindset of capitalism. For example, one of the strongest arguments for CSR, as often postulated by CSR academics, lies in corporate reputation because there is a growing belief that companies that have developed CSR policies perform better (Hirunyawipada & Xiong, 2018; Sroufe & Remani, 2018; Berens & Popma, 2014; Gill & Broderick, 2014; Johansen & Nielsen, 2011; Ellen et al., 2006; Nelson, 2004; Simcic Bronn & Vrioni, 2001; Brown & Dacin, 1997; Creyer, 1997; Murray & Vogel, 1997), consumers are willing to pay more for ethical products (Ruggeri et al., 2021; Namkung & Jang, 2017; Creyer, 1997) and even switch brands for more ethical ones that support charitable organisations (Yoon et al., 2006; for consumer behaviour and CSR see also, Smith & Acorn, 1991;

Corporate social responsibility 63

Creyer, 1997; Murray & Vogel, 1997; Brown & Dacin, 1997; Nelson, 2004; Ellen et al., 2006; Pedersen, 2015; Singh & Misra, 2021; Kolcava et al., 2021). Some authors have argued that "good social performance and charitable donations, in particular, can contribute to higher financial performance by either reducing costs or increasing revenues" (Brammer & Millington, 2008, p. 1328). Another aspect is the assumption that "firms are able to identify the salient actors in their environment, be their governmental or nongovernmental institutions, or stakeholders such as employees, customers, and investors" (ibid, p. 1328). The emphasis on reputation, increased sales and attracting new consumers is immediately disclosed as capitalist because academic works are using capitalist language to entice companies to introduce CSR policies by emphasising corporate benefits and increased sales. Ultimately, this justifies a run after profit and increase of consumption, which then contributes to economic growth and higher employability, but also environmental damage due to high waste and pollution as well as extraction of resources (Salleh, 2000, 1994; Shiva, 1999; Georgescu-Roegen, 1971; Meadows et al., 1972, 2004; d'Eaubonne, [1990] 1997; Ehrlich & Holdren, 1971; Cleveland et al., 1984; Douthwaite, 1999; Mishan, 1967). As argued by Margolis and Walsh (2003), the practical aspect of the stakeholder theory is to justify providing the shareholder value because of its focus on win-win situations where social initiatives return economic benefit to the corporation.

Therefore, academics and activists who push companies to do CSR participate in enforcing capitalism and capitalist focus on consumption and production, and inadvertently environmental degradation. Nevertheless, by putting companies in a situation they have to pay CSR and sustainability managers and employees and invest money into CSR implementation, the money lost in CSR programmes will be further supplemented by aggressive public relations to further increase sales. An argument to this by CSR scholars could be that business can be done sustainably. For example, Foster (2021) argued that many corporations use CSR as an add on rather than a genuine willingness to do business sustainably, and in this, he makes a suggestion (among others) that companies should use resources sustainably especially those that cannot be easily replaced. However, all of these academic debates lead to the question of what is a corporation and even more relevant, how enticing is consumerism and production good for the environment. What is sustainable? What is the sustainable use of resources? And why is it the role of the corporation to be sensitive to society when there is a Government that collects taxes? Obviously, the issue with the Government is an issue of economics and what kind of economics one country wants to lead, e.g. open market with minimum intervention promoted during the 1980s by Ronald Reagan and Margaret Thatcher (Pillay, 2015) or an economy based on abandoning the economic growth, which is promoted by those who argue that resources are being drained in a way that is putting the planet in danger (Salleh, 2000, 1994; Shiva, 1999; Georgescu-Roegen, 1971; Meadows et al., 1972, 2004; Ehrlich & Holdren, 1971; Cleveland et al., 1984;

64 *Corporate social responsibility*

Daly & Morgan, 2019). At best, these questions show the ambiguity of the CSR concept and some logical incoherence in that policy other than seeing it as a very useful public relations tool but that is questionable too given the discussion on catch 22 of CSR communication mentioned above (Morsing et al., 2008).

Some researchers also argued that consumers do not always reward companies for good CSR implementation. For example, in a US study by Dodd (2015), consumers stated they are willing to perform positive word-of-mouth behaviour for socially responsible companies, but social responsibility engagement is not significant when making purchase decisions. A similar finding has been found by the UK Government (2014) and Ethical Consumer (2013). These findings report the growth of ethical purchase in general but not when it comes to personal preferences, that is, quality and price over ethics. However, there is an apparent rise in ethical purchase, which serves as an incentive for companies to showcase their CSR commitments. For example, in a report by Ethical Consumer (2019) on 20 years of ethical purchasing, the organisation reported that the average ethical spending in 2018 was £1,278 as opposed to £202 in 1999. In other words, some research studies point towards financial benefits for companies if they engage in what is perceived as socially responsible behaviour, thus automatically undermining the concept as truly socially responsible and linking it to the interest and profit increase motivation for companies. Nevertheless, academics also argue that reputation attracts better job applicants, investors, the possibility to charge premium prices and opens access to capital markets, and the more the company contribute to the welfare, the higher the reputation and this contributes to the overall success of the company (Fombrun & Shanley, 1990; Tench et al., 2014; Lee, 2019a; Mahmood & Bashir, 2020; Bahta et al., 2020; Singh & Misra, 2021). In other words, companies are incentivised to invest in CSR to further increase productivity and profit, which contributes to environmental damage and does not change the current system of capitalist policies. The search for a sustainable business solution reads as a search for better capitalism or a way to save capitalism.

So, what constitutes CSR? Nowadays, different authors emphasise different elements, and even though these elements are similar, the fact there is no agreement opens room for confusion. For example, Bowie (2012, p. 8) stated that

> corporate social responsibility includes profits for stockholders, high-quality products for consumers, reasonable pay, benefits, and good working conditions for employees, a consistent market for suppliers who are paid promptly for their products, and investment in the local communities where the corporation operates.

This view is clearly in line with Friedman's view of how corporations should do business; however, this is usually deemed as insufficient by proponents of CSR who argue that corporations must look after the interests of all stakeholders. This has then resulted in several scandals because suppliers were not engaged with CSR in their own business or they were violating the rights of workers. While it comes naturally to criticise corporations that violate the rights of workers, it is beyond comprehension that corporations now need to police suppliers and monitor whether they are doing something wrong, all in fear of corporate disrepute. In other words, the Government has shifted the responsibility of controlling and legislating businesses to the general public who are acting as unpaid police and tax officers, and thus the country is essentially regulating itself. Therefore, there is a clear danger that CSR enforcement will result in even more open-market policies and liberalisation where companies will self-regulate, and since research shows that many companies are reacting to external pressure (Kowalczyk & Kucharska, 2019; Topić et al., 2020a; Yu & Choi, 2016; Story & Neves, 2015; Clarkson, 1995; Falck & Heblich, 2007; Wheeler et al., 2002; Gan, 2006), the question who will be pressuring companies on what CSR policies and with what purpose remains. Can we indeed argue that journalists, NGOs and members of the public do not have their own agenda when pushing for CSR? For example, some studies have argued that NGOs form partnerships with corporations to gain access to resources but do not engage with businesses while corporations partner with NGOs for reputational reasons (Arenas et al., 2009; Jamali and Keshishian, 2009; Pedersen & Pedersen, 2013; Rohwer & Topić & Tench, 2018; Eesley and Lenox, 2006), which means corporations are often greenwashing by improving their reputation through collaboration with NGOs while some NGOs are seeking a stake in companies for their own interests (Holzer, 2008).

However, the above discussion leads to a discussion of two main approaches to CSR, with the first one (shareholder) being labelled as irresponsible by mainstream academics (e.g. Jones et al., 2009) whereas the second one (stakeholder) has had the higher moral ground in the literature and seems to impose itself as a socially responsible concept that helps societies even though, as I am arguing, it does nothing more than to preserve the status quo even if this might be unintentional, and in this way, the stakeholder approach presents a clear danger to the environmental cause because justifying CSR as doing good also automatically means justifying the corporate focus on enticing consumption and production to increase profit because corporations can only invest in CSR if they are profitable. In other words, proponents of the stakeholder approach do not seem to have a problem with consumerism and excessive production that drains resources, but simply want a portion of the profit to be returned to the society in a shady decision-making process made by someone in some corporation under unclear terms and with the influence from NGOs and the public who either might have their own interests or might not have enough knowledge to promote policies that would be truly sustainable and useful for society as a whole. Therefore, what are the two main approaches to CSR and what are their main shortcomings?

66 *Corporate social responsibility*

Shareholder vs stakeholder orientation to CSR

The first approach to CSR, nowadays labelled as irresponsible (Jones et al., 2009) is the shareholder approach of Milton Friedman (1962) who argued that liberalism was under attack and that this is done by putting a label conservative on liberalism by imposing objectives such as "welfare and equality rather than freedom" (p. 5). Friedman insisted that he was defending liberalism in its original meaning, or as a principle that advocates freedom. He supported these views by discussing economic and political freedom, and political systems that are able or unable to provide these freedoms. In that, he strongly opposed socialism and communism saying that the so-called *democratic socialism* (which is how he saw proponents of corporate social responsibility) is not possible because no socialist system can offer individual freedom. For Friedman (1962, p. 8), "economic freedom is an end in itself" and the only way towards achieving political freedom. Friedman (1962) argued that only capitalism provides political and economic freedom because it is only capitalism that provides separation of two freedoms. In his view, there is historical evidence that capitalism provides political freedom. After all, capitalism also provides a free market, which is not the case with socialism where economy and politics are intertwined to the extent that people cannot argue for the introduction of capitalism (as they can argue for socialism in capitalist systems) because the political regime controls their employment as well. Friedman (1962) believed that some groups are imposing on people with something they do not want because people need a free exchange. In his words,

> So long as effective freedom of exchange is maintained, the central feature of the market organization of economic activity is that it prevents one person from interfering with another in respect of most of his activities. The consumer is protected from coercion by the seller because of the presence of other sellers with whom he can deal. The seller is protected from coercion by the consumer because of other consumers to whom he can sell. The employee is protected from coercion by the employer because of other employers for whom he can work, and so on. And the market does this impersonally and without centralized authority. Indeed, a major source of objection to a free economy is precisely that it does this task so well. It gives people what they want instead of what a particular group thinks they ought to want. Underlying most arguments against the free market is a lack of belief in freedom itself.
>
> Friedman (1962, pp. 14–15)

In line with this, Friedman opposed not only business ethics as something that will be imposed on businesses through the concept of social responsibility, but he also opposed interventions of Governments in any sphere that has anything to do with the market, such as distribution of income. Friedman

Corporate social responsibility 67

(1962) believed that Governments should not offer any benefits in line with a classic liberal doctrine of "to each according to what he and the instruments he owns produces" (pp. 161–162). This principle and his strong advocacy of liberalism are visible in his hostility to any social welfare policies providing social security such as "public housing, minimum wage laws, farm price supports, medical care for particular groups, special aid programs, and so on" (Friedman, 1962, p. 178). Following this, he clearly opposed the imposition of the notion of social responsibility of companies "that goes beyond serving the interest of their stockholders or their members", and this means that in a free economy,

> there is one and only one social responsibility of business – to use its resources and engage in activities designed to increase its profits so long as it stays within the rules of the game, which is to say, engages in open and free competition, without deception or fraud.
>
> Friedman (1962, p. 133)

Besides, he also identified the social responsibility of labour leaders as a responsibility to their members, and all of us together have to establish a legal framework where this will work (ibid). In other words, this view can be explained as *doing no harm* while maximising profit. Friedman believed that imposing social responsibility on companies other than what has just been described is fundamentally against the freedom principle of the liberal doctrine and can be considered as subversive:

> Few trends could so thoroughly undermine the very foundations of our free society as the acceptance by corporate officials of a social responsibility other than to make as much money for their stockholders as possible. This is a fundamentally subversive doctrine. If businessmen do have a social responsibility other than making maximum profits for stockholders, how are they to know what it is? Can self-selected private individuals decide what the social interest is? Can they decide how great a burden they are justified in placing on themselves or their stockholders to serve that social interest? Is it tolerable that these public functions of taxation, expenditure, and control be exercised by the people who happen at the moment to be in charge of particular enterprises, chosen for those posts by strictly private groups? If businessmen are civil servants rather than the employees of their stockholders then in a democracy they will, sooner or later, be chosen by the public techniques of election and appointment. And long before this occurs, their decision-making power will have been taken away from them.
>
> Friedman (1962, pp. 133–134)

Friedman (1962) opposed any charitable activities of companies arguing this is an "inappropriate use of corporate funds in a free-enterprise society", and

68 *Corporate social responsibility*

this is because a "corporation is an instrument of the stockholders who own it" (p. 135). In other words, whenever a corporation makes a charitable contribution that means that shareholders cannot use the funds as they wish, and this fundamentally undermines freedom. Friedman (1962) believed that this would be reasonable if there would be no corporate tax, but for as long as corporate tax is not abolished, "there is no justification for permitting deductions for contributions to charitable and educational institutions" (p. 135).

In his famous article "The Social Responsibility of Business is to Increase its Profits" (Friedman, 1970), published after his book (Friedman, 1962), he continued defending his position and advocated maximisation of wealth to shareholders, and denied philanthropy as a part of company's responsibility. Friedman (1970, n.p.) argued that reformers (as he called proponents of the social responsibility concept) were advocating prevention of pollution, elimination of discrimination, and that business must have a "social conscience", and some of the businessmen embraced this view and started to advocate these elements as crucial for business. Friedman (1970) believed these businessmen are actually advocating socialism and business people who embraced these views are acting as "unwitting puppets of the intellectual forces that have been undermining the basis of a free society these past decades" (n.p.). Also, Friedman (1970) also believed that debates on the social responsibility of business lack analytical skills and rigour. In that, he asked the following questions:

> What does it mean to say that "business" has responsibilities? Only people have responsibilities. A corporation is an artificial person and in this sense may have artificial responsibilities, but "business" as a whole cannot be said to have responsibilities, even in this vague sense.
>
> n.p.

Following this, Friedman (1970) asserted that the first task for those who advocate social responsibility is to ask "what it implies for whom" (n.p.). According to Friedman (1970), in a free market system where there is a respect of the private property and free enterprise,

> ... corporate executive is an employee of the owners of the business. He has direct responsibility to his employers. That responsibility is to conduct the business following their desires, which generally will be to make as much money as possible while conforming to their basic rules of the society, both those embodied in law and those embodied in ethical custom.
>
> n.p.

Friedman (1970) claimed that at the time when he was writing his article, capitalism was seen as negative and rhetoric used to describe it was based

Corporate social responsibility 69

on "profits", "soulless corporation" and similar, and because of it advocates of the concept of social responsibility were advocating what is today mostly known as CSR (n.p.).

Friedman (1970) kept insisting that a truly free society relies on market freedom, individual freedom and private property, which fits into classical economics and the politics of the open market that liberalism postulates. In such a society,

> no individual can coerce any other, all cooperation is voluntary, all parties to such cooperation benefit or they need not participate. There are no values, no "social" responsibilities in any sense other than the shared values and responsibilities of individuals. Society is a collection of individuals and of the various groups they voluntarily form.
>
> n.p. (emphasis in the original)

However, Friedman (1970) expanded his initial views on social responsibility (Friedman, 1962) to call it a "doctrine of social responsibility" and argued it does not differ much from socialism because it also presents a form of collective identity. In other words, Friedman (1970) believed that enforcing social responsibility means "professing to believe that collectivist ends can be attained without collectivist means" (n.p.). Because of it, he re-enforced his view that this doctrine presents a "fundamentally subversive doctrine" because the only purpose of business in a free society is to "use its resources and engage in activities designed to increase its profits so long as it stays within the rules of the game, which is to say, engages in open and free competition without deception or fraud" (Friedman, 1970, n.p.; see also Friedman, 1962). It can be indeed said that Friedman's remarks on socialism can be mistaken with Europe (Bowie, 2012). This is because it is especially NGOs in the EU that push for CSR implementation and European NGOs are indeed often associated with the political Left by taking over from previous social movements and advocating worker's rights and environmental protection (Morris-Suzuki, 2000). In such an environment, it comes as no surprise that the EU leads the way towards implementation of strong CSR policies (see, e.g. Teach, 2005; Blowfield, 2005; Tench et al., 2007; Nielsen & Thomsen, 2009) and these policies are immediately enforced onto the prospective EU Member States.[6] However, an argument can also be made that those who propose CSR policies are saving capitalism (whether intentionally or not) by inventing financial incentives for companies to reduce their socially damaging behaviour, which could indeed turn into social unrest had companies continued to behave as they did before major scandals, employees losing pensions, underpayment of employees, health hazards for employees, and generally excessive exploitation. The latter still exists; however, it can be argued that with the advent of CSR the focus shifted and some corporate handouts managed to put the situation under control.

70 *Corporate social responsibility*

Nevertheless, companies are in some ways forced into complying with CSR expectations as they often face pressure from their business-to-business customers or the general public, which has embraced the concept. As already mentioned, some research shows that companies are reactive in their CSR implementation which relies on consumer activism, and consumer activism is linked to corporate reputation (Kowalczyk & Kucharska, 2019; Topić et al., 2020; Yu & Choi, 2016; Story & Neves, 2015; Clarkson, 1995; Falck & Heblich, 2007; Wheeler et al., 2002; Gan, 2006). However, the fact companies work in this way and embrace and change CSR policies as per public and media views brings back the criticism of greenwashing and companies doing CSR because they feel they have to due to external pressures (Kowalczyk & Kucharska, 2019; Topić et al., 2020; Yu & Choi, 2016; Story & Neves, 2015; Clarkson, 1995; Falck & Heblich, 2007; Wheeler et al., 2002; Gan, 2006) and media coverage (Carroll & McCombs, 2003; Staw & Epstein, 2000). In that sense, Friedman (1962, 1970) was right when he said that companies are not entirely free to work as they wish in the open market; however, I am arguing that they are restrained to save capitalism rather than destroy it. What is more, Friedman wrote his famous book defending capitalism and the open market in 1962 and an article in 1970, and it is well known that the 1960s are often seen as the main period when capitalism was in crisis, which happened due to the rise of the so-called New Left in the US and elsewhere in the Western world.

The 1960s were the time of political crisis and discontent and this made ground for a rise of the New Left and then the rise of neo-capitalism during the 1970s (Cutrone, n.d.). The protests and political unrest continued until the 1980s and did not happen only in the US but elsewhere too, e.g. in Europe; however, in the US people were rioting and there were high profile assassinations due to discontent with the political and economic situation (Waterhouse, 2017). For example, in 1975, one businessman declared that US capitalism is going through its darkest hour and this was a result of the recession that happened during the 1970s after the boom of the 1960s (ibid). In other words, the 1960s were the time of political protest and in the 1970s this was expanded to include economic protests and discontent with capitalism and businesses. Therefore, Friedman's work needs to be analysed in the context of capitalism and the struggle to preserve the system. It is indeed indicative that amid the crisis in capitalism, a debate on CSR emerged, which further leads towards a question of whether CSR was invented to save capitalism.

In a nutshell, it can be argued that all the mentioned questions remain unanswered despite a major proliferation of academic studies in the field of CSR and the majority of CSR research remains produced by CSR scholars who are preserving the status quo and taking CSR for granted. There are hardly any debates on who constructed the CSR narrative, for what purpose, and what is it that CSR proponents seek to achieve. There are even fewer studies, in fact very few, that question whether CSR was a good idea. Besides, it can be argued that proponents of CSR fail to answer why is it not the Government that needs to regulate business conduct rather than businesses having to impose self-restrictions. Why would businesses have to function as some combination of corporations and NGOs, or corporate NGOs? What could be the possible goal of this policy push where corporations are essentially self-regulating? One possible argument is further marketisation and liberalisation, which could lead Britain to a country where corporations self-regulate in a market freed from the state role, which has always been a central tenet and mantra of liberal economists such as Milton Friedman as already explained.

This leads to the notion of stakeholder orientation, which I have already criticised as preserving the status quo and not helping with making a meaningful change and certainly not in reducing environmental impact. In a stakeholder orientation, different authors emphasise different elements of CSR, but it seems that many agree on worker's rights and environmental protection. Before the stakeholder theory was developed and widely used by R. Edward Freeman (1984), Archie Carroll (1979) recognised the ambiguity of the concept of CSR because there was no agreement on what CSR actually means since many authors debate it in different ways. In other words, Carroll (1979) also identified stakeholders and their importance to the company's ethical business. Carroll (1979, p. 499) defined the social responsibility of business as "economic, legal, ethical, and discretionary expectations that society has of organizations at a given point in time". Economic responsibilities are connected with providing "goods and services to societal members", and "all other business responsibilities are predicated upon the economic responsibility of the firm because without it the others become moot considerations" (Carroll, 1991, pp. 40–41). On the other hand, legal responsibilities are related to the obligation of business to "comply with the laws and regulations promulgated by the federal state, and local governments as the ground rules under which business must operate" (ibid, p. 41). Ethical responsibilities, however, are related to "fairness and justice, ethical responsibilities embrace those activities and practices that are expected or prohibited by societal members even though they are not codified into law" (ibid). Finally, philanthropy,

> encompasses those corporate actions that are in response to society's expectation that businesses be good corporate citizens. This includes actively engaging in acts or programmes to promote human welfare or goodwill. Examples of philanthropy include business contributions to financial resources or executive time, such as contributions to the arts, education, or the community.
>
> ibid (p. 42)

72   *Corporate social responsibility*

However, Carroll's pyramid faced criticism, which led him to re-design his pyramid by conducting a re-examination of the previous model. According to the re-examination, the previous four components model have been unclear because,

> to some, the pyramid framework suggests a hierarchy of CSR domains. One may be led to conclude that the domain at the top of the pyramid, philanthropic responsibilities, is the most important or highly valued domain, that should be strived for by all corporations, while the economic domain at the base of the pyramid is the least valued CSR domain.
>
> Schwartz and Carroll (2003, p. 505)

This has happened in the work of some authors who assumed that the most important part of the pyramid is the philanthropic component while the actual intention was to emphasise that "the economic and legal domains are the most fundamental while philanthropic responsibilities are considered less important than the other three domains" (Carroll, 1991, p. 42). On the other hand, in the re-examination, it appeared that

> ... a pyramid framework cannot fully capture the *overlapping* nature of the CSR domains [...] Such mutuality is an integral characteristic of CSR [...] and of such fundamental importance that it must be included and clearly depicted in any proposed CSR model. Carroll's use of dotted lines separating the domains does not fully capture the non-mutually exclusive nature of the domains, nor does it denote two of the critical tension points among them, the tension between the economic and ethical and the economic and philanthropic domains.
>
> Schwartz and Carroll (2003, p. 505, emphasis in the original)

Schwartz and Carroll (2003) argued that "philanthropic activities are simply an example of an ethically motivated activity". In this, Schwartz and Carroll (2003, p. 506) emphasise that philanthropy is not generally expected from the business for the company to be considered as ethical but ask a question "of exactly when an activity can be considered ethical as opposed to philanthropic according to Carroll's treatment of these two domains". To that end, they raise the following question: "is a corporation's contribution to a charitable organization an ethical activity (i.e., expected by society) or a philanthropic activity (i.e., merely desired by society)?" (ibid). Companies actually donate to charities but society also expects them to do so, and this opens a question as to whether "society now expects corporate philanthropic contributions" (Schwartz & Carroll, 2003, p. 506). However, according to the new model of CSR, it is no longer necessary to have a philanthropic category separated because philanthropy forms part of an ethical domain (Schwartz & Carroll, 2003, p. 506). The Three-Domain Model of CSR, therefore, has three responsibilities: economic, legal and ethical with the philanthropic

Corporate social responsibility 73

dimension now being encompassed by ethical component. All components are equally important and the new model is, to avoid confusion, not set as a pyramid. The new Three-Domain Approach means that "the economic domain captures those activities which are intended to have either a direct or indirect positive economic impact on the corporation in question", and the positive economic impact is based on "(i) the maximization of profits and/ or (ii) the maximization of share value" (Schwartz & Carroll, 2003, p. 508).

However, re-designing the pyramid did not spare Carroll from further criticism. For example, Bowie (2012) found his model misleading because it failed to place legal responsibilities as the foundation together with economic responsibilities. According to his observation, Carroll was not that much different from Friedman because the only aspect of Carroll's pyramid that Friedman denies is philanthropy while he accepts all other parts (economic responsibilities, legal responsibilities and ethical responsibilities) (Bowie, 2012). While Carroll debated CSR and related it with the stakeholder theory, Freeman and his colleagues developed and introduced the stakeholder theory that does not necessarily relate to CSR. The term stakeholder firstly appeared in an internal memorandum of Stanford Research Institute in 1963 and is nowadays accepted in many disciplines (law, health care, public administration, environmental policy, and ethics) (Freeman, 1994). The stakeholder approach is seen as diametrically opposite to the shareholder approach, and the stakeholder theory has been mostly associated with R. Edward Freeman.

Many authors discuss these two approaches in terms of the so-called "Friedman-Freeman debate" even though Freeman denies this dualism, which I agree with because I see both approaches as capitalist and liberal except that the stakeholder approach pretends to do good for societies by making companies give back a portion of profit without questioning whether they need to make so much profit and how consumerism affects the environment. Freeman argues that the stakeholder theory is not a rival to the shareholder theory but that this approach "rejects the very idea of maximizing a single objective function as a useful way of thinking about management strategy. Rather, *stakeholder management* is a never-ending task of balancing and *integrating multiple relationships and multiple objectives*" (Freeman & McVea, 2001, p. 10, my emphasis). However, while Carroll focused on supporting the necessity of ethics when doing business, Freeman and his associates took this view for granted and focused on defining stakeholders and the nature of organisational responsibilities towards these groups (see, e.g. Freeman, 2010). Therefore, the focus of the stakeholder theory is a view that stakeholders are not just shareholders but also customers, suppliers, local communities, and similar people and organisations involved in doing business with a certain company as well as society as a whole. In the words of R. Edward Freeman,

> My thesis is that I can revitalize *the concept of managerial capitalism* by replacing the notion that managers have a duty to stockholders with

74   *Corporate social responsibility*

> the concept that managers bear a fiduciary relationship to stakeholders.
> Stakeholders are those groups who have a stake in or claim on the firm.
>
> Freeman (2001, p. 56, my emphasis)

The statement above already confirms that Freeman is looking into some version of improved capitalism and preserving the system with minor tweaks that enable corporations to give a portion of profit back to society without failing to question consumerism, excessive production, an inequality that is inherent to capitalism and the environmental consequences. His definition, thus, only focuses on identifying who companies should be responsible to, and the narrow definition of stakeholders he proposed encompasses owners, employees, customers, managers, suppliers, and the local community that is vital for the survival of the company while a wider definition encompasses all groups affected by the firm (Freeman, 2001). The stakeholder theorists argue they are interested in the real people and how a business organisation manages the interests of stakeholders to ensure the long-term survival of the firm, thus again supporting competition and the survival of capitalism even if not openly saying this. In other words, stakeholder theorists argue,

> … the stakeholder approach is about concrete "names and faces" for stakeholders rather than merely analysing particular stakeholder roles. As such what is important is developing an understanding of the real, *concrete,* stakeholders who are specific to the firm, and the circumstances in which it finds itself. It is only through this level of understanding that management can create options and strategies that have the support of all stakeholders. And it is only with this support that management can ensure the long-term survival of the firm. It matters less that management understands the reaction of "customers-in-general" to a price rise. It matters much more that they understand how *our actual* customers react, bearing in mind that they have 'tuned' their machinery to our product's specification and bearing in mind the industry annual trade show is next month. It matters less that management understands that "shareholders-in-general" expect steady dividend growth. It matters more that we understand that our shareholders expect us to increase internal investment as fast as possible because they invested expecting us to be "first to market" with the next generation product. Good strategic management, according to this approach, emerges from the specifics rather than descending from the general and theoretical.
>
> Freeman and McVea (2001, p. 12, all emphases in the original)

Freeman and associates further elaborated on this and emphasised that stakeholders are "those groups and individuals who can affect or be affected by actions connected to value creation and trade" (Hörisch et al., 2014, p. 2; see also Freeman, 2010, p. 9). A stakeholder approach emphasises "*active* management of the business environment, relationships and the promotion of shared interests" (Freeman & McVea, 2001, p. 8, emphasis in the

Corporate social responsibility 75

original). In other words, the stakeholder theory "is a theory of organizational management and ethics" because "all theories of strategic management have some moral content, though it is often implicit. This is not to say that all such theories are moral, as opposed to immoral. Moral content, in this case, means that the subject matter of the theories is inherently moral topics" (Philips et al., 2003, p. 480).

Additionally, authors acknowledge that "moral content is frequently taken for granted, or ignored in this manner in management scholarship", and this is where the theory differs from others, i.e. because "it addresses morals and values explicitly as a central feature of managing organizations" (ibid, p. 481). According to stakeholder theorists, companies like already mentioned Enron, WorldCom and Tyco reinforced the view that companies only care for profits, and these corporate scandals led to a situation where managers have to think about how to conceptualise responsible business strategy where stakeholder theory has emerged as a good solution because it presents,

> ... a new narrative to understand and remedy three interconnected business problems – the problem of understanding how value is created and traded, the problem of connecting ethics and capitalism, and the problem of helping managers think about management such that the first two problems are addressed. These problems matter and their effects are not confined to theorizing in management, but cut across a variety of disciplines and ultimately suggest a revision of how we should think about capitalism.
>
> Parmar et al. (n.b., p. 3)

This means that the stakeholder theory is "a managerial conception of organizational strategy and ethics", and,

> the central idea is that an organization's success is dependent on how well it manages the relationships with key groups such as customers, employees, suppliers, communities, financiers, and others that can affect the realization of its purpose. The manager's job is to keep the support of all of these groups, balancing their interests, while making the organization a place where stakeholder interests can be maximized over time. The identification of stakeholder groups is currently among the central debates in the scholarly and popular literature [...], but most scholars would include employees, customers, suppliers, financiers, and local communities, at a minimum.
>
> Freeman and Philips (2002, p. 333)

In other words, for companies to survive in an increasingly critical environment led by critical NGOs and media, which influenced consumers, companies must give something back to preserve their reputation and survive. In that sense, Freeman and all other stakeholder proponents are only finding

76 *Corporate social responsibility*

ways how to save capitalism and improve corporate survival chances and performance, which is not good for the environment because this approach does nothing to suggest a decrease in consumerism and draining resources (Salleh, 2000, 1994; Shiva, 1999; Georgescu-Roegen, 1971; Meadows et al., 1972, 2004; Ehrlich & Holdren, 1971; Trentmann, 2016; Wright & Nyberg, 2015; Krstić & Krstić, 2017; Coghlan, 2009; Corrigan, 1997; Douthwaite, 1999; Mishan, 1967; Ewen & Ewen, 1992; Calder, 1990: Krstić, 2018; Krstić et al., 2018; Fleming & Jones, 2013; Ireland & Pillay, 2008; Sheehy, 2014).

While stakeholder theory emerged as a criticism of the shareholder theory, as with every theory the stakeholder theory also faced criticism; however, this criticism mostly came from the Friedmanite camp that only argued in favour of the old version of capitalism rather than in favour of the so-called improved capitalism that Freeman and other stakeholders seem to propose. Bowie (1991, p. 63) stated that the problem with the stakeholder theory is deciding who to donate to when it comes to managerial decisions on supporting social causes, and managing reactions from stakeholders. For example, Dayton Hudson has been donating for 20 years through their foundation to an organisation *Planned Parenthood* that had opposition among abortion opponents. To avoid participating in abortion debates, the company announced that it will no longer make donations and this caused boycotts of the organisation by pro-choice activists and the company, in only a few days, agreed to continue financing *Planned Parenthood*. That, however, received attention among anti-abortion activists and caused boycotts and demonstrations (Lewin, 1990; De Witt, 1990). This caused anger among management that was heard saying the money belongs to the company, and if people do not like how they spend it then perhaps they should not spend it on charity at all (Bowie, 1991). This situation alone already shows the difficulty of implying that the role of corporations is to serve societies without challenging capitalism and it opens a question on who decides on CSR and whether the concept works at all.

Michael Jensen (2002, p. 236) as the vocal opponent of the stakeholder theory proposed an approach called "Value Maximization Proposition" where he argued that the stakeholder theory is "incomplete as a specification for the corporate purpose or objective function, and therefore cannot logically fulfil that role", and this "incompleteness is not accidental. It serves the private interests of those who promote it, including corporate outsiders as well as many managers and directors of corporations". Jensen (2002, p. 236) defined his proposition for value maximisation by stating that, "managers should make all decisions so as to increase the total long-run market value of the firm. Total value is the sum of the values of all financial claims on the firm – including equity, debt, preferred stock, and warrants". On the other hand, Jensen (2002, p. 237) pointed out that the stakeholder theory is,

> ... fundamentally flawed because it violates the proposition that any organization must have a single-values objective as a precursor to

Corporate social responsibility 77

purposeful or rational behaviour [...] a firm that adopts stakeholder theory will be handicapped in the competition for survival because, as a basis for action, stakeholder theory politicizes the corporation, and it leaves its managers empowered to exercise their own preferences in spending the firm's resources.

Jensen (2002, p. 241) explained the main failure of the stakeholder theory as an impossibility of meeting everybody's expectations. In other words,

> ... customers want low prices, high quality, expensive service, etc. Employees want high wages, high quality working conditions, and fringe benefits including vacations, medical benefits, pensions, and the rest. Suppliers of capital want low risk and high returns. Communities want high charitable contributions, social expenditures by firms to benefit the community at large, stable employment, increased investment, and so on. And so it goes with every conceivable constituency. Obviously any decision criterion – and the objective function is at the core of any decision criterion – must specify how to make the tradeoffs between these often conflicting and inconsistent demands.

This view is proposed by some other scholars. For example, Pedersen (2006) stated that companies cannot engage with all stakeholders because people do not see everything and do not pay attention to everything, while Dalton and Daily (1991, p. 75) stated that companies give more but people also ask too much and proposed to readers to ask themselves the following questions:

> Do customers prefer a higher quality product or service? A better value for the product or service? Do employees prefer more wages? More fringe benefits? More job security? Do managers prefer higher wages? More fringe benefits? Greater ownership positions? More responsibility? Does organized labor prefer more members? More stable employment? Higher wages? More fringe benefits? More job security? Do debtors prefer a higher return? Better risk evaluation? Do suppliers prefer better terms? Do owners prefer higher returns? More equity appreciation? Do governments prefer higher levels of social responsibility? More stability? A higher tax base? Does the public-at-large prefer greater environmental standards? More stability?

Jensen (2002) also argued that managers embraced the stakeholder theory because of,

> ... their own personal short-term interests. Because stakeholder theory provides no definition of better, it leaves managers and directors unaccountable for their stewardship of the firm's resources. With no criteria for performance, managers cannot be evaluated in any principle way.

78 *Corporate social responsibility*

Therefore, stakeholder theory plays into the hands of self-interested managers allowing them to pursue their own interests at the expense of society and the firm's financial claimants. It allows managers and directors to invest in their favourite projects that destroy firm-value whatever they are (the environment, art, cities, medical research) without having to justify the value destruction.

p. 242

Because of this, managers can do whatever they want because there is no guidance or control over what they do. Jensen (2002) also claimed that the,

...stakeholder theory plays into hands of special interests who wish to use the resources of firms for their own ends. With the widespread failure of centrally planned socialist and communist economies, those who wish to use non-market forces to relocate wealth find great solace in the playing field that stakeholder theory opens to them. Stakeholder theory gives them the appearance of legitimate political access to the sources of decision-making power in organizations, and it deprives those organizations of a principles basis for rejecting those claims. The result is to undermine the foundations that have enabled markets and capitalism to generate wealth and high standards of living worldwide.

Jensen (2002, p. 243)

This critique is in line with the criticism of Milton Friedman (1970, 1962) who also stated that managers would use their power to manage resources that normally belong to shareholders. Jensen, again in line with Friedman (1970, 1962), also interconnected the stakeholder theory with socialism by saying that,

...if widely adopted, stakeholder theory will reduce social welfare even as its advocates claim to increase it – just as in the failed communist and socialist experiments of the twentieth century. And [...] stakeholder theorists will often have the active support of managers who wish to throw off the constraints on their power provided by the value-seeking criterion and its enforcement by capital markets, the market for corporate control, and product markets. Indeed we have seen, and will continue to see, more political action limiting the power of these markets to constrain managers. And such actors will continue using the arguments of stakeholder theory to legitimize their positions.

2002, p. 243

An interesting discussion on stakeholder theory in the *Journal of Marketing and Morality* also exposed some flaws of the stakeholder concept. The debate centred on the question of whether companies should be responsible to societies where Barry (2002, 2000) argued in favour of Friedman's model while McCann (2000a, 2000b) defended the stakeholder theory and necessity of businesses acting as moral agents and not just striving for profit. Barry (2000) argued that the "social responsibility thesis is a covert attempt to bring about socialism" (p. 100) and that Friedman's views are accepted by all writers who accept capitalism as an economic system. He also asserted that the plight for social responsibility that goes beyond the legal framework is another attack to free enterprise just that this time there is no obvious attempt to replace the existing market system but to reform it, thus indicating that proponents of the stakeholder approach are trying to reform capitalism. In a way, these two camps could be also seen as classical economists vs Keynesian economists. In other words, both are not challenging capitalism but proposing different ways on how to enhance it, preserve it and make it work. Barry (2000) insisted that "most of business could regulate itself", and that "many of the spectacular business scandals that occur in these markets are the result of over-zealous prosecutors and the myriad of competition-destroying rules" (p. 101), thus openly advocating a free market policy and self-regulation of businesses, which fits into classical economics. Barry (2000) also argued that "Anglo-American capitalism is proving to be superior to its rivals" while some socially oriented markets such as the German one are being threatened by foreign competitors due to "uncompetitive effect of communitarian capitalism" (p. 106, see also Barry, 2002), with which he clearly ignored the fact the US is a country with a poverty issue and a divide between the rich and the poor. For example, in 2019, 34 million people in the US were living in poverty (Semega et al., 2020) and the divide between the rich and the poor has increased further (Menasce Horowitz et al., 2020). Like Bowie (1991), Barry (2000) also believed it is "a manager's fiduciary duty [...] first to act in the best interest of the owners, yet a manager's immediate self-interest lies in protecting his or her job", and managers that promote responsible policies are doing so from self-interest (p. 115). The latter can indeed be seen as truthful as managers are not qualified to decide what benefits society as a whole nor how should a corporation act as a societal agent. As already mentioned, this inevitably brings hierarchy and shows a top-down approach from corporations deciding what to give and to whom, thus again bringing the notion of CSR serving as a free market policy where corporations self-regulate.

In other words, what this debate shows is that arguments between shareholder and stakeholder approaches are actually arguments between capitalists, just those who support different methods and different definitions of capitalism. While shareholders openly support capitalism and the open market initiative where corporations have the freedom to do their business as they please, stakeholders (whether intentionally or not) are actually helping capitalism save itself. As argued by shareholders, there is indeed an excessive criticism of businesses among critical NGOs and media (Brown & Dacin, 1997; Freeman & McVea, 2001; Dawkins, 2004; Buhr & Grafström, 2006; Tench et al., 2007; Krishnamurthy et al., 2007; Inauen & Schoeneborn,

80 *Corporate social responsibility*

2014; Ihlen, 2008; Jones et al., 2009; Grayson, 2009; Johansen & Nielsen, 2011; Grafström & Windell, 2011) and stakeholder approach that pushed for CSR implementation has likely saved capitalism from destruction as it enabled companies to pretend they are also helping societies while actually continuing the push towards consumption, production and draining resources.

While in previous sections, I analysed the literature on CSR and expressed critical views on its capitalist nature and preserving the status quo, two issues remain to enable a full understanding of this concept. One issue is linked to the notion of CSR as capitalist discourse, and that is the role of women in CSR and the other one is the role of the media in CSR with media being also subjected to the analysis in terms of their own social responsibility. The final two sections thus link these two concepts with previously emphasised considerations of CSR as a capitalist smokescreen. However, it needs to be emphasised that CSR is not linked with the social responsibility of the media concept despite the similarity in the name. In other words, while CSR is about corporations giving something to the society and, as I argue, preserving capitalism, social responsibility of the media is about media having a social role and thus not being capitalist enterprises interested in profit and/or serving agenda of their owners or at least, this is not how media should function if they are to fulfil their social role. Instead, social responsibility of the media leans more towards a collectivist approach where media serve a social purpose and many proponents of this approach, myself included, advocate funding for fully independent community media run for the interest of the society rather than capitalist enterprises prone to influences of the market, readers and more dangerously media moguls with vested interests.

CSR and the media

CSR and media have been discussed both in terms of how media write about CSR and businesses but also in terms of media social responsibility, the social responsibility of the press in particular. The latter is an increasingly relevant issue because of the lower trust of the public in mainstream media and the rise of fake news and information distortion on social media (Lee, 2019b; Watson, 2020). For example, in the UK, public polls have been showing a downward trend in trusting journalists and the media. In 2018, a survey from Press Gazette (2018) has shown low trust in journalists, to tell the truth with only 2% of the British public putting great trust in journalists. In 2020, the same organisation recorded that the British public distrusts journalists despite being reliant on the media to provide information about coronavirus pandemic (Press Gazette, 2020b) and the public believes their trust in the media, to tell the truth, has further eroded because of coronavirus pandemic (Press Gazette, 2020c). This led editors to express concerns about the public's trust in the media as the biggest challenge for the press in 2021

Corporate social responsibility 81

and going forward (Press Gazette, 2021). However, despite the lack of trust, the public still gets information from the media who affect their views and due to this influence of mass media in attitude formation and influencing behavioural change, media are often seen in a different way than traditional corporations despite working in the open market and being reliant on external income where they also face market competition (Ingenhoff & Koelling, 2012; Owen & Wildman, 1992; Bardoel & d'Haenens, 2004; Meier & Perrin, 2007; Hou & Reber, 2011). Criticism emerges when media put their commercial interests before social interests, which happens because of shaping content to satisfy needs and to reach audiences who may support certain views (Plaisance, 2000). Because of its major influence, media face more scrutiny in terms of how they report on issues of the day.

Since it is generally recognised that media have a prominent social role because they provide information to citizens, which influences their behaviour and attitudes, media are sometimes called the Fourth Estate as journalists are meant to provide monitoring of power of the legislative, judicial and executive powers, or government, parliament, courts and so on. (Ingenhoff & Koelling, 2012). Van Liedekerke (2004) argued that the role of media in society is more important than the role of, for example, traditional corporations because media have an impact on social norms and values. Many authors argued that media have to be independent, objective, pluralistic and truthful because of the power they have over the public (McQuail, 1997, 2003, 2005; Napoli, 1999). However, since media also compete in the market and have economic goals, many authors argued that economic values replaced social and editorial values, which eroded media social responsibility and threatens democratic standards (Ingenhoff & Koelling, 2012).

Marx ([1849] 1959) argued decades ago that the press has to serve as a watchdog and "the tireless denouncer of those in power, the omnipresent eye, the omnipresent mouthpiece of the people's spirit that jealously guards its freedom" (p. 231, cited from Sandoval, 2013, pp. 44–45). However, for this to happen Marx argued that the press would need to be independent and non-commercial, or as Marx put it "not being a trade" (ibid). Some authors, therefore, argued that media need to be studied within the context of capitalism and as part of the political economy (Sandoval, 2013; Mosco, 2009; Herman & Chomsky, 1988; Garnham, 1998). The main focus of the critical political economy of media is on the dual relationship between an economic aspect of media practice and its social and cultural practice on the other hand (Sandoval, 2013). This means that critical political economists argue that commercial interests are impairing social work of the media because media are generating a private profit and this inevitably includes exploitation of media employees (including journalists), and working in the free market and with a commercial goal means that media fall under the market pressure and this then means also uniformity and conformism (Garnham, [1986] 2006; Smythe, [1977] 1997; Fuchs, 2011, 2010;

82 *Corporate social responsibility*

Horkheimer & Adorno, [1947] 1997; Herman & Chomsky, 1988; Schiller, 1997; McChesney, 2004) as well as a threat to democracy (Schiller & Schiller, 1988). Sandoval (2013) thus argues that any voluntary CSR concept is deeply flawed because corporations will not go the extra mile if it affects their profit and will do what they absolutely have to. Applying this to the media, which are also functioning as corporations; this would mean that the media will not necessarily engage with social interest if it undermines their strive for profit. Sandoval (2013) thus proposes that the media system needs to go beyond CSR and turn CSR on its head and renamed and reconceptualised to Responsibility to Socialise Corporations (RSC). This means that "in order to become truly social, capitalist corporations need to be socialised, so that private wealth turns into common wealth. Socialising the media means to replace the privately controlled commercial media system with a socially controlled non-commercial media system" (p. 52). Therefore, instead of relying on corporate self-conduct and willingness to give something, this approach would "expand democratic social control over corporate conduct and to restrict corporate power. This can be achieved through government regulation on the one hand and pressure from civil society groups on the other hand" (p. 52). With this approach, according to Sandoval (2013), media could contribute towards the common good because they would be free from commercialising pressure and the pressure to maximise profit.

However, there is no agreement on how media should operate and the media obligations and regulation remain a contested issue since the debate emerged during the 1940s when the Commission formed at the University of Chicago issued the first report tackling social responsibility of the press. In other words, the press has been under particular scrutiny since The Hutchins Commission (the Commission on the Freedom of the Press) released a report "A Free and Responsible Press", in 1947, and this interest got exacerbated with the rise of agenda-setting studies in 1962 (McCombs & Shaw, 1972; McCombs, 2014), which confirmed the role of media in placing issues on the public agenda and thus influencing attitudes. Since 1962, hundreds of studies have proven the power of the press in setting the agenda, and the situation has not changed even with the rise of television and social media (Perko et al., 2015; Kim et al., 2015; Meraz, 2011, 2009; Sweetser et al., 2008; Kook Lee, 2007; Lee, 2007; Lim, 2006; Lee et al., 2005; Roberts et al., 2002; King, 1997; Trumbo, 1995; Roberts & McCombs, 1994; Reese & Danielian, 1989; Whitney & Becker, 1982).

What is usually debated when it comes to media responsibility are issues such as accountability, liability and responsibility (Middleton, 2009). According to Plaisance (2000), accountability often means manifesting a claim to responsibility whereas responsibility is the action within the framework of morals and roles. This furthermore means that journalists have to keep the interests of society as their top priority, which would also mean that journalists have a collective responsibility (Middleton, 2009). According to

Corporate social responsibility   83

the already mentioned Hutchins Commission, the press has the following obligations.

- To provide a truthful, comprehensive, and intelligent account of the day's events in a context that gives meaning;
- To serve as a forum for the exchange of comment and criticism;
- To develop a representative picture of the constituent groups in society;
- To be responsible for the presentation and clarification of the goals and values of society;
- To provide full access to the day's intelligence (cited from Bivins, 2004, p. 42).

Hutchins Commission believed that the press needs to participate in creating the well-being of the society and not just merely report on social issues. These recommendations are still used and debated and many scholars recognise them as relevant for understanding the role of the media in societies (Curran, 2011; Bates, 2017).

Since the report on the free and responsible press, Siebert, Peterson and Schramm (1963) developed the theory of social responsibility of the media which was enlisted as one of the four main theories of media along with authoritarian, libertarian and soviet theories. Siebert, Peterson and Schramm (1963) argued that media have to use their powerful position to deliver information to citizens and if media fail in this, then there is a case for media regulation. In other words, according to these authors, media must fairly present the information to be socially responsible and this includes presenting enough information from all sides to citizens so as to enable them to make informed decisions and opinions (ibid). The public interest is, thus, at the heart of this theory as media are seen as powerful in shaping and influencing societies and journalist is seen as intrinsically linked to his or her audiences who read the content (Hoenisch, 2000).

Owens-Ibie (1994) argued that media are responsible to citizens, government, media owners and also to themselves and failing in fulfilling this four-tier responsibility decreases trust and accountability, which then harms responsibility itself. The notion of regulation is defended by Libertarian theorists and this view is grounded in liberalism and the ideas of John Stuart Mill. Libertarians defend media against the regulation using the principles of the free market where ideas are also seen as part of the free market. Thus, the tension between economic and social interests that journalists face when reporting on issues of the day are, according to libertarians, a natural and healthy choice that should not be regulated because it would undermine journalistic autonomy. This view also argues that journalists make up their minds when reporting on issues spontaneously and thus regulation would undermine this autonomy (Middleton, 2009). Journalistic codes are seen as an effective instrument to ensure balanced coverage and integrity of professional standards; however, criticism has emerged over the years as to

84 *Corporate social responsibility*

whether all journalists pay attention to codes and some authors argued that codes are often used by media organisations to justify susceptible behaviour (Plaisance, 2000). Nevertheless, some authors argued that market conditions and corporatism affect journalists (Richards, 2004; McQuail, 2010) who work in the open market and this contradicts ethics and prevents fully ethical practice (Sandoval, 2013).

Supporters of the social responsibility of media argue that media cannot simply report on issues, thus refuting the objectivity and impartiality argument but that it is the role of the media to open a debate. Thus, this view goes directly against Lippman's ([1992] 1997) view of media as an objective observer, which was upheld decades before social responsibility theory emerged. Ward (2008) argued that there was a "disillusionment with the liberal hope that an unregulated press would be a responsible educator of citizens on matters of public interests" (p. 298) and this means that the liberal press is failing to serve its social role. Lasch (1990) argued that societies need debate because merely reporting information can lead to misinformation and manipulation while McNealy (2017) argued that the purpose of the libertarian theory of media was for media to fulfil six functions, "(1) service to the political system; (2) enlightenment of the public; (3) serving as a watchdog; (4) serving the economic system through advertising; (5) acting as a vehicle of entertainment; and (6) maintaining its independence" (p. 3). In other words, it is clear that libertarian theory of the media does not contain debate as a fundamental role of the media but it does contain entertainment and economic aspect of the media coupled up with independence. This led to criticism of the social responsibility of the media where opponents argued that this theory is similar to authoritarian and soviet media theory because of its collectivist nature (Siebert et al., 1963; Pickard, 2015). Proponents responded that social responsibility of the media theory is, in fact, democratic because the free-market orientation of the press does not contribute to democracy, and having a social responsibility approach in the press does not mean a lack of objectivity because the journalistic ideal of objectivity is upheld in this theory through the request of balancing opposing views and factual reporting (Benson, 2008; Nerone, 1995). Thus, social responsibility theory advocates that instead of relying on codes of practices, we should introduce freedom of journalists to report as they please and in return, they cover public issues and contribute towards the well-being of society (Ward, 2008; Klaidman, 1987; Kovach & Rosenstiel, 2001). In addition to this, according to the social responsibility theory, media must remain free from external influence; however, publishing information is not a freedom, but a duty because issues of public interest must have a place on the media agenda (Ward, 2008).

Most commonly cited examples of problematic journalistic practices are media affecting elections and health decisions of citizens, which signal sensationalism and sensationalism can generally be linked with strive for profit as getting people interested sells newspapers or increases online readership,

Corporate social responsibility   85

both of which influence revenues. For example, in politics, a lot of work has been done on media bias in elections and in the way women are represented in the media, with which media affected electoral choices and equality of opportunities. In the US, media have been under scrutiny of scholars for biased reporting on women politicians, with Hillary Rodham Clinton being a commonly cited example. Clinton was scrutinised first as a First Lady when she was involved in the reform of the health care system in the US and where she refused to take a traditional First Lady's role of the supportive wife only (Winfield, 1994, 1997a, 1997b; Templin, 1999; Topić, 2009). Later, when she continued her political career (she was politically active and successful before her husband Bill became a president), media again scrutinised her, first by asking her to quit the presidential race against Barack Obama in a run for the candidate of the Democratic Party, even though she was in the lead at the time (Newport, 2008a, 2008b), and then later also by accusing her to play the gender card (Falk, 2013) even though she was originally presented as a feminist pioneer (Sisco & Lucas, 2015). A similar issue happened in presidential elections in 2016 when she was undermined as a liberal feminist because the media shifted from the support towards liberal feminism to argue that new feminism is needed, thus not openly being anti-feminist but shifting the debate and "whitening" Clinton to undermine her cause (Zacharias & Arthurs, 2008; Topić & Gilmer, 2017). In the UK, for example, recent years saw examples of press reporting on the Labour Party leader Jeremy Corbyn. Cammaerts, De Cillia, Magalhães and Jimenez-Martínez (2016) analysed the coverage of the British press on Jeremy Corbyn, the leader of Labour Party of the time and concluded that media went from the watchdog to the "attackdog" because almost all newspapers (except for *Daily Mirror*, which published 60% of articles that were seen as balanced), had a negative perception of Jeremy Corbyn and expressed bias in their articles, and this includes also the newspapers such as *The Guardian*, commonly seen as centre-left. In the foreword to the study on Jeremy Corbyn and the media, Couldry and Cammaerts (2016) asked,

> to what extent this warranted the acerbic and overtly aggressive media reaction he has consistently received over the last year? Is it acceptable for the media to delegitimise to such an extent a legitimate democratic actor who is the leader of the main opposition party in British politics?
>
> p. 1

Nevertheless, Cammaerts, De Cillia, Magalhães and Jimenez-Martínez (2016) argued that

> the high degree of media power needs to be accompanied by a high degree of media and democratic responsibility, is it then acceptable that the majority of the British newspapers uses its mediated power to attack and delegitimise the leader of the largest opposition party against a

86　*Corporate social responsibility*

right-wing government to such an extent and with such vigour? By posing this question in the way we do, we also imply that this is not merely a political question, but also an ethical and a democratic one. Certainly, democracies need their media to challenge power and offer robust debate, but when this transgresses into an antagonism that undermines legitimate political voices that dare to contest the current status quo, then it is not democracy that is served.

pp. 12–13

Therefore, speaking from the point of media social responsibility theory, journalists and the media failed in providing a balanced coverage and with the violation of equality and through the use of stereotyping they failed to serve the public interest.

In health, scholars warned on the importance of covering health issues in a fair and balanced way because people often make choices based on media writing. Shuchman and Wilkes (1997) reported on sensationalism in health reporting, such as an increased heart disease risk for receivers of channel blockers for hypertension, which resulted in numerous phone calls to surgeries to physicians and some people discontinuing treatment. In the UK, media increased interest in health to the point that it entered the public agenda and news pages. However, this did not come without issues because some studies have shown that media are failing to provide a balanced view of health affairs. In my study on sugar reporting (Topić & Tench, 2018), an analysis of press releases from a charity "Action on Sugar" was driving the coverage of the press in a period between 2010 and 2015 and the data has shown that the media failed in informing the public that reducing sugar is not enough to lead a healthy life because media ignored issues such as sedentary lifestyle, exercise and genetic predispositions, which are all contributors to health issues (Black et al. 2017; Ghobadi et al. 2017; Avery et al. 2017; Jordan et al. 2008; Schneider et al. 2007; Viner and Cole 2005; Reilly et al. 2005; Hancox et al. 2004; Epstein et al. 2002; Miles et al. 2001; Vuori et al. 1998). In the coverage of sugar, the press uncritically repeated views of anti-sugar activists and failed to provide information from the industry, for example, some of whom would have probably argued that buying sugary products is a matter of choice and that people should be generally taught how to lead a healthy life and refrain from many unhealthy practices. However, an argument could also be made that people buy so many sugary products because they are available due to over-production and consumption enticed by corporate advertising and marketing, but the media did not challenge sugar in this way.

This leads back to the notion of CSR and already mentioned question on who promotes which interests and whether we can rely on individuals and interest groups to influence society as a whole, which can also be applied to the media. Therefore, a question can be asked whether journalists having the freedom to report one-sided information (because this can be sensationalised and bring readership) also means that journalists and the media are failing to serve the interests of the society and follow commercial interests. While on the outsight it looks as if they promote social causes, the media have in the case of the sugar debate failed their social responsibility role (if we would argue that the media have a social role) (Topić & Tench, 2018; Topić, 2020a) because the information was partial and the public does not need to be expected to know that the reduction of sugar alone is not enough to achieve a healthy lifestyle. These findings have also shown that it is not necessarily true that media most commonly take business and political sources as more newsworthy as previous research has shown (Lewis et al., 2008), this clearly depends on what the media find as newsworthy and sellable.

However, while many scholars debate media bias, framing and agenda-setting and show that journalists do not always work in the public interest (particularly in reference to bias), media have been engaged in promoting CSR as a concept since the 1980s and the interest and support has intensified since the 1990s (Hamilton, 2003; Buhr & Grafström, 2006; Hannah & Zatzick, 2008; Lee & Carroll, 2011). In other words, despite criticism of media's commercialisation and failing to protect the public interest, media have been active in reporting on CSR and promoting the concept as morally necessary for corporations. The media coverage of CSR is relevant because media have an influence on corporate behaviour and CSR as the most visible part of that behaviour (Baron, 2005; Berman et al., 1999; Chen & Meindl, 1991; Fombrun & Shanley, 1990; Henriques & Sadorsky, 1999; Pollock & Rindova, 2003). In line with agenda-setting studies proving the influence of the media on public opinion, works on corporate reputation have also proven that the firm's behaviour is influenced by media coverage (Fiss & Zajac, 2006). For example, Zyglidopoulos, Georgiadis, Carroll and Siegel (2012) argued that media attention influences CSR policies, particularly in regard to increasing CSR strengths rather than reducing CSR weaknesses. A study by Cahan, Chen, Chen and Nguyen (2015) has also shown that media see companies that perform better in CSR more favourably and this is also linked with the public's preference for socially responsible business practice, which then enticed media to provide more positive coverage of CSR initiatives. Lunenberg, Gosselt and De Jong (2016) argued that CSR is generally covered in a positive way in the news media that promote the concept. This is particularly the case when the organisation is perceived to have CSR embedded in their practice whereas in other cases when CSR is conducted but might not be perceived as part of the business practice, the tone is largely neutral. Therefore, Lunenberg, Gosselt and De Jong (2016) concluded that "CSR fit positively impacts media coverage with regard to framing. CSR misfit, however, does not necessarily lead to a negative framing of organizations and their activities" (p. 950). This is relevant because people remember media coverage and they tend to remember negative coverage longer (Shoemaker & Reese, 1996); however, in a situation where media are inclined to

88 *Corporate social responsibility*

only put positive or neutral framing on news stories on CSR, the message is clear: CSR is a good thing and companies need to embrace this practice.

In addition to this, media often shape public discourses on CSR through setting the tone and framing articles (Wang, 2007; Zhang & Swanson, 2006; Lunenberg et al., 2016), which are standard and much-debated practices in journalism studies and this has an influence on public opinion on CSR when this issue is salient and framed in the media coverage (Carroll & McCombs, 2003). Framing is a concept that

> … essentially involves selection and salience. To frame is to select some aspects of a perceived reality and make them more salient in a communicating text, in such a way as to promote a particular problem definition, causal interpretation, moral evaluation, and/or treatment recommendation for the item described.
>
> Entman (1993, p. 52, emphasis in the original)

Gamson also argued that framing is "a central organizing idea for making sense of relevant events and suggesting what is at issue" (Gamson, 1989, p. 157). Gamson offered a constructionist understanding of framing where he treats media discourse and public opinion "as two parallel systems of constructing meaning" (Gamson & Modigliani, 1989, p. 1). While there is some debate whether framing is a research agenda on its own or a second-level agenda setting,[7] this research concept is also used to analyse CSR coverage and particularly in regard to the tone of the coverage (Hester & Gibson, 2003), which is often conceptualised as positive, neutral and negative (Deephouse, 2000; McCombs & Ghanem, 2001). This practice has an impact on public perceptions of the topic covered in the news media (De Vreese & Boomgaarden, 2006; Kim et al., 2007). In the case of CSR, news coverage had an impact on corporate reputation and public perceptions (Lee & Carroll, 2011; Carroll, 2010, 2009; Deephouse, 2000; Fombrun & Shanley, 1990; Kiousis et al., 2007; Meijer & Kleinnijenhuis, 2006a, 2006b; Padelford & White, 2009; Wartick, 1992).

Hamilton (2003) tracked coverage of CSR topic (or topics that are usually seen to constitute the CSR practice such as environment, health, workers and labour) and has found that the most commonly reported topics in the media are environment, health and the community. These three topics are long-standing CSR initiatives that have been circulating among corporate policies for decades and show media interest in the matter despite some commentators stating that CSR is not newsworthy (Carroll, 2011; Lee & Carroll, 2011). In other words, media often write about CSR affairs without mentioning the term but that does not mean that CSR is not covered. As already emphasised, environmental policies have long constituted CSR policy and activism, but media do not often mention CSR when talking about corporate environmental conduct albeit they do report extensively about it.

A study by Buhr and Grafström (2006) examined assigning meaning to CSR in the *Financial Times* from 1988 to 2003 since CSR has been seen as a natural practice for organisations that want to be seen as embracing good management practice (Margolis & Walsh, 2003). Buhr and Grafström (2006) noted that the meaning of CSR is shaped by individuals, organisations, the non-governmental sector and also the media. In the latter, Buhr and Grafström (2006) note that CSR as a concept gained prominence in the 1960s (which is also the time when Friedman wrote his first main work criticising the concept, Friedman (1962)), but then it lost prominence during the 1980s only to return in 1990s and has grown ever since. Buhr and Grafström (2006) traced coverage of CSR and noted that during the 1980s CSR was mostly linked to job creation and charitable giving but in the 1990s the concept got associated with marketing and advertising; however, in the period from 1999 to 2003, the CSR concept got assigned a wider meaning now including also environmental affairs, disclosures (especially pension funds) and social issues. In addition to that, the meaning of CSR got expanded to also include human rights, poverty, health, working conditions and ecology (climate change and oil spills in particular) (ibid).

However, the meaning media assign to CSR is also often linked to the personal opinion of the journalist. Tench, Bowd and Jones (2007) found that journalists have views on what they would cover on CSR and what the tone of the coverage would be. For example, in their study, journalists stated they are not very likely to cover general expectations such as organisations obeying laws and evolving to meet different expectations. At the same time, journalists also said they would likely positively cover stories on environmental practices, social issues, communities, donations and profitability whereas negative coverage would encompass issues such as environmental practices, health and safety, governance and human rights (ibid). Similarly, journalists participating in a large study of over 700 UK journalists, conducted by Thurman, Cornia and Kunert (2016), said it is extremely important to scrutinise businesses and businesses were seen as more relevant than politics when it comes to journalistic scrutiny (i.e. 33% thought that it is important to scrutinise businesses whereas 29% said the same for politics). At the same time, journalists also said that journalists need to be detached observers (40%) and report things as they are (67%) (ibid), thus showing an inclination towards objectivity and observation in journalism rather than engagement as proposed by media social responsibility theory. However, as already illustrated with Corbyn's example from the UK and Clinton's example from the US and examples from health, this is not always the case.

Sandoval (2013) developed a useful classification of media approaches to CSR, which draws from Hofkirchner's (2003) classification of CSR policies and provides a useful understanding of the link between the mainstream CSR and the way this applied to the media system. In that, media can take four different approaches to CSR, reductionist, projectionist, dualist and

90 *Corporate social responsibility*

dialectical approach. In a reductionist approach, the main beneficiaries of media work are shareholders and owners of the media because this approach supports the view that business interest preceded social interests. The projectionist approach, however, supports the view that media need to meet expectations of the society, and this means that despite commercial orientation, media still need to have some moral values, which is often seen in journalistic codes. The dualist approach then argues that the economic and social responsibilities of the media are separate entities just like journalism and media are two separate entities. For example, Altmeppen (2011, cited from Sandoval, 2013) argued that journalism is not a business model because the work revolved around selecting topics and writing content while the media organisation works towards ensuring business funding and distribution of content. In theory, this means that journalists could be let to their own devices to provide socially responsible coverage and serve the public interest and the media organisation (marketing departments in particular) would be responsible to find a market for this content (cited from Sandoval, 2013). While some authors argue that the separation of journalism is not feasible because it ignores market pressures and argues that advertisers are paying for journalism (Sandoval, 2013), there is another argument to this, i.e. if readers read a certain media outlet, whether in print or online, this presents an incentive for advertisers to pay for media space regarding whether they agree with the position of journalists or not. Finally, the dialectical approach has a position that the economic and social responsibility of the media is mutually shaped and interdependent. In other words,

> from this perspective economic success and profitability of media companies have consequences that impair their social responsibility. At the same time, socially responsible media that resist commercial mechanisms and market pressures are likely to suffer from a lack of resources and visibility.
>
> Sandoval (2013, p. 44)

The UK media are indeed subjected to market forces and competition, and in recent years there have been talks about media ownership due to the fact they are dominated by a handful of billionaires accused of having links with the government, and some of these newspapers, such as Murdoch's *The Sun*, have claimed a significant impact on elections (Iosifidis, 2016). According to the report from the Media Reform organisation (2019), three companies (News UK, DMG and Reach) own 83% of the UK national newspaper market; however, this is just for the press. When online readers are included, five companies dominate 80% of the market (News UK, DMG, Reach, Guardian and Telegraph) (Ramsay, 2019). This media ownership translates into just three rich families owning 68% of national newspapers, i.e. the Murdochs, Rothermeres and Barclays with Lord Rothermere controlling more than a third of national newspapers (Press Gazette, 2020d).

Corporate social responsibility 91

On top of this, gender needs to be considered as gender issues are inextricably intertwined with capitalism, which many feminists (and ecofeminists in particular) see as fundamentally sexist and responsible for masculine domination (Brownhill & Turner, 2020; Salleh, 2017, 2011, 2000, 1994; Mellor, 1992; Đurđjević, 2020; Marjanić, 2020; saed, 2017). As already mentioned in the ecofeminism chapter, the lack of consideration of the position of women is generally a problem in Marxist scholarship, which is how ecofeminism came to be embraced by many feminists who hold Marxist views but feel there is a lack of women's distinctive position in capitalist society in Marxist scholarship, thus joining the position of socialist ecofeminism.

CSR and women

The position of women can be seen as a CSR issue and the current scholarship goes in line with ecofeminist research arguing that women are more likely to support environmental initiatives (Mallory, 2006; Brownhill & Turner, 2019; Goldstein, 2006; Leahy, 2003; McStay & Dunlap, 1983; Poole & Harmon Zeigter, 1985; Shapiro & Mahajan, 1986; Steger & Witt, 1989; Diani, 1989; Schahn & Holzer, 1990; Blaikie, 1992; Franklin & Rudig, 1992; Stern et al., 1993; McAllister, 1994; Hampel et al., 1996; Tranter, 1996; Godfrey, 2005, 2008; Shiva, 1989; Brownhill, 2010; Holy, 2007; Mann, 2011; Stoddart & Tindall, 2011; Giacomini, 2014; Kirk, 1998; McMahon, 1997; Salleh, 1984; Topić, 2020d; Topić et al., 2021). In other words, many studies indicated that women contribute to CSR implementation more than men and that the CSR implementation has increased when women started to join corporate boards.

Authors argued that women are more aware of risks and thus more likely to put CSR policies in place to protect the reputation of companies and also that women have been socialised to care for other people's needs so they recognise the need to help societies with CSR policies (Ciocirlan & Peterson, 2012; Fernandez-Feijoo et al., 2014; Huyn et al., 2016). Women are also seen to have a different conscience in the private sphere, and this is then projected to their behaviour in the public (Bernardi & Threadgill, 2010; Hunter et al., 2004). However, authors also recognise that it is not possible to fully speak of women's impact on CSR implementation because a few women in a large group of men in managerial positions or at boards can also mean women are tokens in organisations (Konrad et al., 2008; Torchia et al., 2011). A study by Fernandez-Feijoo et al. (2014) has shown that companies that have at least three women members on the board are more likely to have sustainability reporting in place, and equally, countries, where gender equality is higher, tend to have more women board members. This is supported with research arguing that women are more likely to contribute to environmental protection such as reducing carbon emissions (Haque, 2017), managing water resources (Alonso-Almeida, 2012), avoiding a conviction for environmental offences (Tauringana et al., 2017) and women board members generally tend

92 *Corporate social responsibility*

to ask for more corporate reporting, transparency and environmental impact and CSR (Ntim, 2016; Hollindale et al., 2019; Liao et al., 2015; Rupley et al., 2012; Nekhilli et al., 2017). Xie et al. (2020) argued that

> female presence on boards has positive effects on promoting proactive environmental strategies, especially *the pollution prevention strategy*, which is found to bring about sustained competitive advantage in both short-term and long-term financial performance, and the *sustainable development strategy*, which is expected to enhance future performance.
>
> p. 2045 (emphasis in the original)

Studies also argued that women have better skills to monitor and advise managers (Bear et al., 2010; Cumming et al., 2015) and they have better connections with an external environment, for example with women customers as they can relate with them and understand their needs (Bear et al., 2010; Hussain et al., 2018; Liao et al., 2018). In addition to that, research shows that companies that have female directors have a higher rating in confidence in the equality policies of the company and this has been linked to attracting a more diverse talent into the workforce (Ali et al., 2014; Isidro & Sobral, 2015; Turban & Greening, 2017) and increased commitment towards employees (Glavas & Kelley, 2014; Valls Martinez et al., 2020). Other studies also emphasise the positive influence of women on boards on the non-financial performance of companies (Ben-Amar et al., 2017; Post et al., 2015; Liao et al., 2018) and disclosure (Tapver et al., 2020). In a study by Liu et al. (2020), research suggested that the quality of female managers influence corporate performance because "firms benefit more when female directors are more well-regarded and influential" (p. 119). This inevitably brings a question on whether women are then proponents of capitalism despite research showing they are more likely to be environmentalists and collectivist than men. While on the outsight this could look like a case to make, the reality is likely different because women who succeed in higher organisational positions are commonly masculine.

In other words, there has indeed been a change in a public debate on the position of women in organisations, at least in the UK. For example, many UK companies started to add statements of the pay gap to their CSR policies (Topić et al., 2020a) outlining how they support pay equality and some are also publishing reports showing what they do to address this issue. This is clearly a welcome development; however, despite CSR policies, equality is far from reality at present, in the UK and elsewhere. Organisational research continually reports on the barriers women face. As already mentioned in the introduction and ecofeminism chapters, organisations remain man's world where women who want to join must be bloke-ified and embrace masculine values (Alvesson, 1998, 2013; Acker, 1990, 2009; Topić & Tench, 2018; Topić, 2020c, 2020e, 2021; Topić & Bruegmann, 2021; Mills, 2014, 2017; Ross, 2001; North, 2016a, 2016b, 2009a, 2009b). Also, historically women have not been able to join corporate boards due to obstacles in career progression (Nguyen et al., 2020; Adams, 2016) despite homogeneous boards not always being able to reach decisions that take into consideration the needs of a diverse community. Nevertheless, the global financial crisis that happened in 2007 and 2008 has been attributed to poor corporate governance but also the lack of diversity (Elmagrhi et al., 2019, 2020; Jeong & Harrison, 2017; Ntim & Soobaroyen, 2013; Post & Byron, 2015).

Therefore, studies reported various reasons for the lack of representation of women; for example, social role theorists argued that women struggle in progressing because of the "think manager-think male" stereotype (Koenig et al., 2011) and women generally struggle because of women being expected to show caring attitudes, which are not associated with leadership (Liu et al., 2020; Eagly & Karau, 2002). Other theorists, such as those using social identity theory, also argued that individuals prefer to working with people they can identify with or find something in common, which explains why men tend to appoint other men to senior positions (Ali et al., 2014). This issue is also known as a problem of boys clubs where men socialise together and this results in career progressions (Broyles and Grow, 2008; Crewe & Wang, 2018; Weisberg and Robbs, 1997; Topić, 2020b, 2020c). Gender socialisation theory also explains socialisation differences between men and women in terms of their behaviour, which lead to differences in the way they do work and lead (Boulouta, 2013). This approach is similar to the already mentioned Different Approach where scholars have been arguing that women and men lead, communicate and behave differently due to the socialisation process, which then conditions and influences career success (Tannen, 1995, 1990, 1986; West & Zimmerman, 1983; Vukoičić, 2013; Merchant, 2012; Yule, 2006; Maltz & Borker, 1982; Christopher, 2008; de la Rey, 2005; van der Boon, 2003; Growe & Montgomery, 2000; Crawford, 1995; Stanford et al., 1995; Alimo Metcalfe, 1995; Anderson et al., 2006; Morgan, 2004; Chemers et al., 2000).

However, research also shows that women often work in less paid roles such as human resources and marketing, and thus the presence of women on boards did not always contribute towards the increase of income for women or closing the pay gap (Cardoso & Winter-Ebmer, 2010; Kulich et al., 2011). Some studies also showed that while senior men offer promotions and positions to other men, women board members do not do this because their presence is not always strong enough (Abendroth et al., 2017), which is known as tokenism. Tokenism has been an issue for women and minority groups for a long time because organisations often appoint these groups to positions and use them as a token to prove equality has been considered, but these groups do not always have the power in the organisation. For example, in public relations, women reported being heads of communications departments and still excluded from business decisions and board meetings or not treated seriously and confined to lower and technical positions (Topić, 2021, 2020e; Van Slyke, 1983; Cline et al., 1986; Miller, 1988; Lance Toth, 1988;

94 *Corporate social responsibility*

Dozier, 1988; Singh and Smyth, 1988; Broom, 1982; Scrimger, 1985; Pratt, 1986; Theus, 1985; Topić et al., 2019, 2020; Lee et al., 2018; Dubrowski et al., 2019; Aldoory and Toth, 2002; Grunig, 1999) whereas in advertising women reported having little influence in the department (Topić, 2020b, 2020c; Weisberg and Robbs, 1997; Broyles and Grow, 2008; Crewe and Wang, 2018).

The fact women are often tokenised and discriminated against is not the only issue. There is also a recognised issue of "queen bees" and also of blokish women or those women who embrace masculine characteristics, such as behaviour and communication, which helps them go ahead, as already mentioned (Mills, 2014, 2017; Gallagher, 2002; Ross, 2001; North, 2009a, 2009b, 2016a, 2016b; Lobo et al., 2017; Alvesson, 2013, 1998; Acker, 1990, 2006, 2009; Bourdieu, 2007; Bourdieu & Wacquant, 1992; Topić & Tench, 2018; Topić, 2020a, 2020b, 2020c, 2021). The issue of blokishness is particularly relevant for this book because this is something explored in journalism first and foremost, and it is also something that has an impact on the journalistic profession and news production. Blokishness is closely linked to the notion of masculinity in journalism where men have historically been journalists and created a culture of hard news, which includes politics and business, for example, whereas health, food, lifestyle were so-called soft news (North, 2016a). The politics and business news were traditionally man's domain whereas women brought the soft coverage to the newspapers and historically covered health, food and lifestyle (Craft & Wanta, 2004; North, 2016b; Christmas, 1997; Everbach & Flournoy, 2007). The situation has not changed until the present day as many studies analysing the coverage and the hard vs soft news approach, as well as masculine domination in journalism, is still overly present (Bawdon, 2012; Cochrane, 2011; Topić & Tench, 2018). The masculine way of doing journalism has also resulted in a masculine newsroom culture where women who want to fit in have to embrace the masculine way of writing and doing the job but also embrace a largely masculine culture of newsrooms and become one of the boys to succeed, fit in and consequentially get ahead in their careers (Mills, 2014, 2017; Gallagher, 2002; Ross, 2001; North, 2009a, 2009b, 2016a, 2016b; Lobo et al., 2017; Alvesson, 2013, 1998; Acker, 1990, 2006, 2009; Bourdieu, 2007; Bourdieu & Wacquant, 1992; Topić & Tench, 2018; Topić, 2020a, 2020b, 2020c, 2021).

In other words, journalism has been a male industry for centuries despite the fact what newspapers and other media cover have relevance and implication not only for men but also for women, and generally for all communities (Christmas, 1997). In the UK, women started to work in journalism in larger numbers during the 1960s, the first female editor was not appointed until 1987 when *News of the World* and *Sunday Mirror* appointed women editors. The career of women, therefore, started first and foremost in tabloids, as both of these newspapers are red top tabloids and the reason they hired women was feature writing, which has always been seen as a woman's strength (ibid). The 1980s present a golden period for women in journalism as this is the time when they started to join the profession in larger numbers

Corporate social responsibility 95

and some became editors and went ahead; however, it is worth noting that women have worked in journalism before the 1960s: for example, Rachel Beer was an editor of *The Observer* in 1891, but during the whole of 20th century there were almost no female editors in UK broadsheet newspapers (Franks, 2013). The fact women struggled to join journalism was exacerbated by the views of male journalists that women are not fit to work in the field because they will bring emotion and have class-bound voices or because wives of journalists would not like their husbands staying overnight with a woman journalist for an assignment. Some male editors also said that women cannot handle "hard news stories…(but) see themselves as experts on women's features" (Franks, 2013, p. 3). Lonsdale (2013) also analysed novels depicting women journalists and journalism newsrooms, using novels as a testimony of the time in which it was produced, and argued that women were seen as a nuisance in newsrooms by male journalists. This is echoed in other organisational research where organisations are seen as fundamentally masculine and organised in a way that benefits men rather than women. For example, and as already emphasised earlier in this book, organisations always worked according to an assumption that men will work while women were always socially expected to stay at home and look after children and the elderly, which resulted in a situation in that masculine world invented after work networking with clients and long working hours, which is causing a myriad of issues for women up to today since social expectations have not changed enough (Saval, 2015; Alvesson, 1998, 2013; Acker, 1990, 2009).

Therefore, it comes as no surprise that women who wanted to succeed had to embrace blokish characteristics and become one of the boys. Graber (1980) has warned in her early research that women have merged into the masculine culture of newsrooms because newsgathering techniques have not changed even though the number of women has risen in journalism, and these findings keep finding confirmation in other research (Christmas, 1997; Djerf-Pierre, 2011). Gallagher (2002) called the culture also laddish and argued that many women cannot or do not want to join that culture. Data shows that women are more educated than men, with more women coming to journalism in the UK with a degree from Oxford or Cambridge; however, men still prevail in number, earn more, have a longer and more successful career and are not forced into freelancing as women are when they reach the 45 years of age, which is seen as the right time for men to progress while women are seen as old and they face redundancies and rejections of freelance work even when they do leave the industry and try to work on their own (Sieghart & Henry, 1998; Franks, 2013; Thurman et al., 2016; Mills, 2014). In addition to this, recent research I conducted also confirmed all of these findings. In that, I conceptualised blokishness through behaviour, communication and views on what constitutes a successful journalist and an editor (Topić & Bruegmann, 2021). It appeared that women have indeed merged into the masculine culture because they emphasise that women need to "be

96 *Corporate social responsibility*

able to give as good as you get in what was traditionally a man's world" and they have to be "very tough, very determined" (Topić & Bruegmann, 2021); however, these views were mainly emphasised by women who merged into the masculine culture of newsrooms and embraced blokish behaviour and communication (North, 2016a, 2016b, 2009a, 2009b; Mills, 2014, 2017; Gallagher, 2002; Topić & Tench, 2018), some even by openly calling it a masculine world and showing acceptance. Those who did not embrace masculine characteristics openly criticised newsrooms as sexist and discouraging for women and said they are sometimes treated as just girls, without any personality or humanity attached to them (Topić & Bruegmann, 2021).

Notes

1 The rise of CSR did coincide with the rise of corporate image programmes during 1970s and 1980s, and this happened because companies were no longer able to keep their business information private as they were facing more demands for disclosure and engagement with publics (Clark, 2000). These changes coincided with increased popularity of the stakeholder approach advocated by Edward Freeman (1984) who saw consumers as part of organisational stakeholders. Clark (2000) argues that the reason why CSR is strongly intertwined with PR lies in the fact that both PR and CSR use similar process to run programmes. For example, Cutlip and Center's (1978) model of four stages of PR planning (fact finding and feedback, planning and programming, action and communication, and evaluation) can easily be applicable to CSR campaigns too. Nevertheless, Preston and Post (1975) have introduced a four-step process of corporate social involvement, which included recognition of an issue, planning and analysis, policy development response and implementation (cited from Clark, 2000, p. 368), and this process is clearly similar to the Cutlip's and Center's four stage of PR model introduced after Preston and Post's model, which further contributes to similarity of the implementation of both PR and CSR. Cutlip's and Center's model later on became a four-step management process that encompasses "defining the problem (or opportunity), planning and programming, taking action and communicating, and evaluating the program" (Clark, 2000, p. 367), and this model later on informed the famous two-way symmetrical communication advocated by Grunig and Hunt (1984).

2 In other words, while Marxist generally criticise economic growth, excessive production aimed at achieving surplus and the labour relations, other economic perspectives focus on different things. In Marxist thought, Mandel (2002 [1962]), as one of the most prominent Marxists has argued that the surplus would not occur for as long as people produce enough to satisfy their own needs and thus division of labour and the capitalist social order would not happen. Following this, as soon as one person produces more than what they need, a question on how to share this surplus emerges, and as soon as someone has more than what they need they join the ruling class, i.e. a section of society producing more than what they personally need become a ruling class, and this leads to emancipation of this class from the class working for them; thus, emancipated ruling class starts to detach from the needs of working classes who are producing a surplus for the ruling class. Mandel (2002 [1962]) argued that when a division of labour and ownership happens,

> the products of each of these two very different types of labour can be defined in different terms. When the producer is performing necessary labour,

Corporate social responsibility 97

he is producing a necessary product. When he is performing surplus labour, he is producing a social surplus product. Thus, social surplus product is that part of social production which is produced by the labouring class but appropriated by the ruling class, regardless of the form the social surplus product may assume, whether this be one of natural products, or commodities to be sold, or money.

p. 6

This naturally leads towards human labour becoming a commodity and having a value assigned to someone's work, and there comes an exchange of commodities. Mandel (2002 [1962]) thus argues that in capitalism commodity production has a higher value whereas production for own purpose is not seen as a commodity or rewarded in any way. For example, making a bowl of soup is production but the labour invested in cooking is not assigned value because it is not produced for mass consumption but for personal use. This economic setup necessarily leads to competition, which is at the essence of capitalism along with free (unlimited) market and this leads to lower prices and more employment and more production and consumption. As a result, capitalists have turned luxury products into essentials, such as for example sugar, which became almost like a necessity (ibid). CSR fits into this notion of the capitalist free market with unlimited competition and exploitation of resources.

3 This statement is not to be confused with a view that Keynesian system is desired in my view. Keynesian economics is also liberal and based on growth. Or in other words, "degrowth and steady-state advocates are allies against the neoclassical-Keynesian ideology of growthism" (Daly & Morgan, 2019, p. 145).

4 Neoliberalism is "a politically guided intensification of market rule" (Brenner et al., 2010, p. 184) or a "programme for destroying collective structures which may impede the pure market logic" (Bourdieu, 1998 cited in Gareau, 2013, p. 42). Gill and Law (1993) argued that Reagan and Thatcher liberalised the private sector from state regulation and deliberately changed ideas on the role of the government, markets and the private enterprise.

5 For example, Enron was a US publicly held company that went bankrupt due to its corruptive activities, which ended with thousands losing their jobs and pension funds. When the scandal was about to be discovered the management engaged in destroying documents to cover it up, and eventually 16 former executives of the company were imprisoned (Silverstein, 2013). On the other hand, WorldCom was a large US company that acquired many other companies in its expansion while the management did not put sufficient efforts into merging newly acquired companies. Its founder also burdened the company with high loans to save it, and that sent the company to bankruptcy. Failed management and merging of the business empire also led to four billion USD debts in expenses that were not allocated properly, phony accounting entries to make it look as if company was more profitable than it was, failure to send bills on time and claim liability against clients who were not paying and so on. Therefore, the company eventually filed for bankruptcy leaving many unemployed and without pension funds (Moberg & Romar, 2003, 2006). Tyco was also a large US company that was engaged with accountancy frauds, false bonuses paid to management and similar activities that eventually led to trial against two senior executives who were charged 600 million USD that they had to give back to the company, which meant personal bankruptcy for them as well as a prison sentence (*USA Today*, 2005).

6 For example, the EU financed a project on CSR that offered awards to companies that implement CSR in Croatia. The project started in 2013 (DOP, 2015), which is also a year when Croatia joined the EU (in July 2013). Croatia

98 *Corporate social responsibility*

is, however, a country where the Constitution asks companies to contribute to the general well-being and avoid doing harm, but there is no requirement to report on CSR, nor does this present a mandatory concept. Citizens, on the other hand, do not express particular interest in CSR and enlist it at the end of their priorities when making purchase decisions (Srbljinović, 2012; Vrdoljak Raguž & Hazdovac, 2014; Omazić, 2012; The Constitution of Croatia, Article 48).

7 McCombs and Ghanem (2001), as an advocate of framing as part of second level agenda setting defined framing as a set of expectations that people use to interpret the social world, and media through framing of issues contribute to this (see also Baran & Davis, 2012; McCombs, 1997), with which he more relied on Goffman's (1974) definition of framing as a primary framework people rely on to interpret the social world, and framing can be social and natural. McCombs (2005) believes that both "framing and attribute agenda setting call attention to the perspectives of communicators and their audiences, how they picture topics in the news and, in particular, to the special status that certain attributes or frames have in the content of a message" (p. 546).

4 The press coverage of economic growth and CSR

As I have argued in previous chapters, I see CSR as a capitalist smokescreen meant to preserve the status quo and an initiative that saved capitalism. In addition to that, I also elaborated on the ecofeminist anti-capitalist view, which sees capitalism as inherently anti-environmentalist and thus incompatible with the protection of Nature. I've also argued that economic growth does not go together with environmentalism as resources are being drained to the point of destruction of Nature and thus capitalism being inherently anti-environmentalist. CSR research has shown that women are more inclined to introduce CSR policies (Ntim, 2016; Hollindale et al., 2019; Liao et al., 2015; Rupley et al., 2012; Nekhilli et al., 2017), and ecofeminist and environmentalist research has shown that women have historically been in support of environmental policies (Mallory, 2006; Brownhill & Turner, 2019; Goldstein, 2006; Leahy, 2003; McStay & Dunlap, 1983; Poole & Harmon Zeigter, 1985; Shapiro & Mahajan, 1986; Steger & Witt, 1989; Diani, 1989; Schahn & Holzer, 1990; Blaikie, 1992; Franklin & Rudig, 1992; Stern et al., 1993; McAllister, 1994; Hampel et al., 1996; Tranter, 1996; Godfrey, 2005, 2008; Shiva, 1989; Brownhill, 2010; Holy, 2007; Mann, 2011; Stoddart & Tindall, 2011; Giacomini, 2014; Kirk, 1998; McMahon, 1997; Salleh, 1984; Topić, 2020d; Topić et al., 2021). Therefore, this opens up the question what the situation is with women journalists and generally, how media write about these two issues, which is relevant given the power of media in creating public attitudes and enticing action, either positive or negative. What is more, the question is whether media report positively about economic growth and CSR and support these economic concepts which can be seen as promoting the status quo because companies need to constantly grow to be able to give something to society; thus the concept is fundamentally based on a capitalist premise.

Economic growth

As already argued in the introduction, my thesis is that environmentalism does not go together with economic growth (Georgescu-Roegen, 1971; Meadows et al., 1972; Ehrlich and Holdren, 1971; Cleveland et al., 1984; Salleh, 2000; Daly & Morgan, 2019). The continuous concentration of world

DOI: 10.4324/9781003091592-4

100 *Press coverage of economic growth and CSR*

economies on fostering economic growth (and thus also consumption) can be seen as problematic and incompatible with environmentalism. This issue is not without a polarisation, and thus there are two camps of thought, those who think that economic growth is associated with excessive consumption and abuse of resources, which harms the environment and on the other side are those who think that economic growth increases the quality of life and income so that people can start putting policies in place to improve environmental protection. In other words, Georgescu-Roegen (1971), Meadows et al. (1972), Ehrlich and Holdren (1971) and Cleveland et al. (1984) argued that high-level of economic activities centred on economic growth (increased production and consumption) inevitably lead towards high consumption of energy and materials and thus create lots of waste and pollution, which can overwhelm the biosphere and decrease the environmental quality resulting in decreased human welfare, and this will happen despite rising incomes (see also Panayotou, 2000). On the other side of this argument are Shafik and Bandyopadhyay (1992), Panayotou (1993), Grossman and Krueger (1991, 1994) and Selden and Song (1994) who argued that economic growth and environmental protection can go together because increased levels of income will result with people demanding better infrastructure and the more preservation of the environment. Panayotou (1993) thus believes that the growth of agriculture and industrialization, for example, caused resource use and the growth of waste but the change towards information-based societies with more focus on services and efficient technology, along with an increased demand for environmental quality, can result in the so-called levelling-off which, in turn, will result with a decline in environmental degradation.

An often-quoted document by those who support the view of economic growth fuelling the destruction of Nature and thus potentially threatening the survival of the planet is *The Limits to Growth* by Meadows et al. (1972)[1] and even though this has been written decades ago, the concern stands today as it did back in the 1970s. In a preface to the report, Watts (1972) argued that the work aimed to tackle,

> the complex of problems troubling men of all nations: poverty in the midst of plenty; degradation of the environment; loss of faith in institutions; uncontrolled urban spread; insecurity of employment; alienation of youth; rejection of traditional values; and inflation and other monetary and economic disruptions.
>
> p. 10

The report continues by saying that the humankind is failing in solving these problems because they are analysed separately without recognising their interconnectedness, i.e.

> it is the predicament of mankind that man can perceive the problematique, yet, despite his considerable knowledge and skills, he does not understand the origins, significance, and interrelationships of its many

components and thus is unable to devise effective responses. This failure occurs in large part because we continue to examine single items in the problematique without understanding that the whole is more than the sum of its parts, that change in one element means change in the others.

Watts (1972, p. 11)

The report thus argues that people are focused on their personal problems and do not participate in environmental affairs as much as they would if they did not have to worry about how to provide for themselves. The report predicted the following:

> 1. If the present growth trends in world population, industrialization, pollution, food production, and resource depletion continue unchanged, the limits to growth on this planet will be reached sometime within the next one hundred years. The most probable result will be a rather sudden and uncontrollable decline in both population and industrial capacity.
> 2. It is possible to alter these growth trends and to establish a condition of ecological and economic stability that is sustainable far into the future. The state of global equilibrium could be designed so that the basic material needs of each person on earth are satisfied and each person has an equal opportunity to realize his individual human potential.
> 3. If the world's people decide to strive for this second outcome rather than the first, the sooner they begin working to attain it, the greater will be their chances of success.

Meadows et al. (1972, pp. 23–24)

The report therefore called for a change in lifestyle and its results and predictions are relevant because it has been 49 years since the report has been published and based on current climate issues, it seems as if authors were not alarmist when they said that in the next 100 years limits of growth will be reached. In other words, the authors suggested that issues will occur around 2072, thus in the lifetime of current children and teenagers. Authors argued that all five elements constituting relevant variables that need to be taken into consideration when thinking of human survival on the planet (population, food production, industrialization, pollution and consumption of non-renewable natural resources) are constantly growing in, what is known as, an exponential growth (Meadows et al., 1972). Industrial output has been increasing even more than the population (which they explain in great details by arguing that in 30 years from 1972 the world population will be around 7 billion people[2]) and that the gap between rich and poor will widen, which has indeed happened.[3] Authors demonstrated in great length which natural and non-renewable sources are being used with consumption and argued that

> the natural ecological systems can absorb many of the effluents of human activity and reprocess them into substances that are usable by,

102 *Press coverage of economic growth and CSR*

or at least harmless to, other forms of life. When any effluent is released on a large enough scale, however, the natural absorptive mechanisms can become saturated. The wastes of human civilization can build up in the environment until they become visible, annoying, and even harmful. Mercury in ocean fish, lead particles in city air, mountains of urban trash, oil slicks on beaches-these are the results of the increasing flow of resources into and out of man's hands.

ibid (pp. 68–69)

The authors argued that the economic growth results in an increased level of pollution, which is not concentrated in the place where the pollution originates from but spreads around to encompass other regions and planet in general, leading towards ecofeminist argument that even though the West produces and consumes more, thus contributing towards pollution, Global South that produces and consumes much less is still affected by the actions of the West (Sandberg & Sandberg, 2010; Griffin, 2020; Salleh, 2000, 1994). Authors also argued that even though it was not known at the time how much pollution can ecosystem absorb before being adversely affected, the fact it can bring about a limit to growth and that the fact the consequences of polluting environment are delayed and not directly observed with an immediate effect already warrants caution (Meadows et al., 1972). Daly and Morgan (2019) also argued that

if the economy grew into the void, it would encroach on nothing, and its growth would have no opportunity cost. But since the economy in fact grows into and encroaches upon the finite and non-growing ecosystem, there is an opportunity cost to growth in scale, as well as a benefit. The costs arise from the fact that the physical economy, like an animal, is a "dissipative structure" sustained by a metabolic flow from and back to the environment. This flow, which we have called "throughput" (adopting the term from engineers) begins with the depletion of low-entropy useful resources from the environment. It is conformed to or followed by the processes of production and consumption, which, despite the connotations of the words, are only physical transformations of existing matter. The flow ends with the return of an equal quantity of high-entropy polluting wastes. Depletion and pollution are costs. Not only does the growing economy encroach spatially and quantitatively on the ecosystem, it also qualitatively degrades the environmental sources and sinks of the metabolic throughput by which it is maintained.

p. 139

Daly, for example, has been an advocate of degrowth for decades and has pointed out that any suggestion of degrowth instigates resistance of neoclassical economists and has had an impact on the ability to publish works that do not support, what Daly calls, growthism (Daly & Morgan, 2019). The view is also perpetuated by the media. For example, Ed Conway, economics editor of Sky News wrote in an op-ed in *The Times* newspaper a day after IPCC Special Report on Climate Change and Land (IPCC, 2019),

> Instead of seeking economic growth, they say governments should be attempting to constrain it. It is hard to know where to begin with this madness ... [Regarding GDP and growth] the more we moan about its deficiencies, the more likely we are to forget that there are few phenomena in the world as magical as economic growth. Growth makes us healthier, it lengthens our lives, it (mostly) makes us happier, it diminishes poverty and narrows the gaps between countries, it expands opportunities and frequently liberates those who are oppressed. Even bearing in mind its faults, it remains one of the world's great miracles ... So by all means let's measure economic growth better. Let's ensure our growth is even cleaner. Let's share it out more equally. But for heaven's sake let's not actively try to stop it.
>
> Conway (2019, n.p.)

In 2004, the authors of *The Limits to Growth* also published *Limits to Growth – The 30-Year Update* (Meadows et al., 2004) arguing that while their predictions on the limits of economic growth were seen as an outrage in 1972, it is increasingly visible they were right and that the Earth is reaching limits of its potential with over-exploitation of natural resources while failing to absorb all pollutants that are being released. An organisation called Footprint Network frequently releases data on country footprint marking in an open data platform and countries that use more than the biodiversity allows in red. The graph screenshotted on 17 January 2021 (Figure 4.1) already confirms comments from ecofeminists that the so-called developed countries, such as the US and the UK, are making a bigger environmental impact than many countries in the Global South (Sandberg & Sandberg, 2010; Griffin, 2020; Salleh, 2000, 1994).

However, the fact Meadows et al. (1972, 2004) published their work and that many things they originally said are clearly happening today, does not mean there is an agreement on economic growth and its limits. De Bruyn (2000) identified and summarised four positions to economic growth. *The radical supporter* of economic growth thinks that growth will fuel technological development, which will, in turn, improve environmental quality. The radical supporter is wary of environmental protection since they can bring paperwork and government's failure (see Simon, 1981). *The conditional supporter* thinks that there are negative effects on economic growth but still supports it because they see it as the only way to achieve good environmental policies (e.g. Grossman & Krueger, 1994). *The weak antagonist* sees economic growth as causing environmental degradation; however, the weak antagonist would support environmental policies as mitigating environmental degradation albeit they recognise that these are less effective

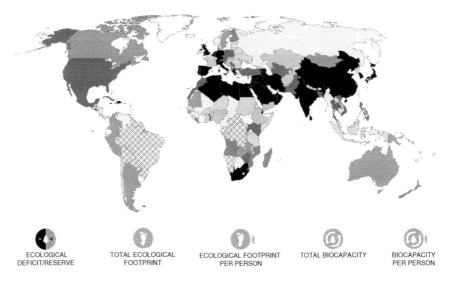

Figure 4.1 Global Carbon Footprint on 17 January 2021.

in a developed economy (e.g. Arrow et al., 1995). *The strong antagonist* believes that economic growth is always bad for the environment and while environmental policies can mitigate some negative impact of the growth, in a long run this is not possible unless the philosophy of economic growth is abandoned altogether (e.g. Meadows et al., 1972; Daly, 1991). De Bruyn (2000) thus summarises four positions and their envisaged policy responses by arguing that radical supporters suggest policies that stimulate growth while preserving the free-market policy. On the other hand, conditional supporters envision the policy of stimulating growth while also implementing environmental policy. The weak antagonist would envision environmental policies that reduce economic growth in the so-called dirty sectors of the economy mostly responsible for environmental degradation while the strong antagonist would propose reducing or abolishing economic growth altogether. However, the dilemma is ultimately summarised in the work of Jackson (2009, pp. 187–188, cited from Morgan, 2017, p. 176):

> Society is faced with a profound dilemma. To resist growth is to risk economic and social collapse. To pursue it relentlessly is to endanger the ecosystems on which we depend. For the most part, this dilemma goes unrecognized in mainstream policy […] The sheer scale of the task is rarely acknowledged […] Never mind that all our institutions and incentive structures continually point in the wrong direction. The dilemma, once recognized, looms so dangerously over our future that we are desperate to believe in miracles. Technology will save us. Capitalism is good at technology. So let's just keep the show on the road and hope for the

Press coverage of economic growth and CSR 105

best. This delusional strategy has reached its limits [...] None of this is inevitable. We can't change ecological limits. We can't alter human nature. But we can and do create and recreate the social world. Its norms are our norms. Its structures and institutions shape and are shaped by those norms and visions. This is where transformation is needed.

I am arguing that environmental protection and economic growth need to be debated and tackled together, as proposed by Meadows et al. (1972) and Watts (1972) decades ago. This means that a change in lifestyle and consumerist habits is necessary or resources will run out and thus humanity needs to tackle population, food production, industrialization, pollution and consumption of non-renewable resources, and this also means the need is to tackle the exponential growth and decrease industrial outputs and pollution (Meadows et al., 1972, 2004). All these issues are interconnected because constant economic growth is based on consumerism and this results in the extraction of resources and pollution, and this has been an ecofeminist argument for decades because it is indeed true that the West produces and consumes more while the Global South produces and consumes less but nevertheless suffers from environmental consequences (Sandberg & Sandberg, 2010; Griffin, 2020; Salleh, 2000, 1994). I see CSR as central to the preservation of this system of incessant growth because companies can greenwash the harm they do to the environment by giving a portion of the profit back to communities, thus CSR effectively preserving a premise on which this policy is based, excessive production, consumerism and a drive for profit while the environment is falling apart. As already emphasised, ecofeminists oppose economic growth as well as technology as a solution to an environmental problem and see technology as a contributor to the problem because it is based on the masculine domination of Nature (Bronson, 2009; Buck et al., 2014; Sikka, 2017; Cross, 2018). Ecofeminism particularly centres on-isms, or racism, sexism and speciesism and anti-capitalist criticism of the current economic and social system embedded in the inequality of races, species and women (Salleh, 2000) and neoliberalism that seeks to enforce a modern form of colonisation on the Global South (Price & Nunn, 2016). This makes ecofeminism a strong antagonist of economic growth and what is needed is a change of thinking and acting, or in other words, we cannot simply rely on technological solutions to fix the damage while continuing to cause damage, we need to change us, our worldviews and our actions (Krstić et al., 2020).

The question is, therefore, where the British press fits on economic growth and CSR.

The coverage of economic growth

After analysing the coverage of the daily press, *Daily Mail* and *The Guardian*, surprisingly, there is more concentration on reporting on the economic growth in *The Guardian* than in *Daily Mail* with *The Guardian*

106   *Press coverage of economic growth and CSR*

Table 4.1 Coverage of Economic Growth in *Daily Mail* (N = 99)

Article Author	Number of Articles	Promotes EC. Growth	Neutral	Negative about EC. Growth
Man	52	45	6	1
Woman	24	10	10	4
Mixed	0	0	0	0
No byline	23	18	5	0
Total	99	73	21	5

Table 4.2 Coverage of Economic Growth in *The Guardian* (N = 352)

Article Author	Number of Articles	Positive towards Economic Growth	Neutral	Negative towards Economic Growth
Man	264	65	185	14
Woman	62	8	47	7
Mixed	16	2	14	0
No byline	3	0	1	2
Editorial	7	5	2	0
Total	352	80	249	23

publishing a total of 352 articles (Table 4.2) and *Daily Mail* a total of 99 articles (Table 4.1).

What is immediately relevant from the data is that it is mostly men who write about economic growth, which goes in line with literature that shows men have historically covered topics such as finance, business, politics and sports while women were predominantly in features, health, lifestyle, food and beauty and fashion (Craft & Wanta, 2004; North, 2016b; Christmas, 1997; Everbach & Flournoy, 2007). The situation is the same here with men publishing 52 articles as opposed to women's 24 articles in *Daily Mail* (Table 4.1) and men publishing a total of 264 articles as opposed to women's 62 in *The Guardian* (Table 4.2), thus showing an astonishing difference between the extent men and women are engaged with business writing, confirming all existing literature on women in journalism showing that business is still a man's domain (Bawdon, 2012; Cochrane, 2011; Topić & Tench, 2018).

This is further exacerbated by the tone of the coverage. In the case of *Daily Mail*, both men and women published more positive articles supporting economic growth (73 out of 99 articles are positive about the need for economic growth); however, more men published positive articles than women arguing in favour of economic politics founded on the economic growth. For example, out of 52 articles on the economic growth that men wrote, 45 are positive, 6 are neutral and one is negative. As opposed to this,

Press coverage of economic growth and CSR 107

women published 10 positive articles, 10 neutral articles and 4 negative articles (Table 4.1). This shows that from one side, women have indeed joined the masculine workforce and are inclined to write positively about economic growth or neutrally, both of which are seen as masculine characteristics. In other words, the politics of economic growth is seen as masculine and the impartiality in journalism is seen as masculine and women have to a large extent merged to this newsroom culture and expectations (Gallagher, 2002; Mills, 2014; Ross, 2001; North, 2009a, 2009b, 2016a, 2016b; Topić & Bruegmann, 2021). However, their numbers are low, and even in these low numbers, four women published a negative article on economic growth as opposed to just one man, thus opening a question of whether the situation would be different if more women joined politics and business sections in newspapers and had a chance to express an opinion about this capitalist policy. In other words, ecofeminist research has been showing for decades that women are more inclined to support environmentalist causes due to their experiences of oppression (Mallory, 2006; Brownhill & Turner, 2019; Goldstein, 2006; Leahy, 2003; McStay & Dunlap, 1983; Poole & Harmon Zeigter, 1985; Shapiro & Mahajan, 1986; Steger & Witt, 1989; Diani, 1989; Schahn & Holzer, 1990; Blaikie, 1992; Franklin & Rudig, 1992; Stern et al., 1993; McAllister, 1994; Hampel et al., 1996; Tranter, 1996; Godfrey, 2005, 2008; Shiva, 1989; Brownhill, 2010; Holy, 2007; Mann, 2011; Stoddart & Tindall, 2011; Giacomini, 2014; Kirk, 1998; McMahon, 1997; Salleh, 1984; Topić, 2020d; Topić et al., 2021), and since out of 24 articles signed by women, 4 were negative as opposed to 52 articles by men of which only one is negative, this opens a question of whether women are not just inclined to support the environmentalist cause but also denounce capitalism and economic growth. This question alone immediately goes back to the fundamental premise of ecofeminism and that is that equality of women is central to improving environmental protection because Nature and women are being dominated in the name of the patriarchal and masculine ideology that ultimately is bringing the world as we know it to the collapse (Gaard, 2015).

In terms of *The Guardian*, the difference between men and women in covering a historically masculine topic of economic growth/business is even higher than in *Daily Mail* with 264 articles signed by men and 62 signed by women (Table 4.2). Given the sheer number of articles on this issue, it seems that *The Guardian* is very interested in placing the concern about the economic growth on the agenda because a total of 362 articles published in a 12 months period signals they published about this issue almost every day of the year. The coverage is mainly neutral, 264 articles out of 352 total (Table 4.2). Of 80 articles that are promoting economic growth, 65 were written by men and 8 by women whereas men wrote a total of 14 negative articles with women signing 7 negative articles. Given the large discrepancy between men and women in writing on this issue, it is again a question of whether things would be different if women had more recognition and opportunities to write about business affairs. In other words, while women published only

108 *Press coverage of economic growth and CSR*

62 articles, 7 were negative towards economic growth and 8 were positive while 47 were neutral and just reporting on the issue, signalling that women have indeed embraced neutrality and impartiality in writing on this issue, and thus merged into masculine newsrooms (Gallagher, 2002; Mills, 2014; Ross, 2001; North, 2009a, 2009b, 2016a, 2016b; Topić & Bruegmann, 2021) but they are also inclined to write negatively and much less positively than men about economic growth. This again opens a question of whether the situation would be different had women had more space in the newspapers to tackle masculine practices such as obsessive concentration on economic growth.

However, what appears when reading articles in depth is that regardless of how journalists write about economic growth, the fundamental premise is the same, all writing is embedded within a neoliberal paradigm and attempts to find solutions to environmental problems without fundamentally changing the economic system centred on economic growth and excessive consumption that drains resources (Georgescu-Roegen, 1971; Meadows et al., 1972; Ehrlich and Holdren, 1971; Cleveland et al., 1984; Douthwaite, 1999; Mishan, 1967; Salleh, 2000). What is more, some articles critical of economic growth also propose neoliberal policies as a solution to the problem and there are an overall reliance and trust in technology to solve environmental problems, which is in ecofeminist scholarship recognised as masculine and as something that will not work (Gaard, 2015).

For example, *The Guardian*, from 7 May 2019, calls for investments in "nature restoration" but proposes to do this by raising,

> the tax burden on companies that degrade wildlife, according to recommendations made to the G7 group of rich nations. The proposals are part of a growing debate on how to radically change humanity's relationship with nature in the wake of a new UN mega-report that showed an alarming decline in the Earth's life-support systems.

Thus, the author calls for a change in priorities that would "redirect economic systems towards natural growth rather than material extraction" but emphasises this would be difficult politically because of lobbying from big companies such as energy and farm lobbies who donate money to political parties, and this also includes stock indexes who are "heavily dependant on mining and petroleum companies". However, the article states that while "millions of jobs are at stake" the potential "economic benefits are far greater" especially because trillions of dollars are being lost due to "climate instability, soil erosion, pollinator loss and water pollution". This author also recognises the,

> growing argument that the concept of capital itself is at the root of the planet's current problems because current economic models are predicated on endless growth, extraction and consumption – which are

Press coverage of economic growth and CSR 109

impossible on a finite planet. Instead of tallying the value of nature in dollars, which could simply lead to further commodification, many people believe nature should be recognised for its essential, incalculable role as the foundation of life. This flips the debate: instead of justifying nature in economic terms, it should be up to businesses to justify their activities in environmental terms. This is not yet on the table of most global conferences. But for the first time in many years, there is a high-level debate about the destructive nature of the current economic model.

Thus, this article comments on issues such as the current economic policy and the saving of the planet and calls for a dialogue on how we manage growth, extraction and consumption critically arguing it is not possible to sustain these policies on a finite planet. However, it proposes to do so within a neoliberal economic paradigm. In other words, it is well known that neoliberal economic policy is centred on Governments first raising money through taxes to pay for policies whereas, for example, Keynesian politics would promote borrowing to invest in policies albeit Keynesian policy is also capitalist just approaching economy differently (e.g. by sheltering prices, Nunn, 2014; Gamble, 1989; Jessop, 2003); however, the media do not even propose this approach and never mind offering any meaningful criticism of neoliberalism. Therefore, even when articles nominally criticise economic growth as damaging for the environment, this is done in a way that fits within the neoliberal paradigm and neoliberal economics, which leads nowhere because neoliberalism is fundamentally based on the open market and freedom for corporations to pursue profit at all cost.

Some other articles mention the problem of the population and argue against the hostility against couples who do not want children for the sake of the planet and argued that

> according to the UN, global population will peak at the end of this century before falling thereafter, transforming the way we think about our once teeming planet. Good news for depleted natural resources, maybe, but a red flag for economic growth – although it should be said that a crucial driver of that growth for the last few decades has been the surge of women going out to work. Funny how the economic upsides of female liberation never get quite so much coverage as the downsides.
>
> *The Guardian* (3 August 2019)

While this article promotes women's right to choose, it also fails to recognise that population in itself is not a problem but consumption and capitalism. This is a common view in deep ecology, which is founded on patriarchal and masculine values (Hallen, 1999; Holy, 2007), similar to the media (Ross, 2001; North, 2016a, 2016b; Topić & Tench, 2018), whereas an ecofeminist position is commonly that population is not a problem but over-consumption in the Global North (Gaard, 2015; D'Eaubonne, [1990] 1997).

110 *Press coverage of economic growth and CSR*

Thus, while some articles call for ending the economic policy of obsessing with economic growth on a finite planet using various arguments (albeit within the neoliberal paradigm), many articles actually express concerns about economic growth stalling. This is particularly present in articles about Brexit where authors expressed concerns about growth stalling because of, for example, "Brexit uncertainty and a slowdown in the global economy has served as a handbrake on business investment". Thus, the author states that

> Britain has three primary economic problems to address from the outset, all arguably made far worse by the spending constraint of the 2010s. [...] First will be to reboot the flatlining productivity growth of the 2010s. Second is the task of rebalancing a fractured nation, by addressing inequalities of wealth, gender, race, education, geography and opportunity. Third will be to decarbonise the UK's economic model, to prevent the climate emergency from turning into catastrophe.
>
> *The Guardian* (5 January 2020)

Therefore, articles on economic growth either propose tackling environmental problems with reducing economic growth using neoliberal policies of first collecting taxes, which signals an incomprehensible and undoable initiative, which can only lead to over-saturation of the environmental coverage but is unlikely to instigate any meaningful action.

What seems to be underlined by those who promote economic growth is also the trust in technology to solve environmental problems. Thus, the same article from *The Guardian* from 5 January 2020 argues that economies will further slip apart, and calls for international cooperation, thus recognising the need for cooperation; however, many countries in the Global South refuse to bear the blame of global warming that has been caused by consumerism in the West (Stiglitz, 2006). In this sense, the author of the article continues by saying that many people will be pushed into poverty by 2030 and that the poorest regions of the world will be mostly hit, e.g. sub-Saharan Africa and South Asia, and that this will cause a migration crisis, after which the author states that

> there are hopes that technological advances could address both the demographic shift and the climate emergency. But like a common thread running through these issues facing Britain in the 2020s, greater government coordination and funding will be required to realise the ambition.
>
> *The Guardian* (5 January 2020)

What is therefore troubling is that even those who link economic growth with resource issue, seem to be advocating in favour of technology as a solution to problems as well as see population as a problem that causes depletion of resources, but they are not mentioning, for example, that women not having

Press coverage of economic growth and CSR   111

control of their bodies in many countries of the world (and attempts are being made to reverse these rights in some Western countries) is what contributes to population rise. What is more, at the heart of ecofeminist critique is not only that all environmental debate seems to be founded on masculine values (e.g. the focus on the population) but also that the debate often fails to acknowledge that the main issue is consumption rather than population (Gaard, 2015; D'Eaubonne, [1990] 1997).

Other authors state that economic growth is "stubbornly low across most of the developed world. The UK economy may expand 1.5% this year, if we're lucky (and Germany even less). Productivity is lousy, consumer confidence poor, and Brexit uncertainty hangs over everything" (*The Guardian*, 11 January 2020) and around elections, some stated that "Britain's next prime minister will take charge of an economy beginning to falter, as Brexit uncertainty and the mounting risk of a no deal scenario serve as a brake on growth, according to a Guardian analysis" (*The Guardian*, 26 June 2019). Articles also speak of the gap between rich and the poor labelling it as "climate apartheid" defined as a situation "in which the rich insulate themselves from the impacts of the climate emergency while the poor and vulnerable are abandoned to their fate" and continues to warn about consequences for humanity if climate change is not addressed by saying,

> nowhere on Earth will be untouched, with the number of people facing water shortages set to leap from 3.6 billion today to 5 billion by 2050. At least 100 million people will be plunged into poverty in the next decade, and in the decades following that, rising sea levels will swamp coastal cities from Miami to Shanghai, wiping $1tn a year from the global economy. Agriculture will become increasingly difficult, with more people displaced as a result, searching for liveable conditions elsewhere [...] And modern adaptation means more than building seawalls. Restoring natural features, such as mangrove swamps and wetlands, can do far more to protect coastal regions, as well as nurturing biodiversity and tourism.
>
> *The Guardian* (12 September 2019)

The article clearly has a human-centric approach where the call for action is directed towards saving humanity with Nature and other species scarcely being mentioned, thus showing the domination of Nature that pervades discussions on climate change, or speciesism in writing. The same article also calls for collaboration and unity, which is a contested issue and also expresses support for technology albeit with some criticism:

> New technology will play a key role, as early warnings of extreme weather give people time to take shelter or protect their property. Engineering climate-ready infrastructure encompasses everything from porous pavements to urban trees to provide shade [...] The view that adapting

112 *Press coverage of economic growth and CSR*

to inevitable climate change should be our priority, over futile and ruinously expensive attempts to cut emissions, has been spread by those who want to continue to emit CO2, come what may. Fossil fuel companies saw adaptation, along with the idea that we could geo-engineer our way out of trouble, as a way to keep selling oil while paying lip service to the climate science. Now it is gaining traction among more respectable thinkers. It's true that spending on adaptation is a good deal. It saves lives, and if used wisely could stave off the climate apartheid that experts foresee. But setting up adaptation versus emissions-cutting as an either-or choice is a grave mistake. Trying to adapt to the consequences of climate change while continuing to burn fossil fuels is like trying to mop up an overflowing sink while the taps are still running. As long as we continue to pump CO2 into the air, we are fuelling rises in temperature. We cannot outrun global heating any more than we can hold back the rising sea with dykes. And the fires blazing through the Amazon show that without action, things could easily get much worse. It can seem that in a world of finite resources, we need to make a binary decision about where to put our efforts. That is an illusion. The truth is that dealing with the climate emergency requires an across-the-board approach, for the simple reason that all of our resources – economic, physical, social – are at stake. If we do not throw everything we can at the problem, there won't be much left anyway. In short, there is no wall high enough to keep out the consequences of inaction on emissions.

The Guardian (12 September 2019)

Some articles correctly recognise that economy and ecology cannot be separated by saying we cannot keep gobbling up resources as we do now because it is "wrecking the planet", thus arguing that

the trouble is that these two universes aren't separate at all: the world in which GDP growth is valued above all else is the same one making life on Earth increasingly difficult, for humans and the ecosystems on which we depend. Treating the economy and ecology as separate worlds didn't happen by accident.

The Guardian (10 May 2019)

The same article is also the only one found in the sample that criticises the human-centric approach to Nature by saying that Nature has "has for centuries been seen as little more than an input to fuel economic growth, whether through digging up and burning coal or planting gargantuan stretches of monoculture for industrial agriculture" and the author then continues to argue about domination and exploitation of women and the indigenous population and recognises that peace between species must be achieved:

That quest for more inputs led the west's captains of industry to extract from people as they did from the Earth, whether through brutal,

Press coverage of economic growth and CSR 113

genocidal colonial expansions snapping up gold, rubber, tobacco and more, or by disciplining women to have more children to throw into factories. The trouble is that we humans are part of nature too, a fact that those more likely to be on the losing end of this unhinged expansion – indigenous communities, in particular – have sounded alarm bells about for generations, pushing for more stringent protections of biodiversity. The logic of extraction, of valuing certain lives more than others, has been a moral horror for as long as it has existed. As this new UN report and our mounting climate crisis each echo, it's an ecological one too. Preventing runaway catastrophe on either of these interconnected fronts means throwing that logic of endless accumulation out the window, pursuing the kind of transformative reorganization scientists are calling for [...] Those interested in heading off mass extinction should see this as a once-in-a-species opportunity to throw out those old rules altogether [...] Properly designed, a Green New Deal could go a long way toward righting humanity's relationship with the non-human nature around us.

The Guardian (10 May 2019)

In *Daily Mail*, which published less on economic growth, the discourse is rather different. Thus, the newspaper predominantly praises the economic growth and expresses criticism of environmentalism and campaigners, in particular Extinction Rebellion. Economic growth is seen as something that has helped people live "longer, healthier lives. Thanks to decades of economic growth and scientific innovation, we are becoming better at diagnosing, preventing and treating diseases" (*Daily Mail*, 21 November 2019). Nevertheless, in response to announcements on coronavirus and its potential impact on the economy, *Daily Mail* further argued that the lack of economic growth is seen as scary because the "economic fallout" could be "just as contagious and dangerous" (*Daily Mail*, 3 February 2020). However, unlike *The Guardian* that is either writing on economic growth neutrally or positively that only concentrates on the economy, or in some small number of cases links economic growth with the destruction of the planet, albeit in a neoliberal way, *Daily Mail* is obsessively focused on the Labour Party and Jeremy Corbyn with lots of articles emphasising the alleged consequences of a Corbyn Government. In an article from 15 December 2019, three days after the General Elections, *Daily Mail* expressed satisfaction with Jeremy Corbyn's electoral defeat by arguing that the economic policy will now be better and, in that, capitalist elements such as personal wealth and investments are particularly emphasised. For example,

So goodbye to Jeremy Corbyn (hopefully sooner rather than later) and his dream of turning the country into a socialist state where wealth creation would have been despised and taxed to the hilt. And a hearty hello to a Government that, touch wood, will now help re-energise the country and with it our own personal and financial fortunes, however modest

114 *Press coverage of economic growth and CSR*

our wealth may be [...] a Labour government would have wreaked havoc with our personal finances and in particular our investments – be they a pension, and Individual Savings Account or a share portfolio.

Daily Mail (15 December 2019)

Extinction Rebellion is seen similarly as Jeremy Corbyn, for example, by linking the movement with disruption to the economy and labelling protesters as middle class:

But making Britain hell for business (and anyone who drives a car) is what Extinction Rebellion stands for [...] Or in other words, to reduce us to a state of mere subsistence, last seen in the pre-industrial age when life was (for the great majority) nasty, brutish and short. [...] There might be some thousands of middle-class students and drop-outs sufficiently aesthetically offended by mass consumerism to vote for such a manifesto, but that would be it. [...] and was cheered by the youthful audience when he demanded action to end economic growth, adding that this meant we've got to go straight to the heart of capitalism and overthrow it.

Daily Mail (15 April 2019)

Gills and Morgan (2020) correctly observed that there is a concerted effort to delegitimize Extinction Rebellion where critique, in this case also *Daily Mail,*

seized on internal dissent, disruptions created by protest (and differences over the effectiveness of these) and on some of the purported claims regarding bleak futures to suggest the movement has been captured by extremists with political agendas that have little to do with the climate issue.

p. 1

Thus, when looking at the way the press writes about economic growth, it appears that *Daily Mail* follows a neoliberal logic of promoting economic growth and expressing criticism of environmental movements that obstruct businesses through protests, as well as political parties that propose different solutions. On the other hand, *The Guardian* provides more coverage of the economic growth, and some voices expressing concerns about the policy of growth and destruction of resources have managed to find a platform, but these remain marginal and solutions are proposed within a neoliberal economic paradigm. What is more, the discourse of writing, whether male or female in authorship, largely leans towards the masculine view of environmental affairs and speciesism where the environmental threat is seen as a threat to humanity and its survival and technology frequently as a solution to the problem. The problem of population is sometimes mentioned, however, outside of the context of women's equality and capitalist consumerism.

Press coverage of economic growth and CSR 115

Thus, there is no mention of the population being a woman's issue because women are still not always in control of their own bodies and reproduction, but also there is no mention of excessive consumerism and consumption. When consumption is mentioned, it seems to be in the context of economic policy, thus consumption being criticised as the only driver of the economy rather than investment, but ultimately both policies are neoliberal.

While there is a meaningful difference between *The Guardian* and *Daily Mail* in a sense that *The Guardian* is not no-platforming critical voices and gives them coverage, the predominant coverage is still centred in both newspapers on economic growth and fostering economic policies that deplete the environment and natural resources, thus both newspapers promoting predominantly a neoliberal discourse of incessant growth as a means to go forward. Whether this growth is based on fossil fuels or green development is irrelevant because there is very little debate on the limits of growth and the necessity to change the economics fundamentally to go forward and save the planet. Speciesism also remains a concern because the way newspapers write is human-centric and very little is being said about Nature and the right of other species to survive and thrive, and there is a sense of alarmism in writing about humanity and the planet. In a nutshell, there is a discourse of hierarchy in which humanity has the right to use resources for its own benefit and progress regardless of how this affects Nature and other species. However, what needs to be emphasised is that both sides do not link economic growth and capitalism generally with environmental problems and this goes so far that *The Guardian* is either proposing neoliberal solutions to the problem while *Daily Mail* is trying to attribute labels to protestors in a way that detaches them from the actual political situation. As eloquently summarized by Gills and Morgan (2020),

> But there is also the systemic issue. The 'political agendas' of climate movement activists encompass a broad spectrum of systemic critiques of capitalism because capitalism is the dominant framework of economy and society in the world. Capitalism is in the main the system in which consequences have been and continue to be produced. This too is important to bear in mind when considering pushback. To suggest that a campaigning organization that criticizes corporations and governments has been 'captured' by political agendas that have little to do with the climate issue implies either that the climate issue is somehow separate from the systemic features of economy and society (domestic and global) within which those issues have arisen or that the system itself is giving rise to timely solutions to the problems that are arising. The latter is clearly false and the former is manifestly contradictory. The main question that should be asked and answered here is one that is more appropriately directed at corporations and governments: does the evidence suggest that the scale and intensity of our economies are compatible with the ecological and climate balance on which we depend? If

116 *Press coverage of economic growth and CSR*

we think of an economy as a material subsystem operating within an earth system, then we must recognize that the kinds of economies we have created exhibit structurally inscribed tendencies which affect that earth system. These are not somehow separate matters. As such, the 'political agendas' of climate activists are not 'capture' they are highly relevant (if sometimes contentious) sources of insight and critique regarding the sources of tendencies.

p. 4

The coverage of CSR

CSR is seen as a "buzz word" in the business literature due to an immense interest of scholars in this field, and some prominent debates surrounding this concept (e.g. Friedman vs Freeman). However, I have argued that CSR is a neoliberal concept that serves as a smokescreen to preserve neoliberalism and capitalism and that, in a way, saved capitalism due to social and political unrest and anti-business sentiments during the 1960s and 1970s, which led to the proliferation of CSR policies (Cutrone, n.d.; Waterhouse, 2017). As explained, CSR is linked to Reaganomics and Thatcherism because Reagan and Thatcher operationalized CSR while at the same time reducing the pressure on the corporation and liberalising markets, which also meant abandoning Keynesian politics of state intervention and sheltering markets and prices (Pillay, 2015; Nunn, 2014; Gamble, 1989; Jessop, 2003; Gareau, 2013).

When looking into coverage of all media in the country, they published a total of 110 articles on CSR of which 42 are public relations pieces with no byline announcing various CSR events, awards that companies got because of their commitment to CSR, and so on (Table 4.3). This immediately confirms the results of previous studies that argued that media are willing to publish positive achievements of companies and thus create a meaning of CSR as a must-have (Buhr & Grafström, 2006; Tench et al., 2007).

In terms of the gender of the author, more articles have been published by women than men albeit the difference is not high (39 vs 29, respectively), and women published exclusively positive articles expressing support towards

Table 4.3 CSR Coverage Overall (*N* = 110)

Article Author	Number of Articles	Positive towards CSR Initiatives	Neutral	Negative towards CSR Initiatives
Man	29	26	2	1
Woman	39	39	0	0
Mixed	0	0	0	0
No byline	42	41	1	0
Total	110	106	3	1

CSR initiatives while men published one negative article and 2 neutral articles (Table 4.3). This goes in line with literature arguing that women are inclined to support CSR initiatives (Ben-Amar et al., 2017; Post et al., 2015; Liao et al., 2018; Tapver et al., 2020); however, it also goes in line with the literature arguing there is large support for CSR in the media (Buhr and Grafström, 2006) and that women have merged into masculine media (Gallagher, 2002; Mills, 2014, 2017; Topić & Tench, 2018; Ross, 2001; North, 2009a, 2009b, 2016a, 2016b; Topić & Bruegmann, 2021, thus showing support towards the capitalist policy of CSR.

However, it seems that CSR is mostly of interest to regional newspapers who publish PR pieces on awards and achievements of local companies working in the community because the daily press does not seem to be that concerned with CSR. In *The Guardian*, for example, only 23 articles met the criteria for inclusion, and a total of 14 articles had a positive tone, 9 had a neutral tone and no negative tones have been recorded. More men than women wrote articles but the difference is again not large (13 vs 10, respectively) (Table 4.4), thus showing that both men and women support this initiative, which goes in line with literature from journalism showing that women merged to masculine newsrooms and embraced the masculine way of reporting (Mills, 2014; Gallagher, 2002; Graber, 1980; Topić & Tench, 2018; Topić & Bruegmann, 2021).

In addition to that, *The Guardian* did not publish negative articles challenging the CSR concept, thus going in line with literature that argued media are inclined to support the concept (Buhr and Grafström, 2006) and this indeed links with the coverage of economic growth that rarely challenges growth and corporations. *The Guardian*'s coverage of CSR is largely placed in a dichotomy between being anti-business and pro-environment with a particular focus on fossil fuel industries. So, when trying to make sense of their CSR coverage, this is linked with their editorial policy discussed in the next chapter where *The Guardian* has focused on criticising fossils industries by for example deciding not to take any further advertising money from

Table 4.4 CSR Coverage in *The Guardian* ($N = 23$)[a]

Article Author	Number of Articles	Positive towards CSR Initiatives	Neutral	Negative towards CSR Initiatives
Man	13	8	5	0
Woman	10	6	4	0
Mixed	0	0	0	0
No byline	0	0	0	0
Total	23	14	9	0

a Only two articles from *Daily Mail* appeared in searches on CSR. Thus, these two articles have been analysed in the overall analysis of the coverage of CSR but not separately as with *The Guardian* that published 23 articles.

118 *Press coverage of economic growth and CSR*

these industries. In the same way, their CSR coverage is centred on criticising businesses who can be seen as dirty, such as fossil fuels, which echoes the weak antagonist position in De Bruyn's (2000) classification (see also Arrow et al., 1995). This is visible in *The Guardian*'s coverage of the fossil fuels industry and CSR so for example, one article cheered a resolution "calling on the world's biggest miner company to end its links to controversial lobbyists for the fossil fuel industry" (*The Guardian*, 10 October 2019). However, some articles express cynical views of CSR by saying that CSR is a part of woke culture because,

> many of them have developed their pre-existing corporate social responsibility programmes into a performance of 'wokeness', to both generate headlines and head off some of our boredom and scepticism. Whether it's Dove soap challenging body fascism in the beauty industry or Gillette attempting to tackle toxic masculinity in the name of selling razors, our woke pounds are there for the taking.
>
> *The Guardian* (11 August 2019)

Nevertheless, some articles call CSR "the second-biggest con of 2019" arguing that companies are not credible and one cannot trust them because they do not genuinely look to do good. For example, in an article from 29 December 2019, a journalist criticises initiative of the Business Roundtable where an association of 192 CEOs in the US made a commitment to respect the interests of all of their stakeholders only to soon after refuse worker's demands to raise wages and ending outsourcing jobs, cutting worker's medical benefits for part-time workforce, freezing pensions to cut costs, laying off staff, and so on. Thus, a journalist expresses criticism that companies did not meet an expectation they set out and looked after the interests of their staff against corporate profit-making interests, showing that corporations are expected to fulfil social obligations largely present in discussions surrounding CSR and the media coverage going in line with existing research on CSR and unquestionable support towards the concept, driven internally from the media (Gulyas, 2009). The same journalist who criticised corporations for not looking after workers while making a stakeholder commitment then proposed that

> the only way to make corporations socially responsible is through laws requiring them to be – for example, giving workers a bigger voice in corporate decision-making, making corporations pay severance to communities they abandon, raising corporate taxes, busting up monopolies, and preventing dangerous products (including faulty aeroplanes) from ever seeing the light of day [...] The only way to get such laws enacted is by reducing corporate power and getting big money out of politics. The first step is to see corporate social responsibility for the con it is.

Therefore, journalists from one side promoted economic growth and CSR policies while expressing criticism of corporations that do not meaningfully engage with policies constitutive of CSR, such as employee rights. This brings to the fore the already asked question of why corporations are supposed to act as NGOs and the writing brings the same sentiment as with anti-business protests in the 1970 and 1980s that led towards the operationalisation of CSR (Pillay, 2015) and leads towards further liberalisation of the market where corporations self-govern. These operationalising policies of CSR have been done in the context of neoliberalism of Ronald Reagan and Margaret Thatcher who were looking into companies giving more, with which they also saved capitalism as the unease with businesses was growing at the time. In the same way, writing in the press echoes this and asks businesses to do more and be more genuine in their social responsibility, thus again opening a question from Chapter 3 on CSR and asking whether the society is sinking towards more market policies and self-regulation while the role of the government is weakening with media and citizens policing corporations on whether they give some bits back to the society while media fail to challenge the threat to humanity in the form of consumption and depletion of resources. In other words, as mentioned in the section on economic growth, not much criticism of consumption and current neoliberal policies is being put forward, while the discourse on CSR again goes along with neoliberal policies of fostering growth on the one hand and then policing corporations to give some of it back while market opens up further.

But most of the coverage of CSR falls on the environment and criticising corporations which go in line with research on journalists showing that journalists think businesses need to be scrutinised equally or more than politics (Thurman et al., 2016; Tench et al., 2007), environmentally focused coverage looks at cutting down on carbon emissions and invites employees to engage with this to foster CSR focus on this matter, such as cutting down on travel and how to travel more sustainably (*The Guardian*, 18 January 2020) praising CSR initiatives that focus on the environment such as the work of CSR activists and organisations (*The Guardian*, 2 January 2020). As it seems to be common in the coverage of environmental affairs, the fashion industry appears a lot in criticism and the CSR coverage fashion is labelled as carbon-heavy with coverage centred on how to reduce carbon emissions and praising brands that engage with these practices (e.g. *The Guardian*, 12 November 2019), thus giving them publicity. But again, this coverage does not meaningfully tackle the environmental problems because authors are not challenging the current status quo or neoliberal policies with which the policy of economic growth accompanied with CSR is further supported in coverage.

In regional press, which published more on CSR specifically than the daily press, the vast amount of coverage goes to business awards for various CSR programmes, which brings about the notion that businesses are incentivised to have CSR to gain earned media coverage and thus free PR. The

120 *Press coverage of economic growth and CSR*

extensive focus of these awards is on helping local communities and with youth employment, the latter being a focus of British CSR policies since Thatcherism. For example, Thatcher's Conservative Government during the 1980s enforced CSR policies by asking businesses to offer youth training programmes to tackle unemployment (Moon, 2004, 2005) and the Labour Government led by Tony Blair extended this policy and introduce partnerships between private and public sectors such as school programmes offering placements, community programmes and specialist courses (Moon, 2004). This resulted in a stronger CSR focus of British companies and the increased likelihood of forming partnerships with NGOs (ibid). But what all of these policies show is neoliberalism and a founding view that businesses can be a solution to societal problems rather than being part of the problem. However, there is nothing to quote in this coverage to make sense of conceptualisation of CSR beyond the mere description of what regional press writes about because the coverage is visibly and exclusively based on copy-pasting press releases, which opens up a question on journalism standards in the local press and the influence of PR on driving the media coverage. In other words, it became known that journalists are more likely to publish positive CSR coverage and support CSR initiatives (Buhr and Grafström, 2006; Tench et al., 2007) and this now seems to be exploited by companies and their PR departments in driving a positive reputation for companies.

In summary, it can be argued that the line of argumentation in the media falls within the neoliberal paradigm where the media either openly support economic growth and CSR policies or they advocate for changes using falsely constructed concerns for the environment by using CSR-y arguments such as focusing on the so-called dirty industries or by proposing that it is the role of the corporation to look after environment and stakeholders, which has been central to a stakeholder orientation of CSR. However, other than criticising corporations for their impact on the environment, the journalists do not express criticism of the capitalist system and consumerism that leads towards environmental issues but rather engage with criticism and policing of industries and corporations. What is more, the media often openly support economic growth as good for humanity and in some cases express hostility towards environmental movements (*Daily Mail*) or they give a platform to environmental movements but fail to challenge the very reason why these movements are necessary in the first place (*The Guardian*). In either case, there is a sense of hierarchy and domination over Nature in which humans are seen as rightfully using resources and the only question being whether these resources will run out and how to "fix" the environment so it works for humans again. Nonetheless, in the latter, the fix is often found in masculine ideology by relying on technology to solve environmental problems and by challenging population numbers without challenging patriarchal structures that led to the alleged population problem. Not surprisingly, women largely lack among economy writers, except with CSR, but they also largely show merging within masculine newsrooms by producing either neutral articles

Press coverage of economic growth and CSR 121

or going in line with the same argumentation as found in the work of male journalists; however, this opened up the question whether the situation would be different had more women joined these sections in newspapers given a tiny advantage in pro-environmental and anti-capitalist writing that was identified among women writers.

Notes

1 Before this report, Mishan (1967) argued that economic growth is bringing consequences for the environment as well as the quality of life. Mishan (1967) called the policy of the economic growth a "no-choice myth" and to claim otherwise a blasphemy, with the focus on economic growth being imported from the US and this policy is obsessively focused, among others, on foreign trade. Instead, Mishan (1967) argues that consequences for human welfare are grave and that markets do not need to expand but that it is possible, and desirable, to produce less and have more leisure time instead. This view is also present in the work of Douthwaite (1999) who argued that economic growth enriched the few, impoverished the masses and it is destroying the planet, thus again focusing also on the negative impact on humanity refuting the view that economic growth is a good thing for the humanity. In other words, an argument in these works that economic growth is not good either for humanity or Nature.

2 In 2002, the world population was estimated to 6,273 billion and it 2019 it reached 7, 674 billion (World Bank, n.d.), thus the author's calculation was 17 years from the actual situation, and if we apply the same error to limits of growth then it might take longer for this to be reached than the author predicted but this does not mean it will not happen, given all warning about the climate change and a potential for ensuing chaos.

3 Keeley (2015) conducted research for OECD and has indeed confirmed this data. According to this OECD report, the gap widened further in a period between 1985 and 2005.

5 The press coverage of environmental affairs

Global warming, plastic and the food waste

In the previous chapter, I outlined how media write about economic growth and CSR and commented on the neoliberal nature of coverage where there is hardly any challenge of capitalist and consumerist culture that led to environmental degradation in the first place. In addition to that, I also argued that media write in a CSR-y way by criticising corporations and asking them to give to societies but not challenging their role and profit-driven aspect of capitalism that can be linked with depletion of resources. In this chapter, I am looking into three environmental issues that have a prominent place on the media agenda and in public debates, global warming, plastic and food waste.

Global warming

Houghton (2005) argued that global warming became one of the best known environmental issues and defined it as

> the effect on the climate of human activities, in particular the burning of fossil fuels (coal, oil and gas) and large-scale deforestation—activities that have grown enormously since the industrial revolution, and are currently leading to the release of about 7 billion tonnes of carbon as carbon dioxide into the atmosphere each year together with substantial quantities of methane, nitrous oxide and chlorofluorocarbons (CFCs). These gases are known as greenhouse gases.
>
> p. 1346

A report from the Intergovernmental Panel on Climate Change (IPCC) (Allen et al., 2018) on global warming indicated that human-induced warming of the planet has increased by approximately 1°C (0.8–1.2) and this has been increasing per decade. The report identifies global warming as "an increase in combined surface air and sea surface temperatures averaged over the globe and over a 30-year period" (Allen et al., 2018, p. 51). Global warming means that there are changes in regions and seasons where there is higher average warming on land and oceans and while lands and regions

DOI: 10.4324/9781003091592-5

are experiencing global warming greater than the global average, oceans are warming at a slightly lower rate. The majority of regions in the world, which host the majority of the global human population has already experienced global warming of more than 1.5°C above pre-industrial levels (ibid). There is also a sea rise, which is a result of past emissions so even if past emissions do not contribute directly to global warming they still contribute to sea rise (ibid). The report, thus, argues that immediate reduction in emissions would help in reducing global warming, results of which would be visible within the next two to three decades (0.5°C) and less than 0.5°C over a century (ibid). Houghton (2004) argued that "in the absence of efforts to curb the rise in the emissions of carbon dioxide, the global average temperature will rise by about a third of a degree Celsius every ten years – or about three degrees in a century" (p. 10).

However, as is often the case with reports from international organisations, there is again a sense of neoliberalism and reliance on technology to resolve environmental problems. For example, the report proposes for countries to accept proposals from the Paris agreement and for countries to unite and work towards eradicating poverty and ensure sustainable development and this is further linked to the UN's sustainable goals thus proposing that the world tackles global warming through "climate adaptation" which means the world should "manage impacts of climate change by reducing vulnerability and exposure to its harmful effects and exploiting any potential benefits" and an obstacle towards adjusting and managing the climate, according to the report, lies in lack of information, finance and technology, social values and attitudes and other constraints (e.g. institutional), lack of capacity to use sustainable energy for example and so on (Allen et al., 2018). The report is essentially proposing dominating Nature to reverse the trend and seems to believe that technology can tackle climate problems as well as sustainable development, thus a form of better capitalism. As already emphasised, the demographic pushing for controlling Nature is male and the control men seek to achieve is "anthropocentric and oriented towards and instrumentalist view of nature" and the technology designed to achieve changes in nature are aligned with "masculine temperament of abstraction, objectivity, precision and calculation" (Buck et al., 2014, p. 653). Nevertheless, it has been a long-standing view in ecofeminist theory that our current relationship with Nature is hierarchical and fragmented because it is "rooted in a culture where science and technology are posited as the epitome of reason in contract with pre-modernity, which was centred around nature, myth and religion" (Cross, 2018, p. 29).

The issue with these views on climate is that it belongs to the so-called climate governance approach, which is embedded within a *neoliberalisation* of environmentalism (e.g. Goldman, 2006; Conca, 2006; Fieldman, 2011; Ciplet & Roberts, 2017). Ciplet et al. (2015) argued that the climate regime came as a result of interactions between various stakeholders (states, businesses, civil society organisations), more insecure international relations

124 *Press coverage of environmental affairs*

(e.g. the decrease of the influence of the US and the rise of China), fragmentation in the Global South where countries no longer always subscribe to North vs. South discourse in tackling climate change, economic recessions, the rise of libertarian and populist ideologies, which traditionally express antagonism towards any form of state intervention which includes environmental protection and so on. Houghton (2004) argued that the 1980s and the 1990s brought an increased warming up of the planet,[1] and while it is not yet known how will climate change and global warming play out in the world, there is a reason for concern. For example, Houghton (2004) argued that global warming might destroy some parts of the world and make them less inhabitable, but it might as well create better conditions in some other parts of the world, thus showing that national borders bear no relevance in fighting the climate change because changes can happen anywhere. However, Houghton (2004) also argues that

> while some parts of the world experience more frequent or more severe droughts, floods or significant sea level rise, in other places crop yields, may increase due to the fertilising effect of carbon dioxide. Other places, perhaps for instance in the sub-arctic, may become more habitable. Even there, though, the likely rate of change will cause problems: large damage to buildings will occur in regions of melting permafrost, and trees in subarctic forests like trees elsewhere will need time to adapt to new climatic regimes.
>
> p. 10

While this at the outset might mean that people could continue living as they do and then save themselves through migrations and reshuffling the world, it is enough to look at neoliberal policies and the rise of the Far Right in the West that promotes these policies to see how this will not work. For example, in recent years, immigration became prominent on the public agenda in the West with many popular votes being driven by immigration (Goodwin & Milazzo, 2017; Esipova et al., 2015; Halla et al., 2017; Lonsky, 2021), and thus one can only guess how would neoliberal West react if the Global South faced adverse climate conditions which instigated migration to the West where the land became more fertile, for example. It is also worth noting that many works discussing global warming speak of the population rise as a contributing factor to global warming. As already emphasised, Gaard (2015) argued that the over-consumption of the North is the problem because it contributes to greenhouse gases to a total of 80% of world emissions. She thus argues,

> reducing third world population becomes increasingly important when first-world overconsumers realize that the severe climate change outcomes already heading for the world's most marginalized communities will create a refugee crisis and urgent migrations of poor people. Since

the growing population of the Two-Thirds World will be hardest hit by climate change effects and will seek asylum in One-Thirds nations – a migration perceived as a threat to the disproportionate wealth (i.e. "security") of the North – the spectre of climate refugees has inspired arguments for increased militarization as protection against migration.

Gaard (2015, p. 16)

What is more, ecofeminism has historically been critical of militarism and border controls (the latter being also a subject of discussion in socialist theory) and thus, it is not unreasonable to worry that increased pressure on migration to the West can result in further militarism and even more patriarchy and masculinity in environmental policies if Global South gets hit with climate change more harshly and an immigration increases. This has already been visible in the way the West tackled immigration that came as a result of wars waged by the Western countries in the Middle East and where refugees were then used by the Far Right and portrayed by the media as a threat, which resulted with votes such as Brexit in the UK and appointing Donald Trump as a president of the US (Garett, 2019; Fox, 2020; Johnson & Cuison-Villazor, 2019).

Many scholars identified neoliberal environmentalism or market environmentalism as a trend towards *neoliberalising* Nature (McCarthy, 2004; Mansfield, 2004; Bridge, 2004; Prudham, 2004; Ciplet & Roberts, 2017). For supporters of this approach, environmental problems could be solved with privatisation, commercialisation and commodification of natural resources and ecosystems, reduced role of the government in favour of markets self-regulating and with public-private partnerships as well as private sector dominating the environmental protection (Bakker, 2005, 2007; Corson, 2010). Therefore, international initiatives such as the Montreal Protocol, Basel Convention, the UN's Conference on the Law of the Sea, the UNFCCC and the Paris agreement can all be seen as neoliberal initiatives where countries are invited to self-regulate and commit to changing climate change, and Ciplet & Roberts (2017) argue that "in the context of the international environmental governance, this view seeks to recognize and affirm asymmetries of resources and power between states in governance arrangements, rather than mitigate them" (p. 150). However, as some authors argue, by all states committing to reducing climate change, the responsibility for environmental damage is shared too despite over-consumption of the North and thus the strategy is not based on the "polluter pays principle" (ibid), thus leaving the responsibility for the environment to state and non-state actors with limited resources and power to solve the problem caused by neoliberal states (Shamir, 2008). Stiglitz (2006), however, argued that the biggest polluter and over-consumer is the US and that the environmental damage the country causes to the world is greater than any war waged so far. Stiglitz (2006) thus argues that the US boycott of international environmentalist protocols results also in developing countries not being able to do anything

126 *Press coverage of environmental affairs*

even though they will become polluters of the future. Thus, he proposes an international mechanism to force the US to comply such as, for example, refusing to import US products that use high levels of energy or at least tax them at a higher rate. However, simply reducing emissions, taxing to collect money to put into environmental affairs can again be seen as environmental governance grounded in neoliberalism.

What is more, not only does the neoliberal approach to environmentalism dominate societies in the North that shifted towards a market-based approach to corporate governance including environmental governance, but there is also an increase of importance of the private sector in scientific and corporate decision-making processes (Lucier & Gareau, 2015; McCormick, 2006; Newell & Patterson, 2009). However, some authors identified the issue of the so-called transparency as a way neoliberalism sells its policy because all of the information is shared as if sharing information alone with solve problems (Mason, 2008). Gupta (2008, p. 5) argued that "information (including scientific information) is neither value neutral, nor universally valid, and thus information alone is not likely to resolve normative and political conflicts" that arise in environmental governance and expectations that all countries of the world will suddenly unite in a common cause and peacefully collaborate after centuries of wars and competition. Mason (2008) argued that "the normative agenda here, often unexamined, is the scaling back of mandatory environmental regulation (nationally and internationally), the privatization of environmental resources, and the framing of information disclosure options in terms of individual lifestyle choices" (p. 10). What is more, developing countries refuse to agree to pollute less than developed countries that have been polluting for decades, while the US refuses to accept any environmental initiative (no matter how neoliberal) until developing countries are put in line and made to abide by the same standards (Stiglitz, 2006).

The environmental governance criticism is linked to the Kyoto Protocol which is commonly labelled as neoliberal due to its focus on making peace between businesses and environmentalism, which does not go together because the Kyoto Protocol is also centred on economic growth and a view that businesses can be part of the solution to environmental issues (Brundtland Commission, 1987; Newell & Roberts, 2007). However, Ciplet and Roberts (2017) argued that the Kyoto Protocol was later incorporated into UNFCCC just with an addition that new policies of transparency and accountability were introduced, but the UNFCCC system,

> is largely reduced to cheerleading for private and voluntary national action on climate change. The main institutional framework of the regime to achieve mitigation targets is that of the Nationally Determined Contributions, and while reporting rules (modalities, procedures and guidelines) are being hammered out in the 2016–2018 period, it is very unlikely that equity or justice concerns will be meaningfully included.
>
> p. 154

The coverage of global warming

When it comes to global warming, which is seen as a direct cause of climate change, the number of published articles immediately signals that the issue is on the media agenda with *Daily Mail* publishing a total of 112 articles and *The Guardian* 313 articles (Tables 5.1 and 5.2).

What is interesting here is that *The Guardian* has an editorial policy on global warming and has published a total of eight editorials outlining their position on global warming; however, the number of articles is roughly similar to the number of articles on economic growth, thus showing that the newspaper is equally concerned with economic growth and global warming. However, since the majority of articles in *The Guardian* on economic growth are either neutral (the majority) or positive and voices critical of economic growth still marginal and grounded in a neoliberal paradigm, the question emerges what is the position of the newspaper on global warming. According to data (Table 5.2), *The Guardian* published more neutral articles (178 overall); however, they also published 135 articles with a positive tone, thus showing more support for tackling global warming than tackling economic growth. In *Daily Mail*, the majority of articles are neutral (47 overall) but this is closely followed with negative coverage of global warming (37 overall)

Table 5.1 Coverage of Global Warming in *Daily Mail* (N = 112)

Article Author	Number of Articles	Positive about Reducing Global Warming	Negative about Reducing Global Warming	Neutral about Global Warming
Man	57	14	24	19
Woman	27	13	5	9
Mixed	6	2	3	1
No byline	22	3	5	14
Total	112	32	37	43

Table 5.2 Coverage of Global Warming in *The Guardian* (N = 313)

Article Author	Number of Articles	Positive towards Reducing Global Warming	Neutral	Negative towards Reducing Global Warming
Man	165	76	89	0
Woman	122	41	81	0
Mixed	11	6	5	0
No byline	7	4	3	0
Editorial	8	8	0	0
Total	313	135	178	0

128 *Press coverage of environmental affairs*

and positive coverage (32 overall), showing a slightly ambiguous attitude of *Daily Mail* towards this issue.

When it comes to gender, men wrote more negative articles on global warming than women in *Daily Mail*, whereas in *The Guardian* neither men nor women wrote negative articles (Tables 5.1 and 5.2), and the difference in reporting between men and women in the tone of articles is roughly similar; however, it was men who wrote negatively in *Daily Mail* than women, but they also published more articles than women. In *The Guardian*, both men and women wrote a similar number of articles in a neutral tone with women lacking in positive articles due to the lower number of women writing about the issue, but the way journalists write seems very similar. The fact more men than women write about environmental affairs brings back a question already recognised in byline research on whether women get pushed out when a traditional woman's area enters the public agenda. This has already been recognised in health reporting where in my study of bylines, women have indeed been pushed out on writing about sugar debate and supermarkets, both topics historically being woman's area and labelled as soft news (Topić & Tench, 2018). However, now that these topics have come to the agenda, more men write about it and it seems that environmental affairs are not much different despite women historically being more involved in environmentalist movements than men (Mallory, 2006; Brownhill & Turner, 2019; Goldstein, 2006; Leahy, 2003; McStay & Dunlap, 1983; Poole & Harmon Zeigter, 1985; Shapiro & Mahajan, 1986; Steger & Witt, 1989; Diani, 1989; Schahn & Holzer, 1990; Blaikie, 1992; Franklin & Rudig, 1992; Stern et al., 1993; McAllister, 1994; Hampel et al., 1996; Tranter, 1996; Godfrey, 2005; Shiva, 1989; Brownhill, 2010; Godfrey, 2008; Holy, 2007; Mann, 2011; Stoddart & Tindall, 2011; Giacomini, 2014; Kirk, 1998; McMahon, 1997; Salleh, 1984; Topić, 2020d; Topić et al., 2021). The tone of the coverage also follows the masculine agenda of neutrality and detachment in reporting and a libertarian approach of the media to just report on issues of the day. This is particularly the case in *The Guardian* which published many more articles on the issue of global warming than *Daily Mail* and with both men and women publishing neutral articles more than positive or negative ones (Table 5.1).

When making sense of writing on global warming, *The Guardian* is sounding quite an alarmist on the issue asking for change, particularly focusing on reducing emissions. This is backed with writing about weather changes and threats to humanity, thus again bringing about the issue of speciesism but the coverage fundamentally lacks criticism of economic growth and capitalist policies centred on consumption except for one article in the sample, which explicitly takes a hit on economic growth as a reason for global warming but this remains a marginal voice in a pool of voices shouting about global warming, zero carbon emissions without proposing solutions on how to go about this or opening a meaningful debate on how we live our lives, how advertising and marketing departments are selling us stuff we do not need, and the impact of consumerism on the environment

Press coverage of environmental affairs 129

(Georgescu-Roegen, 1971, Meadows et al., 1972; Ehrlich and Holdren, 1971; Cleveland, 1984; Salleh, 2000).

Thus, the coverage in *The Guardian* concentrates on criticising the UK government for not introducing green policies and links this with some other policies in other countries that have done so. For example, in an editorial from 26 April 2019, the author states that "climate change is becoming hard to ignore" and links this with extreme weather suggesting that

> the question is not whether this country should achieve a net zero target, but when. Presently the UK is committed in law to reduce greenhouse gas emissions by at least 80% by 2050 compared to 1990 levels. This is not ambitious enough [...] If other modern European societies are willing to accept the costs of transitioning to a greener and sustainable existence, it is hard to see why the UK could not.
>
> *The Guardian* (editorial, 26 April 2019)

Other articles also focus on weather conditions and warn that too many people around the world do not accept climate change as a real problem. For example, in an editorial from March 2019, *The Guardian* states that too many people do not accept climate change as a real problem and thus calls for BBC to include climate change coverage in their weather reports arguing also that climate change does not make the news in other media outlets, thus indirectly criticising the media for irresponsible behaviour,

> Still, and in defiance of decades worth of scientific evidence, vast numbers of people around the world refuse to accept that we are in the process of drastically altering the climate. Vast numbers more lack the information they need to interpret what is going on. This is a global problem whose importance cannot be overstated. It has no single solution. But giving up on trying to halt the damage to life on our planet is not an option. And in this context, this week's suggestion by the former BBC weather presenter Bill Giles, that forecasts should be adapted to include information about climate change as well as local weather conditions, is extremely welcome. [...] Weather and climate are not the same thing, and to confuse them would be unhelpful. But the rapidly developing science of weather attribution means that experts are now able to analyse extreme events including floods and heatwaves to determine the contribution of manmade climate change. Last summer's UK heatwave, for example, was made 30 times more likely by greenhouse gases. Findings such as this could feature in the remodelled broadcasts, and play a valuable role in increasing public understanding. So could information about globally important climate-related events, such as updates on melting ice sheets in Greenland or Antarctica. Currently such items are treated as news, if they feature in current affairs schedules at all. But often they do not, and there is certainly no systematic effort on the

130 *Press coverage of environmental affairs*

part of such programmes to keep their audiences apprised of what climate scientists think is going on. If taken up, Mr Giles's proposal could lead to a re-evaluation of weather broadcasting – and a consideration of whether it is appropriate, in the era of global warming, to treat weather as the cheery endnote, delivered by a friendly face, that viewers have learned to expect.

The Guardian (editorial, 19 March 2019)

A lot of coverage, and editorials, are centred on the interplay between climate change and the weather changes and in this, *The Guardian* tends to use science to back up its claims and in some cases, the promotion of technology emerges. For example, in an editorial from April 2019, *The Guardian* stated that we "struggle to give the global warming and wildlife crisis the attention they deserve" and this happens despite having "science, with predictions of manmade greenhouse effect dating back to the 1890s". However, *The Guardian*'s editorial continues the criticism of ignoring the problem of climate change by also arguing that

we have some, although not all, of the knowledge and technology we need to wean us off our addiction to fossil fuels: wind and solar energy; healthy alternatives to meat; bicycles and trains. Many nations have laws to help us transition to a low-carbon future.

The Guardian (editorial, 23 April 2019)

These claims are then backed up with references to the Paris agreement and other UN conventions, which have been labelled as neoliberal (Ciplet & Roberts, 2017). So, the author calls for action "to stop emitting greenhouse gases as soon as possible", without saying how one might do that without fundamentally changing the economic system.

Some of the coverage addresses the issue of globality and calls for unity in solving these problems by recognising people in the Global South are more affected by climate change. For example, in an article from 17 October 2019, *The Guardian* elaborates on weather changes and emphasises that hot summers are a sign of climate change, and then links climate problems with problems of migration by arguing that extreme weather conditions are not,

just "weather", however, and we follow their impact: the buckling European road and rail infrastructure not suitable for the new climate era, the desperate search for water in Chennai and the Greenland residents traumatised by the climate emergency as life becomes more precarious and social problems such as alcoholism intensify [...] Climate can also lie at the root of other stories. Failed harvests and rising food prices can often be the final straw that triggers political upheaval, in recent years notably the Arab spring, but we are now seeing in real time how the climate emergency is affecting migration patterns. As Donald Trump

Press coverage of environmental affairs 131

attempted to close the US border to Central American migrants, in some cases separating children from their parents, we spoke to those in Guatemala who after a decade of intense droughts and late rains have seen crops fail and wages fall one too many times. "I have to find a way to travel north, or else my children will suffer even more," subsistence farmer Esteban Gutiérrez told reporter Nina Lakhani.

The Guardian (17 October 2019, emphasis in the original)

However, as with the coverage of economic growth and its link with environmental issues, what emerges is speciesism and all coverage is centred on the threat to humanity not care for Nature as a whole system or other species. What is more, migration can be seen as a neoliberal concern about the threat to the economic system and wealth in the Western countries because if people migrate in large numbers, this can strengthen the Far Right which is already obsessively centred on immigration (Goodwin & Milazzo, 2017; Esipova et al., 2015; Halla et al., 2017; Lonsky, 2021). What is at the root of the problem is the call for collaboration, which emerges throughout the coverage of economic growth and global warming, which is a contested issue because collaboration is a discourse that comes from the US refusing to accept any deals to tackle climate change unless everyone commits (Stiglitz, 2006). However, data continually shows that the Global North over-consumes and not just historically but by the present day, thus the onus needing to be on the North to reduce consumption, but as visible in coverage on economic growth, even when authors link economic growth and environmental affairs, a link with over-consumption rarely emerges. It is unrealistic to expect an average reader to figure this out by themselves especially since their daily reality is full of adverts and popular culture selling them a lifestyle of consumption as something everyone should strive to achieve, within a neoliberal logic of individualism.

However, the coverage of global warming is also leaning towards CSR expectations of companies to tackle this issue. For example, in an article from January 2020, *The Guardian* writes about the Royal Dutch Shell and their failures to invest in green energy projects, thus arguing that this is "likely to raise concern that oil companies are not moving fast enough to help tackle the climate crisis" (*The Guardian*, 3 January 2020), this writing showing that *The Guardian* from one point is calling on the government to invest into legislation on green policies, people to start taking climate change seriously and then also companies to take action and reduce emissions and invest into green businesses. However, the call for businesses to invest in becoming green is futile because many companies are basing their businesses exclusively on the anti-green business model such as burning fossil fuels and using coal. As argued by Pollin (2019, n.p.), neoliberalism is "a driving force causing climate crisis" and this is also because neoliberalism goes further than classical liberalism which offered everyone the freedom to pursue their own interests in a capitalist market setting. Instead, neoliberal

132 *Press coverage of environmental affairs*

systems create a situation in which governments allow corporations to work in the free market, pursue profit and governments intervene when this profit gets threatened. Therefore, Pollin (2019, n.p.) argues that what oil companies are doing when they burn oil, coal and gas to produce energy that elevates global warming is actually within the neoliberal paradigm and did exactly what they are allowed to do, legally do everything possible to protect their profit. Thus, defeating neoliberalism is at the centre of the Green New Deal policy; however, the coverage in *The Guardian* – while supportive of the Green New Deal – again proposes this as a minor part of their coverage and without tackling, what is at the heart of neoliberalism, excessive consumption and inequality between the use of resources between the South and the North. What is also concerning is that lots of talk about the Green New Deal are also centred on proposing solutions that would make a profit to companies, just that the profit would be taken through greener business, which brings a shadow to the whole initiative. For example, some commentators argued that

> unequal and exploitative power relations are at the root of our environmental crisis. So it's essential that any policy calling itself a Green New Deal lives up to these standards. No durable solution to this catastrophe can be based on our model of extractive capitalism — on Friedman's "Father Greed" and the growth needed to feed it.
>
> Adler and Wargan (2019, n.p.)

Nevertheless, Adler and Wargan (2019) argue that any green deal cannot be based on the capitalist premise of corporations running after profit with different means but that a whole economic system needs changing and going back to the government intervention to ensure stability and equality. A commonly cited proposal is a Green New Deal proposed by two US senators, Alexandria Ocasio-Cortez and Ed Markey, and this proposal is aiming for net-zero greenhouse emissions that do not undermine the rights of workers and communities while also creating millions of jobs and prosperity (Galvin & Healy, 2020). The proposal is based on Keynesian economics where the government is meant to create money to pay for projects by collecting taxes, fees and issuing bonds rather than raising money first from taxes, fees and borrowing before spending on projects (ibid). What is more, the Green New Deal proposal is based on addressing inequality in all its forms, racial and gender included too (ibid), thus trying to decarbonise the economy as well as tackle all forms of inequality. According to some studies, there is evidence that inequality directly contributes to emissions. For example, the rich contribute to emissions through over-consumption while the poor contribute by not having the money to decarbonise their homes (Jorgenson et al., 2016, 2015; Chancel & Piketty, 2015; Galvin & Healy, 2020). The Global North also produces more emissions and pollutions (Sandberg & Sandberg, 2010; Griffin, 2020; Salleh, 2000, 1994). Some authors argued that 90 companies had produced two-thirds of emissions and this is not always linked to the

Press coverage of environmental affairs 133

extent of business but to the fact that those companies that contribute to emissions use their excess wealth to exercise power over political processes to stop regulation and to influence the public discourse to reduce objections (Stiglitz, 2013; Supran & Oreskes, 2017). Nevertheless, Galvin and Healy (2020) correctly observed that the cost of decarbonising cannot be done by slashing jobs in favour of environmental protection because this will (a) affect the poor communities disproportionately and (b) cause a backlash. Thus, the green new deal has to make sure nobody gets left behind and that the cost is not put on the public through excessive taxation of workers and the poor (Adler & Wargan, 2019), which is not just unfair but could also cause a backlash against environmental policies (Galvin & Healy, 2020). What is more, gender inequality is prevalent in the current economic system with the majority of organisations being dominated by men, and this also applies to the clean energy economy (Muro et al., 2019). Daly and Morgan (2019), however, correctly argue that at the root of the New Green Deal is the "unwillingness to identify growth as *the* root cause" (p. 148, emphasis in the original) of climate change and somehow the view is constantly going back to non-renewable fossil fuels and shifting to renewable sources of energy (ibid), but this is also problematic because it focuses too much on the so-called dirty industries rather than a problem as a whole. In other words, fossil fuels have allowed humanity, for the past 200 years, to use more energy than what was naturally available to them through the wind, for example (Asefi-Najafabady et al., 2020). However, Asefi-Najafabady, Villegas-Ortiz and Morgan (2020) argue that there is no evidence it is possible to either continue this way or even go back and manage the consequences. At the same time, it is known and widely recognised that the Earth has passed capacity to repair the damage caused by human activity and the current rates of extinction of species and pollution of oceans and climate change issues are showing tensions and leading towards a collapse (Ripple, 2020; Ceballos et al., 2017; Lenton et al., 2020).

The Guardian formally endorsed the New Green Deal policy introduced in the US, and argued that this is the right way to go and that the UK Government should move away from putting the burden of carbon offsetting to people through higher taxes towards a more progressive approach of investing into a green economic model, arguing that "humanity will run out of limited global resources long before the US runs out of dollars. Britain needs something like Ms Ocasio-Cortez's Green New Deal. And we need it now – before it is too late" (*The Guardian*, editorial, 12 May 2019). The editorial correctly presented the New Green Deal and its elements of employment, equality and sustainability and this writing is further exacerbated by another editorial saying,

> costs are concentrated in the power and construction sectors. New energy sources such as hydrogen need infrastructure, while wind and solar must be scaled up. New technologies such as carbon capture and storage require trials. Buildings must become energy-efficient as gas

134 *Press coverage of environmental affairs*

boilers, 1m of which are installed each year, are phased out. Huge numbers of trees need planting, with one-fifth of all agricultural land turned over to forests, peatland or energy crops. People should be encouraged to make different choices, eating less beef, lamb and dairy. The report suggests a target of 2030 for ending the sale of petrol and diesel cars, but then wrongly settles for 2035. Currently, transport emissions are still going up [...] A "green new deal" has become popular currency on the progressive side of politics in the UK, US and Spain. This idea usefully links technological and environmental change with the prospect of a renewed social contract and the questions of justice often emphasised by environmentalists [...] Finding ways to counter this, and build the future into our politics, is a challenge not just for politicians, environmentalists and civil society groups, but for human civilisation as a whole.

The Guardian (editorial, 2 May 2019)

Thus, some articles call for a government that will "balance the ecosystem, rather than obsessing with balancing its budget" and rightfully recognise that

the market won't deliver technological change on its own. The state is needed to design regulation so environmental and social objectives can be met. The UK ought to copy California and require carmakers to sell a fixed proportion of their overall sales as electric cars. It must start subsidising bus routes, not cut funding for them. Big cities will need mass transport systems. Agriculture will have to peel itself away from oil-intensive farming. Perhaps the biggest challenge is the heating of homes and businesses, 90% of which rely on fossil fuels. That needs a hydrogen economy built almost from scratch. All this is feasible; the technologies are available and could become much cheaper if they were widely deployed. What has been missing is the political ambition; it is a shame that Mrs May only supplied this as she is departing.

The Guardian (editorial, 12 June 2019)

The Guardian calls for government intervention and funding to sort out greening of the country and offsetting carbon emissions; however, these articles still do not go into details on how this can be done, that everyone would benefit, nor do articles directly call for an end to consumption and the change of the economic model. The obsessive focus is on the weather and global cooperation and then, in some instances emphasises that the UK would not be as affected by global warming and climate change as other countries and that the public needs to be informed better:

As our heating planet turns from a threat into an emergency, with emissions still increasing, we must reject passivity in favour of action. Climate change won't affect the UK as severely as it will poorer

Press coverage of environmental affairs 135

countries, or those more vulnerable to desertification or flooding. Our target of 80% reductions in greenhouse gases by 2050 is already more ambitious than many comparable countries. But the government should be far more active in advancing public understanding. It is no longer permissible to pretend that ice-creams in February are a quirk of nature.

The Guardian (editorial, 26 February 2019)

This article in itself raises the question, why and how is the government supposed to educate people on the need to change some habits? This is entirely unclear and opens up a question of media responsibility. Due to a large reach of media outlets and if we embrace social responsibility of the media approach (Ward, 2008; Klaidman, 1987; Kovach & Rosenstiel, 2001), then it becomes clear it would be the role of the responsible media to educate citizens on the need to change how they live. However, given that media also operate as capitalist enterprises and are neoliberal in many ways, the coverage often shifts responsibility to not only the government (which is alright for carbon-reducing initiatives, because that is indeed the role of the government that has the power to make changes) but also the public, thus failing to recognise the history of selling neoliberalism to the public and the fact many media outlets still scaremonger about changes to neoliberal practice and imply that, for example, people will lose jobs if societies move towards a green economy, and overemphasise the cost towards insulating their homes. While it is clear that the New Green Deal policies do not propose to place the cost of decarbonisation to the public, it is not clear that this is not what *The Guardian* is suggesting especially since there is so much coverage promoting economic growth and CSR policies both of which go hand in hand with consumerism that fuels growth and then corporate profit, which then leads to CSR. What is more, telling people in the UK they will not be as affected by climate change without providing a context in which this happens and educating them about the actions of the North that are causing climate chaos in the South, can only instigate views that climate change is someone else's problem. Nevertheless, in a country such as the UK, which has promoted neoliberal policies of individualism and individual responsibility and where individualism is still considerably higher than, for example, in some other countries in the world and Europe for that matter (Eurobarometer, 2017), is irresponsible and dangerous because some populist political parties, many of whom support neoliberal policies and capitalist status quo, could exploit this and turn into a manipulative campaign to defend neoliberalism using migration, as it has been done in many campaigns before. Or, in other words, populists and supporters of neoliberalism often scapegoat migrants for economic problems to divert attention that migrants only come to serve capitalism as cheap labour (Shiva, 1989), and in the case of climate change, they will come because of consumption of the Global North (Gaard, 2015).

136 *Press coverage of environmental affairs*

The coverage in *The Guardian* is, however, followed up with updating style guide on how to cover these issues to create a crisis and make people realise the world is in crisis, and in this, *The Guardian* resorts to speciesism by arguing that "The phrase 'climate change', for example, sounds rather passive and gentle when what scientists are talking about is a catastrophe for humanity" (*The Guardian*, 17 May 2019). The speciesism, as already emphasised, runs through the coverage frequently because most of the coverage centres on threat towards humanity. While it is true that people are more likely to respond to threats to their own kind, it is also true that this does not create compassion and a sense of justice which are also powerful tools in fostering a social change. However, to further exacerbate the problem some articles are openly linking the New Green Deal and the lack of economic growth with the loss of jobs. For example, in an article on 17 June 2019, *The Guardian* states the following:

> The world's wealthiest countries need to consume, on average, 416kg of materials and 111kg of energy products to generate $1,000 of GDP. [...] Replacing the world's growth model and reliance on GDP as the barometer of success is challenging. It would require people to stop buying stuff and that would put a lot of people out of work. That would only work if income was decoupled from labour, and that feels like an idea that is some way off. The concept of degrowth is promoted by some more radical economists, calling for a focus on wellbeing and pushing for a reduction of production and consumption in developed nations. A focus on sufficiency is demanded, rather than relying on the ability of technology and productivity gains to solve ecological problems. At its core the movement argues that growth is typically unjust, unsustainable for the environment and that there never can be such thing as "enough".
>
> *The Guardian* (17 June 2019)

While the article above continues with statements from experts who propose various solutions, the damage is done by mentioning job losses and putting a question mark on whether the green world is feasible. Later on, in January 2020, *The Guardian* decided not to accept advertising from oil and gas companies (29 January 2020), thus again bringing the notion of the weak antagonist coverage where the focus in environmental protection is on the so-called dirty industries (De Bruyn, 2000) but not consumerism and capitalism as a whole. This is also further exacerbated with the change of policy with images to focus on the effects of global warming on humans rather than animals by replacing the image policy and deciding that photos of human suffrage will drive the coverage to instigate action:

> We know, from years of experience, that people love polar bears and pandas, so it is easy to see how these appealing creatures have become the emblems for the topics of endangered species and what we previously

Press coverage of environmental affairs 137

termed as global warming. Often, when signalling environmental stories to our readers, selecting an image of a polar bear on melting ice has been the obvious – though not necessarily appropriate – choice. These images tell a certain story about the climate crisis but can seem remote and abstract – a problem that is not a human one, nor one that is particularly urgent. So it made sense when we heard that research conducted by the team at Climate Visuals has shown that people respond to human pictures and stories. Images that show emotion and pictures of real situations make the story relevant to the individual. Rather than choosing, say, an image of a smoke stack pumping out pollution or a forest on fire, such as this: ... we should consider showing the direct impact of environmental issues on people's daily lives as well as trying to indicate the scale of the impact, such as these: (...) But as we have reported, the science tells us a much more sinister story of regular heatwaves and unseasonal weather being a defining indicator of the climate crisis. So, although scenes of children playing in fountains and everyone racing to the beach can be uplifting and irresistible, we have to be mindful of the tone of our journalism. This summer, the British media published dramatic headlines issuing climate warnings and covered in detail the negative impact of the crisis, but the images were typically of people taking pleasure in the environment. The contradiction in messaging, between the headlines and imagery, can undermine the effect of the reporting and how we perceive the risks.(...) It is an example of how, as picture editors and photographers, we are having to think again about finding the right focus. Many of the impacts to communities, biodiversity, agriculture, water and food supply represent the escalating crisis our planet faces, yet visually they can be far more challenging to depict. We need new imagery for new narratives. This can be challenging in a fast-paced newsroom but it is important to be nuanced and creative with search terms to unearth photography beyond the usual keywords of climate change, heatwave and floods.

The Guardian (18 October 2019)

However, while *The Guardian* seems to be backing the right initiatives on global warming, the question emerges on newsworthiness and media economic model. In other words, editorial policy backs environmentalism and gives a platform to environmental activists and those who promote the end to economic growth (albeit, again, in a neoliberal way). But these are shadowed with excessive coverage that goes in favour of neoliberalism or coverage that fails to challenge it, which indeed opens up a question of media social responsibility, running after profit and media business model. In other words, it seems *The Guardian* is on the right track but the likely issue might be the need to create profit through clicks and selling newspapers because of which lots of coverage, inconsistent with editorial policy, gets in so *The Guardian* stumbles around with inconsistency with its editorial policy.

138 *Press coverage of environmental affairs*

But the question of media responsibility becomes even more relevant when the coverage in *Daily Mail* is reviewed. Unlike *The Guardian* whose editorial policy supports the environmental initiatives and whose journalists do not criticise environmental activists, *Daily Mail* aggressively criticises the Extinction Rebellion group by labelling them as middle-class and disruptive of hard-working people. For example, an article from 7 October 2019, calls activists "eco zealots" and accuses them of "causing chaos" in London, while another article places the blame on the environmental movement for people's hardship in jobs and labels them as hypocrites:

> Was anything more galling this week than the sight if eco-warrior Zoe Jones in tears when she heard that a man had failed to reach his dying father's bedside in time to say goodbye because of her protest group's roadblock? [...] Quite apart from the intolerable disruption to hard-working people's lives, police and politicians have been warning for months that the Extinction Rebellion protests could result in deaths because of ambulance crews, doctors, fire engines and police cars being held up in traffic.
>
> *Daily Mail* (20 July 2019)

With the above coverage, *Daily Mail* created a negative image of the organisation and the article (this one or the others) rarely mention what the movement stands for, what the fight is and why are people willing to get arrested and abused by the public. Instead, *Daily Mail* labels the movement as middle class and eco zealots/eco-warriors and this heavy framing creates negative images among the public. This labelling policy is what is likely going to undermine the movement in the eyes of the public because *Daily Mail* uses very strong language and attempts to divide people according to class lines. For example, environmentalism is labelled as a toy of the rich who contribute more to global warming but then preach to everyone else:

> Enough of tiresome lectures from these paragons of privilege. The rich and famous love to tell us how to live our lives. As they clamber out of costly electric cars into private jets, or gather at impossibly expensive resorts to discuss the need for universal sacrifice, they give off a golden glow of virtue that can be seen for miles and probably contributes to global warming. Prince Harry thinks we should limit ourselves to two children for the sake of the planet. His wife Meghan guest-edits the super-rich fashionista's magazine Vogue, earnestly displaying her circle of beautiful people with beautiful opinions [...] Wealth and privilege now go with renewable energy, vegan diets, and perhaps a past brush with drugs, now bravely overcome [...] Do these supposed paragons begin to realise just how irritating this posturing is to those whose days are filled with school runs, frazzling childcare, jammed roads and

crammed trains, last-minute shopping and trying to stretch limited, often shrinking incomes to stay in the same place?

Daily Mail (4 August 2019)

While one could disregard the class issue and say it is not relevant, this is hardly the case in contemporary Britain where social background still affects one's life chances and is thus a point of contestation (Social Mobility Commission, 2020b). Previous research has also shown that working-class women, for example, are less likely to support environmental affairs because of the lack of agency and financial means to make that choice (Topić et al., 2021). Thus, one of the largest newspapers in the country contributing to this discourse instead of contributing to the meaningful debate is fundamentally irresponsible and brings a traditionally unpopular question of whether we need press regulation. In other words, scientific research shows the seriousness of the crisis, every person is witnessing extreme weather conditions and natural catastrophes which have been increasing in the recent decade, and while the pressure on governments rises to take action, the most influential newspaper in the country undermines the plight, which eventually could save the planet. At the same time, the newspaper claims to agree with the need to tackle pollution but states that it needs to be done slowly to allow people to adjust and indirectly calls for government support:

> The Mail agrees that particulate pollution must be tackled and that the principle of an emissions charge is not unreasonable. But surely it could have been phased in a lower price to give people a chance to adjust. And whatever happened to all that talk of a compensatory scrappage scheme?
>
> *Daily Mail* (8 April 2019)

What is more, *Daily Mail* is criticising the Extinction Rebellion but at the same time shows appraisal to initiatives that could reduce meat consumption. For example, in an article from 4 August 2019, a journalist praises technological solutions to create stem cell–based chicken, and the appraisal is linked to helping the planet by reducing global warming and ending world hunger with the aid of technology, thus seeing technology as a solution to human problems rather than abandoning capitalism:

> It may sound like science-fiction but thanks to a chicken called Ian – the first bird to have his stem cells harvested in 2017 – the technology is now so advanced that Tetrick and other entrepreneurs claim to have come up with a solution to end world hunger, eradicate food-borne illnesses and reduce global warming [...] Environmental benefits could be huge. At the moment, traditional cattle farming uses 70 per cent of world's non-ice covered land, and the methane produced by cows is a major contributor to global warming. Moreover, a cow takes 18 months to

140   *Press coverage of environmental affairs*

get to slaughter, compared to two weeks to produce lab-grown beef [...] Eating a chicken nugget that tastes as good as, if not better than, one from McDonald's and knowing no animal had to die in the process was a profound experience. If I had a choice, and if I knew the lab-made meat was 100 per cent safe, I would choose it every time. I've tasted the future and it tastes like chicken. Thank you, Ian.

Daily Mail (4 August 2019)

In addition to that, *Daily Mail* launched some initiatives to help environmental cause such as its Christmas campaign to plant trees by outlining reasons why planting trees is necessary, thus attempting to make a meaningful change and help the planet:

Today the Daily Mail announces its Christmas campaign calling on our army of loyal readers to plant trees for a greener Britain. At a time when we traditionally gather around a tree, we are urging readers to Be a Tree Angel and Make Britain Greener. We are appealing for donations to help plant more woodlands and create a more beautiful country. So please take part. Trees create beauty, provide habitats for birds and wildlife and play a vital role in keeping our planet healthy. They can also contribute to beating some of the alarming threats facing the UK: global warming, pollution and flooding. They soak up the greenhouse gas carbon dioxide and air pollution in their leaves, absorb excess water in their roots and prevent soils from eroding.

Daily Mail (13 November 2019)

However, at the heart of this initiative seems to again be the preservation of capitalism and there is again inconsistency, which brings back the question of media privatisation. In other words, some authors have argued that societies need media that work for the public interest, challenge those in power (Marx, [1849] 1959, cited from Sandoval, 2013) or what Sandoval (2013) called socialisation of corporations, which means de-privatising the media and turning their private wealth into common wealth and media would be part of the socially controlled non-commercial media system.

When looking at the coverage of global warming alone, it is difficult to disagree with statements that media are failing the public and it seems likely that the inconsistency in otherwise environmentally-friendly Guardian comes from the fact it works for-profit and competes in the market. Because of that, newspapers have to write and produce coverage, and since digitalisation, this means even more coverage because journalists now need to fill in print pages as well as digital newspaper pages (Brédart, 2017). On top of that, in newspapers owned by billionaires such as *Daily Mail*, who traditionally promote neoliberalism and harshly criticise anything they perceive as left or liberal, the situation is even worse and the newspaper openly scaremongers and preaches hostility towards environmentalists, thus not only failing the public in not helping provide solutions but also not actively being the part of the problem. However, what is underlying all coverage, in both newspapers, is speciesism where humanity is the only species perceived as threatened with hardly any consideration on the impact on Nature and other living and non-living organisms, thus showing hierarchy. The latter is also linked to patriarchalism in the coverage where a consensus seems to be that technology will save the world, and not only is this unquestioned in the coverage, but the Government is also criticised for not taking advantage of technology more to "save" the environment. In other words, Nature is being dominated by humans and the newspapers seem to look for solutions how to continue to do so without becoming extinct all the while, while also suggesting that humans could dominate Nature with technology and perhaps "tame" the wilderness that is causing natural catastrophes and global warming with the use of masculine technology and domination.

Plastic pollution

Plastic pollution has been one of the most debated environmental issues in the past years. As colourfully illustrated by Boucher and Billard (2019), "it is not only our feet which leave a footprint on sandy beaches – our heavy reliance on plastic materials is creating a visible yet pervasive "plastic footprint" in the environment" (p. 68). According to the Our World in Data website, which collects information on plastic and its environmental impact, plastic was firstly produced in 1907 but its use has grown during the 1950s and since then, it has increased around 200-fold to 381 million tonnes in 2015 alone, which is around the mass of two-thirds of the world population (Ritchie & Roser, 2018, see also Geyer et al., 2017; Rhodes, 2018). Rhodes (2018) argues that the amount of plastic produced from 2004 to 2015 amounts to the total amount produced in the previous century. In addition to that, between 1950 and 2015,

> a total of 6.3 billion tonnes of primary and secondary (recycled) plastic waste was generated, of which around 9% has been recycled, and 12% incinerated, with the remaining 79% either being stored in landfills or having been released directly into the natural environment.
>
> ibid (p. 217)

Besides, according to Ellen MacArthur Foundation (2017), on the future of plastics and rethinking plastic pollution, authors concluded that around 40% of plastic packaging goes to landfill, 32% leaks out of the collection system and thus ends up directly in the environment (e.g. not collected, mismanaged, illegally dumped). According to Van Sebille, Spathi and Gilbert (2016), plastic pollution happens through illegal dumping, ineffective waste management, industrial activities, insufficiently filtered wastewater, coastal littering, discharge of stormwater, combined sewer overflows, natural disasters, fishing, shipping, gas platforms and undersea explorations.

142 *Press coverage of environmental affairs*

Many scholars and activists predicted that if something is not done, by 2050, there will be more plastic than fish in oceans. Plastic is, thus, considered as one of the major threats to both humanity and wildlife and plastic waste is seen as causing an unprecedented environmental crisis since approximately 10 million tonnes are leaking into the marine environment every year (see also Boucher & Billard, 2019; UN Environment, 2018; Boucher & Friot, 2017; Borrelle et al., 2017; The Ellie MacArthur Foundation, 2017; Wilcox et al., 2015). According to the data collected by Our World in Data, high-income countries generate more plastic waste per person than low-income countries and emphasises that effective waste-management needs to be established around the world to stop polluting oceans with plastic. The authors also recognise that plastic has benefits, for example, to avoid food waste through plastic packaging that preserves food longer; however, they also call for effective plastic management (ibid; Ritchie & Roser, 2018; Boucher & Friot, 2017). But when we look at plastic waste production, a link with previously mentioned over-consumption immediately emerges because the US (0.34 kg per person) is recognised as a country that produces the most plastic waste followed by the UK (0.21 kg per person), as two largest polluters in the world (Ritchie & Roser, 2018). According to Ritchie and Roser (2018), the most plastic waste is produced by packaging (which has been hit by consumer activism, as emphasised above), then building and construction, textiles, consumer products, transportation, electrics, industrial and other industries.

A commonly used term in the plastic pollution debate is the "Great Pacific Garbage Patch", which is an area between the Western Garbage Patch that comes from Japan and the Eastern Garbage Patch (that comes from the side of Hawaii and California). This area has a high concentration of plastic, chemical sludge and other debris that pollutes the ocean (Rhodes, 2018; Lebreton et al., 2018), which clearly presents a threat to oceans and life in the water. However, some authors warn that the predicted growth of plastic pollution is higher than efforts to reduce plastic. Borrelle and associates (2020) argued that "the petrochemical industry announced over $204 billion U.S. in investment driven by the shale gas boom, leading to a projected acceleration in virgin plastic production" (p. 1515), which can mitigate efforts of environmental, government and international organisations that are trying to reduce plastic emissions (e.g. Resolution EA.4/L9, the United Nations Environment Assembly Resolutions Marine Litter and Microplastics, and Goal 14.1 of the United Nations Sustainable Development Goals; governments banning and putting levies on single-use consumer plastic, organisations trying to clean beaches, etc.). Haward (2018) argued that there is a challenge in addressing plastic pollution and these challenges are not new. For example, in 1967, the world community focused on saving the world's seas and oceans by calling them the common heritage and since 2017, the UN's Environment Assembly resolution on marine plastic serves a similar purpose, to save oceans but this time the organisation recognises that the marine plastic pollution is a major threat. Haward (2018) thus argues that

Press coverage of environmental affairs   143

international agreements are difficult to develop and international initiatives need support from scientific research and committed governments that would encourage communities to act in disposing and reducing the use of plastic. This view echoes the previously expressed view of Borrelle and associates (2017) who called for international agreement on marine plastic pollution by arguing that

> tiny particles of plastic debris (often called microplastics) are so pervasive in aquatic ecosystems that we find them in seafood and table salt. Marine organisms ingest or are entangled by plastic, sometimes with fatal consequences. Research suggests plastic pollution may impact biodiversity, ecosystem services, food security, and human health. In short, plastic pollution is a global threat.
>
> n.p.

Van Sebille, Spathi and Gilbert (2016) also argued that ingestion is an issue and a direct danger from plastic pollution and not only for humans but also for marine life. For example, authors argue that more than 250 marine species have been affected by ingestion of plastic litter, and this caused damage or blockage of the intestinal tract leading, in many cases, to infection, starvation, reproductive disorders and death in some cases. Other issues, according to the same authors, lie in entanglement and ghost fishing (where fishing nets can entangle marine life and cause fatal injuries and abandoned nets continue to ghost fish and trap marine life) and transport of non-native and invasive species (where floating litter can entice marine life to move and adapt to new conditions, which in turn can threaten other marine life) (ibid). Authors also argue that the loss of oceans and marine life will reduce social benefits for humanity because it will reduce recreational opportunities and cause a loss of aesthetic value due to beaches being full of litter (ibid).

What is more, Borrelle and associates (2017) argued that plastic affects all organisms at every level of biology by, for example,

> altering gene expression, cells and tissues, causing death, and altering population size and community structure. Microplastics can impair reproduction and development and alter how species function, disperse, and assemble. These impacts, combined with evidence for accelerating plastic production and emissions into the environment, suggest the international community should come together to limit future emissions of plastic now, before they transform ecosystems irreparably.
>
> n.p.

Other authors suggested collaboration and also educational campaigns to preserve the environment by reducing plastic pollution (Xanthos & Walker, 2017).

144 *Press coverage of environmental affairs*

The plastic debate in the UK started to increase in significance after BBC' documentary Blue Planet, which was picked up by the press and then developed into a public agenda. The issue of plastic pollution and its impact on animal life and oceans has poured into CSR strategies and many businesses now tackle packaging, for example, in an attempt to reduce plastic. Therefore, biodegradable bags and products increased in popularity due to the decision of the UK Government, in 2015, to introduce charges of 5p for single-use plastic bags from 2016, which obliged the industry to report on how much plastic they produce and to charge for single-use bags (DEFRA, 2015). Besides, supermarkets, for example, have started to reduce plastic packaging and/or change packaging materials. The latter is consumer-driven as the British public became active in campaigning for plastic reduction by contacting supermarkets and asking them to take action (Topić et al., 2020a). Ahead of the proposed legislative change, WRAP conducted consumer research in 2014 and asked consumers to what extent they use single-use plastic bags concluding that consumer under-estimate their actual single-plastic use; however, nearly three-fifth of respondents supported charges on plastic bags (WRAP, 2014). According to the consumer research from YouGov, one of the largest polling companies in the UK, more than 70% of respondents stated they bring their own bag for shopping all of the time with a further 18% saying fairly often (YouGov, 2021), thus showing that 88% of the respondents are conscious about plastic pollution. In 2020, YouGov also asked the British public whether they would support an increase of price for single-use plastic bags to 10p, and 47% said they strongly support with 25% saying they somewhat support (YouGov, 2020). This survey was done in response to an announcement from the British Government that the price of plastic bags will increase to 10p and small producers will no longer be exempted (Smithers, 2020), thus showing that the UK Government has moved towards, what is in the literature recognised, as local action to tackle plastic pollution. However, surveying of the population in Britain has also shown that the public struggles to identify plastic in products despite expressing concerns about plastic consumption (Baverstock, 2020) and worryingly, almost half of the population said that the risk of climate change is real but consequences likely over-hyped by the media and the Government (Ibbetson, 2020), thus bringing back one of the questions this book addresses, that is, whether the media are causing damage by over-saturated coverage of environmental affairs but without offering a real solution.

The coverage of plastic

When it comes to plastic, the interest of the media follows the interest in global warming, with even more coverage of the issue in the press, with *Daily Mail* publishing a total of 268 articles (Table 5.3) and *The Guardian* a total of 426 articles (Table 5.4).

Press coverage of environmental affairs 145

Table 5.3 Coverage of Plastic in *Daily Mail* (*N* = 268)

Article Author	Number of Articles	Positive towards Reducing Plastic	Neutral	Negative towards Reducing Plastic
Man	127	39	77	11
Woman	89	66	20	3
Mixed	2	2	0	0
No byline	50	7	43	0
Total	268	114	140	14

Table 5.4 Coverage of Plastic in *The Guardian* (*N* = 426)

Article Author	Number of Articles	Positive towards Reducing Plastic	Neutralc	Negative towards Reducing Plastic
Man	151	72	78	1
Woman	251	115	136	0
Mixed	11	5	6	0
No byline	10	6	4	0
Editorial	3	3	0	0
Total	426	201	224	1

In the case of plastic, most of the coverage of *Daily Mail* is neutral (a total of 140 articles) and the situation is the same with *The Guardian* that published 224 neutrally toned articles. However, in the case of both newspapers the neutral number of articles is closely followed by positive ones, i.e. 114 vs. 140 in *Daily Mail* and 201 vs. 224 in *The Guardian*, respectively, thus signalling that both newspapers both have plastic on the agenda based on the number of articles they published and both newspapers write similarly about the issue in terms of the ratio of neutral vs. positive articles. However, *The Guardian* again published editorials, thus showing that the newspaper has a formal view of the issue that is followed by the coverage, but with coverage leaning towards the libertarian view of the media as an unbiased observer.

When it comes to gender ratio, in *Daily Mail* more men than women wrote articles on plastic (127 vs. 89), thus again signalling that when a historically feminine issue came to the agenda, men took over to write about the issue (Topić & Tench, 2018). In *The Guardian*, however, the situation is the opposite and more women than men wrote articles on this issue, 251 bylines signed by a woman as opposed to 151 by a man (Table 5.4). However, in *Daily Mail*, even though fewer women wrote about the issue of plastic (89 vs. 127), they still published 66 positive articles vs. 39 positive articles signed by men (Table 5.3),

146 *Press coverage of environmental affairs*

thus signalling women's inclination to support environmental causes, which has been a historical ecofeminist argument (Mallory, 2006; Brownhill & Turner, 2019; Goldstein, 2006; Leahy, 2003; McStay & Dunlap, 1983; Poole & Harmon Zeigter, 1985; Shapiro & Mahajan, 1986; Steger & Witt, 1989; Diani, 1989; Schahn & Holzer, 1990; Blaikie, 1992; Franklin & Rudig, 1992; Stern et al., 1993; McAllister, 1994; Hampel et al., 1996; Tranter, 1996; Godfrey, 2005; Shiva, 1989; Brownhill, 2010; Godfrey, 2008; Holy, 2007; Mann, 2011; Stoddart & Tindall, 2011; Giacomini, 2014; Kirk, 1998; McMahon, 1997; Salleh, 1984; Topić, 2020d; Topić et al., 2021). This again opens up a question of whether the situation with decreasing support for capitalism and increasing support for the preservation of Nature would be more prominent on the media agenda had women had more power and influence in newspapers. In the case of *The Guardian*, women also wrote more positive articles than men; however, as with the previous analysis, it needs to be said that the number they wrote, in general, is much higher. Thus, it cannot be said that men write negatively when they write much less than women on this issue.

When making sense of newspaper coverage on plastic, *The Guardian* has editorial policies published which appeared in the sample. In that, a little neoliberal leaning and speciesism of *The Guardian* becomes instantly visible. For example, in an editorial from May 2019, *The Guardian* expressed speciesism by calling for saving humanity from extinction and by instrumentalising Nature and other species by emphasising we need them to save ourselves, thus using a pragmatist approach to instigate human action:

> We humans pride ourselves on our ability to look beyond immediate concerns and think on a grander scale. While other creatures preen for mates, hunt prey or build homes, only humans ponder the nature of time, explore our place in the universe or are troubled by the question of what wiped out the dinosaurs. Yet we are often poor at focusing on and understanding the things which really matter. A new mass extinction is under way, and this time we are mostly responsible [...] Real change will require a depth of imagination, ambition and sheer determination which humans have historically struggled to muster. Yet if we cannot summon the required concern for a million species, we could at least focus on one: our own. We may not be charmed by Earth's 5.5 million insect species, but we need them to pollinate crops, disperse seeds and break down waste to enrich the soil. Through ignorance, greed, laziness and simple lack of attention we are wiping out the very creatures upon whom we ourselves depend.
>
> *The Guardian* (editorial, 7 May 2019)

In an editorial from June 2019, *The Guardian* also emphasised that

> it is possible that rising awareness of the scale and effects of plastic pollution could lead to significant changes in shopping habits over time, if initiatives like Waitrose's were to become widespread. But the

Press coverage of environmental affairs 147

seriousness of the pollution problem means there isn't time to wait and see. Environmental regulation is needed urgently.

The Guardian (4 June 2019)

While at the outset, this seems like an environmental engagement, it is actually a weak antagonist position recognising some negative effects of economic growth but still supporting it along with some environmental regulation (De Bruyn, 2000), thus going along with neoliberalism and environmental governance as a solution to the problem. Therefore, there is a clear link between speciesism and neoliberal policies of environmental regulation that do not challenge, or not sufficiently, economic growth and current economic policies but call for managing environmental affairs and using Nature to preserve humanity. These views are also reinforced in some other articles where journalists narrated their attempts to reduce plastic and then call for environmental regulation. For example, a Guardian journalist attempted a plastic-free month and tried to carry everything consumed in a bag only to realise the consumption of plastic is so big that it is impossible to carry all of that, thus arguing,

what I learned from my month of privileged, cashed-up western failure is that it's going to take the regulation of plastic production, distribution and supply by global governments to make anywhere "plastic-free". Single-use-plastic-bag bans are not enough. Recycling is not enough. Governments must legislate to enforce the use of alternatives, starting yesterday. A dead albatross is hanging around our necks, it's full of plastic waste ... but we're the ones who will choke on the stuff.

The Guardian (19 August 2019)

However, all this coverage of environmental affairs and calling for action, shows itself as futile because it is not only that economic growth is not challenged enough, as explained in the previous chapter, but it is also that consumerism is promoted instead of challenged. Therefore, *The Guardian* frequently writes about Christmas shopping and provides lengthy guides on what to buy, and while some of the coverage is wrapped into environmentalism by suggesting eco gifts, the message of consumerism is still the same, we need to buy things we do not need. For example, in an article from December 2019, the journalist asks the readers "Are you dreaming of a green Christmas?" and then carries on by emphasising that

households and individuals across the UK are turning their backs on the vulgarity of Christmas consumerism and waste by cutting back on obvious and most visible areas of excess such as unwanted gifts, plastic trees and decorations and unrecyclable wrapping paper. But the scale of our extravagance remains shocking.

The Guardian (16 December 2019)

148 *Press coverage of environmental affairs*

The article then continues with offering advice on how to shop in a more environmentally friendly way by reducing plastic, shopping locally and so on, which brings a question of what is less vulgar in eco shopping from other shopping when both are done in the name of consumerism. What is more, coverage like this can only instigate resentment among readers who cannot afford to shop eco-friendly products, which are still more expensive, and this leads to the notion of *Daily Mail* and its promotion of environmentalism as a middle-class thing that hard-working people simply cannot afford.

The plastic coverage is the only section where equality and domination of Nature emerged in regard to human pollution of the planet. In an article from July 2019, a journalist writes a colourful story about Anne LaBastille and her work on women in the wilderness, based on her own experience of living alone in Adirondacks for decades. In that, journalist emphasises that women do not aim to dominate Nature, which links to ecofeminist theory that sees women as more likely to embrace Nature and protection of the environment (Mallory, 2006; Brownhill & Turner, 2019; Goldstein, 2006; Leahy, 2003; McStay & Dunlap, 1983; Poole & Harmon Zeigter, 1985; Shapiro & Mahajan, 1986; Steger & Witt, 1989; Diani, 1989; Schahn & Holzer, 1990; Blaikie, 1992; Franklin & Rudig, 1992; Stern et al., 1993; McAllister, 1994; Hampel et al., 1996; Tranter, 1996; Godfrey, 2005; Shiva, 1989; Brownhill, 2010; Godfrey, 2008; Holy, 2007; Mann, 2011; Stoddart & Tindall, 2011; Giacomini, 2014; Kirk, 1998; McMahon, 1997; Salleh, 1984; Topić, 2020d; Topić et al., 2021) and also that women environmentalists, especially women of colour, are largely missing from environmental literature. Journalist boldly states that

> the white-male-against-nature narrative has played out horribly. We have seen what has happened when the last big game are hunted and stuffed, the great old forests logged, Everest is polluted with bodies and plastic, and shorelines have been developed. The outdoorsman protagonist has become the antagonist. We need new narratives. We need a different kind of hero. LaBastille wanted to see women as a "major force" in conservation. She felt that retreating to nature would allow you to first "inspire yourself, then calm yourself" – and periodically emerge with enough energy and insight to fight short battles. Many of the conservationists I know are exhausted. The stakes are high, the anti-environmental counter current is strong, and species and ecosystems are crashing around us: the Great Barrier Reef, right whales, the Amazon, the last forest in Miami, coastlines.
>
> *The Guardian* (17 July 2019, all emphases in the original)

In other words, this is the article that directly tackles the masculine domination of Nature and pollution. These views are echoed in an article from 2020 which finds that eco-products are labelled as women's products and marketed to women, thus noticing an "eco gender gap" in which "green branding might as well be pink". The journalist continues by tackling precisely an

Press coverage of environmental affairs 149

ecofeminist notion of women being more caring of the planet but expresses criticism that because caring for the planet is perceived as feminine men do not seem to engage with environmentalism as much:

> The idea is already insidious due to the persistent portrayal of women as caregivers – even of the planet. Janet K Swim, a professor of psychology at Pennsylvania State University who has done extensive research into the social consequences of environmentally friendly behaviour, points to a political cartoon showing Theodore Roosevelt, the US president from 1901 to 1909, wearing an apron, "trying to mock him as feminine" for his conservation policies. [...] While it is true that women are more likely than men to be green, in the past that gender gap has been attributed to personality differences. Research from the mid-90s to early 00s pointed to women's greater tendency to be prosocial, altruistic and empathetic; to display a stronger ethic of care; and to assume a future-focused perspective. "Research suggests that women have higher levels of socialisation to care about others and be socially responsible, which then leads them to care about environmental problems and be willing to adopt environmental behaviours," says Rachel Howell, a lecturer in sustainable development (a subject that is, she notes, studied overwhelmingly by women at undergraduate level) at the University of Edinburgh. Whether women are born caring about the planet or learn to do so, there is evidence to suggest that femininity and "greenness" have come to be cognitively linked (by men and women) – and that this, as absurd as it may sound, is partly what puts off men from doing their bit [...] Even arguments about meaningful action on the climate crisis are are split down gender lines. Another study by Swim, published in the journal Global Environmental Change last year, showed that men preferred arguments that centred on science and business and tended to "attribute negative feminine traits" to men who argued on the basis of ethics and environmental justice – as women typically did. Women tend to have less trust in institutions, Howell says, which may mean they have less faith in the ability of science, technology and the government to address the issues that face us. Men, however, having been historically well served by the status quo, "are much more inclined to believe that, if they accept there is a problem, then somebody or some technology will sort it all out – that we don't need to change our lifestyle". Misogyny has been shown to be a factor in climate denial. A 2014 paper in the International Journal for Masculinity Studies found that: "For climate sceptics, it was not the environment that was threatened; it was a certain kind of modern industrial society built and dominated by their form of masculinity." As Martin Gelin wrote last year in the New Republic, the highest-profile climate campaigners in the world today are two young women: Greta Thunberg and Alexandria Ocasio-Cortez. Those shouting them down are primarily older conservative men.
>
> *The Guardian* (6 February 2020)

150   *Press coverage of environmental affairs*

This one part of the one out of the only two articles on environmentalism and women summarises all ecofeminist theory that has been developed over the decades. However, these voices are marginal and while it can be appreciated that *The Guardian* published them, much more needs to be done to push this narrative forward and enlighten the masses that environmental affairs are everybody's problem; however, since they have been constructed as feminine, the success is lacking.

Other articles continue in a similar tone as with economic growth and environmental affairs and focus on speciesism such as health problems as a result of plastic pollution. For example, in an article from 14 March 2019, a journalist writes lengthily about washing the laundry and the impact detergents have on the ocean but also health because,

> there's the discovery of synthetic fibres in human faeces, confirming that plastic pollution is making its way into our bodies either from our food, our drink, or both. Some researchers have speculated that plastic particles in the gut could affect our immune response, or transmit toxic chemicals.
>
> *The Guardian* (14 March 2019)

In other words, while the impact of plastic pollution on oceans and life within oceans is mentioned briefly, the article lengthily explains harms to human health to call for action, thus again demonstrating speciesism.

But media is criticised for not paying enough attention to the destruction of the planet in an article from May 2019 where the journalist writes about the collapse of life on Earth but points out this is not in the news because of interests of billionaire owners who have an interest in pushing these stories aside (*The Guardian*, 9 May 2019), which links to general coverage aimed at criticising businesses. Thus, a long article from October 2019 emphasises that "business and economics are right at the centre of the climate emergency" because "companies are among the biggest polluters in the world – and are key to meeting the Paris agreement's target of limiting global warming to 1.5C". The article thus uses the Paris agreement as a way to save the environment. This agreement has been labelled as neoliberal because it also focuses on self-regulation of companies and committing to tackle climate change, which is seen as market environmentalism and *neoliberalisation* of Nature (McCarthy, 2004; Mansfield, 2004; Bridge, 2004; Prudham, 2004; Ciplet & Roberts, 2017). The article, however, proceeds to suggest that businesses need to make changes by saying,

> from giant fossil fuel companies to agricultural and food businesses, retailers, airlines and car manufacturers – all must make big changes, for the sake of the planet, the global economy and their own future sustainability, providing goods and services and employment.
>
> *The Guardian* (17 October 2019)

Press coverage of environmental affairs 151

The article essentially calls for a neoliberal practice where the market regulates itself and companies engage with practices that benefit society through CSR policies to avoid criticism such as this one, and potential consumer activism. The article then non-critically continues with emphasising that the writing of the newspaper is,

> questioning whether traditional capitalism, which aims for perpetual growth, can ever deal with the huge challenges of climate emergency, or whether a new slow-capitalism or green growth – which does not pursue profit at all costs – must come. We are reporting on the changes being made by corporate executives – and alerting readers to those who fall short,
>
> ibid

thus again re-enforcing the notion of CSR and reporting on companies who fail to comply with social/media expectations but without offering a meaningful solution. For example, some companies simply cannot change their business model because it is, for example, based on fossil fuels or coal and they are not doing anything illegal when continuing to work and pollute (Pollin, 2019) because it should be the government that needs to ban these resource depletions.

On the other hand, *Daily Mail* continues linking all environmental affairs with relentless attacks against the Extinction Rebellion and the criticism of this movement is also accompanied by celebrating Londoners for taking matters into their own hands. Thus, an article from October 2019 celebrates "fed-up Londoners" who "took matters in their own hands" by dragging down protesters from trains on Jubilee Line, which the newspaper calls an "uprising at last! Hurrah". The Mail labelled signs that protesters carried 'Business As Usual-Death' as "enraging" and again as "eco-warriors" who "may turn their noses up at capitalism, this is what stops this country from turning into one giant mud field, with a few turnips rotting in the gutters where Kent once stood". The coverage then carries on with class divide and labelling the public as hard-working average people sick of elites telling them what to do while environmentalists are labelled also as "eco-terrorist chums" and saying that the Extinction Rebellion is acting in an act of civil disobedience:

> However, the only business going down at Canning Town was the bubbling frustration of the commuters. Who are as mad as hell and are not going to take this any more. Look at them. They are the normals, the everyday civilians, the overlooked ordinary Joes just trying to get to work. Or desperate to get home after a draining night shift. Hard-working people who never get a favour or a lucky break or the opportunity to smugly tell everyone about how they have just offset their carbon footprint and have solar panels on the swimming pool roof. The only footprints they make are on the commuter trudge to and from work — only this time to find themselves thwarted by smug do-gooders protesting about the state

152 *Press coverage of environmental affairs*

of the planet. Somebody threw a cup of tea over them right at the beginning, so matters were clearly fraught [...] The right to protest ends when you violate the rights of others to go about their daily business. That is not protest, it is civil disobedience [...] There is no way that holding up commuters is going to make them sympathetic to your cause — surely Extinction Rebellion and their pathetic celebrity eco-terrorist chums must see this is a warning of what is to come?

Daily Mail (18 October 2019)

The journalist continues by saying there is something good in the cause of Extinction Rebellion but then complains at their methods and engage with climate change denial by arguing that

they preach an apocalyptic rhetoric of death, claiming billions of people are going to die soon because of climate change [...] They talk of imminent catastrophe, mass suffering and deaths, but science doesn't back this up. (Hallam has said it is 'great fun taking down capitalists'. So at least he's honest about that.) The alarmist language is bad enough, but a lot of goodwill is being washed away by their hardline stance and the utter ghastliness of many of their supporters. The well-to-do grandparents, the trust fund kids, the anarchists, the Octavias, the Ruperts, the Buddhist students, the grungsters, the unemployed, the bored, the Benedict Cumberbatches and the rest. The elites are on the wrong side on this one, supporting this mass, inchoate movement so fond of hysterics and superglue. Once, XR fought against public indifference. Now, they must contend with public rage. Good.

Daily Mail (18 October 2019)

Thus, the article engages with climate change denial and complaint on methods as well as class divide where protesters are labelled as "elites". While there is some truth in a claim that middle classes are engaged with environmental activism and that working classes oppose it because of lack of power to choose environmental options or because they cannot afford to go to protests (Topić et al., 2021) and while there is some truth in arguing that methods of Extinction Rebellion can be seen as aggressive, it is also the truth that *Daily Mail* does not propose a solution to the problem and articles are not only about criticising methods of the movement but generally undermining the cause. With this, *Daily Mail* engages with denial of the threat that capitalism – it clearly supports –poses. Many articles engage with this rhetoric and undermine the cause with populist writing emphasising, for example, that activists have smartphones and then carry on by emphasising the environmental cost of technological devices such as phone and also slave labour:

No self-respecting eco-warrior can go without their shiny, up-to-date smartphone. How else could they film their marches and share them on social media, or stay abreast of the latest howls of outrage on Twitter about the destruction of the planet? [...] For they are a big part of the problem, too. More than 50 million tonnes of 'e-waste', the term for discarded electronics products, is now generated every year [...] The phones aren't just aluminium, plastic and glass, they contain precious materials which are in limited global supply: gold and copper in the wiring, silver and platinum for the main printed circuit board, lithium in the batteries, cobalt and aluminium. Some of these materials come with a devastating price — one that reveals the hypocrisy at the heart of today's eco-brigade [...] Environmental campaigners have applauded Apple for going in the right direction. But one only needs to look in the cramped, dangerous holes in Africa — where children as young as six slave away, mining for precious metals that often end up in our phones — to see that.

Daily Mail (7 June 2019)

This writing, criticising environmental movements, is also further exacerbated with articles criticising the government for "suddenly [...] falling over itself in order to make gestures on climate change", criticising also the government for leaping "aboard every passing bandwagon, without thinking through what it is doing, it is in danger of imposing huge costs on the economy and causing considerable public resentment — while making emissions worse". The article then carries on expressing criticism some from the socialist side of the argument have expressed too by saying that the cost of going green cannot be placed on the back of workers (Adler & Wargan, 2019; Galvin & Healy, 2020):

The fact is, if the public are to bear the cost of all this, we should be wary. For past evidence shows that good intentions can go horribly awry when the dead hand of the State is involved [...] But there is a serious issue of fairness here. Would it really be acceptable for owners of modest homes to be forced to pay through the nose to eliminate their carbon emissions so that the likes of Emma Thompson can continue to enjoy their transatlantic jaunts while lecturing the rest of us on our climate sins? Government ministers don't exactly set a good example either, flying off to Davos to deliver lectures on climate change. The point is that the Government needs to think very seriously before thoughtlessly committing itself willy-nilly to carbon reduction targets. Because there are unforeseen consequences everywhere.

Daily Mail (3 May 2019)

This is a valid point, however, in the context of expressing resentment against all environmental affairs, it reads as if environmentalism is a middle-class obsession because people have nothing else to do, which is the sentiment that runs through the coverage. Nevertheless, environmentalism is sometimes

154 *Press coverage of environmental affairs*

mocked as a sect directly undermining that the movement emerged not from the fanaticism of the new religion, as *Daily Mail* portrays it, but as a result of scientific research showing changes in the climate:

> Years ago in a satirical spirit, I suggested that ecologists, Guardian columnists and BBC environment reporters (sorry, 'analysts') were elevating theories about climate change to the status of religious truths, to be questioned on pain of punishment for heresy. I pictured these eco-maniacal faithful at prayer meetings of their sect, chanting in unison a rewritten version of the Creed, beginning: 'I believe that the Earth, and everything in it, is on the brink of destruction by man-made global warming.' [...] If the Church is now to add offences against the environment to the catalogue of transgressions that must be confessed, I fear I would have to detain the poor priest for days on end. 'Bless me, Father, for I have sinned: I failed to wash up my yoghurt pot before putting it in the recycling; I've bought single-use plastic bags at Sainsbury's many times; I used disposable, unrecyclable coffee mugs; over the years, I've flown off on holiday to Italy, France, Greece, New York, India and Spain; in idle moments, I've fired off facetious text messages and emails, further increasing my internet provider's prodigious consumption of energy ...' and so the list would go on.
>
> *Daily Mail* (6 December 2019)

And the article carries on by insulting Greta Thunberg and questioning data and scaremongering readers about going back to the pre-industrial age of stone and hunger, thus again linking environmentalism with decreasing standards of life, building popular antagonism towards the environmental movement:

> Look, I grant you that environmental campaigners are on to something. I admit, too, that for the sake of future generations we owe a duty of care to the planet and all God's creatures. So the more trees we plant, and the less we pollute the atmosphere, the better for our lives and our souls alike [...] By the same token, we may be wise to believe in man-made global warming. In this case, for eternal damnation read planetary extinction. But hardened old sceptic that I am, I can't help wondering if the facts are really as clear-cut as we're encouraged to believe by the eco-fanatics, under their new-found prophetess of doom — that little crosspatch Greta Thunberg. Instead of bludgeoning humanity back into a pre-industrial stone age of poverty and hunger, which is the course seemingly preferred by the Swedish schoolgirl's most fervent worshippers, I put my faith in technology's ability to come up with eco-friendly answers.
>
> *Daily Mail* (6 December 2019)

Press coverage of environmental affairs 155

The notion of poverty and people losing jobs is central to the coverage including economic growth, which is praised as the only way forward along with some version of environmentalism. Thus, an article from January 2020 says,

> Preaching climatic Armageddon is easy. Much more difficult is suggesting ways we can achieve zero carbon emissions without destroying the global economy and throwing billions into poverty [...] But William is to be applauded for launching an award, the Earthshot Prize, to reward people who come up with practical solutions to help us work towards zero emissions while continuing to grow the economy.
>
> *Daily Mail* (1 January 2020)

However, despite attacks to environmental activists and calling for economic growth and preservation of capitalism by criticising environmentalists for wanting to take Britain to the pre-industrial age, *Daily Mail* launched also an action to tackle plastic pollution by calling readers for joining the "Great British Spring Clean" to clean plastic waste and litter from the community (*Daily Mail*, 27 January 2020). Lots of reporting is then dedicated to this action with articles reporting on the course of action, its success in a tone that is largely supportive of the problem:

> Ever since the Daily Mail launched its brilliant attack on single-use plastic, I have been on a mission to cut back. Our family of five now saves around 190kg of plastic waste each year (enough to fill an entire bathroom), but I know I am going to have to turn up the volume in the next few weeks if I'm going to get on top of the sparkling, crackling, unrecyclable Christmas excess. Thankfully, this Christmas looks set to be one of the most eco-friendly ever, with supermarkets and department stores offering plastic-free crackers, cards, wrapping and packaging, and big name eco-voices such as Emma Thompson publicly swearing to forgo presents altogether in a bid to minimise plastic waste and help protect the environment.
>
> *Daily Mail* (15 December 2019)

> This time last year the Mail asked you, our remarkable readers, to lead a fightback against the scourge of litter that blights our precious landscape and coastline. We asked for 500,000 volunteers, scarcely daring to hope we could ever meet such an audacious target. In the end we not only met it but soared past it, making the 2019 Great British Spring Clean – organised in partnership with Keep Britain Tidy – the biggest single environmental action ever known in this country. A staggering 563,000 of you came together and collected 4,300 tonnes of litter from our cities, towns and countryside, making life infinitely more pleasant for us all.
>
> *Daily Mail* (25 January 2020)

156 *Press coverage of environmental affairs*

Therefore, it seems as if *Daily Mail* seems to think that human-made pollution can be sorted out by inviting humans to clean communities. While these actions are useful and can be applauded, they fall short of addressing the real problem that capitalism does not go with environmentalism (Georgescu-Roegen, 1971, Meadows et al., 1972; Ehrlich and Holdren, 1971; Cleveland, 1984; Douthwaite, 1999; Mishan, 1967; Salleh, 2000). Ultimately, it is possible to clean what humans litter, but the underlying problem of over-consuming and littering as a result of consumption remains, along with the problem of pollution that affects all life on the planet and disproportionately the Global South.

In summary, plastic as an issue is portrayed from one point as a human-made problem, and how this problem should be tackled depends on the editorial position of the newspaper where *The Guardian* advocates for the protection of the environment while *Daily Mail* proposes a solution for the public to clean litter and keep the country clean. However, neither newspaper engaged with neoliberalism and the underlying cause of this human behaviour, which is from one side already mentioned consumerism, but also entitlement similar to the one that runs through the coverage where humans are put on a pedestal while other species and Nature as a whole are to be dominated and organised. What is more, articles barely challenge (except for two articles in *The Guardian*) masculinities and domination that preceded environmental degradation and that is at the core of the problem. The fact, for example, that it is masculinity that is intertwined with capitalism and that masculine technology will not solve a masculine problem of capitalism and neoliberalism, or that master's tools will not dismantle the master's house (Rudy, 2006, p. 107). What is more, women journalists have overall written more positively towards the need to reduce plastic in both newspapers, thus again opening up a question what would happen if they were better represented across all section and if newspapers are not masculine organisations where women need to merge into the masculine culture to succeed.

Food waste

Food waste is another topic that has received interest from activists, policy-makers and the general public albeit the topic has been, to an extent, overshadowed by issues such as global warming and plastic even though food waste also forms a part of environmental politics and has a connection with over-sconsumption and consumerism. Nevertheless, food waste is also associated with greenhouse emissions and resource depletion and private households have been identified as crucial in tackling this environmental problem (Schanes et al., 2018; Stancu et al., 2016; Hall et al., 2009; WRAP, 2009; Quested et al., 2013; Parfitt et al., 2010; Gustavson et al., 2011) and it has been outlined as one of UN's sustainable goals (UN, 2015). Food waste captures losses at the distribution and consumption stage, globally representing around 24% of all food supplied to humans (Kummu et al., 2012; Gustavson et al., 2011). There is a difference in who bears responsibility for food waste. In high-income

Press coverage of environmental affairs 157

countries, food waste comes from distribution and households while in low-income countries agricultural and postharvest stages are responsible for the loss of food (Kummu et al., 2012; Parfitt et al., 2010). In the US and Europe food waste is estimated to represent 60% or 50% of all food production respectively (Griffin et al., 2009), thus clearly linking food waste with capitalism and consumerism where the Global North over-consumes and purchases more than needed, which contributes to global warming and emissions (Salleh, 2000; Griffin, 2020; Sandberg & Sandberg, 2010; Gaard, 2015).

Previous consumer research has shown that consumers dislike food waste because they perceive it as a waste of money rather than an environmental problem (Brook Lyndhurst, 2007; Watson & Meah, 2013). According to Quested and associates (2013), 7.2 million tonnes of food and drink was waste in the UK in 2010, and 4.4 million tonnes was avoidable. In other words, some food that was waste (bread slices, meat, etc.) were edible at some point before it was wasted. This waste totals 160 kg per household per year and it is around 12% of all food and drink purchases by UK households. WRAP (2020) also estimated that in 2018 at around 9.5 million tonnes, of which 70% was supposed to be consumed by people, and this food had a value of £19 billion a year and more than 25 million tonnes of greenhouse emissions. According to the same report, more than 85% of this wasted food (by weight) comes from households and food manufacturing. With just two crops, strawberry and lettuce, £30 million of food were wasted (ibid). WRAP (2020) also estimates that food waste contributes to $984 billion in economic losses globally per year, >£19 billion is the worth of food waste in the UK annually (WRAP, 2021). At the same time, FareShare (2021) reports that 8.4 million people in the UK do not have enough food to feed themselves, or in other words, the equivalent of the whole London population does not have enough food on the table while billions are being wasted.

According to Quested and associates (2013), avoidable food waste contributed to approximately 17 million tonnes of CO2 in greenhouse emissions. As with the use of single plastic bags, some studies have shown that people under-estimate how much food they waste (Quested et al., 2011) and there are some differences in demographics. For example, over 65s are less likely to waste food than other demographics but this is not because of environmental reasons but because they often see it as wrong without any particular reason specified or because over 65s have lived during periods of austerity and food rationing, and thus see food waste as wrong (British Social Attitudes, 2011; WRAP, 2007; Quested et al., 2013).

When it comes to food waste, both newspapers published fewer articles than on plastic and global warming, thus signalling that global warming and plastic are seen as more relevant issues for the environment. In *Daily Mail*, a total of 56 articles was published (Table 5.5) with *The Guardian* publishing 109 articles overall (Table 5.6), thus again signalling *The Guardian's* concern with environmental affairs and giving more space to this issue.

In the case of food waste, the coverage in both newspapers leans towards neutral covering on the topic, but this is again closely followed by positive

158 *Press coverage of environmental affairs*

Table 5.5 Coverage of Food Waste in *Daily Mail* (*N* = 56)

Article Author	Number of Articles	Positive towards Reducing FoodWaste	Neutral	Negative towards Reducing Food Waste
Man	28	5	19	4
Woman	18	13	3	2
Mixed	1	1	0	0
No byline	9	3	6	0
Total	56	22	28	6

Table 5.6 Coverage of Food Waste in *The Guardian*

Article Author	Number of Articles	Positive towards Reducing Food Waste	Neutral	Negative towards Reducing Food Waste
Man	52	28	24	0
Woman	55	23	31	1
Mixed	1	1	0	0
No byline	1	0	1	0
Total	109	52	56	1

coverage. For example, in the case of *Daily Mail*, a total of 28 neutrally toned articles were published as opposed to 22 with a positive tone (Table 5.5), whereas *The Guardian* published 56 neutral articles and 52 positive articles (Table 5.6). With gender, in *Daily Mail*, again more men than women covered the topic with more women writing positively about the need to reduce food waste whereas in *The Guardian* slightly more women wrote about the issue than men (55 bylines signed by women as opposed to 52 signed by men) but more men wrote positively about the need to reduce food waste whereas more women wrote neutrally about the issue.

When making sense of how newspapers write about food waste, and unlike for other sections, a stronger anti-business discourse emerges here. So, for example, in *The Guardian*, journalists criticise the meat diet as a contributor to the environmental problems, including food waste, by saying that if,

> one in five people in richer countries adopted low-meat diets, and threw away a third less food than they currently do, while poor countries were assisted to preserve their forests and restore degraded land, the world's agricultural systems could be absorbing carbon dioxide by 2050 instead of adding massively to global heating as they do at present.
>
> *The Guardian* (21 October 2019)

Press coverage of environmental affairs 159

This is, however, accompanied by criticism of companies that are attempting to reduce waste. For example, in an article from June 2019, *The Guardian* expressed criticism of food waste practice by calling Waitrose's initiative to reduce plastic and waste as PR and by asking that the onus is taken off the consumer because supermarkets should pay for their waste, and this money could fund other initiatives:

> It is all positive PR and puts Waitrose on par with rival supermarkets who, facing predicted "polluter pay" legislation (more on that later), are suddenly super-keen to prove their green packaging credentials. Market-style loose vegetable aisles are being rolled out at Booths; Asda has removed the plastic wrap from its swedes; Morrisons has unsheathed its cucumbers (for part of the year), and both Iceland and Tesco are trialling schemes to pay customers to recycle plastic bottles (5.5bn worth of which are currently burned or dumped annually). Tesco is even experimenting with collecting and recycling "soft plastics" such as crisp packets, which local authorities generally cannot reprocess [...] But instead of celebrating this change, it feels to me like another of those fashionable supermarket spasms (trials selling misshapen veg; pushes on unfashionable sustainable fish like mackerel), that will ultimately change little. It will achieve traction with an already self-motivated minority, but then what? [...] Take the onus off the consumer. Make supermarkets pay for their waste, immediately. Feed that money into recycling and, just as the sugar tax forced manufacturers to redesign their fizzy drinks, we will see supermarkets moving swiftly to innovate new packaging solutions. For now, they are just pootling around the edges of the problem.
>
> *The Guardian* (5 June 2019)

While at the outset, this seems like a reasonable criticism and a sign that *The Guardian* is not supporting neoliberalism, the problem is much more complex. As explained earlier, it is a sign of neoliberalism when governments are first supposed to collect taxes to fund initiatives such as food waste in this case (Galvin & Healy, 2020). Instead, what environmentalists propose is a return to the Keynesian economic policy where the government intervenes and this can happen through collecting taxes but also borrowing to invest and affect change rather than wait to collect enough taxes to invest (Galvin & Healy, 2020; Nunn, 2014; Gamble, 1989; Jessop, 2003) albeit it needs re-emphasising that this approach either does not address consumerism and environmental degradation sufficiently. The latter policy is how countries ended up not investing sufficiently in environmental protection because waiting to collect enough taxes is simply not enough to fuel meaningful change. In addition to that, criticising corporations for reducing or not reducing waste again brings back the CSR element and media imposition of the concept, which preserves the open market policy and brings about self-regulation.

160 *Press coverage of environmental affairs*

Daily Mail, on the other hand, calls food waste staggering and calls waste that poisons animals who eat it distressing, but there is no proposal for a solution:

> Britons throw away a staggering £494 million worth of food every year. Cooking is one of our favourite pastimes, but research released for Stop Food Waste Day reveals UK shoppers still throw away an average 40 per cent of things they put in their weekly shopping basket.
>
> *Daily Mail* (24 April 2019)

> They should be grazing on pastures in their lush forest habitat. Instead, these distressing images show a different and worrying reality. Ponies and donkeys roam the streets of a tourist spot, ripping into black plastic sacks and gorging on the rubbish inside. There are fears the wild horses of the New Forest National Park in Hampshire are regularly swallowing harmful plastics, as well as food waste that could be poisonous to them.
>
> *Daily Mail* (1 March 2019)

The issue of food waste is arguably least prominent in the coverage than other two issues, global warming and plastic; however, as with corporations that change their CSR policies depending on how consumers and media feel about it (Topić et al., 2020a), a similar situation is with the media that obsess with plastic and global warming because this is where the scientific debate is and also largely because of BBC documentary Blue Planet, which has instigated a debate. But it remains open to see whether and how the debate will change.

What is central to the existing debate is the CSR-y discourse of focusing on forcing corporations to instigate social problems, thus bringing about an issue on what is a corporation. Or, in other words, the discourse throughout the coverage seems to be on environmental governance that implies corporations are supposed to be part of the solution to environmental issues rather than seeing them as a problem and the cause of the environmental problem. How two newspapers go about arguing this issue differs and ranges from notorious pro-capitalism and anti-environmentalism in *Daily Mail* with some journalists writing in a way that can only be described as rage to *The Guardian* that advocates environmental protection but enforces a view of the environmental governance where businesses are imposed with CSR by the media; however, as businesses do not genuinely engage with CSR, not much action is happening.

Note

1 Delworth and Knutson (2000) state that global warming firstly occurred in "a distinct 20-year periods, from 1925 to 1944 and from 1978 to the present" (p. 2246), which is in line with Houghton (2004) who concentrates on the period from the 1980s onwards.

6 The wheel of neoliberalism and the responsibility of the press

After all the discussion in this book, a question remains on the role of the press and its intertwined nature with neoliberalism. My view is that the press, as well as CSR, is part of a wheel of neoliberalism where different practices perpetuate themselves in a never-ending cycle that preserves the status quo. This cycle starts with patriarchy, then continues with capitalism due to its intertwined nature with patriarchy. This then feeds into a neoliberal economic policy of the economic growth, which is perpetuated and preserved with CSR practice, and results with the environmental governance approach and belief that technology will solve problems masculine culture created, and all these policies are perpetuated by the liberal media and result with the degradation of the environment (Figure 6.1).

What this means in practice is that patriarchy works as a system embedded in cultural masculinity where things are done in line with traditionally masculine ways and this same way of managing relations is then projected to Nature. In ecofeminist terms, there is a duality of oppression of women and Nature (Mallory, 2012) and this dual oppression comes from the ideology of hegemonic masculinity and patriarchy, which are intertwined with capitalist practices (von Werlhof, 2007; Merchant, 1992; Stoddart & Tindall, 2011; Radford Ruether, 2012; Henderson, 1997; Maclaran & Stevens, 2018; Gaard, 1997; Ling, 2014; Warren, n.d.; Đurđević & Marjanić, 2020). In this research monograph, this became visible in the way media write about economic growth, environmental affairs and the position of women. In other words, the press advocates economic growth from one side, and management of the environment on the other side with a biased view of technology as a saviour of humanity. Gaard (2015) argued that "climate change and the first world consumption are produced by masculinist ideology, and will not be solved by masculinist techno-science approaches" (p. 4). What is more, the press is one of the bastions of masculinity where women are underrepresented in business and news sections and thus have very little voice on environmental affairs. While there is a sense that women have merged into the masculine culture in the way they advocate for solutions, there is also a sense that things might be different had more women managed to join traditionally masculine beats because even with low numbers and merging into

DOI: 10.4324/9781003091592-6

162 *The wheel of neoliberalism*

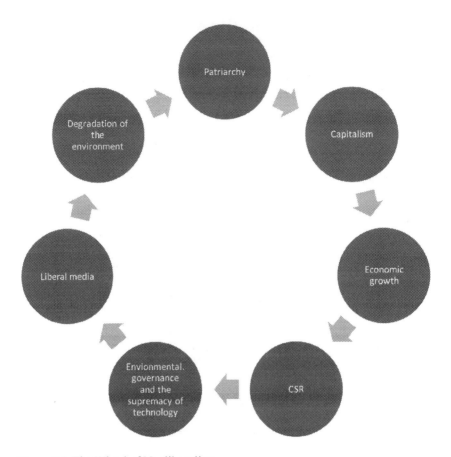

Figure 6.1 The Wheel of Neoliberalism.

masculine view of economy and environment, more women than men in most cases wrote more anti-capitalist and more pro-environmental articles, which goes in line with all data of women being more inclined to support environmental affairs (Mallory, 2006; Brownhill & Turner, 2019; Goldstein, 2006; Leahy, 2003; Salleh, 1989; McStay & Dunlap, 1983; Poole & Harmon Zeigter, 1985; Shapiro & Mahajan, 1986; Steger & Witt, 1989; Diani, 1989; Schahn & Holzer, 1990; Blaikie, 1992; Franklin & Rudig, 1992; Stern et al., 1993; McAllister, 1994; Hampel et al., 1996; Tranter, 1996; Godfrey, 2005, 2008; Holy, 2007; Shiva, 1989; Brownhill, 2010; Mann, 2011; Stoddart & Tindall, 2011; Giacomini, 2014; Kirk, 1998; McMahon, 1997; Salleh, 1984; Topić, 2020d; Topić et al., 2021). Therefore, with the current media support for neoliberal policies, there is little chance for rearrangement of production and reproduction between men and women as well as Nature (Salleh, 1991) and d'Eaubonne's (1994) view of the planet "placed in the feminine" seems

The wheel of neoliberalism   163

a far-reaching goal. The connection between the domination of Nature and women (Gersdorf, 2006) seems pervasive.

What the press does in their coverage is perpetuating market competition models and economic growth, which is incompatible with environmentalism (Besthorn & Pearson McMillen, 2002; Salleh, 2000, 1994; Shiva, 1999; d'Eaubonne, [1990] 1997; Georgescu-Roegen, 1971; Meadows et al., 1972, 2004; Ehrlich & Holdren, 1971; Cleveland et al., 1984; Douthwaite, 1999; Mishan, 1967). As argued by Salleh (2000) the global economic system is aggressive and deepens tensions between species and the writing in the press is linked with speciesism because even when the call for action is done it is always embedded into a call to save humanity. However, not even this is done properly as the patriarchal and masculine system is perpetuated with free trade policies, competition and exporting (Salleh, 2000) or with policies of economic growth that are supported not only by the neoliberal Government but also by the press. As argued by D'Eaubonne ([1990] 1997),

> capital, now in the imperialist stage, will only disappear with an ecological solution of production (and of consumption) which will constitute the only possible elimination of the outdated structures of dominance, aggressiveness, competitiveness, and absolutism in order to replace them with those of cooperation and equality between individuals (thus between sexes), and of the species with the environment.
>
> p. 2

However, based on the press coverage and a sense-making analysis of the environmental coverage this seems far from happening. In other words, instead of developing a "partnership ethic that treats humans (including male and female partners) as equals in personal, household and political relations and humans as equal partners with (rather than controlled by or dominant over) nonhuman nature" (Merchant, 1992, p. 18), the press' coverage is hierarchical and deeply entrenched within a neoliberal paradigm. In other words, humans should refrain from destructive behaviour that contributes towards natural disasters and showing compassion towards all living life and Nature, or that humanity should adopt an ecofeminist view "that the existing economic order must be understood as a continuation not only of the history of capitalism but also of the history of patriarchy" (Clarke, 2001, p. 87). Capitalism, as I have argued using ecofeminist theory in this book, is at the heart of the social and environmental crisis and capitalism is intertwined with patriarchy (saed, 2017; Brownhill & Turner, 2020). The capitalist regime relies on the domination of Nature, turning it into a corporate commodity and assigning it value and this is done through a masculine ideology that produces "an irrational male-produced social order" (Salleh, 1984, p. 8). As argued by Cross (2018), "in order to protect the earth from irreparable ecological destruction we need to change the relationship we have with the natural world from one which is hierarchical and fragmented

164   *The wheel of neoliberalism*

to one which is ecologically responsive" (p. 29). Instead, capitalism (and corporate media) perpetuate the paradigm of modernity and relies on science led by "masculine way of thinking of the world" (Bordo, 1986, p. 441). This way of thinking, grounded in Cartesian dualistic objectivism, instrumentalises Nature and denies the connection of humanity and Nature and leans towards dominating Nature (Singer, 2002) and extracting resources for corporate gains. In this view, and this is visible in the press coverage, humans have the right to exploit Nature due to their central place in the universe (Godfrey, 2008), which creates us vs them discourse in relationship with Nature, the latter being othered by capitalism and patriarchy and dominated. This view led to the rise in scientific experiments and "masculine" rationalist paradigm (Singer, 2002, p. 198) ultimately resulting in the rise of technology, nowadays seen as a solution to environmental problems rather than confronting capitalism and consumption as a solution to environmental problems. This relationship presents a particular hierarchy where humanity is seen as superior to Nature and this is present in the coverage of environmental affairs where the media speak only on humanity and there are even direct interventions to change the environmental coverage to focus on the impact on humans to instigate action as there is no sense of empathy among people to react on the destruction of Nature alone. While at the outset, it may appear that the media are trying to instigate action in any way possible, which would be admirable, the problem is that the media do not challenge patriarchal and capitalist structures that brought about climate change in the first place. Because of the capitalist inequality and a system in which eco products are often more expensive and promoted by middle classes, working-class people are often alienated due to the lack of agency and purchase power to participate in the eco-movement (Topić et al., 2021). This is then also dangerously perpetuated by the media, in the case of *Daily Mail* by directly playing into this sentiment, or in the case of *The Guardian*, likely unintentionally, by writing Christmas shopping lists of eco products that often cost more and are not easily available to people who might be working on zero-hour contracts and thus having several jobs or working long hours when work is available. Leahy (2003) argues that some working-class people see the environmental movement as a middle-class movement that pushes for one particular agenda without consideration of an effect on working classes while some middle-class people will see the environmental movement as a threat to capitalist enterprises from which they profit, and thus those part of middle classes who advocate for environmental protection are sometimes seen as traitors of their class. It is indeed true that the environmental movement has always had links with anti-consumerism (Roszak, 1992) and often with the middle classes. As Hugo Blanco (a former peasant leader in Peru) wrote,

> at first sight, environmentalists or conservationists are nice, slightly crazy guys whose main purpose in life is to prevent the disappearance

The wheel of neoliberalism 165

of blue whales or pandas. The common people have more important things to think about, for instance how to get their daily bread...

Blanco (1991, cited from Martínez-Alier, 1997, p. 97)

This discourse has been identified in *Daily Mail*, as already mentioned, and thus presents a challenge for the success of the environmentalist movement and making a positive change in the way we treat Nature, especially since even newspapers that nominally support the environmental cause do this within a neoliberal paradigm of fostering economic growth and the use of resources (*The Guardian*).

This leads to the question of how this capitalist system perpetuates itself without conflict. As I have argued throughout the book, CSR can be seen as one of the tools that help perpetuate capitalism and preserves the status quo and with the mere existence of this concept, based on consumption and economic growth, environmental damage is unavoidable (Salleh, 2000, 1994; Shiva, 1999; d'Eaubonne, 1997; Georgescu-Roegen, 1971; Meadows et al., 1972, 2004; Ehrlich & Holdren, 1971; Cleveland et al., 1984; Trentmann, 2016; Wright & Nyberg, 2015; Krstić & Krstić, 2017; Coghlan, 2009; Corrigan, 1997; Douthwaite, 1999; Mishan, 1967; Ewen & Ewen, 1992; Calder, 1990; Krstić, 2018; Wright & Nyberg, 2015; Krstić et al., 2018; Fleming & Jones, 2013; Ireland & Pillay, 2013; Sheehy, 2014). CSR can also be seen, speaking in ecofeminist terms, as a hierarchical policy where some corporate managers take information from consumers and react with changes to CSR policies in an attempt to influence public perceptions and contribute to public relations activities (Topić et al., 2020a; Sandoval, 2013; Alves, 2009). As argued in some research studies, companies do not do good of their own will but because this discourse has been imposed onto them. While some authors argued this is a sign of socialist undermining of the free market system (Friedman, 1962, 1970), I am arguing this imposition saved capitalism. What is particularly relevant, and the reason I see CSR as part of the wheel of neoliberalism is that the concept emerged at the time of debates on businesses and their role in society, and the concept got operationalised during Reagan's and Thatcher's *neoliberalisation* of economies (Pillay, 2015) and consequentially the environment and environmental affairs.

In other words, the rise of CSR is linked to the rise on debates on sustainable development, and the first initiatives achieved the only institutionalising neoliberal approaches to sustainability, e.g. Brundtland Report by the World Commission on Environment and Development in 1987; this report was then further promoted at UNCED Earth Summit in Rio de Janeiro in 1992 (Böhm et al., 2012; Chatterjee & Finger, 1994; Bernstein, 2002; Bruno & Kerliner, 2002). These initiatives promoted a view, which is also promoted by the press,

1) that free trade regimes and high economic growth rates are not only compatible with, but are important preconditions for, environmental

166 *The wheel of neoliberalism*

sustainability, and, 2) that market-based tools are the most appropriate instruments to apply in efforts to achieve that goal.

Bernstein (2002, p. 101)

The Kyoto Protocol of 1997 for tackling climate change is part of this neoliberal agenda too (Böhm et al., 2012) and this is especially the case since the proposal for the Kyoto Protocol is based on a premise that countries need to create profit to invest into the decarbonising global economy (Newell & Paterson, 2010). In addition to this, some authors argued that neoliberal and market-driven initiatives are not addressing a problem such as climate change, and have a negative social, environmental and economic impact while benefiting the elite in developed countries and exploiting the under-privileged (Lohmann, 2006, 2008a, 2008b, 2009a, 2009b, 2010; Whiteman et al., 2010). Nevertheless, there is no agreement in the Global North on reducing or abandoning the economic growth and even scholars and activists are still polarised about the issue where some argue that constant economic growth leads towards increased consumption and creates waste and pollution which are overwhelming the biosphere and the environment (e.g. Georgescu-Roegen, 1971; Meadows et al., 1972, 2004; d'Eaubonne, [1990] 1997; Ehrlich & Holdren, 1971; Cleveland et al., 1984) while others argue that economic growth can go together with environmental protection because an increase in income will make people pay attention to environmental affairs more and this will also be addressed with the growth of the information society (Shafik and Bandyopadhyay, 1992; Panayotou, 1993; Grossman & Krueger, 1991, 1994; Selden & Song, 1994). Marx and Engels (1975) argued that capitalism constantly pushes for economic development and this often goes beyond the limits of controllable growth, which is why major crises tend to occur. These crises include global economic crashes (e.g. 2008) and environmental crises and this results from "capitalism's persistent tendency to deplete natural resources and generate externalities, i.e. environmental costs that are 'dumped' onto nature and society without being accounted for within the capitalist processes of valuation, production and exchange" (Böhm et al., 2012, p. 3). However, these crises so far did not endanger capitalism to a large extent and the system always re-invents itself with new accumulations and legitimations that are being introduced (Moore, 2010; Marx & Engels, 1964; 1975; Marx, 1981). Therefore, I am arguing that CSR can also be seen as part of capitalism's new re-invention where corporations are seen to doing good to society but what lies underneath is excessive production and consumption that depletes resources and causes damage that will become beyond repair unless a meaningful change in economic policy is done.

In other words, it was during the 1970s that popular discontent arose against business also because of recession and inflation, which led to increased talks on CSR (Latapí Agudelo et al., 2019), and during the 1980s CSR got operationalised. This operationalisation came as a result of the

The wheel of neoliberalism 167

Reagan and Thatcher administrations, both keen on reducing the pressure on corporations. Reagan and Thatcher saw the growth and strengthening of economies as an imperative for maintaining the free market environment and minimum state intervention (Pillay, 2015). Thatcherism as a politics was predominantly oriented towards the weakening of working classes, adoption of monetarism, public expenditure cuts, privatisation, attacks on the position of organised labour and opening the economy towards international collaboration, thus replacing Keynesian style of the economy centred on sheltering labour markets and prices (Nunn, 2014; Gamble, 1989; Jessop, 2003). Reaganomics and Thatcherism became symbols of neoliberalism, and CSR operationalisation was born in this context and from two neoliberal politicians, thus signalling the use of CSR as a means to save capitalism in the time of unrest and anti-corporate discourse that developed in the West.

The opening of markets in the situation of social discontent led to the situation that corporations were still facing public hostility and especially from various interest groups to fulfil social role so scholars started to look at business ethics and various concepts of CSR (Carroll, 2008; Wankel, 2008). As argued by Latapí Agudelo et al. (2019) there were different societal concerns during the 1980s and this included sustainable development accompanied by corporate behaviour, and,

> some of the initiatives that happened at the time were the creation of the European Commission's Environment Directorate-General (1981), the establishment of the World Commission on Environment and Development chaired by the Norwegian Prime Minister Gro Harlem Brundtland (1983), the Chernobyl nuclear disaster (1986), the publication of the report Our Common Future presented by the Brundtland Commission which provided a definition of sustainable development (1987), the United Nations (UN) adoption of the Montreal Protocol (1987), and the creation of the Intergovernmental Panel on Climate Change (IPCC) (1988).
>
> n.p.

Therefore, environmental protection and corporate conduct came to the public agenda through increased awareness of environmental concerns and sustainable development, which was then linked with corporate behaviour. Carroll (2008) argued that the major societal concerns about corporate conduct during the 1980s were "environmental pollution, employment discrimination, consumer abuses, employee health and safety, quality of work-life, deterioration of urban life, and questionable/abusiveness practices of multinational corporations" (p. 36). This, according to Carroll (2008) prompted scholars to look into business ethics and stakeholder management instead, for example, the role of capitalism in environmental degradation. However, this is the period when CSR implementation and scholarship started to rise. This was further exacerbated during the 1990s when the concept of CSR

168 *The wheel of neoliberalism*

gained international recognition, with prominent documents and events influencing this change, such as,

> the creation of the European Environment Agency (1990), the UN summit on the Environment and Development held in Rio de Janeiro which led to the Rio Declaration on Environment and Development, the adoption of Agenda 21 and the United Nations Framework Convention on Climate Change (UNFCCC) (1992), and the adoption of the Kyoto Protocol (1997).
>
> Latapí Agudelo et al. (2019, n.p.)

This leads to the media and CSR. The view I promoted in this book is that while the CSR concept is incomprehensible for a variety of reasons and that CSR serves to save capitalism, media have responsibilities towards societies. van Liedekerke (2004) argued that the role of media in society is more important than the role of, for example, traditional corporations because media have an impact on social norms and values. Many authors argued that media have to be independent, objective, pluralistic and truthful because of the power they have over the public (McQuail, 1997, 2003, 2005; Napoli, 1999). However, since media also compete in the market and have economic goals, many authors argued that economic values replaced social and editorial values, which eroded media social responsibility and threatens democratic standards (Ingenhoff & Koelling, 2012). Marx ([1849] 1959) argued decades ago that the press has to serve as a watchdog and "the tireless denouncer of those in power, the omnipresent eye, the omnipresent mouthpiece of the people's spirit that jealously guards its freedom" (p. 231, cited from Sandoval, 2013, pp. 44–45). However, for this to happen Marx argued that the press would need to be independent and non-commercial, or as Marx put it, "not being a trade" (ibid). Some authors therefore argued that media need to be studied within the context of capitalism and as part of the political economy (Sandoval, 2013; Mosco, 2009; Herman & Chomsky, 1988; Garnham, 1998), which is what I did in this book by analysing the media and their coverage not just of environmental affairs but also economic growth and CSR.

It can indeed be argued that commercial interests are impairing the social work of the media because media are generating a private profit and this inevitably includes working in the free market and with a commercial goal means that media fall under the market pressure and this then means also uniformity and conformism (Garnham, [1986] 2006; Smythe, [1977] 1997; Fuchs, 2011, 2010; Horkheimer & Adorno, [1947] 1997; Herman & Chomsky, 1988; Schiller, 1997; McChesney, 2004) as well as a threat to democracy (Schiller & Schiller, 1988). Sandoval (2013) thus argued that any voluntary CSR concept is deeply flawed because corporations will not go the extra mile if it affects their profit and will do what they absolutely have to. Applying this to the media, which are also functioning as corporations, this would mean that the

The wheel of neoliberalism 169

media will not necessarily engage with social interest if it undermines their strive for profit. Sandoval (2013) thus proposes that the media system needs to go beyond CSR and turn CSR on its head and renamed and reconceptualised to Responsibility to Socialise Corporations (RSC). This means that "in order to become truly social, capitalist corporations need to be socialised, so that private wealth turns into common wealth. Socialising the media means to replace the privately controlled commercial media system with a socially controlled non-commercial media system" (p. 52). Therefore, instead of relying on corporate self-conduct and willingness to give something, this approach would "expand democratic social control over corporate conduct and to restrict corporate power. This can be achieved through government regulation on the one hand and pressure from civil society groups on the other hand" (p. 52). With this approach, according to Sandoval (2013), media could contribute towards the common good because they would be free from commercialising pressure and the pressure to maximise profit.

What appeared in the analysis done for this book is that the media coverage falls within the neoliberal paradigm and environmental degradation regardless of intentions, for example of *The Guardian*. This is because media promote capitalist policies of economic growth, the domination of Nature and work within patriarchal structures in which women have very little power in news sections such as economy. If we apply the analysis from this book to recommendations from the Hutchins Commission, it becomes clear that the press failed in "serving as a forum for the exchange of comment and criticism" (Bivins, 2004) because the communication and editorial policies seem very asymmetrical and as one-way communication, while the press also fails in providing a "truthful, comprehensive, and intelligent account of the day's events in a context that gives meaning" (ibid) because, as shown in the analysis in this book, the press does not provide meaningful coverage of environmental affairs but either criticise the environmental movement thus causing damage to Nature and humanity alike or they nominally support environmental affairs but fail to meaningfully engage with solutions and thus risk saturating the coverage and causing the lack of action from readers due to an incessant and excessive coverage that does not lead to a sustainable solution. The question remains whether a normally unpopular suggestion of press regulation should be considered or perhaps turning the media system into not-for-profit organisations which would be independently funded? It is hard to imagine a meaningful change while the press competes in the open market and falls under the influence of media owners, many of whom are billionaires and thus naturally have an interest in keeping the status quo. Owens-Ibie (1994) correctly argued that media are responsible to citizens, government, media owners and also to themselves and failing in fulfilling this four-tier responsibility decreases trust and accountability, which then harms responsibility itself.

The notion of regulation is opposed by Libertarian theorists and this view is grounded in liberalism and the ideas of John Stuart Mill. Libertarians

170 *The wheel of neoliberalism*

defend media against the regulation using the principles of the free market where ideas are also seen as part of the free market. Thus, the tension between economic and social interests that journalists face when reporting on issues of the day are, according to libertarians, a natural and healthy choice that should not be regulated because it would undermine journalistic autonomy. This view also argues that journalists make up their minds when reporting on issues spontaneously and thus regulation would undermine this autonomy (Middleton, 2009). Journalistic codes are seen as an effective instrument to ensure balanced coverage and integrity of professional standards; however, criticism has emerged over the years as to whether all journalists pay attention to codes and some authors argued that codes are often used by media organisations to justify susceptible behaviour (Plaisance, 2000). Nevertheless, some authors argued that market conditions and corporatism affect journalists (Richards, 2004; McQuail, 2010) who work in the open market and this contradicts ethics and prevents fully ethical practice (Sandoval, 2013). However, as argued by Ward (2008) this view presents a "disillusionment with the liberal hope that an unregulated press would be a responsible educator of citizens on matters of public interests" (p. 298) and this means that the liberal press is failing to serve its social role. It seems, indeed, to be the truth that the free-market orientation of the press does not contribute to democracy or well-being of the society due to climate change, with which media abuse their social influence and can be seen as causing harm for corporate interests by perpetuating neoliberalism in their coverage. Thus, instead of relying on codes of practices, we should introduce freedom of journalists to report as they please and in return, they cover public issues and contribute towards the well-being of society (Ward, 2008; Klaidman, 1987; Kovach & Rosenstiel, 2001). In addition to this, media should be free from external influence; however, publishing information is not a freedom but a duty because issues of public interest must have a place on the media agenda (Ward, 2008). In other words, we do not necessarily need to regulate the press, but we need to look into ways of de-privatising it and creating socially responsible media outlets. While it would be incomprehensible to nationalise existing media corporations in a neoliberal Britain, what needs to be done is creating funding for not-for-profit media organisations that could, through public funding, eventually compete with the mainstream media and force change while not being reliant on the open market and its rules of competition, masculinity and hierarchy.

If no meaningful change in the media system happens, the wheel of neoliberalism will continue to perpetuate itself and while, in the future, the concept of CSR might diminish in relevance, there will be some other initiative that will perpetuate capitalism and consumption. Therefore, a meaningful change is necessary to make the press socially responsible so that people are not continually fed one-sided views of the economic system, in this case, capitalist, but for people to receive impartial information from all sides on the society in which they live in, and on personal obligations on each of us

The wheel of neoliberalism 171

to make a meaningful change. At the moment, calls on the public to act in this or that way only leads towards further liberalisation of the market and corporations self-regulating with some shady policing from the neoliberal media and the public. A meaningful change towards preserving Nature, and this includes humanity, can only happen if we fundamentally change how we live and if we change the economic system from capitalism, economic growth and excessive consumption to a more sustainable world that respects the rights of all living and non-living species in Nature and that does not abuse resources for profit. The press has the power to instigate this change and truly serve the interests of the society in which they work; however, this will not happen while the press is privatised and commercialised as is the case at the present.

References

Abendroth, A.-K., Melzer, S., Kalev, A., & Tomaskovic-Devey, D. (2017). Women at work: Women's access to power and the gender earnings gap. *Industrial and Labor Relations Review*, 70(1), 190–222.

Acker, J. (2009). From glass ceiling to inequality regimes. *Sociologie du travail*, 51(2), 199–217.

Acker, J. (2006). Inequality regimes: Gender, class, and race in organizations. *Gender & Society*, 20(4), 441–464.

Acker, J. (1990). Hierarchies, jobs, bodies: A theory of gendered organizations. *Gender & Society*, 4(2), 139–158.

Adams. C. (2017). Derrida and the sexual politics of meat. In – Potts, A. (ed), *Meat Culture*. Leiden: Brill, pp. 31–54.

Adams, R. B. (2016). Women on boards: The superheroes of tomorrow? *Leadership Quarterly*, 27(3), 371–386.

Adams, C. (2010). Why feminist-vegan now? *Feminism & Psychology*, 20(3), 302–317.

Adams, C. (2007). Caring about suffering. In – Adams, C., & Donovan, J. (eds), *The Feminist Care Tradition in Animal Ethics*. New York: Columbia University Press, pp.170–196.

Adams, C. (1991). *The Sexual Politics of Meat. A Feminist-Vegetarian Critical Theory*. New York: Continuum.

Adler, D., & Wargan, P. (2019). Stop polluting our green new deal. *Jacobin*, 6th November. Retrieved from https://jacobinmag.com/2019/06/green-new-deal-europe-capitalism.

Agarwal, B. (1992). The gender and environment debate: Lessons from India. *Feminist Studies*, 18(1), 119–158.

Aldoory, L., & Toth, E. (2002). Gender discrepancies in a gendered profession: A developing theory for public relations. *Journal of Public Relations Research*, 14(2), 103–126.

Allen, M. R., Dube, O. P., Solecki, W., Aragón-Durand, F., Cramer, W., Humphreys, S., Kainuma, M., Kala, J., Mahowald, N., Mulugetta, Y., Perez, R., Wairiu, M., & Zickfeld, K. (2018). Framing and context. In – Masson-Delmotte, V., Zhai, P., Pörtner, H.-O., Roberts, D., Skea, J., Shukla, P. R., Pirani, A., Moufouma-Okia, W., Péan, C., Pidcock, R., Connors, S., Matthews, J. B. R., Chen, Y., Zhou, X., Gomis, M. I., Lonnoy, E., Maycock, T., Tignor, M., & Waterfield, T. (eds), Global warming of 1.5°C. An IPCC. *Special Report on the Impacts of Global Warming of 1.5°C above Pre-industrial Levels and Related Global Greenhouse Gas Emission*

174 *References*

Pathways, in the Context of Strengthening the Global Response to the Threat of Climate Change, Sustainable Development, and Efforts to Eradicate Poverty. Retrieved from https://www.ipcc.ch/site/assets/uploads/sites/2/2019/05/SR15_Chapter1_Low_Res.pdf.

Alonso-Almeida, M. d. M. (2012). Water and waste management in the Moroccan tourism industry: The case of three women entrepreneurs. *Women's Studies International Forum*, 35(5), 343–353.

Ali, M., Ng, Y. L., & Kulik, C. T. (2014). Board age and gender diversity: A test of competing linear and curvilinear predictions. *Journal of Business Ethics*, 125(3), 497–512.

Alimo Metcalfe, B. (1995). An investigation of female and male constructs of leadership and empowerment. *Women in Management Review*, 10(2), 3–8.

Alloun, E. (2015). Ecofeminism and animal advocacy in Australia: Productive encounters for an integrative ethics and politics. *Animal Studies Journal*, 4(1), 148–173.

Alves, I. M. (2009). Green spin everywhere: How greenwashing reveals the limits of the CSR paradigm. *Journal of Global Change and Governance*, II(1), 1–26.

Alvesson, M. (2013). *Understanding Organisational Culture*, 2nd edition. London: SAGE.

Alvesson, M. (1998). Gender relations and identity at work: A case study of masculinities and femininities in an advertising agency. *Human Relations*, 51(8), 969–1005.

Anderson, N., Lievens, F., Van Dam, K., & Born, M. (2006). A construct-driven investigation of gender differences in a leadership-role assessment center. *Journal of Applied Psychology*, 91, 555–566.

Archambault, A. (1993). A critique of ecofeminism. *Canadian Woman Studies/les cahiers de la femme*, 13(3), 19–22.

Arenas, D., J. M. Lozano, & L. Albareda. 2009. The role of NGOs in CSR: Mutual perceptions among stakeholders. *Journal of Business Ethics*, 88(1), 175–197.

Arrow, K. J., Bolin, R., Constanza, P., Dasgupta, C., Folke, S., Holling, B. O., Jansson, S., Levin, K. G., Maler, C., Perrings, & Pimentel, D. (1995). Economic growth, carrying capacity, and the environment. *Science*, 268, 520–521.

Asefi-Najafabady, S., Villegas-Ortiz, L., & Morgan, J. (2020). The failure of integrated assessment models as a response to 'climate emergency' and ecological breakdown: The emperor has no clothes. *Globalizations*, https://doi.org/10.1080/14747731.2020.1853958.

Ashforth, B. E., & Gibbs, B. W. (1990). The double-edge of organizational legitimation. *Organization Science*, 1(2), 177–194.

Avery, A., Anderson, C., & McCullough, F. (2017). Associations between children's diet quality and watching television during meal or snack consumption: A systematic review. *Pediatric Obesity/Etiology*, 13, 124–28.

Bakker, K. (2007). The commons versus the commodity: Alter-globalization, anti-privatization and the human right to water in the global south. *Antipode*, 39(3), 430–455.

Bakker, K. (2005). Neoliberalizing nature? Market environmentalism in water supply in England and Wales. *Annals of the Association of the American Geographers*, 95(3), 542–565.

Bahofen, J. J. (1990). *Matrijarhat*. Sremski Karlovci: Izdavačka knjižnica Zorana Stojanovića.

References   175

Bahta, D., Yun, J., Rashidul Islam, M., & Bikanyi, K. J. (2020). How does CSR enhance the financial performance of SMEs? The mediating role of firm reputation. *Economic Research-Ekonomska Istraživanja*. Retrieved from https://www.tandfonline.com/doi/pdf/10.1080/1331677X.2020.1828130.

Bajželj, B., Richards, K. S., Allwood, J. M., Smith, P., Dennis, J. S., Curmi, E., & Gillian, C. A. (2014). Importance of food-demand management for climate mitigation. *Nature Climate Change*, 4, 924–929.

Bandyopadhyay, J. (1999). Chipko movement: Of floated myths and flouted realities. *Economic and Political Weekly*, April 10, 880–882.

Banerjee, S. B. (2014). A critical perspective on corporate social responsibility: Towards a global governance framework. *Critical Perspectives on International Business*, 10(1–2), 84–95. Retrieved from https://openaccess.city.ac.uk/id/eprint/6083/.

Banford, A., & Froude, C. K. (2015). Ecofeminism and natural disasters: Sri Lankan women post-tsunami. *Journal of International Women's Studies*, 16(2), 170–187.

Baran, S. J., & Davis, D. K. (2012). *Mass Communication Theory: Foundations, Ferment, and Future* (6th edition). Boston, MA: Wadsworth Cengage Learning.

Bardoel, J., & d'Haenens, L. (2004). Media meet the citizen: Beyond market mechanisms and government regulations. *European Journal of Communication*, 19(2), 165–194.

Baron, D. P. (2005). Competing for the public through the news media. *Journal of Economics and Management Strategy*, 14, 339–376.

Barry, N. (2002). The stakeholder concept of corporate control is illogical and impractical. *The Independent Review*, 6(4), 541–554.

Barry, N. (2000). Do corporations have any responsibility beyond making a profit? *Journal of Markets & Morality*, 3(1), 100–107.

Bates, S. (2017). Is this the best philosophy can do? Henry R. Luce and a free and responsible press. *Journalism & Mass Communication Quarterly*, 95(3), 811–834.

Baverstock, A. (2020). Majority of Brits can't identify plastics in multiple household items. *IPSOS Mori*. Retrieved from https://www.ipsos.com/ipsos-mori/en-uk/majority-brits-cant-identify-plastics-multiple-household-items#:~:text=A%20new%20Omnibus%20survey%20by, household%20items%20that%20contain%20plastics.&text=Overall%2C%20almost%20eight%20in%20ten, by%20unnecessary%20use%20of%20plastic.

Bawdon, F. (2012). Seen but not heard: how women make front page news. *Report for Women in Journalism Organisation*. Retrieved from http://womeninjournalism.co.uk/wp-content/uploads/2012/10/Seen_but_not_heard.pdf.

Bear, S., Rahman, N., & Post, C. (2010). The impact of board diversity and gender composition on corporate social responsibility and firm reputation. *Journal of Business Ethics*, 97(2), 207–221.

Ben-Amar, W., Chang, M., & McIlkenny, P. (2017). Board gender diversity and corporate response to sustainability initiatives: Evidence from the carbon disclosure project. *Journal of Business Ethics*, 142(2), 369–383.

Benson, R. (2008). Normative theories of journalism. In – Donsbach, W. (ed), *The Blackwell International Encyclopedia of Communication* (Vol. VI). London: Blackwell, pp. 2591–2597.

Berens, G., & T. Popma, W. T. (2014). Creating consumer confidence in CSR communications. In – Tench, R., Sun, W., & Jones, B. (eds), *Communicating Corporate Social Responsibility: Perspectives and Practice* (pp. 383–405). Howard House: Emerald Books.

176 *References*

Berman, S. L., Wicks, A. C., Kotha, S., & Jones, T. M. (1999). Does stakeholder orientation matter? The relationship between stakeholder management models and firm financial performance. *Academy of Management Review*, 42, 488–506.

Bernardi, R. A., & Threadgill, V. H. (2010). Women directors and corporate social responsibility. *Electronic Journal of Business Ethics and Organizational Studies*, 15(2), 15–21.

Bernstein, S. (2002). *The Compromise of Liberal Environmentalism*. New York: Columbia University Press.

Besthorn, F. H., & Pearson McMillen, D. (2002). The oppression of women and nature: Ecofeminism as a framework for an expanded ecological social work. *Families in Society: The Journal of Contemporary Human Services*, 83(3), 221–232.

Birkeland, J. (1995). Disengendering ecofeminism. *Trumpeter*, 12(4), 2–6. Retrieved from http://www.icaap.org/iuicode?6.12.4.10.

Birth, G., & Illia, L. (2008). Communicating CSR: Practices among Switzerland's top 300 companies. *Corporate Communications: An International Journal*, 13(2), 182–196.

Bivins, T. (2004). *Mixed Media: Moral Distinctions in Advertising, Public Relations, and Journalism*. Mahwah: Lawrence Erlbaum Associates Publishers.

Black, L., Matvienko-Sikar, K., & Kearney, P. M. (2017). The association between childcare arrangements and risk of overweight and obesity in childhood: A systematic review. *Pediatric Obesity/Etiology*, 18, 1170–1190.

Blaikie, N. (1992). The nature and origins of ecological world views: An Australian study. *Social Science Quarterly*, 73(1), 144–165.

Bloch, R. H. (1978). American feminine ideals in transition: The rise of the moral mother, 1785–1815. *Feminist Studies*, 4(2), 101–126.

Blowfield, M., & Frynas, J. G. (2005). Setting new agendas: Critical perspectives on corporate social responsibility in the developing world. *International Affairs*, 81(3), 499–513.

Blowfield, M. (2005). Corporate social responsibility: Reinventing the meaning of development? *International Affairs*, 81(3), 515–524.

Boero, N. (2007). All the news that's fat to print: The American "obesity epidemic" and the media. *Qualitative Sociology*, 30(1), 41–60.

Böhm, S., Misoczky, M. C., & Moog, S. (2012). Greening capitalism? A Marxist critique of carbon markets. *Organization Studies*, 1–22. Retrieved from https://core.ac.uk/download/pdf/16387374.pdf.

Boomgaarden, H. G., & Vliegenthart, R. (2007). Explaining the rise of anti-immigrant parties: The role of news media content. *Electoral Studies*, 26(2), 404–417.

Booth, A. (2000). Ways of knowing: Acceptable understandings within bioregionalism, deep ecology, ecofeminism, and native American culture. *The Trumpeter*, 16(1), 1–14.

Bordo, S. (1986). The Cartesian masculinity of thought. *Journal of Women in Culture and Society*, 11(3), 439–456.

Borrelle, S. B., Ringma, J., Lavender, K., Law, C., Monnahan, C., Laurent Lebreton, L., McGivern, A., Murphy, E., Jambeck, J., George, H. L., Hilleary, M. A., Eriksen, M., Possingham, H. P., De Frond, H., Gerber, L. R., Polidoro, B., Tahir, A., Bernard, M., Mallos, N., Barnes, M., & Rochman, C. M. (2020). Plastic pollution: Predicted growth in plastic waste exceeds efforts to mitigate plastic pollution. *Science*, 369, 1515–1518. Retrieved from https://conservation-innovation.lab.asu.edu/wp-content/uploads/2020/09/Borrelle_etal_2020.pdf.

References 177

Borrelle, S. B., Rochman, C. M., Liboiron, M., Bond, A. L., Lusher, A., Bradshaw, H., & Provencher, J. F. (2017). Opinion: Why we need an international agreement on marine plastic pollution. *PNAS: Proceedings of the National Academy of Sciences of the United States of America. PNAS*, September 19, 114(38), 9994–9997. Retrieved from https://doi.org/10.1073/pnas.1714450114 https://www.pnas.org/content/114/38/9994.

Bourdieu, P. (2007). *Masculine Domination*. Cambridge: Polity Press.

Bourdieu, P., & Wacquant, L. (1992). *An Invitation to Reflexive Sociology*. Cambridge: Polity Press.

Bowen, H. (1953). *The Social Responsibility of the Businessman*. New York: Harper.

Bowie, N. E. (2012). *Corporate Social Responsibility in Business. A Commissioned Background Paper about Corporate Social Responsibility in Business as It Relates to the Creation of Public Value*. Retrieved from http://www.leadership.umn.edu/documents/Bowie5-30.pdf.

Bowie, N. E. (1991). New directions in corporate social responsibility. *Business Horizons*, 34(4), 56–65.

Boucher, J., & Billard, G. (2019). The challenges of measuring plastic pollution. Field actions. *Science Reports*, 19. Retrieved from http://journals.openedition.org/factsreports/5319.

Boucher, J., & Friot. D. (2017). *Primary Microplastics in the Oceans: A Global Evaluation of Sources*. IUCN. Retrieved from https://www.iucn.org/content/primary-microplastics-oceans.

Boulouta, I. (2013). Hidden connections: The link between board gender diversity and corporate social performance. *Journal of Business Ethics*, 113(2), 185–197.

Braidotti, R., Charkiewicz, E., Hausler, S., & Wieringa, S. (1995). *Women, the Environment and Sustainable Development: Towards a Theoretical Synthesis*. London: Zed Books.

Brammer, S., & Millington, A. (2008). Does it pay to be different? An analysis of the relationship between corporate social and financial performance. *Strategic Management Journal*, 29, 1325–1343.

Branco, M. C., & Rodrigues, L. L. (2007). Positioning stakeholder theory within the debate on corporate social responsibility. *EJBO: Electronic Journal of Business Ethics and Organization Studies*, 12(1), 5–15.

Branco, M. C. (2006). Communication of corporate social responsibility by Portuguese banks: A legitimacy theory perspective. *Corporate Communications: An International Journal*, 11(3), 232–248.

Brédart, H. (2017). Burnout among journalists, a symptom of discontent in newsrooms. *Hesamag*, 15, 12–16. Retrieved from https://www.etui.org/sites/default/files/Hesamag_15_EN_12-16.pdf.

Breed, W. (1955). Newspaper opinion leaders and the process of standardization. *Journalism Quarterly*, 32, 277–284.

Brenner, N., Peck, J., & Theodore, N. (2010). Variegated neoliberalization: Geographies, modalities, pathways. *Global Networks*, 10(2), 182–222.

Bridge, G. (2004). Mapping the bonanza: Geographies of mining investment in an era of neoliberal reform. *The Professional Geographer*, 56(3), 406–421.

British Social Attitudes (2011). Retrieved from http://www.natcen.ac.uk/study/british-socialattitudes-28th-report.

Bronson, D. (2009). Geoengineering: A gender issue? *Isis International Publication*, 2, 83–87. Retrieved from http://www.isiswomen.org/index.php?option=com_content&view=article&id=1389:geoengineering-a-gender-issue&catid=162.

178 *References*

Brook Lyndhurst (2007). *Food Behaviour Consumer Research – Findings from the Quantitative Survey*. Briefing paper UK: WRAP.

Broom, G. M. (1982). A comparison of sex roles in public relations. *Public Relations Review*, 8(3), 17–22.

Brown, T. J., & Dacin, P. A. (1997). The company and the product: Corporate associations and consumer product responses. *Journal of Marketing*, 61, 68–84.

Brownhill, L., & Turner, T. E. (2020). Ecofeminist ways, ecosocialist means: Life in the post-capitalist future. *Capitalism Nature Socialism*, 31(1), 1–14.

Brownhill, L., & Turner, T. E. (2019). Ecofeminism and the heart of ecosocialism. *Capitalism, Nature Socialism*, 30(1), 1–10.

Brownhill, L. (2010). Earth democracy and ecosocialism: What's in a name? *Capitalism Nature Socialism*, 21(1), 96–99.

Broyles, S. L., & Grow, J. M. (2008). Creative women in advertising agencies: Why so few "babes in Boyland"? *Journal of Consumer Marketing*, 25(1), 4–6. Retrieved from https://epublications.marquette.edu/cgi/viewcontent.cgi?referer=https://www.google.com/&httpsredir=1&article=1021&context=comm_fac&sei-redir=1.

Brundtland Commission (1987). *Our Common Future: Report of the World Commission on Environment and Development. UN Documents Gathering a Body of Global Agreements*. Retrieved from https://sustainabledevelopment.un.org/content/documents/5987our-common-future.pdf.

Bruno, K., & Karliner, J. (2002). *Earthsummit.Biz: The Corporate Take-over of Sustainable Development*. Oakland, CA: Food First Books.

Buck, H. J., Gammon, A. R., & Preston, C. (2014). Gender and geoengineering. *Hypatia*, 29(3), 651–669.

Buckingham, S. (2004). Ecofeminism in the twenty-first century. *The Geographical Journal*, 170(2), 146–154.

Buhr, H., & Grafström, M. (2006). *The Making in the Media: The Case of Corporate Social Responsibility in the 'Financial Times', 1988–2003*. Retrieved from http://www.fek.uu.se/gems/publications/Buhr_Grafstrom_CSR_2006.pdf.

Burchell, J., & Cook, J. (2006). It's good to talk? Examining attitudes towards corporate social responsibility dialogue and engagement processes. *Business Ethics*, 15(2), 154–170.

Buzov, I. (2020). Socijalna perspektiva ekofeminizma. In – Marjanić, S., & Đurđević, G. (eds), *Ekofeminizam – između ženskih i zelenih studija*. Zagreb: Durieux, pp. 81–101.

Cahan, S. F., Chen, C., Chen, L., & Nguyen, N. H. (2015). Corporate social responsibility and media coverage. *Journal of Banking & Finance*, 59, 409–422.

Calder, L. G. (1990). *Financing the American Dream: A Cultural History of Consumer Credit*. Princeton, NJ: Princeton University Press.

Cammaerts, B., DeCillia, B., Magalhães, J., & Jimenez-Martínez, C. (2016). Journalistic representations of Jeremy Corbyn in the British Press: From watchdog to attackdog. *London School of Economics and Political Science – Academic Report on Journalistic Representations of Jeremy Corbyn*. Retrieved from https://www.lse.ac.uk/media-and-communications/assets/documents/research/projects/corbyn/Cobyn-Report.pdf.

Campbell, A. (2016). The lady vanishes. *Women in Journalism Organisation Report* (n.d). Retrieved from http://womeninjournalism.co.uk/the-lady-vanishes-at-45/.

References   179

Campbell, J. L. (2007). Why would corporations behave in socially responsible ways? An institutional theory of corporate social responsibility. *Academy of Management Review,* 32(3), 946–967.

Canavan, G., Klarr, L., & Vu, R. (2010). Embodied materialism in action: An interview with Ariel Salleh. *Polygraph,* 22, 183–1999.

Cardoso, A. R., & Winter-Ebmer, R. (2010). Female-led firms and gender wage policies. *Industrial and Labor Relations Review,* 64(1), 143–163.

Carlassare, E. (1994). Essentialism in ecofeminist discourse. In – Merchant, C. (ed), *Ecology.* Atlantic Highlands, NJ: Humanities Press.

Carroll, C. E. (2011). Media relations and corporate social responsibility. In – Øyvind, I., Bartlett, J. L., & May, S. (eds), *The Handbook of Communication and Corporate Social Responsibility,* 1st edition. PLACE: John Wiley & Son.

Carroll, C. E. (2010). Should firms circumvent or work through the news media? *Public Relations Review,* 36(4), 278–280.

Carroll, C. E. (2009). The relationship between firms' media favorability and public esteem. *Public Relations Journal,* 6(4), 1–32.

Carroll, A. B. (2008). A history of corporate social responsibility: Concepts and practices. In – Crane, A., Matten, D., Moon, J., & D. Siegel (eds), *The Oxford Handbook of Corporate Social Responsibility* (pp. 19–46). New York: Oxford University Press.

Carroll, C. E., & McCombs, M. (2003). Agenda-setting effects of business news on the public's images and opinions about major corporations. *Corporate Reputation Review,* 6(1), 36–46.

Carroll, A. B. (1991). The pyramid of corporate social responsibility: Toward the moral management of organizational stakeholders. *Business Horizons,* 34, 39–48.

Carroll, A. B. (1979). A three-dimensional conceptual model of corporate performance. *Academy of Management Review,* 4(4), 497–505.

Ceballos, G., Ehrlich, P. R., & Dirzo, R. (2017). Biological annihilation via the ongoing sixth mass extinction signaled by vertebrate population losses and declines. *Proceedings of the National Academy of Sciences,* 114(30), E6089–E6096, https://doi.org/10.1073/pnas.1704949114.

Chaffe, S. H., & Metzger, M. J. (2001). The end of mass communication? *Mass Communication & Society,* 4(4), 365–379.

Chaffee, E. C. (2017). The origins of corporate social responsibility. *University of Cincinnati Law Review,* 85, 347–373.

Chancel, L., & Piketty, T. (2015). *Carbon and Inequality: From Kyoto to Paris. Trends in the Global Inequality of Carbon Emissions (1998–2013) & Prospects for an Equitable Adaptation Fund. Paris School of Economics.* Retrieved from https://wid.world/document/chancel-l-piketty-t-carbon-and-inequality-from-kyoto-to-paris-wid-world-working-paper-2015-7/.

Chatterjee, P., & Finger, M. (1994). *The Earth Brokers: Power, Politics and World Development.* London: Routledge.

Chemers, M. M., Watson, C. B., & May, S. T. (2000). Dispositional affect and leadership effectiveness: A comparison of self-esteem, optimism, and efficacy. *Personality and Social Psychology Bulletin,* 26, 267–277.

Chen, C. C., & Meindl, J. R. (1991). The construction of images in the popular press. *Administrative Science Quarterly,* 36, 521–551.

180 *References*

Chomsky, N. (2002). *Media Control*. New York: Seven Stories Press.

Christensen, L. J., Peirce, E., Hartman, L. P., Hoffman, W. M., & Carrier, J. (2007). Ethics, CSR, and sustainability in the *Financial Times* top 50 global business schools: Baseline data and future research directions. *Journal of Business Ethics*, 73, 347–368.

Christmas, L. (1997). Women in journalism: Chaps of both sexes? – Women decision-makers in newspapers: Do they make a difference? *Report for Women in Journalism Organisation* (1997). Retrieved from http://womeninjournalism.co.uk/wp-content/uploads/2012/10/Chaps-of-both-Sexes.pdf.

Christopher, B. (2008). Why are women so strange and men so weird? *Business Credit*, 110, 4–8.

Cifrić, I. (1990). *Ekološka adaptacija i socijalna pobuna*. Zagreb: Radničke novine.

Ciocirlan, C., & Petterson, C. (2012). Does workforce diversity matter in the fight against climate change? An analysis of Fortune 500 companies. *Corporate Social Responsibility Management*, 19(1), 47–62.

Ciplet, D., & Roberts, T. (2017). Climate change and the transition to neoliberal environmental governance. *Global Environmental Change*, 46, 148–156.

Ciplet, D., Roberts, J. T., & Khan, M. (2015). *Power in a Warming World: The New Global Politics of Climate Change and the Remaking of Environmental Inequality*. Cambridge: MIT Press.

Clare, K. (2013). The essential role of place within the creative industries: Boundaries, networks and play. *Cities*, 34, 52–57.

Clark, C. E. (2000). Differences between public relations and corporate social responsibility: An analysis. *Public Relations Review*, 26(3), 363–380.

Clarke, J. P. (2001). Alan Dordoroy and Mary Mellor's "ecosocialism and feminism". *Capitalism Nature Socialism*, 12(1), 87–91.

Clarkson, M. B. E. (1995). A stakeholder framework for analyzing and evaluating corporate social performance. *The Academy of Management Review*, 20(1), 92–117.

Cleveland, C. J., Costanza, R., Hall, C. A. S., & Kaufmann, R. (1984). Energy and the US economy; a biophysical perspective. *Science*, 225, 890–897.

Cline, C., Toth, E., Turk, J., Walters, L., Johnson, N., & Smith, H. (1986). *The Velvet Ghetto: The Impact of the Increasing Percentage of Women in Public Relations and Business Communication*. San Francisco, CA: IABC Foundation.

Cochrane, C. (2011). Why is British public life dominated by men? *Women in Journalism Report*. Retrieved from http://womeninjournalism.co.uk/why-is-british-public-life-dominated-by-men/.

Coghlan, A. (2009). Consumerism is 'eating the future'. *The New Scientist*, 7 August. Retrieved from https://www.newscientist.com/article/dn17569-consumerism-is-eating-the-future/?ignored=irrelevant.

Collard, A., & Contrucci, J. (1988). *Rape of the Wild: Man's Violence against Animals and the Earth*. Bloomington: Indiana University Press.

Conca, K. (2006). *Governing Water. Contentious Transnational Politics and Global Institution Building*. Massachusetts Institute of Technology. Cambridge: London.

Condorcet (2012). *Political Writings. Edited by Steven Lukes and Nadia Urbinati*. Cambridge: Cambridge University Press.

Connell, R. (1987). *Gender and Power: Society, the Person and Sexual Politics*. Cambridge: Polity Press.

Conway, E. (2019). Talking up 'degrowth' is not clever or funny." *The Times*, 9th August.

Corrigan, P. (1997). *The Sociology of Consumption: An Introduction*. London: SAGE.

References 181

Corson, C. (2010). Shifting environmental governance in a neoliberal world: US AID for conservation. *Antipode*, 42(3), 576–602.

Couldry, N., & Cammaerts, N. (2016). Foreword. Journalistic representations of Jeremy Corbyn in the British Press: From watchdog to attackdog. *London School of Economics and Political Science – Academic Report on Journalistic Representations of Jeremy Corbyn*. Retrieved from https://www.lse.ac.uk/media-and-communications/assets/documents/research/projects/corbyn/Cobyn-Report.pdf.

Craft, S., & Wanta, W. (2004). Women in the newsroom: Influences of female editors and reporters on the news agenda. *Journalism and Mass Communication Quarterly*, 81(1), 124–138.

Crane, A., & Glozer, S. (2016). Researching corporate social responsibility communication: Themes, opportunities and challenges. *Journal of Management Studies*, 53(7), 1223–1252.

Crawford, M. (1995). *Talking Difference: On Gender and Language*. London: SAGE.

Creyer, E. H. (1997). The influence of firm behaviour on purchase intention: Do consumers really care about business ethics? *Journal of Consumer Marketing*, 14(6), 421–432.

Crewe, L., & Wang, A. (2018). Gender inequalities in the city of London advertising industry. *Environment and Planning: Economy and Space*, 50(3), 671–688.

Cross, C. L. (2018). Ecofeminism and an ethic of care: Developing an eco-jurisprudence. *Acta Academica*, 1, 28–40.

Cumming, D., Leung, T. Y., & Rui, O. (2015). Gender diversity and securities fraud. *Academy of Management Journal*, 58(5), 1572–1593.

Curran, J. (2011). *Media and Democracy*. New York: Routledge.

Cushion, S., Kilby, A., Thomas, R., Morani, M., & Sambrook, R. (2018). Newspapers, impartiality and television news. *Journalism Studies*. Online first http://www.tandfonline.com/doi/pdf/10.1080/1461670X.2016.1171163.

Cushion, S., Kilby, A., Thomas, R., Morani, M., & Sambrook, R. (2016). Newspapers, impartiality and television news: Intermedia agenda-setting during the 2015 UK general elections campaign. *Journalism Studies*, 19(2), 162–181.

Cutlip, S. M., & Center, A. H. (1978). *Effective Public Relations* (5th edition, pp. 316–317). Englewood Cliffs, NJ: Prentice-Hall.

Cutrone, C. (n.d.). When was the crisis of capitalism? The legacy of the 1960s new left. *Philosophers of Change*. Retrieved from https://philosophersforchange.org/2014/11/04/when-was-the-crisis-of-capitalism-the-legacy-of-the-1960s-new-left/.

Ćorić, D. (2014). Ecofeminism as a way of resolving some environmental issues. *Zbornik Matice srpske za društvene nauke*, 148, 551–558. Retrieved from https://www.researchgate.net/publication/273294507_Ecofeminism_as_a_way_of_resolving_some_environmental_issues.

Dalton, D. R., & Daily, C. M. (1991). The constituents of corporate responsibility: Separate, but not separable, interests? *Business Horizons*, 34(4), 74–78.

Daly, H., & Morgan, J. (2019). The importance of ecological economics: An interview with Herman Daly. *Real World Economics*, 90. Retrieved from http://eprints.leedsbeckett.ac.uk/id/eprint/6397/8/TheImportanceOfEcologicalEconomicsAnInterviewWithHermanDalyPV-MORGAN.pdf.

Daly, H. E. (1991). *Steady State Economics. Second Edition with New Essays*. Washington, D.C.: Island Press.

Daly, M. (1978). *Gyn/Ecology: The Metaethics of Radical Feminism*. Boston, MA: Beacon Press.

182 *References*

Daly, M. (1973). *Beyond God the Father: Toward a Philosophy of Women's Liberation.* Boston, MA: Beacon Press.

DEFRA (2015). Review of standards for biodegradable plastic carrier bags. *Presented to Parliament Pursuant to Section 18 of the Single Use Carrier Bags Charges (England) Order 2015.* Department of Food and Rural Affairs. Retrieved from https://assets.publishing.service.gov.uk/government/uploads/system/uploads/attachment_data/file/485904/carrier-bag-biodegradable-report-2015.pdf.

Diers-Lawson, A. (2020). Applying the stakeholder relationship model as an issue management and risk communication tool. In – Sabuncuoglu Peksevgen, B. (eds), *Themes in Issues, Risk, and Crisis Communication: A Multi-Dimensional Perspective.* Berlin: Peter Lang.

Douthwaite, R. (1999). *The Growth Illusion.* Devon: Green Books.

Dubrowski, M., McCorkindale, T., & Rickert, R. (2019). *Mind the Gap: Women's Leadership in Public Relations.* Retrieved from https://instituteforpr.org/wp-content/uploads/IPR.KPMG-WIL-Study-FINAL041219-compressed.pdf.

d'Eaubonne, F. ([1990] 1997). What could an eco-feminist society be? In – *Liberty, Equality and Women? Anthology,* (Harmattan). Retrieved from http://richardtwine.com/ecofem/deaubonne.pdf.

d'Eaubonne, F., & Michel, A. (1997). An open letter to the pope. *Ecofem Journal.* Retrieved from http://richardtwine.com/ecofem/pope.pdf.

d'Eaubonne, F. (1994). The time for ecofeminism. In – Merchant, C. (ed), *Key Concepts in Critical Theory: Ecology* (pp. 174–197). Atlantic Highlands, NJ: Humanities Press.

Ewen, S., & Ewen, E. (1992). *Channels of Desire: Mass Images and the Shaping of American Consciousness.* Minneapolis: University of Minnesota Press.

Dawkins, J. (2005). Corporate responsibility: The communication challenge. *Journal of Communication Management, 9*(2), 108–119.

Dearing, J. W., & Rogers, E. M. (1996). *Agenda-Setting, Vol. 6.* Thousand Oaks, CA: SAGE.

De Bruyn, S. M. (2000). *Economic Growth and the Environment.* Amsterdam: Springer Science.

Deephouse, D. L. (2000). Media reputation as a strategic resource: An integration of mass communication and resource-based theories. *Journal of Management, 26*(6), 1091–1112.

De la Rey, C. (2005). Gender, women and leadership. *Agenda, 19*(65), 4–11.

Delveaux, M. (2001). Transcending ecofeminism: Alice Walker, spiritual ecowomanism, and environmental ethics. *Ecofem Journal.* Retrieved from http://richardtwine.com/ecofem/walkera.pdf.

Delworth, T. L., & Knutson, T. R. (2000). Simulation of early 20th century global warming. *Science, 287,* 2246–2250. Retrieved from https://www.researchgate.net/profile/Thomas_Delworth/publication/12585354_Simulation_of_Early_20th_Century_Global_Warming/links/00b7d52389be2aade5000000.pdf.

De Vreese, C. H., & Boomgaarden, H. G. (2006). Media effects on public opinion about the enlargement of the European Union. *Journal of Common Market Studies, 44*(2), 419–436.

De Witt, K. (1990). *Company Resumes Planned Parenthood Gift.* Retrieved from http://www.nytimes.com/1990/09/21/us/company-resumes-planned-parenthood-gift.html.

Dhanesh, G. S. (2014). A dialectical approach to analyzing polyphonic discourses of corporate social responsibility. In – Tench, R., Sun, W., & Jones, B.

References 183

(eds), *Communicating Corporate Social Responsibility: Perspectives and Practice* (pp. 157–179). Howard House: Emerald Books.

Diani, M. (1989). Italy: The "list Verdi". In – Muller-Rommel, F. (ed), *New Politics in Western Europe: The Rise and Success of Green Parties and Alternative Lists*. San Francisco, CA: Westview Press.

Didulica, D. (2020). Negativni učinci suvremenih prehrambenih trendova na pokret za prava životinja. In Marjanić, S., & Đurđević, G. (eds), *Ekofeminizam – između ženskih i zelenih studija*. Zagreb: Durieux, pp. 179–199.

Dimitropolous, S. (2018). Women against climate change. *Womankind*, 18, 76–84.

Djerf-Pierre, M. (2011). The difference engine: Gender equality, journalism and the good society. *Feminist Media Studies,* 11(1), 43–51.

Dobers, P., & Springett, D. (2010). Corporate social responsibility: Discourse, narratives and communication. *Corporate Social Responsibility and Environmental Management*, 17(2), 63–69.

Dobson, A. (1990). *Green Political Thought*. London: Harper Collins.

Dodd, M. D. (2015). Examining the impact of advertising vs. public relations in consumer engagement with social responsibility. *PRism*, 12(2), 1–13. Retrieved from http://www.prismjournal.org/homepage.html.

DOP (2015). *O projektu*. Retrieved from http://www.dop.hr/?page_id=2.

Donovan, J. (1990). Animal rights and feminist theory. *Journal of Women in Culture and Society*, 15(2), 350–375.

Dozier, D. M. (1988). Breaking public relations glass ceiling. *Public Relations Review*, 14(3), 6–14.

Đurđević, G., & Marjanić, S. (2020). Predgovor ekofem-zborniku: na rubu zenskih I zelenih studija. In – Marjanić, S., & Đurđević, G. (eds), *Ekofeminizam – između ženskih i zelenih studija*. Zagreb: Durieux, pp. 9–15.

Đurđević, G. (2020). Uvodnik: na rubu mogućeg ili uspon ka vrhu. In – Marjanić, S., & Đurđević, G. (eds), *Ekofeminizam – između ženskih i zelenih studija*. Zagreb: Durieux, pp. 15–19).

Eagly, A. H., & Karau, S. J. (2002). Role congruity theory of prejudice toward female leaders. *Psychological Review*, 109(3), 573.

Eesley, C., & Lenox, M. (2006). Secondary stakeholders and firm self-regulation. *Strategic Management Journal*, 27, 765–781.

Eckersley, R. (1992). *Environmentalism and Political Theory: Toward an Ecocentric Approach*. Albany, NY: State University of New York Press.

Ehrlich, P. R., & J. P. Holdren (eds) (1971). *Global Ecology: Readings Toward a Rational Strategy for Man*. New York: Harcourt Brace Jovanovich.

Eichenbaum, L., & Orbach, S. (1999). *What do Women Want? Exploding the Myth of Dependency*. New York: Berkley Books.

Eisenstein, H. (1983). *Contemporary feminist thought*. Boston: G. K. Hall.

Eisler, R. (1990). The Gaia tradition and the partnership future: An ecofeminist manifesto. In – Diamond, I., & Orenstein, G. (eds), *Reweaving the World*. San Francisco, CA: Sierra Club Book, pp. 22–34.

Eisler, R. (1987a). *The Gaia Tradition and the Partnership Future: An Ecofeminist Manifesto*. Retrieved from www.dhushara.com/book/renewal/voices2/eisler.htm.

Eisler, R. (1987b). *The Chalice and the Blade*. San Francisco, CA: Harpers.

Ellen, P. S., Webb, D. J., & Mohr, L. A. (2006). Building corporate associations: Consumer attributions for corporate socially responsible programs. *Journal of the Academy of Marketing Science*, 34(2), 147–157.

184 *References*

Elmagrhi, M. H., Ntim, C. G., Wang, Y., & Zalata, A. (2020). Corporate governance disclosure index– executive pay nexus: The moderating effect of governance mechanisms. *European Management Review*, 17(1), 121–152.

Elmagrhi, M. H., Ntim, C. G., Elamer, A. A., & Zhang, Q. (2019). A study of environmental policies and regulations, governance structures and environmental performance: The role of female directors. *Business Strategy and the Environment*, 28(1), 206–220.

Ellen MacArthur Foundation (2017). *The New Plastics Economy.* Retrieved from https://www.ellenmacarthurfoundation.org/publications/the-new-plastics-economy-rethinking-the-future-of-plastics-catalysing-action.

Emel, J. (1995). Are you man enough, big and bad enough? Ecofeminism and wolf eradication in the USA. *Environment and Planning: Society and Space*, 13, 707–734.

Enloe, C. (1993). *The Morning After: Sexual Politics at the End of the Cold War.* Berkeley: University of California Press.

Entman, R. M. (1993). Framing: Toward clarification of a fractured paradigm. *Journal of Communication*, 43(4), 51–58.

Epstein, L. H., Paluch, R. A., Consalvi, A., Riordan, K., & Scholl, T. (2002). Effects of manipulating sedentary behaviour on physical activity and food intake. *Journal of Pediatrics*, 140, 334–39.

Esipova, N., Ray, J., & Pugliese, A. (2015). How the world views migration. *International Organization for Migration (IOM).* Geneva. Retrieved from https://publications.iom.int/system/files/how_the_world_gallup.pdf.

Ethical Consumer (2019). *Twenty Years of Ethical Consumerism.* Retrieved from https://www.ethicalconsumer.org/sites/default/files/inline-files/Twenty%20 Years%20of%20Ethical%20Consumerism%202019.pdf.

Ethical Consumer (2013). *Ethical Consumer Markets Report.* Retrieved from http://www.ethicalconsumer.org/portals/0/downloads/ethical_consumer_markets_report_2013.pdf.

Everbach, T., & Flournoy, C. (2007). Women leave journalism for better pay, work conditions. *Newspaper Research Journal*, 28(3), 52–64.

Eurobarometer (2017). *Special Eurobarometer 467: Future of Europe – Social Issues.* November 2017. Retrieved from https://ec.europa.eu/commfrontoffice/publicopinion/index.cfm/Survey/index#p=1&yearFrom=1974&yearTo=2017.

Fakier, K., & Cock, J. (2018). Eco-feminist organizing in South Africa: Reflections on the feminist table. *Capitalism, Nature, Socialism*, 29(1), 40–57.

Falck, O., & Heblich, S. (2007). Corporate social responsibility: Doing well by doing good. *Business Horizons*, 50, 247–254.

Falk, E. (2013). Clinton and the playing-the-gender-card metaphor in campaign news. *Feminist Media Studies*, 13(2), 192–207.

Faludi, S. (1991). *Backlash: The Undeclared War against American Women.* New York: Doubleday.

FareShare (2021). *Food Waste and Hunger in the UK.* Retrieved from https://fareshare.org.uk/what-we-do/hunger-food-waste/.

Fawkes, J. (2007). Public relations models and persuasion ethics: A new approach. *Journal of Communication Management,* 11(4), 313–331.

Frankental, P. (2001). Corporate social responsibility – a PR invention? *Corporate Communications: An International Journal,* 6(1), 18–23.

Fernandez-Feijoo, B., Romero, S., & Ruiz-Blanco, S. (2014). Women on boards: Do they affect sustainability reporting? *Corporate Social Responsibility and Environmental Management*, 21, 351–364.

References   185

Figenschou, T. U., Beyer, A., & Thorbjornsrud, K. (2015). The moral police: Agenda-setting and framing effects of a new(s) concept of immigration. *Nordicom Review*, 36(1), 65–78.

Fieldman, G. (2011). Neoliberalism, the production of vulnerability and the hobbled state: Systemic barriers to climate adaptation. *Climate Development*, 3(2), 159–174.

Fiss, P. C., & Zajac, E. J. (2006). The symbolic management of strategic change: Sensegiving via framing and decoupling. *Academy of Management Review*, 49, 1173–1193.

Fleming, P., & Jones, M. T. (2013). *The End of Corporate Social Responsibility: Crisis and Critique*. London: SAGE.

Fombrun, C., & Shanley, M. (1990). What's in a name? Reputation building and corporate strategy. *Academy of Management Journal*, 33(2), 233–258.

Foster, J. M. (2021). Does CSR activity amount to socially responsible management? *Philosophy of Management*. Retrieved from https://link.springer.com/article/10.1007/s40926-020-00158-6.

Fox, B. (2020). Trump leaves mark on immigration policy, some of it lasting. *AP News*. Retrieved from https://apnews.com/article/joe-biden-donald-trump-politics-immigration-united-states-a5bfcbea280a468b431a02e82c15a150.

Fox, W. (1995). The deep ecology – Ecofeminism debate and its parallels. In – Sessions, G. (ed), *Deep Ecology for the 21st Century: Readings on the Philosophy and Practice of the New Environmentalism*. Boston, MA: Shambhala Publications, pp. 269–290.

Franklin, B. (2014). The future of journalism in an age of digital media and economic uncertainty. *Journalism Studies*, 15(5), 481–499.

Franklin, M. N., & Rudig, W. (1992). The green voter: In the 1989 European elections. *Environmental Politics*, 4, 129–159.

Franks, S. (2013). *Women and Journalism*. London: I.B. Tauris.

Fraser, N. (2014). Behind Marx's hidden abode: For an expanded conception of capitalism. *New Left Review*, 86, 55–72.

Frederickson, M. (2020). *COVID-19's Gendered Impact on Academic Productivity*. Retrieved from https://github.com/drfreder/pandemic-pub-bias/blob/master/README.md.

Freeman, I., & Hasnaoui, A. (2011). The meaning of corporate social responsibility: The vision of four nations. *Journal of Business Ethics*, 100, 419–443.

Freeman, R. E. (2010). *Strategic Management: A Stakeholder Approach*. Cambridge: Cambridge University Press.

Freeman, R. E., & Philips, R. A. (2002). Stakeholder theory: A libertarian defense. *Business Ethics Quarterly*, 12(3), 331–349.

Freeman, R. E. (2001). Stakeholder theory of the modern corporation. *Perspectives in Business Ethics*, 3, 38–48. Retrieved from http://academic.udayton.edu/LawrenceUlrich/Stakeholder%20Theory.pdf.

Freeman, R. E., & McVea, J. (2001). A stakeholder approach to strategic management. *Working Paper No. 01-02*, Darden Graduate School of Business Administration. Retrieved from http://papers.ssrn.com/paper.taf?abstract_id=263511.

Freeman, R. E. (1994). The politics of stakeholder theory: Some future directions. *Business Ethics Quarterly*, 4(4), 409–421.

Freeman, R. E. (1984). *Strategic Management: A Stakeholder Approach*. Cambridge: Cambridge University Press. Reprint from 2010.

Friedman, M. (1970). The social responsibility of business is to increase its profits. *The New York Times Magazine*, September 13. Retrieved from http://www.colorado.edu/studentgroups/libertarians/issues/friedman-soc-resp-business.html.

186 *References*

Friedman, M. (1962). *Capitalism and Freedom*. Chicago, IL: University of Chicago Press.

Friend, T. (2019). Can a burger help solve climate change? Eating meat creates huge environmental costs. Impossible foods thinks it has a solution. *The New Yorker*, 30 September. Retrieved from https://www.newyorker.com/magazine/2019/09/30/can-a-burger-help-solve-climate-change.

Fuchs, C. (2011). *Foundations of Critical Media and Information Studies*. New York: Routledge.

Fuchs, C. (2010). Labor in informational capitalism and on the internet. *The Information Society*, 26(3), 179–196.

Gallagher, M. (2002). Women, media and democratic society: In pursuit of rights and freedoms. United Nations: Division for the advancement of women (DAW). *Expert Group Meeting on 'Participation and Access of Women to the Media, and the Impact of Media on, and Its Use as an Instrument for the Advancement and Empowerment of Women'*. Retrieved from http://www.un.org/womenwatch/daw/egm/media2002/reports/BP1Gallagher.PDF.

Galić, B. (2020). Ekofeminizam – novi identitet žene. In – Marjanić, S., & Đurđević, G. (eds), *Ekofeminizam – između ženskih i zelenih studija*. Zagreb: Durieux, pp. 61–81.

Gamble, A. (1989). The politics of Thatcherism. *Parliamentary Affairs*, 42(3), 350–361.

Gaard, G. (2015). *Ecofeminism and Climate Change. Author's Accepted Paper Version of a Paper for Women's Studies International Forum*. Retrieved from https://www.academia.edu/11875214/Ecofeminism_and_Climate_Change.

Gaard, G. (2011). Ecofeminism revisited: Rejecting essentialism and re-placing species in a material feminist environmentalism. *Feminist Formations*, 23(2), 26–53.

Gaard, G. (2002). Vegetarian ecofeminism: A review essay. *Frontiers*, 23(3), 117–146.

Gaard, G. (1997). Toward a queer ecofeminism. *Hypatia*, 12(1), 137–155.

Gaard, G. (1993). Living interconnections with animals and nature. In – Gaard, G. (ed), *Women, Animals, Nature* (pp. 1–12). Philadelphia, PA: Temple University Press.

Galvin, R., & Healy, N. (2020). The green new deal in the United States: What it is and how to pay for it. *Energy Research & Social Science*, 67. Retrieved from https://www.sciencedirect.com/science/article/pii/S2214629620301067.

Gamson, W. A., & Modigliani, A. (1989). Media discourse and public opinion on nuclear power: A constructionist approach. *American Journal of Sociology*, 95(1), 1–37.

Gamson, W. A. (1989). News as framing. *American Behavioral Scientist*, 33(2), 157–161.

Gan, A. (2006). The impact of public scrutiny on corporate philanthropy. *Journal of Business Ethics*, 69(3), 217–236.

Garnham, N. ([1986] 2006). Contribution to a political economy of mass communication. In – Durham, M. G., & Kellner, D. (eds), *Media and Cultural Studies: KeyWorks* (pp. 201–229). Malden, Oxford, Carlton: Blackwell.

Garnham, N. (1998). Political economy and cultural studies: Reconciliation or divorce. In – Sorey, J. (ed), *Cultural Theory and Popular Culture: A Reader* (pp. 600–612). Edinburgh: Pearson.

Gareau, Brian J. (2013). *From Precaution to Profit: Contemporary Challenges to Environmental Protection in the Montreal Protocol*. New Haven, CT and London: Yale University Press.

Garett, A. (2019). The refugee crisis, Brexit, and the reframing of immigration in Britain. *Europe Now*. Retrieved from https://www.europenowjournal.org/2019/09/09/the-refugee-crisis-brexit-and-the-reframing-of-immigration-in-britain/.

References 187

Geiger Zeman, M., & Zeman, Z. (2010). *Uvod u sociologiju održivih zajednica.* Zagreb: Institut društvenih znanosti Ivo Pilar.

Geiger, M. (2006a). Kontroverze kulturalnog ekofeminizma. *Kruh i ruže*, 30, 34–41.

Geiger, M. (2006b). Kako je okoliš postao feminističko pitanje ili što je zapravo ekofeminizam? *Kruh i ruže*, 30, 13–22.

Geiger, M. (2002). Spiritualni aspekti ekofeminizma. *Socijalna ekologija*, 10(1–2), 15–27.

Georgescu-Roegen, N. (1971). *The Entropy Law and the Economic Process.* Cambridge: Harvard University Press.

Gerber, P. J., Steinfeld, H., Henderson, B., Mottet, A., Opio, C., Dijkman, J., Falcucci, A., & Tempio, G. (2013). Tackling climate change through livestock – A global assessment of emissions and mitigation opportunities. *Food and Agriculture Organization of the United Nations (FAO)*, Rome. Retrieved from http://www.fao.org/3/i3437e/i3437e.pdf.

Gersdorf, K. (2006). Nature and body: Ecofeminism, land art, and the work of Ana Mendieta (1948–1985). In – Ernst, W., & Bohle, U. (eds), *Geschlechterdiskurse zwischen Fiktion und Faktizität.* Retrieved from https://studenttheses.universiteitleiden.nl/access/item%3A2662556/download.

Geyer, R., Jambeck, J. R., & Law, K. L. (2017). Production, use, and fate of all plastics ever made. *Science Advances*, 3(7). Retrieved from https://advances.sciencemag.org/content/3/7/e1700782.

Ghobadi, S., Hassanzadeh-Rostami, Z., Salehi-Marzijarani, M., Bellissimo, N., Brett, N. R., Totosy de Zepetnek, J. O., & Faghia, S. (2017). Association of eating while television viewing and overweight/obesity among children and adolescents: A systematic review and meta-analysis of observational studies. *Pediatric Obesity/Etiology*, 19, 313–320.

Giacomini, T., Turner, T., Isla, A., & Brownhill, L. (2018). Ecofeminism against capitalism and for the commons. *Capitalism, Nature, Socialism*, 29(1), 1–6.

Giacomini, T. (2014). Ecofeminism and system change. Women on the frontlines of the struggle against fossil capitalism and for the solar commons. *Canadian Woman Studies*, 31(1–2), 95–100.

Gill, D., & Broderick, A. (2014). Brand heritage and CSR credentials: A discourse analysis of M&S reports. In – Tench, R., Sun, W., & Jones, B. (eds), *Communicating Corporate Social Responsibility: Perspectives and Practice* (pp. 179–201). Howard House: Emerald Books.

Gill, R. (2014). Unspeakable inequalities: Post-feminism, entrepreneurial subjectivity and the repudiation of sexism among cultural workers. *Social Politics*, 21(4), 509–528.

Gill, S., & Law, D. (1993). Global hegemony and the structural power of capital. In – Gill, S. (ed), *Gramsci, Historical Materialism and International Relations.* Cambridge: Cambridge University Press.

Gilligan, C. (1993). *In a Different Voice: Psychological Theory and Women's Development.* Cambridge, MA: Harvard University Press.

Gills, B., & Morgan, J. (2020). Economics and climate emergency. *Globalizations*, https://doi.org/10.1080/14747731.2020.1841527.

Gills, B., & Morgan, J. (2019). Global climate emergency: After COP24, climate science, urgency, and the threat to humanity. *Globalizations*, https://doi.org/10.1080/14747731.2019.1669915.

Glavas, A., & Kelley, K. (2014). The effects of perceived corporate social responsibility on employee attitudes. *Business Ethics Quarterly*, 24(2), 165–202.

188 *References*

Godfrey, P. C. (2008). Ecofeminist cosmology in practice: Genesis farm and the embodiment of sustainable solutions. *Capitalism Nature Socialism*, 19(2), 96–114.

Godfrey, P. (2005). Diane Wilson vs Union Carbide: Ecofeminism and the elitist charge of 'essentialism'. *Capitalism Nature Socialism*, 16(4), 37–56.

Goffman, E. (1974). *Frame Analysis: An Essay on the Organization of Experience.* Boston, MA: Northeastern University Press.

Goldman, M. (2006). *Imperial Nature: The World Bank and Struggles for Social Justice in the Age of Globalization.* New Haven, CT: Yale University Press.

Goldstein, J. (2006). Ecofeminism in theory and praxis. *Capitalism Nature Socialism*, 17(4), 96–102.

Golob, U., & Bartlett, J. L. (2007). Communicating about corporate social responsibility: A comparative study of CSR reporting in Australia and Slovenia. *Public Relations Review*, 33, 1–9.

Goodwin, M., & Milazzo, C. T. (2017). Taking back control? Investigating the role of immigration in the 2016 vote for Brexit. *The British Journal of Politics and International Relations*, 19(3), 450–464.

Govedić, N., & Marjanić, S. (2008). Prvo lice životinjske jednine. *Treća*, 1(X), 5–13.

Graber, D. (1980). *Crime News and the Public.* New York: Praeger.

Grabher, G. (2004). Learning in projects, remembering in networks? Communality, sociality, and connectivity in project ecologies. *European Urban and Regional Studies*, 11(2), 103–123.

Grafström, M., & Windell, K. (2011). The role of infomediaries: CSR in the business press during 2000–2009. *Journal of Business Ethics*, 103, 221–237.

Grampp, W. D. (1965). *Economic Liberalism, vol. 2 The Classical View.* New York: Random House.

Grayson, D. (2009). *Corporate Responsibility and the Media.* Doughty Centre Corporate Responsibility. Retrieved from http://www.som.cranfield.ac.uk/som/dinamic-content/research/doughty/crandthemediafinal.pdf.

Gregory, M. R. (2009). Inside the locker room: Male homosociability in the advertising industry. *Gender, Work and Organization*, 16(3), 323–347.

Grossman, G. M., & Krueger, A. B. (1994). Economic growth and the environment. *NBER Working Series, Working Paper No. 4634.* Retrieved from https://www.nber.org/system/files/working_papers/w4634/w4634.pdf.

Grossman, G., & Kreuger, A. (1991). Environmental impacts of a North American free trade agreement. *NBER Working Paper Series, Working Paper 3914.* Retrieved from https://www.nber.org/system/files/working_papers/w3914/w3914.pdf.

Grow, J. M., & Deng, T. (2015). Tokens in a man's world: Women in creative advertising departments. *Media Report to Women*, 43(1), 6–23.

Growe, R., & Montgomery, P. (2000). *Women and the Leadership Paradigm: Bridging the Gender Gap.* Retrieved from https://www.researchgate.net/publication/242783132_Women_and_the_leadership_paradigm_bridging_the_gender_gap?enrichId=rgreq-e352348da05955595828f718a88d2ecd-XXX&enrichSource=Y292ZXJQYWdlOzI0Mjc4MzEzMjtBUzozNzI2OTMzOTMyNjQ2ND-FAMTQ2NTg2ODQzNzI5OA%3D%3D&el=1_x_2&_esc=publicationCoverPdf.

The Green Belt Movement (n.d.). The official website. Retrieved from: http://www.greenbeltmovement.org/.

Griffin, S. (2020). Održivost i duša. In – Marjanić, S., & Đurđević, G. (eds), *Ekofeminizam – između ženskih i zelenih studija.* Zagreb: Durieux, pp. 19–29.

Griffin, S. (2015). *Woman and Nature.* Newburyport, MA: Open Road Media.

References 189

Griffin, S. (2004). *Woman and Nature. The Roaring Inside Her.* Berkeley, CA: Counterpoint.

Griffin, M., Sobal, J., & Thomas A. Lyson, T. A. (2009). An analysis of a community food waste stream. *Agriculture and Human Values*, 26, 67–81.

Griffin, S. (1990). Curves along the road. In – Diamond, I., & Orenstein, G. (eds), *Reweaving the World*. San Francisco, CA: Sierra Club Books, pp. 87–99.

Griffin, S. (1978). *Women and Nature: The Roaring Inside Her.* New York: Harper and Row.

Gruen, L. (1993). Dismantling oppression: An analysis of the connection between women and animals. In Gaard, G. (ed), *Ecofeminism Ethics and Action*. Philadelphia, PA: Temple University.

Grunig, L. A. (1999). Implications of culture and gender for governmental public affairs. *Journal of Communication Management*, 3(3), 248–259.

Grunig, J. E., & Hunt, T. (1984). *Managing Public Relations*. New York: Holt, Rinehart and Winston.

Gulyas, A. (2009). Corporate social responsibility in the British media industries – preliminary findings. *Media, Culture & Society*, 31(4), 657–668.

Gupta, A., & Asselt, H. (2017). Transparency in multilateral climate politics: Furthering (or distracting from) accountability? *Regulation & Governance*, 13(1), 18–34.

Gupta, A. (2008). Transparency under scrutiny: Information disclosure in global environmental governance. *Global Environmental Politics*, 8(2), 1–7.

Gustavson, J., Cederberg, C., Sonesson, U., van Otterdijk, R., & Meybeck, A. (2011). *Global Food Losses and Food Waste: Extent, Causes and Prevention*. Rome: Food and Agriculture Organization of the United Nations. Retrieved from https://www.madr.ro/docs/ind-alimentara/risipa_alimentara/presentation_food_waste.pdf.

Haque, F. (2017). The effects of board characteristics and sustainable compensation policy on carbon performance of UK firms. *The British Accounting Review*, 49(3), 347–364.

Hamilton, J. T. (2003). Media coverage of corporate social responsibility. *The Joan Shorenstein Center on the Press, Politics and Public Policy Working Paper Series*. Cambridge, MA: Harvard University.

Hall, K. D., Guo, J., Dore, M., Chow, C. C. (2009). The progressive increase of food waste in America and its environmental impact. *PLOS ONE*, 4(11), e7940. Retrieved from https://doi.org/10.1371/journal.pone.0007940.

Halla, M., Wagner, A. F., & Zweimüller, J. (2017). Immigration and voting for the far right. *Journal of the European Economic Association*, 15(46), 1341–1385.

Hallen, P. (1999). The ecofeminism-deep ecology dialogue: A short commentary on the exchange between Karen Warren and Arne Naess. In – Witoszek, N., & Brennan, A. (eds), *Philosophical Dialogues: Arne Naes and the Progress of Ecophilosophy*. London: Rowan and Littlefield.

Hallen, P. (1987). Making peace with nature: Why ecology needs feminism. *The Trumpeter*, 4.

Hamilton, J. T. (2004). *All The News that's Fit to Sell: How the Market Transforms Information into News*. Princeton, NJ: Princeton University Press.

Hampel, B., Boldero, J., Holdsworth, R. (1996). Gender patterns in environmental consciousness among adolescents. *ANZJS*, 32(1), 58–71.

Hancox, R. J., Milne, B. J., & Poulton, R. (2004). Association between child and adolescent television viewing and adult health: A longitudinal birth cohort study. *Lancet*, 364, 257–262.

190   *References*

Hannah, D., & Zatzick, C. (2008). An examination of leader portrayals in the U.S. business press following the landmark scandals of the early 21st century. *Journal of Business Ethics*, 79(4), 361–377.

Hatfield Edwards, H. (2015). Social responsibility and the evolution of corporate philanthropy: An analysis of successful corporate-cause partnerships in an era of the global corporate citizen. *PRism*, 12(2), 1–14. Retrieved from https://www.researchgate.net/publication/331844029_Social_responsibility_and_the_evolution_of_corporate_philanthropy_An_analysis_of_successful_corporate-cause_partnerships_in_an_era_of_the_global_corporate_citizen

Haward, M. (2018). Plastic pollution of the world's seas and oceans as a contemporary challenge in ocean governance. *Nature Communications*, 9, 667. Retrieved from https://doi.org/10.1038/s41467-018-03104-3.

Henderson, K. A. (1997). Ecofeminism and experiential education. *The Journal of Experiential Education*, 20(3), 130–222.

Henriques, I., & Sadorsky, P. (1999). The relationship between environmental and managerial perceptions of stakeholder importance. *Academy of Management Journal*, 42, 87–99.

Herman, E. S., & Chomsky, N. (1988). *Manufacturing Consent. The Political Economy of the Mass Media*. London: Vintage Books.

Hester, J. B., & Gibson, R. (2003). The economy and second-level agenda setting: A time series analysis of economic news and public opinion about the economy. *Journalism & Mass Communication Quarterly*, 80(1), 73–90.

Hill Collins, P. (1990). *Black Feminist Thought*. Cambridge, MA: Unwin.

Hirunyawipada, T., & Xiong, G. (2018). Corporate environmental commitment and financial performance: Moderating effects of marketing and operations capabilities. *Journal of Business Research*, 86, 22–31.

Hoenisch, S. (2000). Habermas' theory of discourse ethics. *Journal of Communication Inquiry*, 24(1), 19–40.

Hofkirchner, W. (2003). A new way of thinking and a new world view. On the philosophy of self-organisation I. In – Arshinov, V., & Fuchs, C. (eds), *Causality, Emergence, Self-Organisation* (pp. 131–149). Moscow: NIA-Parioda.

Holy, M. (2008). Žene – glasnogovornice životinja? *Treća*, 1(X), 87–106.

Holy, M. (2007). *Mitski aspekti ekofeminizma*. Zagreb: TIM Press.

Hollindale, J., Kent, P., Routledge, J., & Chapple, L. (2019). Women on boards and greenhouse gas emission disclosures. *Accounting & Finance*, 59(1), 277–308.

Holm, J., & Jokkala, T. (2008). *Stočarska industrija i klima: Europska Unija loše čini gorim*. Zagreb: Lotusgraf.

Holzer, B. (2008). Turning stakeseekers into stakeholders a political coalition perspective on the politics of stakeholder influence. *Business and Society*, 47, 50–67.

Horkheimer, M., & Adorno, T. W. ([1947] 1997). *Dialectic of Enlightenment*. London, New York: Verso.

Hörisch, J., Freeman, R. E., & Schaltegger, S. (2014). Applying stakeholder theory in sustainability management: Links, similarities, dissimilarities, and a conceptual framework. *Organization & Environment*, 27(4), 328–346.

Hösle, V. (1996). *Filozofija ekološke krize*. Zagreb: Matica Hrvatska.

Houde, L. J., & Bullis, C. (1999). Ecofeminist pedagogy: An exploratory case. *Ethics and the Environment*, 4(2), 143–174.

Hou, J. H., & Reber, B. H. (2011). Dimensions of disclosures: Corporate social responsibility (CSR) reporting by media companies. *Public Relations Review*, 37, 166–168.

References 191

Houghton, J. (2005). Global warming. *Reports on Progress in Physics*, 68, 1343–1403.

Houghton, J. (2004). *Global Warming: The Complete Briefing* (3rd edition). Cambridge: Cambridge University Press. Retrieved from http://117.239.19.55:8080/xmlui/bitstream/handle/123456789/160/pdf679.pdf?sequence=1&isAllowed=y.

Hui, L. T. (2017). Implications on corporate social responsibility and corporate sustainability. In – Hui, L.T. (ed), *Practising Corporate Social Responsibility in Malaysia*. Cham: Palgrave Macmillan, pp. 159–172.

Hulme, M. (2014). *Can Science Fix Climate Change: A Case against Climate Engineering*. Cambridge: Polity Press.

Hunter, L., Hatch, A., & Johnson, A. (2004). Cross-national gender variation in environmental behaviours. *Social Science Quarterly*, 85(3), 677–694.

Hussain, N., Rigoni, U., & Orij, R. P. (2018). Corporate governance and sustainability performance: Analysis of triple bottom line performance. *Journal of Business Ethics*, 149(2), 411–432.

Huyn, E., Yang, D., Jung, H., & Hong, K. (2016). Women on boards and corporate social responsibility. *Sustainability*, 8, 1–26.

Ibbetson, C. (2020). *Quarter of Brits Think Climate Change Risk is Overstated*. YouGov, January 22. https://yougov.co.uk/topics/science/articles-reports/2020/01/22/quarter-brits-think-climate-change-risk-overstated.

Ihlen, Ó (2008). Mapping the environment for corporate social responsibility. *Corporate Communications: An International Journal*, 13(2), 135–146.

ILO (2020). *Global Wage Report 2020-21: Wages and Minimum Wages in the Time of COVID-19*. Retrieved from https://www.ilo.org/wcmsp5/groups/public/—dgreports/—dcomm/—publ/documents/publication/wcms_762534.pdf.

Inauen, S., & Schoeneborn, D. (2014). Twitter and its usage for dialogic stakeholder communication by MNC's and NGOs. In – Tench, R., Sun, W., & Jones, B. (eds), *Communicating Corporate Social Responsibility: Perspectives and Practice* (pp. 283–311). Howard House: Emerald Books.

Ingenhoff, D., & Koelling, A. M. (2012). Media governance and corporate social responsibility of media organizations: An international comparison. *Business Ethics: A European Review*, 21(2), 154–167.

Investopedia (2021). *Economic Growth*. Retrieved from https://www.investopedia.com/terms/e/economicgrowth.asp.

Iosifidis, P. (2016). Media concentration in the UK. In – E. Noam (ed), *Who Owns the World's Media?: Media Concentration and Ownership around the World* (pp. 425–454). New York: Oxford University Press.

Iovino, S. (2013). Loving the alien. Ecofeminism, animals, and Anna Maria Ortese's poetics of otherness. *Feminismols*, 177–203. Retrieved from https://www.researchgate.net/publication/304560853_Loving_the_alien_Ecofeminism_animals_and_Anna_Maria_Ortese's_poetics_of_otherness.

IPCC (2019). IPCC special report on climate change, desertification, land degradation, sustainable land management, food security, and greenhouse gas fluxes in terrestrial ecosystems. *Summary for Policymakers*, 7th August.

Ireland, P., & Pillay, R. (2008). Corporate social responsibility in a neoliberal age. In – Utting, P., & Marques, J. C. (eds), *Corporate Social Responsibility and Regulatory Governance: Towards Inclusive Development?* (pp. 77–104). New York: Palgrave-Macmillan.

Isidro, H., & Sobral, M. (2015). The effects of women on corporate boards on firm value, financial performance, and ethical and social compliance. *Journal of Business Ethics*, 132(1), 1–19.

192 References

Iyengar, S., & Simon, A. (1993). News coverage of the gulf crisis and public opinion: A study of agenda-setting, priming, and framing. *Communication Research,* 20(3), 365–383.

Jahan, S., Mahmud, A. S., & Papageorgiou, C. (2014). What is Keynesian economics? *Finance & Development,* 51(3). Retrieved from https://www.imf.org/external/pubs/ft/fandd/2014/09/pdf/basics.pdf.

Jain, S. (1984). Women and people's ecological movement: A case study of women's Role in the Chipko Movement in Uttar Pradesh. *Economic and Political Weekly,* 19(41), 1788–1794.

Jamali, D., & Keshishian. T. (2009). Uneasy alliances: Lessons learned from partnerships between businesses and NGOs in the context of CSR. *Journal of Business Ethics,* 84(2), 277–295.

Jarvis, H., & Pratt, A. C. (2006). Bringing it all back home: The extensification and 'overflowing' of work: The case of San Francisco's new media households. *Geoforum,* 37(3), 331–339.

Jensen, M. (2002). Value maximization, stakeholder theory, and the corporate objective function. *Business Ethics Quarterly,* 12(2), 235–256.

Jeong, S.-H., & Harrison, D. A. (2017). Glass breaking, strategy making, and value creating: Meta-analytic outcomes of women as CEOs and TMT members. *Academy of Management Journal,* 60(4), 1219–1252.

Johansen, T. S., & Nielsen, A. E. (2011). Strategic stakeholder dialogues: a discursive perspective on relationship building. *Corporate Communications: An International Journal,* 16(3), 204–217.

Johnson, K. R., & Cuison-Villazor, R. (2019). The Trump administration and the war on immigration diversity. *UC Davis Legal Studies Research Paper Series.* Retrieved from https://www.immigrationresearch.org/system/files/SSRN-id3381885.pdf.

Johnson, P., & Kossykh, Y. (2008). Early years, life chances and equality: A literature review. *Research Report 7, Equality and Human Rights Commission.* Retrieved from https://www.equalityhumanrights.com/sites/default/files/research-report-7-early-years-life-chances-and-equality-literature-review.pdf.

Jones, B., Bowd, R., & Tench, R. (2009). Corporate irresponsibility and corporate social responsibility: Competing realities. *Social Responsibility Journal,* 5(3), 300–310.

Jordan, A. B., Kramer-Golinkoff, E. K., & Strasburger, V. C. (2008). Does adolescent media use cause obesity and eating disorders? *Adolescent Medicine,* 19, 431–49.

Jorgenson, A., Schor, J., Knight, K., & Huang, X. (2016). Domestic inequality and carbon emissions in comparative perspective. *Sociological Forum,* 31, 770–786.

Jorgenson, A., Schor, J., Huang, X., & Fitzgerald, J. (2015). Income inequality and residential carbon emissions in the United States: A preliminary analysis. *Human Ecology Review,* 22(1), 93–105.

Jessop, B. (2003). From Thatcherism to new labour. In – Overbeek, H. (ed), *The Political Economy of European Employment* (pp.137–154). London: Routledge.

Judi Bari official website (n.d). Retrieved from http://www.judibari.org/#History.

Kailo, K. (2003). *Cyber/Ecofeminism – From Violence and Monoculture Towards Eco-socialist Sustainability.* Paper presented at Gender and Power in the New Europe, the 5th European Feminist Research Conference, August, 20–24. Retrieved from https://cdn.atria.nl/epublications/2003/Gender_and_power/5thfeminist/paper_803.pdf.

References   193

Kamble, B. P. (2012). Ecofeminism: Issues and areas. *International Indexed & Referred Research Journal*, 3(32), 1–2.

Karunamoorthy, S., Mutharasu, S. A., & Filipe, J. A. (2013). Marketing strategies to add economic value. Reactions on corporate social responsibility advertising in print media. An Indian company case. *International Journal of Latest Trends in Finance & Economic Sciences*, 3(1), 372–388.

Kaur, G. (2012). Postcolonial ecofeminism in Indian novels in English. *International Journal of Social Science and Humanity*, 2(5), 384–390.

Keeley, B. (2015). Income inequality: The gap between rich and poor. *OECD Insights*. Paris: OECD Publishing. Retrieved from https://espas.secure.europarl.europa.eu/orbis/sites/default/files/generated/document/en/011539le.pdf.

Kelsey, S., Morris. C., & Crewe, L. (2019). Yellow-sticker shopping as competent, creative consumption. *Area*, 51(1), 64–71.

Keynes, J. M. (1937). Some economic consequences of a declining population. *Eugenics Review*, XXIX, 14.

Kheel, M. (2009). Communicating care: An ecofeminist view. *Media Development*, 56(2), 45–50.

Kim, J. Y., Kiousis, S., & Xiang, Z. (2015). Agenda building and agenda setting in business: Corporate reputation attributes. *Corporate Reputation Review*, 18(1), 25–36.

Kim, S.-H., Han, M., & Scheufele, D. A. (2010). Think about him this way: Priming, news media, and South Koreans' evaluation of the president. *International Journal of Public Opinion Research*, 22(3), 299–319.

Kim, S. H., Carvalho, J. P., & Cooksey, C. E. (2007). Exploring the effects of negative publicity: News coverage and public perceptions of a university. *Public Relations Review*, 33, 233–235.

Kim, S. H., Scheufele, D., & Shanahan, J. (2002). Think about it this way: Attribute agenda-setting function of the press and the public's evaluation of a local issue. *J&MC Quarterly*, 79(1), 7–25.

King, P. (1997). The press, candidate images, and voter perceptions. In – McCombs, M., Shaw, D. L., & Weaver, D. (eds), *Communication and Democracy*. Mahwah, NJ: Lawrence Erlbaum Associates, pp. 29–40.

Kiousis, S., Popescu, C., & Mitrook, M. (2007). Understanding influence on corporate reputation: An examination of public relations efforts, media coverage, public opinion, and financial performance from an agenda-building and agenda-setting perspective. *Journal of Public Relations Research*, 19(2), 147–165.

Kirk, G. (1998). Ecofeminism and Chicano environmental struggles: Bridges across gender and race. In – Peña, D. G. (ed), *Chicano Culture, Ecology, Politics: Subversive Kin* (pp. 177–200). Tucson: University of Arizona Press.

Klaidman, S. (1987). *The Virtuous Journalist*. Oxford: Oxford University Press.

Klein, N. (2014). *This Changes Everything: Capitalism vs the Climate*. New York: Simon & Schuster.

Koenig, A. M., Eagly, A. H., Mitchell, A. A., & Ristikari, T. (2011). Are leader stereotypes masculine? A meta-analysis of three research paradigms. *Psychological Bulletin*, 137(4), 616–642.

Kolcava, D., Scholderer, J., & Bernauera, T. (2021). Do citizens provide political rewards to firms engaging in voluntary environmental action? *Journal of Cleaner Production*, 279, 123–564.

Kook Lee, J. (2007). The effect of the internet on homogeneity of the media agenda: A test of the fragmentation thesis. *J&MC Quarterly*, 84(4), 745–760.

194   *References*

Konrad, A., Kramer, V., & Erkut, S. (2008). Critical mess: The impact of three or more women on corporate boards. *Organizational Dynamics*, 37, 145–164.

Kovach, B., & Rosenstiel, T. (2001). *The Elements of Journalism: What News People Should Know and What the Public Should Expect*. New York: Crown.

Kowalczyk, R., & Kucharska, W. (2019). Corporate social responsibility practices incomes and outcomes: Stakeholders' pressure, culture, employee commitment, corporate reputation, and brand performance. A Polish–German cross-country study. *Corporate Social Responsibility and Environmental Management*, 27(2), 595–615.

Krishnamurthy, S., Chew, W. N., Soh, T. T., & Luo, W. (2007). *Corporate Social Responsibility and Public Relations: Perceptions and Practices in Singapore*. Conference paper from the 14th International Public Relations Symposium, Bled, Slovenia. Retrieved from http://195.130.87.21:8080/dspace/bitstream/123456789/511/1/Corporate%20social%20responsibility%20and%20public%20relations%20perceptions%20and.pdf.

Krstić, M., Filipe. J. A., & Chavaglia, J. (2020). Higher education as a determinant of the competitiveness and sustainable development of an economy. *Sustainability*, 12. Retrieved from https://doi.org/10.3390/su12166607.

Krstić, B., Krstić, M., & Đekić, I. (2018). Sustainability of development and growth – Crisis, distribution of income and inequality. *Economics of Sustainable Development*, 2(1), 1–12.

Krstić, M. (2018). Dimensions of sustainable development. *Economics of Sustainable Development*, 2(2), 19–29.

Krstić, B., & Krstić, M. (2017). Theoretical frameworks of sustainable development. *Economics of Sustainable Development*, 1(1), 1–9.

Kulich, C., Trojanowski, G., Ryan, M. K., Alexander Haslam, S., & Renneboog, L. D. (2011). Who gets the carrot and who gets the stick? Evidence of gender disparities in executive remuneration. *Strategic Management Journal*, 32(3), 301–321.

Kummu, M., de Moel, H., Porkka, M., Siebert, S., Varis, O., & Ward, P. J. (2012). Lost food, wasted resources: Global food supply chain losses and their impacts on freshwater, cropland, and fertiliser use. *Science of the Total Environment*, 438, 477–489. Retrieved from http://dx.doi.org/10.1016/j.scitotenv.2012.08.092.

Lahar, S. (1991). Ecofeminist theory and grassroots politics. *Hypatia*, 6, 28–45.

Lance Toth, E. (1988). Making peace with gender issues in public relations. *Public Relations Review*, 14(3), 36–47.

Lantos, G. P. (2001). The boundaries of strategic corporate social responsibility. *Journal of Consumer Marketing*, 18(7), 595–630.

Lasch, C. (1990). *Journalism, publicity and the lost art of argument. Gannett center journal: Publicity*. New York: Columbia University Press. Retrieved from http://j647commethics.weebly.com/uploads/6/4/2/2/6422481/lasche_article.pdf

Latapí Agudelo, M. A., Jóhannsdóttir, L., & Brynhildur Davíðsdóttir (2019). A literature review of the history and evolution of corporate social responsibility. *International Journal of Corporate Social Responsibility*, 4(1), https://doi.org/10.1186/s40991-018-0039-y. Open access version retrieved from https://jcsr.springeropen.com/articles/10.1186/s40991-018-0039-y.

Latouche, S. (1993). *In the Wake of the Affluent Society*. Translated by O'Connor, M., & Arnoux, R. London: Zed Books.

Lee, T. (2019a). The global rise of "fake news" and the threat to democratic elections in the USA. *Public Administration and Policy: An Asia-Pacific Journal*, 22(1), 15–24.

References   195

Lee, Y. (2019b). Toward a communality with employees: The role of CSR types and internal reputation. *Corporate Reputation Review*, 23, 13–23.

Levashova, Y. (2014). The role of corporate social responsibility in international investment law: The case of tobacco. In – Tench, R., Jones, B., & Sun, W. (eds), *Communicating corporate social responsibility: Perspectives and practice* (Critical Studies on Corporate Responsibility, Governance and Sustainability, Vol. 6), Emerald Group Publishing Limited, Bingley, pp. 131–153.

Lewis, J., & Cushion, S. (2017). Think tanks, television news and impartiality. *Journalism Studies*, 11(10), 1–20.

Lewis, J., Williams, A., & Franklin, B. (2008). A compromised fourth estate? UK news journalism, public relations and news sources. *Journalism Studies*, 9, 1–20.

Liao, L., Lin, T., & Zhang, Y. (2018). Corporate board and corporate social responsibility assurance: Evidence from China. *Journal of Business Ethics*, 150(1), 211–225.

Liu, Y., Lei, L., & Buttner, E. H. (2020). Establishing the boundary conditions for female board directors' influence on firm performance through CSR. *Journal of Business Research*, 121, 112–120.

Lobo, P., Silveirinha, M. J., da Silva, M. T., & Subtil, F. (2017). 'In journalism, we are all men': Material voices in the production of gender meanings. *Journalism Studies*, 18(9), 1148–1166.

Lofgren-Nilsson, M. (2010). "Thinkings" and "doings" of "gender". *Journalism Practice*, 4(1), 1–16.

Lohmann, L. (2010). Uncertainty markets and carbon markets: Variations on Polanyian themes. *New Political Economy*, 15, 225–254.

Lohmann, L. (2009a). Neoliberalism and the calculable world: The rise of carbon trading. In Böhm, S. & Dabhi, S. (eds), *Upsetting the Offset: The Political Economy of Carbon Markets* (pp. 25–37). London: Mayfly. Retrieved from http://mayflybooks.org/?page_id=21.

Lohmann, L. (2009b). Toward a different debate in environmental accounting: The cases of carbon and cost-benefit. *Accounting, Organizations and Society*, 34, 499–534.

Lohmann, L. (2009c). Climate as investment. *Development and Change*, 40, 1063–1083.

Lohmann, L. (2008a). Carbon trading, climate justice and the production of ignorance: Ten examples. *Development*, 51, 359–365. Retrieved from www.thecornerhouse.org.uk/pdf/document/IgnoranceFinal.pdf.

Lohmann, L. (2008b). Hold the applause: A critical look at recent EU climate claims. *The Corner House*. Retrieved from www.thecornerhouse.org.uk/resource/hold-applause.

Lohmann, L. (ed) (2006). *Carbon Trading: A Critical Conversation on Climate Change, Privatisation and Power*. Uppsala: The Dag Hammarskjöld Foundation.

Leahy, T. (2003). Ecofeminism in theory and practice: Women's responses to environmental issues. *Journal of Interdisciplinary Gender Studies*, 7(1–2), 106–125.

Lebreton, L., Slat, B., Ferrari, F., Sainte-Rose, B., Aitken, J., Marthouse, R., Hajbane, S., Cunsolo, S., Schwarz, A., Levivier, A., Noble, K., Debeljak, P., Maral, H., Schoeneich-Argent, R., Brambini, R., & Reisser, J. (2018). Evidence that the Great Pacific Garbage Patch is rapidly accumulating plastic. *Scientific Reports*, 8, Article No. 4666. Retrieved from https://www.nature.com/articles/s41598-018-22939-w.

Lee, H., Place, K. R., & Smith, B. G. (2018). Revisiting gendered assumptions of practitioner power: An exploratory study examining the role of social media expertise. *Public Relations Review*, 44(2), 191–200.

196 *References*

Lee, Y., Wanta, W., & Lee, H. (2015). Resource-based public relations efforts for university reputation from an agenda-building and agenda-setting perspective. *Corporate Reputation Review*, 18(3), 195–209.

Lee, S. Y., & Carroll, C. E. (2011). The emergence, variation, and evolution of corporate social responsibility in the public sphere, 1980-2004: The exposure of firms to public debate. *Journal of Business Ethics*, 104(1), 115–131.

Lee, J. K. (2007). The effect of the internet on homogeneity of the media agenda: A test of the fragmentation thesis. *Journalism & Mass Communication Quarterly*, 84(4), 745–760.

Lee, B., Lancendorfer, K. M., & Lee, K. J. (2005). Agenda-setting and the Internet: The intermedia influence of internet bulletin boards on newspaper coverage of the 2000 general election in South Korea. *Asian Journal of Communication*, 15(1), 57–71.

Lenton, T. M., Rockstrom, J., Gaffney, O., Rahmstorf, S., Richardson, K., Steffen, W., & Schellnuber, H. J. (2020). Climate tipping points too risky to bet against. *Nature*, 575(7784), 592–595.

Lewin, T. (1990). *Ending aid to family planning, large retailer is caught in storm.* Retrieved from http://www.nytimes.com/1990/09/15/us/ending-aid-to-family-planning-large-retailer-is-caught-in-storm.html

Liao, L., Luo, L., & Tang, Q. (2015). Gender diversity, board independence, environmental committee and greenhouse gas disclosure. *The British Accounting Review*, 47(4), 409–424.

Lim, J. (2006). A cross-lagged analysis of agenda setting among online news media. *Journalism & Mass Communication Quarterly*, 83(2), 298–312.

Ling, C. (2014). The background and theoretical origin of ecofeminism. *Cross-Cultural Communication*, 10(4), 104–108.

Lippmann, W. ([1992] 1997). *Public Opinion.* New York: MacMillan Co. First published 1922.

Lonsdale, S. (2013). We agreed that women were a nuisance in the office, anyway: The portrayal of women journalists in early twentieth-century British fiction. *Journalism Studies*, 14(4), 461–475.

Lonsky, J. (2021). Does immigration decrease far-right popularity? Evidence from Finnish municipalities. *Journal of Population Economics*, 34, 97–139.

Lorentzen, L. A., & Eaton, H. (2002). Ecofeminism: An overview. *The Forum on Religion and Ecology at Yale.* Retrieved from https://skat.ihmc.us/rid=1174588237 625_665601541_9501/ecofeminism.pdf.

Lucier, C., & Gareau, B. (2015). From waste to resources: Interrogating 'race to the bottom' in global environmental governance. *Journal of World Systems Research*, 21(2), 495–520.

Lunenberg, K., Gosselt, J. F., & De Jong, M. D. T. (2016). Framing CSR fit: How corporate social responsibility activities are covered by news media. *Public Relations Review*, 42, 943–951.

Lyon, T. P., & Montgomery, A. W. (2015). The means and end of greenwash. *Organization & Environment*, 28(2), 223–249.

MacCormack, C. (1980). Nature, culture and gender: A critique. In MacCormack, C, & Strathern, M. (eds), *Nature, Culture and Gender.* Cambridge: Cambridge University Press, pp. 1–25.

MacGregor, S. (2004). From care to citizenship: Calling ecofeminism back to politics. *Ethics & the Environment*, 9(1), 56–84.

References 197

MacKinnon, C. (1989). *Toward a Feminist Theory of the State.* Cambridge, MA, Harvard University Press.

Maclaran, P., & Stevens, L. (2018). Thinking through feminist theorizing: Poststructuralist feminism, ecofeminism and intersectionality. In Dobscha, S. (ed), *Handbook of Research in Gender and Marketing.* London: Edward Elgar. Retrieved from https://westminsterresearch.westminster.ac.uk/download/44b124eceb20a-c2e49e17daab506c20a58e08a55aa80efc7f594bd74a4637b60/134885/18th%20 June%20Perspectives%20on%20Feminist%20Theorising.docx%20-%20latest%20%28Autosaved%292.pdf.

MacPherson, C. B. (1962). *The Political Theory of Possessive Individualism: Hobbes to Locke.* London: Oxford University Press.

Magdoff, F., & Foster, J. B. (2010). What every environmentalist needs to know about capitalism. *Monthly Review,* March 2010. Retrieved from https://monthlyreview.org/2010/03/01/what-every-environmentalist-needs-to-know-about-capitalism/.

Mahmood, A., & Bashir, J. (2020). How does corporate social responsibility transform brand reputation into brand equity? Economic and noneconomic perspectives of CSR. *International Journal of Engineering Business Management,* 12, 1–13.

Mallory, C. (2012). Locating ecofeminism in encounters with food and place. *Journal of Agricultural and Environmental Ethics,* 26, 171–189.

Mallory, C. (2006). Ecofeminism and forest defence in Cascadia: Gender, theory and radical activism. *Capitalism, Nature, Socialism,* 17(1), 32–49.

Maltz, D. N., & Borker, R. A. (1982). A cultural approach to male-female miscommunication. In – Gumperz, J. J. (ed), *Studies in Interactional Sociolinguistics 2.* Cambridge: Cambridge University Press, pp. 196–216.

Mann, S. A. (2011). Pioneers of U.S. ecofeminism and environmental justice. *Feminist Formations,* 23(2), 1–25.

Mandel, E. (2002, [1962]). *An Introduction to Marxist Economic Theory.* London: Resistance Books.

Manheim, J. B., & Albritton, R. B. (1984). Changing national images: International public relations and media agenda setting. *The American Political Science Review,* 78(3), 641–657.

Mansfield, B. (2004). Neoliberalism in the oceans: Rationalization, property rights, and the commons question. *Geoforum,* 35(3), 313–326.

Margolis, J. D., & Walsh, J. P. (2003). Misery loves companies: Rethinking social initiatives by business. *Administrative Science Quarterly,* 48, 268–305.

Marjanić, S. (2020). Ekofeminizam o 'etici' medijski zataškane priče: utjecaj mesne i mliječne industrije na globalno zatopljenje. In – Marjanić, S., & Đurđević, G. (eds), *Ekofeminizam – između ženskih i zelenih studija.* Zagreb: Durieux, pp. 209–239.

Marjanić, S. (2019). Medijska slika svijeta o globalnom zagrijavanju ili "is the Earth fucked?" (Brad Werner). *Media Res,* 8(14), 2169–2180.

Marjanić, S. (2017). "Na čemu si ti?" Primjer viševrsne etnografije / antropologije životinja i veganskoga ekofeminizma/feminističko-vegetarijanske teorije. *NU,* 54(2), 27–48.

Marjanić, S. (2008). Ekofeminizam o "etici" zataškane priče: utjecaj mesne i mliječne industrije na globalno zatopljenje. *Treća,* X(1), 65–86.

Martínez-Alier, J. (1997). Environmental justice (local and global). *Capitalism Nature Socialism,* 8(1), 91–107.

Marx, K. (1981). *Capital* (Vol. 3). London: Penguin Books.

Marx, K. (1976 [1967]). *Capital.* Translated by B. Fowkes. London: Pelican.

198 *References*

Marx, K., & Engels, F. (1975). *Collected Works*. New York: International Publishers.

Marx, K., & Engels, F. (1964). *The Communist Manifesto*. New York: Monthly Review Press.

Mason, M. (2008). Transparency for whom? Information disclosure and power in global environmental governance. *Global Environmental Politics*, 8(2), 8–13.

May, S. K., & Zorn, T. E. (2003). Forum communication and corporate social responsibility: Forum introduction. *Management Communication Quarterly*, 16, 595–598.

Mayer, S. (2006). Literary studies, ecofeminism, and the relevance of environmentalist knowledge production in the humanities. In – Gersdorf, C., & Mayer, S. (eds), *Nature in Literary and Cultural Studies: Transatlantic Perspectives on Ecocriticism* (pp. 111–128). Amsterdam: Rodopi.

Mazzei, A. (2014). A multidisciplinary approach for a new understanding of corporate communication. *Corporate Communications: An International Journal*, 19(2), 216–230.

McCann, D. P. (2000a). Do corporations have any responsibility beyond making a profit? A response to Norman P. Barry. *Journal of Markets & Morality*, 3(1), 108–114.

McCann, D. P. (2000b). Do corporations have any responsibility beyond making a profit? A response to Norman P. Barry. *Journal of Markets & Morality*, 3(1), 120–126.

Meijer, M. M., & Kleinnijenhuis, J. (2006a). Issue news and corporate reputation: Applying the theories of agenda setting and issue ownership in the field of business communication. *Journal of Communication*, 56(3), 543–559.

Meijer, M. M., & Kleinnijenhuis, J. (2006b). News and corporate reputation: Empirical findings from the Netherlands. *Public Relations Review*, 32(4), 341–348.

McAllister, I. (1994). Dimensions of environmentalism: Public opinion, political activism and party support in Australia. *Environmental Politics*, 3(1), 22–42.

McCann, D. P. (2000a). Do corporations have any responsibility beyond making a profit? A response to Norman P. Barry. *Journal of Markets & Morality*, 3(1), 108–114.

McCann, D. P. (2000b). Do corporations have any responsibility beyond making a profit? A response to Norman P. Barry. *Journal of Markets & Morality*, 3(1), 120–126.

McCarthy, J. (2004). Privatizing conditions of production: trade agreements as neoliberal environmental governance. *Geoforum*, 35(3), 327–341.

McChesney, R. W. (2004). *The Problem of the Media. U.S. Communication Politics in the 21st Century*. New York: Monthly Review Press.

McChesney, R. W. (1997). The mythology of commercial broadcasting and the contemporary crisis of public broadcasting. *The 1997 Spry Memorial Lecture*. Retrieved from http://www.ratical.com/coglobalize/RMmythCB.html.

McCombs, M., & Stroud, N. J. (2014). Psychology of agenda-setting effects: Mapping the paths of information processing. *Review of Communication Research*, 2(1), 68–93.

McCombs, M. (2014). *Setting the Agenda: The Mass Media and Public Opinion* (2nd edition). Cambridge: Polity.

McCombs, M., Holbert, R. L., Kiousis, S., & Wanta, W. (2011). *The News and Public Opinion: Media Effects on Civic Life*. Cambridge: Polity.

McCombs, M. (2005). A look at agenda-setting: Past, present and future. *Journalism Studies*, 6(4), 543–557.

References 199

McCombs, M. (2004). *Setting the Agenda: The Mass Media and Public Opinion.* Cambridge: Polity Press.

McCombs, M. (2003). *The Agenda-Setting Role of the Mass Media in the Shaping of Public Opinion.* Retrieved from http://www.infoamerica.org/documentos_pdf/mccombs01.pdf.

McCombs, M., & Ghanem, S. I. (2001). The convergence of agenda setting and framing. In – Reese, S. D., Gandy, O. H., & Grant, A. E. (eds), *Framing Public Life: Perspectives on Media and Our Understanding of the Social World* (pp. 67–81). Mahweh, NJ: Lawrence Erlbaum Associates Inc.

McCombs, M. (1997). Building consensus: The news media's agenda-setting roles. *Political Communication,* 14, 433–443.

McCombs, M., & Shaw, D. L. (1972). The agenda-setting function of mass media. *Public Opinion Quarterly,* 36(2), 176–187.

McCormick, S. (2006). The Brazilian anti-dam movement knowledge contestation as communicative action. *Organization & Environment,* 19(3), 321–346.

McDowell, L. (1997). *Capital Culture. Gender at Work in the City.* Oxford: Wiley-Blackwell.

McQuail, D. (2010). *Mass Communication Theory* (6th edition). London: SAGE.

McQuail, D. (2003). *Media Accountability and Freedom of Publication.* Oxford: Oxford University Press.

McQuail, D. (2005). *McQuail's Mass Communication Theory.* London: SAGE.

McQuail, D. (1997). Accountability of media to society: principles and means. *European Journal of Communication,* 12(4), 511–529.

McLeod, C., O'Donohoe, S., & Townley, B. (2011). Pot noodles, placements and peer regard: creative career trajectories and communities of practice in the British advertising industry. *British Journal of Management,* 22(1), 114–131.

McMahon, M. (1997). From the ground up: Ecofeminism and ecological economics. *Ecological Economics,* 20, 163–173.

McNealy, J. E. (2017). Disparaging trademarks and social responsibility. *Sport, Ethics and Philosophy,* 12, 304–16.

McStay, J. R., Dunlap, R. E. (1983). Male-female differences in concern for environmental quality. *International Journal of Women's Studies,* 6(4), 291–301.

Meadows, D., Randers, J., & Dennis Meadows, D. (2004). *Limits to Growth: The 30-Year Update.* White River Junction: Chelsea Green Publishing.

Meadows, D., Meadows, D., Randers, J., & Behrens, WW. (1972). *The Limits to Growth.* New York: Universe Books.

Meier, W. A., & Perrin, I. (2007). Media concentration and media governance. *Communications,* 32(3), 336–343.

Mellicker, R. (2016). *The feminism of fashion.* Retrieved from https://www.huffpost.com/entry/the-feminism-of-fashion_b_9705262.

Mellor, M. (1992). *Breaking the boundaries: Towards a feminist, green socialism.* London: Virago.

Menasce Horowitz, J., Igielnik, R., & Kochhar, R. (2020). Trends in income and wealth inequality. *Pew Social Trends Survey.* Retrieved from https://www.pewsocialtrends.org/2020/01/09/trends-in-income-and-wealth-inequality/.

Merchant, C. (2020). Ekofeminizam i feministička teorija. In – Marjanić, S., & Đurđević, G. (eds), *Ekofeminizam – između ženskih i zelenih studija.* Zagreb: Durieux, pp. 29–35.

Merchant, K. (2012). How men and women differ: Gender differences in communication styles, influence tactics, and leadership styles. *CMS Senior Theses,*

200 *References*

Paper 513, retrieved from http://scholarship.claremont.edu/cgi/viewcontent.cgi?article=1521&context=cmc_theses.

Merchant, C. (1992). Perspectives on ecofeminism. *Environmental Action*, 18–19. Retrieved from https://nature.berkeley.edu/departments/espm/env-hist/articles/37.pdf.

Merchant, C. (1990). *The Death of Nature: Women, Ecology and the Scientific Revolution*. San Francisco, CA: Harper.

Meraz, S. (2011). Using time series analysis to measure intermedia agenda-setting influence in traditional media and political blog networks. *J&MC Quarterly*, 88(1), 176–194.

Meraz, S. (2009). Is there an elite hold? Traditional media to social media agenda setting influence in blog networks. *Journal of Computer-Mediated Communication*, 14, 682–707.

Meraz, S. (2008). The blogosphere's gender gap: Differences in visibility, popularity, and authority. In – Poindexter, P. (ed), *Women, Men, and News*. New York: Routledge, pp. 142–167.

Middleton, M. (2009). *Social Responsibility in the Media*. Retrieved from http://www.mediafutureweek.nl/wp-content/uploads/2014/05/SR_media1.pdf.

Mies, M. (1986). *Patriarchy and Accumulation on a World Scale*. London: Zed Books.

Milardović, A. H. (2016). *Hrana i ekologija*. Čakovec: Dvostruka duga.

Miles, A., Rapoport, L., Wardle, J., Afuape, T., & Duman, M. (2001). Using the mass-media to target obesity: An analysis of the characteristics and reported behaviour change of participants in the BBC's 'fighting fat, fighting fit' campaign. *Health Education Research: Theory and Practice*, 16, 357–72.

Miller, D. A. (1988). Women in public relations graduate study. *Public Relations Review*, 14(3), 29–35.

Mills, E. (2017). How to deal with men. *British Journalism Review*, 28(4), 5–7.

Mills, E. (2014). Why do the best jobs go to men? *British Journalism Review*, 25(3), 17–23.

Millett, K. (1969). *Sexual Politics*. New York: Doubleday.

Mishan, E. J. (1967). *The Costs of Economic Growth*. London: Pelican Books.

Mishra T. K., Maiti S. K., Banerjee S., & Banerjee S. K. (2021). From genesis to awaited success of joint forest management in India. In – Shit, P. K., Pourghasemi, H. R., Das, P., & Bhunia, G. S. (eds), *Spatial Modeling in Forest Resources Management. Environmental Science and Engineering*. Cham: Springer. https://doi.org/10.1007/978-3-030-56542-8_26.

Moberg, D., & Romar, E. (2006). *WorldCom case study update. Markkula center for applied ethics*. Retrieved from https://www.scu.edu/ethics/focus-areas/business-ethics/resources/worldcom-case-study-update/

Moberg, D., & Romar, E. (2003). *WorldCom. Markkula center for applied ethics*. Retrieved from https://www.scu.edu/ethics/focus-areas/business-ethics/resources/worldcom/

Moore, N. (2011). Eco/feminism and rewriting the ending of feminism: From the Chipko movement to Clayoquot Sound. *Feminist Theory*, 12(1), 3–21.

Morgan, J. (2019) Will we work in twenty-first century capitalism? A critique of the fourth industrial revolution literature. *Economy and Society*, 48(3), 371–398.

Morgan, J. (2017). Methodological and ideological options: Piketty and the growth dilemma revisited in the context of ecological economics. *Ecological Economics*, 136, 169–177.

References 201

Morgan, M. J. (2004). Women in a man's world: Gender differences in leadership at the military academy. *Journal of Applied Psychology*, 34(12), 2482–2502.

Morris-Suzuki, T. (2000). For and against NGOs. *New Left Review*, 2, 63–84.

Morsing, M., Schultz, M., & Nielsen, U. (2008). The "Catch 22" of communicating CSR: Findings from a Danish study. *Journal of Marketing Communications*, 14(2), 97–111.

Morsing, M., & Schultz, M. (2006). Corporate social responsibility communication: Stakeholder information, response and involvement strategies. *Business Ethics: A European Review*, 15(4), 323–338.

Mortimer, N. (2016). Why women in ad land are working in a 'toxic culture'. *Advertising Week*, 27 September. Retrieved from https://laurafegley.com/the-3-movements-elephant-on-madison-avenue.

Moore, J. W. (2010). The end of the road? Agricultural revolutions in the capitalist world-ecology, 1450–2010. *Journal of Agrarian Change*, 10, 389–413.

Moon, J. (2005). An explicit model of business-society relations. In – Habisch, A., Jonker, J., Wegner, M., & Schmidpeter, R. (eds), *Corporate Social Responsibility Across Europe*. Berlin: Springer, pp. 51–65.

Moon, J. (2004). Government as a driver of corporate social responsibility. No. 20-2004. *ICCSR Research Paper Series*, ISSN 1479-5214, 1–27.

Mosco, V. (2009). *The Political Economy of Communication*. London: SAGE.

Muro, M., Tomer, A., Shivaram, R., & Kane, J. (2019). *Advancing Inclusion Through Clean Energy Jobs*. Brookings Institute, 18 November. Retrieved from https://think-asia.org/bitstream/handle/11540/10116/2019.04_metro_Clean-Energy-Jobs_Report_Muro-Tomer-Shivaran-Kane_updated.pdf?sequence=1.

Murray, K. B., & Vogel, C. M. (1997). Using a hierarchy-of-effects approach to gauge the effectiveness of corporate social responsibility to generate goodwill toward the firm: Financial versus nonfinancial impacts. *Journal of Business Research*, 38, 141–159.

Naes, A. (1989). *Ecology, Community and Lifestyle*. Cambridge: Cambridge University Press.

Namkung, Y., & Jang, S. (2017). Are consumers willing to pay more for green practices at restaurants? *Journal of Hospitality & Tourism Research*, 41(3), 329–356.

Napoli, P. M. (1999). Deconstructing the diversity principle. *Journal of Communication*, 49(4), 7–34.

Nekhilli, M., Nagati, H., Chtioui, T., & Nekhili, A. (2017). Gender-diverse board and the relevance of voluntary CSR reporting. *International Review of Financial Analysis*, 50, 81–100.

Nelson, J. A. (2004). *Beyond small-is-beautiful: A buddhist and feminist analysis of ethics and business*. Global Development and Environment Institute. Working paper No. 04-01, 1–18. Retrieved from http://www.ase.tufts.edu/gdae/publications/working_papers/04-01beyondsmall.pdf

Nerone, J. (1995). Social responsibility theory. In – *Last Rights: Revisiting Four Theories of the Press*. Urbana: University of Illinois Press. Retrieved from http://www.mmc.twitbookclub.org/MMC910/Readings/Week%2003/Social%20Responsibility%20Theory.pdf.

Newell, P., & Paterson, M. (2010). *Climate Capitalism: Global Warming and the Transformation of the Global Economy*. Cambridge: Cambridge University Press.

Newell, P., & Paterson, M. (2009). *The Politics of the Carbon Economy. The Politics of Climate Change: A Survey*. London: SAGE, pp. 80–99.

202 *References*

Newell, P. J., & Roberts, J. T. (2007). *The Globalization and Environment Reader.* London: Wiley- Blackwell.

Newport, F. (2008a, January 28). *New York Poll: Clinton, McCain have wide leads; New York Republican Vote Appears Very Fluid, However. (Hillary Rodham Clinton and 236 John McCain) (Survey).* Retrieved from http://www.highbeam.com/doc/1G1-186196010.html.

Newport, F. (2008b, January 28). *California Poll: Clinton Leads, McCain and Romney Close; One-Fifth of California Voters Already Voted Via Absentee Ballot. (Hillary Rodham Clinton, John McCain and Mitt Romney) (Survey).* Retrieved from http://www.highbeam.com/doc/1G1-186196009.html.

Nguyen, T. H. H., Ntim, C. G., & Malagila, J. (2020). Women on corporate boards and corporate financial and non-financial performance: A systematic literature review and future research agenda. *International Review of Financial Analysis,* 71, 1–24.

Nguyen, H., & Faff, R. (2006). Impact of board size and board diversity on firm value: Australian evidence. *Corporate Ownership and Control,* 4(2 A), 24–32.

Niehans, J. (1987). Classical monetary theory, new and old. *Journal of Money, Credit and Banking,* 19(4), 409–424.

Nicolotti Squires, C. (2016). Jobs for the girls. *British Journalism Review,* 27(1), 7–8.

Nielsen, A. E., & Thomsen, C. (2009). CSR communication in small and medium-sized enterprises. *Corporate Communications: An International Journal,* 14(2), 176–189.

Nielsen, A. E., & Thomsen, C. (2007). Reporting CSR – What and how to say it? *Corporate Communications: An International Journal,* 12(1), 25–40.

No author a (2005). Ecofeminism in two worlds. *Capitalism, Nature Socialism,* 16(4), 145–147.

No author b (2011). On ecosocialism, objectives, and the role of the natural sciences. *Capitalism Nature Socialism,* 22(3), 1–7.

North, L. (2016a). 'Still a blokes club': The motherhood dilemma in journalism. *Journalism,* 17(3), 315–330.

North, L. (2016b). The gender of 'soft' and 'hard' news: Female journalists' views on gendered story allocations. *Journalism Studies,* 17(3), 356–373.

North, L. (2009a). 'Blokey' newsroom culture. *Media International Australia,* 132, 5–15.

North, L. (2009b). *The Gendered Newsroom: How Journalists Experience the Changing World of Media.* Cresskill, NJ: Hampton Press.

Ntim, C. G. (2016). Corporate governance, corporate health accounting, and firm value: The case of HIV/AIDS disclosures in Sub-Saharan Africa. *International Journal of Accounting,* 51(2), 155–216.

Ntim, C. G., & Soobaroyen, T. (2013). Black economic empowerment disclosures by South African listed corporations: The influence of ownership and board characteristics. *Journal of Business Ethics,* 116(1), 121–138.

Nunn, A. (2015). Saving world market society from itself? The new global politics of inequality and the agents of world market society. *Spectrum: Journal of Global Studies,* 7(2), 68–88.

Nunn, A. (2014). The contested and contingent outcomes of Thatcherism in the UK. *Capital & Class,* 38(2), 303–321.

Ocler, R. (2006). Making sense of social responsibility: The French discourse. *Tamara Journal* 5(3–4), 1532–5555.

References 203

Omazić, M. A. (ed) (2012). *Zbirka studija slučaja društveno odgovornog poslovanja.* Zagreb: HRPSOR & EFZG. Retrieved from http://www.dop.hr/wp-content/uploads/zbirka_studija_slucaja_DOP.pdf.

Omolade, B. (1989). We speak for the planet. In Harris, A., & King, Y. (eds), *Rocking the Ship of State. Toward a Feminist Peace Politics.* Boulder: Westview Press, pp. 171–190.

Owen, B. M., & Wildman, S. S. (1992). *Video Economics.* Cambridge, MA: Harvard University Press.

Owens-Ibie, N. (1994). Press responsibility and public opinion in political transition. *Africa Media Review,* 8(1), African Council for Communication Education, pp. 69–80.

Padelford, W., & White, D. (2009). The shaping of a society's economic ethos: A longitudinal study of individuals' morality of profit-making worldview. *Journal of Business Ethics,* 85(1), 67–75.

Pallin, R. (n.d.). Green new deal as an anti-neoliberal program. *Triple Crisis: Global Perspectives on Finance, Development and Environment.* Retrieved from http://triplecrisis.com/the-green-new-deal-as-an-anti-neoliberal-program/.

Panayotou, T. (2000). Economic growth and the environment. *CID Working Paper Series.* Cambridge, MA: Harvard University, July 2000. Retrieved from https://dash.harvard.edu/bitstream/handle/1/39570415/056.pdf?sequence=1.

Panayotou, T. (1993). Empirical tests and policy analysis of environmental degradation at different stages of economic development. *Working Paper WP238 Technology and Employment Programme. Geneva: International Labor Office.* Retrieved from https://www.ilo.org/public/libdoc/ilo/1993/93B09_31_engl.pdf.

Parfitt, J., Barthel, M., & Macnaughton, S. (2010). Food waste within food supply chains: Quantification and potential for change to 2050. *Philosophical Transactions of the Royal Society B: Biological Sciences,* 365(1554), 3065–3081. Retrieved from http://dx.doi.org/10.1098/rstb.2010.0126.

Parkins, I. (2006). Building a feminist theory of fashion. *Australian Feminist Studies,* 23(58), 501–515.

Parmar, B. L., Freeman, R. E., Harrison, J. S., Wicks, A. C., de Colle, S., & Purnell, L. (n.b.). *Stakeholder theory: The state of the art.* Retrieved from http://www.esade.edu/itemsweb/content/produccion/4004902.pdf

Pedersen, E. R. G. (2015). *Corporate Social Responsibility.* Thousand Oaks, CA: SAGE.

Pedersen, G. E., & Pedersen, J. (2013). The rise of business-NGO partnerships. *Journal of Corporate Citizenship,* 50(1), 6–19.

Pedersen, E. R. (2006). Making corporate social responsibility (CSR) operable: How companies translate stakeholder dialogue into practice. *Business and Society Review,* 111(2), 137–163.

Perko, T., Mays, C., Valuch, J., & Nagy, A. (2015). Mass and new media: Review of framing, treatment and sources in reporting on Fukushima. *Mass Communication and Journalism,* 5(3), 1–5. Online pre-printed version, http://dx.doi.org/10.4172/2165-7912.1000252.

Pickard, V. (2015). *America's Battle for Media Democracy: The Triumph of Corporate Libertarianism and the Future of Media Reform.* New York: Cambridge University Press.

Picard, R. G. (2014). Public opinion, party politics, policy, and immigration news in the United Kingdom. *Working Paper, Reuters Institute for the Study of*

204 *References*

Journalism. Retrieved from http://reutersinstitute.politics.ox.ac.uk/sites/default/files/News%20and%20Immigration%20Working%20Paper.pdf.

Pillay, R. (2015). *The Changing Nature of Corporate Social Responsibility: CSR and Development – The Case of Mauritius*. New York: Taylor & Francis.

Philips, R., Freeman, R. E., Wicks, A. C. (2003). What stakeholder theory is not. *Business Ethics Quarterly*, 13(4), 479–502.

Plaisance, P. L. (2000). The concept of media accountability reconsidered. *Journal of Mass Media Ethics*, 15(4), 257–268.

Plumwood, V. (1996). Does ecofeminism need the master subject? A response to Janis Birkeland. *Trumpeter*. Retrieved from http://trumpeter.athabascau.ca/index.php/trumpet/article/view/236/337.

Plumwood, V. (1993). *Feminism and the Mastery of Nature*. London: Routledge.

Plumwood, V. (1991). Nature, self and gender: Feminism, environmental philosophy and the critique of rationalism. *Hypatia: A Journal of Feminist Philosophy*, 6(1), 3–27.

Poole, K. T., & Harmon Zeigter, L. (1985). *Women, Public Opinion, and Politics: The Changing Political Attitudes of American Women*. New York: Longman.

Pollin, R. (2019). The Green New Deal as an anti-neoliberalism program. *Dollars & Sense: Real World Economics*. Retrieved from http://www.dollarsandsense.org/archives/2019/1119pollin.html

Pollock, T. G., & Rindova, V. P. (2003). Media legitimation effects in the market for initial public offerings. *Academy of Management Journal*, 46(5), 631.

Pomering, A., & Johnson, L. W. (2009). Advertising corporate social responsibility initiatives to communicate corporate image: Inhibiting skepticism to enhance persuasion. *Corporate Communications: An International Journal*, 14(4), 420–439.

Post, C., & Byron, K. (2015). Women on boards and firm financial performance: A meta-analysis. *Academy of Management Journal*, 58(5), 1546–1571.

Post, C., Rahman, N., & McQuillen, C. (2015). From board composition to corporate environmental performance through sustainability-themed alliances. *Journal of Business Ethics*, 130(2), 423–435.

Pratt, C. (1986). Professionalism in Nigerian public relations. *Public Relations Review*, 12(4), 27–40.

Press Gazette (2021). *Trust, Truth and Making News Pay: Editors Outline the Biggest Challenges for Journalism in 2021*. Retrieved from https://pressgazette.co.uk/trust-truth-and-making-news-pay-editors-outline-the-biggest-challenges-for-journalism-in-2021/.

Press Gazette (2020a). *UK National Newspaper ABC Circulation Figures: November 2020 and Historic Data*. Retrieved from https://www.pressgazette.co.uk/most-popular-newspapers-uk-abc-monthly-circulation-figures/.

Press Gazette (2020b). *Coronavirus: Public Distrust Journalists Despite Relying on News Media for Daily Updates, Survey Shows*. Retrieved from https://www.pressgazette.co.uk/coronavirus-public-distrust-journalists-despite-relying-on-news-media-for-daily-updates-survey-shows/.

Press Gazette (2020c). *Press Gazette Poll Shows Half Believe Trust in Journalism Has Fallen Since Covid-19 Outbreak*. Retrieved from https://www.pressgazette.co.uk/press-gazette-poll-shows-half-believe-trust-in-journalism-has-fallen-since-covid-19-outbreak/.

Press Gazette (2020d). *Who Owns the Media? Top Newspaper, Website and Magazine Owners Charted*. Retrieved from https://www.pressgazette.co.uk/digital-diversity-or-age-of-consolidation-media-ownership-2020/.

References 205

Press Gazette (2018). *Just Two Per cent of Brits Put 'Great Deal' of Trust in Journalists to Tell Truth, New Research Finds.* Retrieved from https://www.pressgazette.co.uk/just-two-per-cent-of-brits-put-great-deal-of-trust-in-journalists-to-tell-truth-new-research-finds/.

Preston, C. J. (2012). Ethics and geoengineering: Reviewing the moral issues raised by solar radiation management and carbon dioxide removal. *WIREs Climate Change*, 4, 23–37.

Preston, L. E., & Post, J. E. (1975). *Private Management and Public Policy: The Principle of Public Responsibility.* Englewood Cliffs, NJ: Prentice-Hall.

Price, S., & Nunn, A. (2016). Managing neo-liberalisation through the sustainable development agenda: the EU-ACP trade relationship and world market expansion. *Third World Thematics: A TWQ Journal*, 1(4), 454–469.

Prudham, S. (2004). Poisoning the well: Neoliberalism and the contamination of municipal water in Walkerton, Ontario. *Geoforum*, 35(3), 343–359.

Puleo, A. H. (2017). What is ecofeminism? *Quaderns de la Mediterrania*, 25, 27–34.

Quested, T. E., Marsh, E., Stunell, D., & Parry, A. D. (2013). Spaghetti soup: The complex world of food waste behaviours. *Resources, Conservation and Recycling.* Retrieved from http://analyseplatformen.dk/Data/madspildsmonitor/HTML_madspildsplatform/assets/quested-et-al_2013_spaghetti-soup_the-complex-world-of-food-waste-behaviours.pdf.

Quested, T. E., Parry, A. D., Easteal, S., Swannell, R. (2011). Food and drink waste from households in the UK. *Nutrition Bulletin*, 36, 460–467.

Rademacher, L., & Remus, N. (2014). Correlating leadership style, communication strategy and management fashion: An approach to describing the drivers and settings of CSR institutionalization. In – Tench, R., Sun, W., & Jones, B. (eds), *Communicating Corporate Social Responsibility: Perspectives and Practice.* Howard House: Emerald Books, pp. 81–110.

Radford Ruether, R. (2012). Ecofeminism – The challenge to theology. *DEP*, 20, 23–34.

Radulović, N. (2020). A/simetrija životinja i žena. In – Marjanić, S., & Đurđević, G. (eds), *Ekofeminizam – između ženskih i zelenih studija.* Zagreb: Durieux, pp. 161–179.

Rakow, L. F., & Nastasia, D. I. (2009). Feminist theory of public relations: An example from Dorothy E. Smith. In – Oyvind, I., van Ruler, B., & Fredriksson, M. (eds), *Public Relations and Social Theory* (pp. 252–277). London: Routledge.

Ramsay, G. (2019). *Who Owns the UK Media? Media Reform Organisation.* Retrieved from https://www.mediareform.org.uk/wp-content/uploads/2019/03/FINALonline2.pdf.

Razak, A. (1990). Toward a womanist analysis of birth. In – Diamond, I., & Orenstein, G. (eds)., *Reweaving the World.* San Francisco, CA: Sierra Club, pp. 165–172.

Rhodes, C. J. (2018). Plastic pollution and potential solutions. *Science Progress*, 101(3), 207–260. Paper 1800271, https://doi.org/10.3184/003685018X15294876706211.

Ripple, W. J., Wolf, C., Newsome, T. M., Barnbard, P., Moomaw, W. R., & 11,258 signatories (2020). World scientists' warning of a climate emergency. *BioScience*, 70(1), 8–12, https://doi.org/10.1093/biosci/biz152.

Roberts, M., Wants, W., & Tzong-Horng, D. (2002). Agenda setting and issue salience online. *Communication Research*, 29(4), 452–465.

Roszak, T. (1992). *The Voice of the Earth.* New York: Simon and Schuster.

Reardon, B. A. (1985). *Sexism and the War System.* New York: Teachers College Press.

206 *References*

Reese, S. D., & Danielian, L. H. (1989). Intermedia influence and the drug issue: Converging on cocaine. In – Shoemaker, P. J. (ed), *Communication Campaigns about Drugs*. Hillsdale, NJ: Lawrence Erlbaum Associates, pp. 29–45.

Reilly, J. J., Armstrong, J., Dorosty, A. R., Emmett, P. M., Ness, A., Rogers, I., Steer, C., & Sherriff, A. (2005). Avon longitudinal study of parents and children study team. Early life risk factors for obesity in childhood: Cohort study. *BMJ*, 330, 302–310.

Richards, I. (2004). Stakeholders vs. shareholders: Journalism, business and ethics. *Journal of Mass Media Ethics*, 19(2), 119–129.

Ripple, W., Smith, P., Haberl, H. et al. (2014) Ruminants, climate change and climate policy. *Nature Climate Change*, 4, 2–5, https://doi.org/10.1038/nclimate2081.

Ritchie, H., & Roser, M. (2018). Plastic pollution. *Our World in Data*. Retrieved from https://ourworldindata.org/plastic-pollution?utm_source=newsletter.

Roach, C. (1991). Loving your mother: On the woman-nature relation. *Hypatia*, 6, 45–57.

Roberts, M., & McCombs, M. (1994). Agenda setting and political advertising: Origins of the news agenda. *Political Communication*, 11(3), 249–262.

Rohwer, L., & Topić, M. (2018). The communication of corporate–NGO partnerships: Analysis of Sainsbury's collaboration with comic relief. *Journal of Brand Management*, 26 (1), 35–48.

Ross, K. (2001). Women at work: Journalism as en-gendered practice. *Journalism Studies*, 2(4), 531–544.

Rudy, A. (2006). On the ecofeminist editorial: "Moving to an embodied materialism". *Capitalism Nature Socialism*, 17(4), 105–114.

Ruether, R. R. (1975). *New Woman/New Earth: Sexist Ideologies and Human Liberation*. New York: The Seabury Press.

Ruggeria, G., Corsia, S., Naygab, R. M. (2021). Eliciting willingness to pay for fairtrade products with information. *Food Quality and Preference*, 87, 329–356.

Rupley, K. H., Brown, D., & Marshall, R. S. (2012). Governance, media and the quality of environmental disclosure. *Journal of Accounting and Public Policy*, 31(6), 610–640.

saed (2017). From the October revolution to revolutionary Rojava: An ecosocialist reading. *Capitalism, Nature, Socialism*, 28(4), 3–20.

Salleh, A. K. (2017). *Ecofeminism as Politics: Nature, Marx and the Postmodern*. London: Zed Books.

Salleh, A. K. (2013). Moving to an embodied materialism. *Capital Nature Socialism*, 16(2), 9–14.

Salleh, A. (2011). Fukushima: A call for women's leadership. *Journal of Environmental Thought and Action*, 5(4), 45–52. Retrieved from http://www.arielsalleh.info/theory/eco-feminism/fuku-jete/11_AS_Fuku_JETE.pdf.

Salleh, A. (2010). Embodied materialism in action. *Polygraph: Special Issue on Ecology and Ideology*, 22, 183–199. Retrieved from www.duke.edu/web/polygraph/cfp.html

Salleh, A. (2006). Towards an inclusive solidarity on the left: Editor's introduction. *Capitalism Nature Socialism*, 17(4), 32–37.

Salleh, A. (2005). Moving to an embodied materialism. *Capitalism Nature Socialism*, 16(2), 9–14.

Salleh, A. (2003). Ecofeminism as sociology. *Capitalism Nature Socialism*, 14(1), 61–74.

References   207

Salleh, A. (2001a). Ecofeminism. In – Taylor, V., & Winquist, C. (eds), *The Postmodern Encyclopaedia* (p. 109). London: Routledge. Retrieved from https://www.arielsalleh.info/theory/ecofeminism.html.

Salleh, A. (2001b). Sustaining Marx or sustaining nature? An ecofeminist response to Foster and Burkett. *Organization & Environment*, 14(4), 443–450.

Salleh, A. (2000). The meta-industrial class and why we need it. *Democracy & Nature*, 6(1), 27–36.

Salleh, A. (1994). Nature, woman, labor, capital: Living the deepest contradiction. In – O'Connor, M. (ed), *Is Capitalism Sustainable?* (pp. 106–124). New York: Guilford.

Salleh, A. K. (1993). Class, race, and gender discourse in the ecofeminism/deep ecology debate. *Environmental Ethics*, 15(3), 225–244.

Salleh, A. K. (1992). The ecofeminism/deep ecology debate: A reply to patriarchal reason. *Environmental Ethics*, 14, 195–216.

Salleh, A. (1991). 'Essentialism' – and eco-feminism. *Arena*, 94, 167–173.

Salleh, A. K. (1989). Environmental consciousness and action: An Australian perspective. *The Journal of Environmental Education*, 20, 26–31.

Salleh, A. K. (1984). Deeper than deep ecology: The ecofeminist connection. *Environmental Ethics*, 6, 339–345.

Salleh, A. (1984). From feminism to ecology. *Social Alternatives*, 4(3), 8–12.

Sandberg, L. A., & Sandberg, T. (eds) (2010). *Climate Change – Who's Carrying the Burden? The Chilly Climates of the Global Environmental Dilemma*. Ottawa, Canada: Canadian Centre for Policy Alternatives.

Sandiland, C. (1999). *The Good-Natured Feminist: Ecofeminism and the Quest for Democracy*. Boston, MA: University of Minnesota Press.

Sandoval, M. (2013). Corporate Social (ir)responsibility in media and communication industries. *Javnost – The Public: Journal of the European Institute for Communication and Culture*, 20(3), 39–57. Retrieved from http://openaccess.city.ac.uk/2906.

Saunders, M., Lewis, P., & Thornhill, A. (2012). *Research Methods for Business Students* (6th edition). Harlow: Pearson.

Saval, N. (2015). *Cubed: A Secret History of the Workplace*. New York: Anchor Books.

Schahn, J., & Holzer, E. (1990). Studies of individual environmental concern: The role of knowledge, gender and background variables. *Environment and Behaviour*, 22(6), 767–786.

Schanes, K., Doberniga, K., & Gözeta, B. (2018). Food waste matters – A systematic review of household food waste practices and their policy implications. *Journal of Cleaner Production*, 182, 978–991.

Scharff, V. (1995). Are earth girls easy? Ecofeminism, women's history and environmental history. *Journal of Women's History*, 7(2), 164–175.

Schiller, H. (1997). Manipulation and the packaged consciousness. In – Golding, P., & Murdock, G. (ed), *The Political Economy of the Media* (Vol. I, pp. 423–437). Cheltenham, Brookfield: Elgar.

Schiller, H., & Schiller, A. (1988). Libraries, public access to information, and commerce. In V. Mosco and J. Wasko (eds), *The Political Economy of Information* (pp. 146–166). Madison: The University of Wisconsin Press.

Schneider, M., Fridlund Dunton, G., & Cooper, D. M. (2007). Media use and obesity in adolescent females. *Obesity*, 15, 2328–2335.

208   *References*

Schwartz, M. S., & Carroll, A. B. (2003). Corporate social responsibility: A three-domain approach. *Business Ethics Quarterly*, 13(4), 503–530.

Scott, L. M. (2006). *Fresh Lipstick: Redressing Fashion and Feminism*. London: Palgrave Macmillan.

Scrimger, J. (1985). Profile: Women in Canadian public relations. *Public Relations Review*, 11(3), 40–46.

Seager, J. (1993). *Earth Follies: Feminism, Politics and the Environment*. London: Earthscan.

Selden, T. M., & Song, D. (1994). Environmental quality and development: Is there a Kuznets curve for air pollution emissions? *Journal of Environmental Economics and Management*, 27, 147–162.

Shamir, R. (2008). The age of responsibilization: On market-embedded morality. *Economy & Society*, 37(1), 1–19.

Sheehy, B. (2014). Defining CSR: Problems and solutions. *Journal of Business Ethics*, 131, 625–648.

Semega, J., Kollar, M., Shrider, E. A., & Creamer, J. F. (2020). Income and Poverty in the United States: 2019. Retrieved from https://www.census.gov/content/dam/Census/library/publications/2020/demo/p60-270.pdf.

Shafik, N., & Bandyopadhyay, S. (1992). Economic growth and environmental resources. *Journal of Environmental Economics and Management*, 4, 1–24.

Shaw, E. F. (1979). Agenda-setting and mass communication theory. *International Communication Gazette*, 25, 96–105.

Shoemaker, P. J., & Reese, S. D. (1996). *Mediating the Message: Theories of Influences on Mass Media Content*. White Plains, NY: Longman.

Shuchman, M., & Wilkes, M. S. (1997). Medical scientists and health news reporting: A case of miscommunication. *Annals of Internal Medicine*, 126(12), 976–982.

Siebert, F., Peterson, T. B., & Schramm, W. (1963). *Four Theories of the Press: The Authoritarian, Libertarian, Social Responsibility, and Soviet Communist Concepts of What the Press Should Be and Do*. Chicago: University of Illinois Press.

Siegel, D. S. (2007). Vitaliano DF. An empirical analysis of the strategic use of corporate social responsibility. *Journal of Economics and Management Strategy*, 16, 773–792.

Sieghart, M. A., & Henry, G. (2016). The cheaper sex: How women lose out in journalism. *Women in Journalism Report (1998)*. Retrieved from http://womeninjournalism.co.uk/wp-content/uploads/2012/10/CheaperSex.pdf.

Sikka, T. (2017). Technofeminism and ecofeminism: An analysis of geoengineering research. In – Vakoch, D. A., & Mickey, S. (eds), *Ecofeminism in Dialogue*. Lanham, MD: Lexington Books, pp. 107–129.

Silverstein, K. (2013). Enron, ethics and today's corporate values. *Forbes,* 14 May. Retrieved from https://www.forbes.com/sites/kensilverstein/2013/05/14/enron-ethics-and-todays-corporate-values/?sh=4a4579835ab8

Simon, J. L. (1981). *The Ultimate Resource*. Princeton, NJ: Princeton University Press.

Singer, P. (2002). *Animal Liberation*. New York: Harper Collins Publisher.

Singh, K., & Misra, M. (2021). Linking corporate social responsibility (CSR) and organizational performance: The moderating effect of corporate reputation. *European Research on Management and Business Economics*, 27(1), 100–139.

Singh, R., & Smyth, R. (1988). Australian public relations: Status at the turn of the 21st century. *Public Relations Review*, 26(4), 387–401.

References 209

Sisco, T., & Lucas, J. (2015). Flawed vessels. *Feminist Media Studies*, 15(3), 492–507.

Shapiro, R. Y., & Mahajan, H. (1986). Gender differences in policy preferences: A summary of trends from the 1960s to the 1980s. *Public Opinion Quarterly*, 50, 42–61.

Shaw, C. (2017). A men-only meritocracy. *British Journalism Review*, blog entry (2011). Retrieved from http://www.bjr.org.uk/blog+february_2011.

Shiva, V. (1999). *Biopiracy: The Plunder of Nature and Knowledge*. Berkeley, CA: North Atlantic Books.

Shiva, V. (1996). *Trading our lives away: Free trade, women and ecology* (DURGA-BAI DESHMUKH MEMORIAL LECTURE-1996). Retrieved from https://csdindia.org/wp-content/uploads/2017/04/1996-Memorial-Lecture-Dr.-Vandana-Shiva.pdf

Shiva, V. (1989). *Staying Alive: Women, Ecology and Survival in India*. London and New Delhi: Kali for women and Zed Books.

Shiva, V., & Bandyopadhyay, J. (1986). The evolution, structure, and impact of the Chipko movement. *Mountain Research and Development*, 6(2), 133–142.

Shuck, A. R. T., & de Vreese, C. H. (2006). Between risk and opportunity: News framing and its effects on public support for EU enlargement. *European Journal of Communication*, 21(1), 5–32.

Simcic Bronn, P., & Vrioni, A. B. (2001). Corporate social responsibility and cause-related marketing: An overview. *International Journal of Advertising*, 20, 207–222.

Slicer, D. (1995). Is there an ecofeminism-deep ecology debate? *Environmental Ethics*, 17, 151–169.

Smith, S. M., & Acorn, D. S. (1991). Cause marketing: A new direction in the marketing of corporate social responsibility. *Journal of Consumer Marketing*, 8(3), 19–35.

Smithers, R. (2020). *Price of Single-Use Plastic Bags in England to Double to 10p 31 August*. Retrieved from https://www.theguardian.com/environment/2020/aug/31/price-of-single-use-plastic-bags-in-england-to-double-to-10p.

Smythe, D. W. ([1977] 1997). Communications. Blindspots of Western Marxism. In – P. Golding, & G. Murdock (eds), *The Political Economy of the Media* (Vol. I, pp. 438–464). Cheltenham, Brookfield: Elgar.

Social Mobility Commission (2020a). *Monitoring Social Mobility 2013–2020: Is the Government Delivering on Our Recommendations?* Retrieved from https://assets.publishing.service.gov.uk/government/uploads/system/uploads/attachment_data/file/891155/Monitoring_report_2013-2020_-Web_version.pdf.

Social Mobility Commission (2020b). *Social Mobility Barometer Poll Results 2019*. Retrieved from https://www.gov.uk/government/publications/social-mobility-barometer-poll-results-2019.

Social Mobility Commission (2019). *State of the Nation 2018-19: Social Mobility in Great Britain*. Retrieved from https://assets.publishing.service.gov.uk/government/uploads/system/uploads/attachment_data/file/798404/SMC_State_of_the_Nation_Report_2018-19.pdf.

Spretnak, C. (1990). Ecofeminism: Our roots and flowering. In – Diamond, I., & Orenstein, G. (eds), *Reweaving the World*. San Francisco, CA: Sierra Club Books, pp. 3–14.

Srbljinović, M. (2012). Utjecaj društvene odgovornosti poduzeća na ponašanje potrošača u Hrvatskoj. *Zbornik Ekonomskog fakulteta u Zagrebu*, 10(2), 161–180.

210 References

Sroufe, R., & Remani, G. (2018). Management, social sustainability, reputation, and financial performance relationships: An empirical examination of U.S. firms. *Organization & Environment*. Online First, 1–32.

Stancu, V., Haugaard, P., & Lähteenmäki, L. (2016). Determinants of consumer food waste behaviour: Two routes to food waste. *Appetite*, 96, 7–17.

Stanford Encyclopedia of Philosophy (2020). *Liberal Feminism*. Retrieved from https://plato.stanford.edu/entries/feminism-liberal/.

Stanford, J. H., Oates, B. R., & Flores, D. (1995). Women's leadership style: A heuristic analysis. *Women in Management Review*, 10(2), 9–16.

Staw, B. M., & Epstein, L. D. (2000). What bandwagons bring: Effects of popular management techniques on corporate performance, reputation, and CEO pay. *Administrative Science Quarterly*, 45, 523–556.

Steger, M. A., & Witt, S. L. (1989). Gender differences in environmental orientations: A comparison of publics and activists in Canada and the US. *Western Political Quarterly*, 4, 627–649.

Stein, L. (2017). Advertising is still a boy's club, *AdAge*, 31 May. Retrieved from https://adage.com/article/news/advertising-a-boy-s-club/309166.

Steinfeld, H., Gerber, P., Wassenaar, T., Castel, V., Rosales, M., & de Haan, C. (2006). *Livestock's Long Shadow: Environmental Issues and Options*. Rome: Food and Agriculture Organization of the United Nations. Retrieved from http://www.fao.org/3/a0701e/a0701e00.htm.

Stepanović, N. (2020). Radikalna empatija: feminizam, nejedenje mesa i aktivističke prakse. In – Marjanić, S., & Đurđević, G. (eds), *Ekofeminizam – između ženskih i zelenih studija*. Zagreb: Durieux, pp. 199–209.

Stern, P. C., Dietz, T., & Kalof, L. (1993). Value orientations, gender and environmental concern. *Environment and Behaviour*, 25(3), 322–348.

Stiglitz, J. (2013). *The Price of Inequality*. London: Penguin.

Stiglitz, J. E. (2006). A new agenda for global warming. *Economists' Voice*, 1–4 July. Retrieved from https://www.degruyter.com/document/doi/10.2202/1553-3832.1210/html.

Stoddart, M. C. J., & Tindall, D. B. (2011). Eco-feminism, hegemonic masculinity and environmental movement participation in British Columbia, Canada, 1998-2007, "women always clean up the mess". *Sociological Spectrum*, 31(3), 342–368.

Stone, G. C., & McCombs, M. E. (1981). Tracing the Time Lag in Agenda-Setting. *Journalism Quarterly*, 58(1):51–55.

Story, J., & Neves, P. (2015). When corporate social responsibility (CSR) increases performance: Exploring the role of intrinsic and extrinsic CSR attribution. *Business Ethics: A European Review*, 24(2), 111–124.

Sturgeon, N, (1997). *Ecofeminist Natures: Race, Gender, Feminist Theory and Political Action*. London: Routledge.

Supran, G., & Oreskes, N. (2017). Assessing ExxonMobil's climate change communications (1977–2014). *Environmental Research Letters*, 12(8). Retrieved from https://iopscience.iop.org/article/10.1088/1748-9326/aa815f.

Sweetser, K. D., Guy, J. G., & Wanta, W. (2008). Intermedia agenda setting in television, advertising, and blogs during the 2004 election. *Mass Communication and Society*, 11(2), 197–216.

Sydee, J., & Beder, S. (2001). Ecofeminism and globalism: A critical appraisal. *Democracy and Nature*, 7(2), 281–302. Retrieved from https://ro.uow.edu.au/artspapers/31/.

Tan, Y., & Weaver, D. H. (2013). Agenda diversity and agenda setting from 1956 to 2004. *Journalism Studies*, 14(6), 773–789.

References 211

Tannen, D. (1995). The power of talk: Who gets heard and why. *Harvard Business Review*, September–October, pp. 139–149.

Tannen, D. (1990). *You Just Don't Understand*. New York: Penguin Random House.

Tannen, D. (1986). *That's Not What I Meant!* New York: Penguin Random House.

Tapver, T., Laidroo, L., & Gurvits-Suits, N. A. (2020). Banks' CSR reporting – Do women have a say? *Corporate Governance*, 20(4), 639–651.

Tarascio, V. J. (1971). Keynes on the sources of economic growth. *The Journal of Economic History*, 31(2), 429–444.

Tauringana, V., Radicic, D., Kirkpatrick, A., & Konadu, R. (2017). Corporate boards and environmental offence conviction: Evidence from the United Kingdom. *Corporate Governance: The International Journal of Business in Society*, 17(2), 341–362.

Teach, E. (2005). Two views of virtue: The corporate social responsibility movement is picking up steam. Should you worry about it? *CFO*, 31–33.

Templin, C. (1999). Hillary Clinton as threat to gender norms: Cartoon images of the first lady. *Journal of Communication Inquiry*, 23(1), 20–36.

Tench, R., & Topić, M. (2017). One step forward, two steps back? An analysis of public relations practitioners' views on the position of women in the PR industry (2009-2015). *Current Politics and Economics of Europe*, 28(1), 83–105.

Tench, R., Moreno, Á., & Topić, M. (2017). Male and female communication, leadership styles and the position of women in public relations. *Interactions: Studies in Communication and Culture*, 8(2–3), 231–248.

Tench, R., Sun. W., & Jones, B. (2014). Introduction: CSR Communication as an emerging field of study. In – Tench, R., Sun, W., & Jones, B. (eds), *Communicating Corporate Social Responsibility: Perspectives and Practice*. Howard House: Emerald, pp. 3–21.

Tench, R. (2014). Community and society: Corporate social responsibility (CSR). In – Tench, R., & Yeomans, L. (eds). *Exploring Public Relations*. Longman: Pearson.

Tench, R., Bowd, R., & Jones, B. (2007). Perceptions and perspectives: Corporate social responsibility and the media. *Journal of Communication Management*, 11(4), 348–370.

Terkildsen, N., & Schnell, F. (1997). How media frames move public opinion: An analysis of the women's movement. *Political Research Quarterly*, 50(4), 879–900.

The Guardian Staff and Agencies (2016). Mail on Sunday backs remain as major papers declare sides in EU referendum. *The Guardian*, 19 June. Retrieved from https://www.theguardian.com/politics/2016/jun/19/mail-on-sunday-backs-remain-as-major-papers-declare-sides-in-eu-referendum.

The Mail on Sunday Editorial (2016). The Mail on Sunday comment: Vote remain for a safer, freer, more prosperous – And, yes, an even Greater Britain. *The Mail on Sunday*, 19 June. Retrieved from https://www.dailymail.co.uk/debate/article-3648681/THE-MAIL-SUNDAY-COMMENT-Vote-Remain-safer-freer-prosperous-yes-GREATER-Britain.html.

Theofilou, A., & Watson, T. (2014). Sceptical employees as CSR ambassadors in times of financial uncertainty. In – Tench, R., Sun, W., & Jones, B. (eds), *Communicating Corporate Social Responsibility: Perspectives and Practice* (pp. 355–383). Howard House: Emerald Books.

Theus, K. T. (1985). Gender shifts in journalism and public relations. *Public Relations Review*, 11(1), 42–50.

212 *References*

Thompson-Whiteside, H., Turnbull, S., & Howe-Walsh, L. (2020). Advertising: Should creative women be expected to 'fake it? *Journal of Marketing Management*, online first. Retrieved from https://www.tandfonline.com/doi/full/10.1080/0267257X.2019.1707704.

Thurman, N., Cornia, A., & Kunert, J. (2016). *Journalists in the UK*. Oxford: Reuters Institute for the Study of Journalism. Retrieved from https://reutersinstitute.politics.ox.ac.uk/sites/default/files/research/files/Journalists%2520in%2520the%2520UK.pdf.

Tixier, M. (2003). Soft vs. hard approach in communicating on CSR. *Thunderbird International Business Review*, 45(1), 71–91.

Tobitt, C. (2016). Daily Mail and Mail on Sunday readers agree on second Brexit referendum despite disparity in editorial stance, Yougov poll shows. *The Press Gazette*, 19 September. Retrieved from https://www.pressgazette.co.uk/daily-mail-and-mail-on-sunday-readers-agree-on-second-brexit-referendum-despite-disparity-in-editorial-stance-yougov-poll-shows/.

Topić, M., Diers Lawson, A., & Kelsey, S. (2021, in press). Women and the squander cycle in food waste in the United Kingdom: An ecofeminist and feminist economic analysis. *Social Ecology/Socijalna Ekologija*.

Topić, M., & Bruegmann, C. (2021). 'The girls at the desk': Timeless blokishness in the newsroom culture in the British Press? *Journalism Studies*, 22(1), 77–95.

Topić, M. (2021). Fluffy PR and 'comms girls': Banter, social interactions and the office culture in public relations in England. *International Journal of Organizational Analysis*. Online first https://www.emerald.com/insight/content/doi/10.1108/IJOA-09-2020-2423/full/html.

Topić, M., Bridge, G., & Tench, R. (2020a). Mirroring the zeitgeist: An analysis of CSR policies in the UK's food, soft drink and packaging industries. *Journal of Global Responsibility*, 12(1), 62–75.

Topić, M., Cunha, M. J., Reigstad, A., Jelen Sanchez, A., & Moreno, Á. (2020b). Women in public relations (1982-2019). *Journal of Communication Management*, 24(4), 391–407.

Topić, M., & Polić, M. (2020). Fashion public relations. In – Tench, R., & Waddington, S. (eds), *Exploring Public Relations* (5th edition). Longman: Pearson.

Topić, M. (2020a). The sourcing of stories on sugar and the supermarket industry in the British Press. *The Qualitative Report*, 25(5), 1196–1214. Retrieved from https://nsuworks.nova.edu/tqr/vol25/iss5/3.

Topić, M. (2020b). Two Englands? Blokishness, masculine habitus and the north-south divide in the advertising industry. *Gender in Management: An International Journal*. EarlyCite, https://www.emerald.com/insight/content/doi/10.1108/GM-12-2019-0263/full/html.

Topić, M. (2020c). 'It's something that you should go to HR about' – Banter, social interactions and career barriers for women in the advertising industry in England. *Employee Relations*. EarlyCite, https://www.emerald.com/insight/content/doi/10.1108/ER-03-2020-0126/full/html.

Topić, M. (2020d). Ekofeministička analiza vrijednosti i filozofija globalnih eko-selâ: Jesu li žene sklonije kolektivizmu i anti-hijerarhiji nego muškaraci? (An ecofeminist analysis of values and philosophies of global eco-villages: Are women more inclined towards collectivism and anti-hierarchy than men?). In – Đurđević, G., & Marjanić, S. (eds), *Ekofeminizam: Izmedju zelenih i ženskih studija (Ecofeminism: Between Green and Women's Studies)*. Zagreb: Durieux. (In Croatian).

Topić, M. (2020e). Women in public relations in England. *EUPRERA Report* (Vol. 2, No. 1). Leeds/Brussels: Creative Media and Communications Research Ltd & EUPRERA. Retrieved from http://eprints.leedsbeckett.ac.uk/id/eprint/6774/1/EUPRERAReportVol2No1PV-TOPIC.pdf.

Topić, M., Cunha, M. J., Reigstad, A., Jelen-Sanchez, A., Diers Lawson, A., Polić, M., Moreno, A., Zurbano, Berenguer, B., Damian-Gaillard, B., Sanz, P., Fuentes Lara, C., Cesarec Salopek, N., Saitta, E., Cruz, C., Simeunović Bajić, N., Vandenberghe, H., Bibilashvili, L., & Kaladze, N. (2019). Women in public relations – a literature review (1982-2019). *EUPRERA Report* (Vol. 1, No. 1). Leeds/Brussels, Creative Media and Communications Research Ltd. and EUPRERA. Retrieved from http://eprints.leedsbeckett.ac.uk/id/eprint/6138/12/EupreraReport PV-TOPIC.pdf.

Topić, M., & Tench, R. (2018). Evolving responsibility or revolving bias? The role of the media in the anti-sugar debate in the UK Press. *Social Sciences*, 7(10), 181. Retrieved from https://www.mdpi.com/2076-0760/7/10/181/htm.

Topić, M. (2018). Not bloke-ified enough? Women journalists, supermarket industry and the debate on sugar in the British Press (2010-2015). *Newspaper Research Journal*, 39(4), 433–442.

Topić, M., & Gilmer, E. C. (2017). Hillary Clinton and the media: From expected roles to the critique of feminism. *The Qualitative Report*, 22(10), 2533–2543. Retrieved from https://nsuworks.nova.edu/tqr/vol22/iss10/1.

Topić, M., & Rodin, S. (2012). *Cultural Diplomacy and Cultural Imperialism: European Perspective(s)*. Frankfurt a. M.: Peter Lang.

Topić, M. (2009). Media bias in elections: How Barack Obama won against Hillary Rodham Clinton. *Teme (Themes)*, XXIII(1), 215–238.

Torchia, M., Calabro, A., & Huse, M. (2011). Women directors on corporate boards: From tokenism to critical mass. *Journal of Business Ethics*, 102(2), 299–317.

Tranter, B, (1996). The social bases of environmentalism in Australia. *Australian and New Zealand Journal of Sociology*, 32(2), 85.

Trentmann, F. (2016). *Empire of Things: How We Became a World of Consumers, from the Fifteenth Century to the Twenty-First*. London: Penguin UK.

Trumbo, C. (1995). Longitudinal modeling of public issues: An application of the agenda setting process to the issue of global warning. *Journalism Monographs*, 152, 1–57.

Turban, D. B., & Greening, D. W. (2017). Corporate social performance and organizational attractiveness to prospective employees. *Academy of Management Journal*, 40(3), 658–672.

Twine, R. T. (2001a). Ma(r)king essence-ecofeminism and embodiment. *Ethics & Environment*, 6(2), 31–58.

Twine, R. (2001b). Ecofeminism in process. *Ecofem Journal*. Retrieved from http://richardtwine.com/ecofem/ecofem2001.pdf.

Tyner, K. E., & Ogle, J. P. (2009). Feminist theory of the dressed female body: A comparative analysis and applications for textiles and clothing scholarship. *Clothing & Textiles Research Journal*, 27(2), 98–121.

UN (2015). *Sustainable Developments Goals: Goal 12: Ensure Sustainable Consumption and Production Patterns. United Nations*. Retrieved from http://www.un.org/sustainabledevelopment/sustainable-consumption-production.

UNDP (2020). *Equal Pay for Work of Equal Value*. Retrieved from https://www.un.org/en/observances/equal-pay-day.

214   *References*

UN Environment (2018). *Mapping of Global Plastics Value Chain and Plastics Losses to the Environment (with a Particular Focus on Marine Environment)*. *United Nations Environment Programme*. Nairobi, Kenya. Retrieved from https://wedocs.unep.org/handle/20.500.11822/26745.

UK Government (2014). Public views on ethical retail. *Research Series No. 177*. Retrieved from https://www.gov.uk/government/uploads/system/uploads/attachment_data/file/322624/Public-views-on-ethical-retail.pdf.

USA Today (2005). Timeline of the Tyco International scandal. *USA Today*, 17 June. Retrieved from http://usatoday30.usatoday.com/money/industries/manufacturing/2005-06-17-tyco-timeline_x.htm.

Valls Martinez, M. C., Cervantes, P. A. M., & Rambaud, S. C. (2020). Women on corporate boards and sustainable development in the American and European markets: Is there a limit to gender policies? *Corporate Social Responsibility & Environmental Management*, 27, 2642–2656.

Van der Boon, M. (2003). Women in international management: An international perspective on women's way of leadership. *Women in Management Review*, 18(3), 132–146.

van Liedekerke, L. (2004). Media ethics: From corporate governance to governance, to corporate social responsibility. *Communications*, 29(1), 27–42.

Van Liere, K. D., & Dunlap, R. E. (1980). The social bases of environmental concern: A review of hypotheses, explanations and empirical evidence. *Public Opinion Quarterly*, 44(2), 181–197.

Van Sebille, E., Spathi, C., & Gilbert, A. (2016). The ocean plastic pollution challenge: Towards solutions in the UK. *Grantham Institute, Briefing Paper No. 19*. Retrieved from https://www.imperial.ac.uk/media/imperial-college/grantham-institute/public/publications/briefing-papers/The-ocean-plastic-pollution-challenge-Grantham-BP-19_web.pdf.

Van Slyke, J. K. (1983). On the job: Corporate communications in the United States and the United Kingdom. *Public Relations Review*, 9(3), 55.

Van Zoonen, L. (2004). *Entertaining the Citizen: When Politics and Popular Culture Converge*. New York, Boulder, CO: Rowman and Littlefield.

Vidaver Cohen, D., & Simcic Bronn, P. (2013). Reputation, responsibility, and stakeholder support in Scandinavian firms: A comparative analysis. *Journal of Business Ethics*, 127, 49–64.

Viner, R. M., & Cole, T. J. (2005). Television viewing in early childhood predicts adult body mass index. *Journal of Pediatrics*, 147, 429–35.

Vrdoljak Raguž, I., & Hazdovac, K. (2014). Društveno odgovorno poslovanje i hrvatska gospodarska praksa. *Oeconomica Jadertina*, 1, 40–58.

Von Werlhof, C. (2013). Destruction through "creation" – The "critical theory of patriarchy" and the collapse of modern civilization. *Capitalism Nature Socialism*, 24(4), 68–85.

Von Werlhof, C. (2007). No critique of capitalism without a critique of patriarchy! Why the left is no alternative. *Capitalism Nature Socialism*, 18(1), 13–27.

Vukoičić, J. (2013). Radical feminism as a discourse in the theory of conflict. *Sociological Discourse*, 3(5), 49.

Vuori, I., Paronen, O., & Oja, P. (1998). How to develop local physical activity promotion programmes with national support: The Finnish experience. *Patient Education and Counselling*, 33, 111–20.

References 215

Waldron, D. (2003). Eco-feminism & the reconstruction of *The Burning Times*. Retrieved from https://www.academia.edu/2168627/_Ecofeminism_and_the_Reconstruction_of_the_Burning_Times_.

Wang, A. (2007). Priming, framing and position on corporate social responsibility. *Journal of Public Relations Research*, 10(2), 123–145.

Wankel, C. (2008). *21st Century Management: A Reference Handbook*. Thousand Oaks, CA: SAGE.

Warren, K. J. (2000). *Ecofeminist Philosophy: A Western Perspective on What It Is and Why It Matters (Studies in Social, Political, and Legal Philosophy)*. New York: Rowman and Littlefield.

Warren, K. (1996). *Ecological Feminist Philosophies*. Bloomington: University of Indiana Press.

Warren, K. (1994). Introduction. In – Warren, K. J. (ed), *Ecological Feminism*. London: Routledge, pp. 1–8.

Warren, K. (1990). The power and the promise of ecological feminism. *Environmental Ethics*, 9, 3–20.

Warren, K. (1987). Feminism and ecology: Making connections. *Environmental Ethics*, 9, 3–20.

Warren, K. (n.d.). Introduction to ecofeminism. *Lilith Press Magazine*. Retrieved from http://www.lilithpress.ca/Environment-Introduction-to-Ecofeminism.html.

Ward, S. (2008). Journalism ethics. In – Wahl-Jorgensen K., & Hanitzsch, T. (eds), *The Handbook of Journalism Studies*. London: Routledge, pp. 295–310.

Wartick, S. (1992). The relationship between intense media exposure and change in corporate reputation. *Business and Society*, 31(1), 33–49.

Waterhouse, B. C. (2017). The personal, the political and the profitable: Business and protest culture, 1960s-1980s. *Financial History*, Spring edition. Retrieved from https://www.moaf.org/publications-collections/financial-history-magazine/121/_res/id=Attachments/index=0/Business%20and%20Protest.pdf.

Watson, M., & Meah, A. (2013). Food, waste and safety: Negotiating conflicting social anxieties into the practices of domestic provisioning. *The Sociological Review*, 60, 102–120. Retrieved from http://dx.doi.org/10.1111/1467-954x.12040.

Watson, A. (2020). Fake news – Statistics & facts. *Statista*. Retrieved from https://www.statista.com/topics/3251/fake-news/#dossierSummary__chapter4.

Watts, W. (1972). Foreword. In – Meadows, D., Meadows, D., Randers, J., & Behrens, WW. (eds), *The Limits to Growth*. New York: Universe Books, pp. 9–12.

WRAP (2014). *Carrier Bags Usage and Attitudes: Consumer Research in England*. Retrieved http://www.wrap.org.uk/sites/files/wrap/Carrier%20Bags%20Usage%20and%20Attitudes%20Consumer%20Research%20in%20England.pdf.

Weisberg, L., and Robbs, B. (1997). Creative department still boys' playground. *Advertising Age*, 68(47), 28.

Weiss, C. (1974). What America's leaders read. *Public Opinion Quarterly*, 38, 1–22.

West, C., & Zimmerman, D. H. (1983). Small insults: A study of interruptions in conversations between unacquainted persons. In – Thorne, B., Kramerac, C., & Henley, N. (eds), *Language, Gender and Society* (pp. 102–117). Rowley: Newbury House.

Wheeler, D., Fabig, H., & Boele, R. (2002). Paradoxes and dilemmas for stakeholder responsive firms in the extractive sector: Lessons from the case of Shell and the Ogoni. *Journal of Business Ethics*, 39, 297–318.

216 *References*

Whiteman, G., Dorsey, M., & Wittneben, B. (2010). Business and biodiversity: They would say that. *Nature*, 466, 435.

Whitney, D. C., & Becker, L. B. (1982). Keeping the gates for gatekeepers – The effects of wire news. *Journalism Quarterly*, 59(1), 60–65.

Wilson, E. (2010). *Pomirenje: jedinstvenost znanja*. Zagreb: Algoritam.

Winfield, B. H. (1994). 'Madame president': Understanding a new kind of first lady. *Media Studies Journal*, 8(2), 59–71.

Winfield, B. H. (1997a). The first lady, political power, and the media: Who elected her anyway? In – Norris, P. (ed), *Women, Media and Politics* (pp. 166–179). New York: Oxford University Press.

Winfield, B. H. (1997b). The making of an image: Hillary Rodham Clinton and American journalists. *Political Communication*, 14, 241–253.

Winter, J., & Eyal, C. (1981). Agenda setting for the civil rights issue. *Public Opinion Quarterly*, 45, 376–383.

Wilcox, C., Van Sebille, E., & Denise Hardesty, B. (2015). Threat of plastic pollution to seabirds is global, pervasive, and increasing. *PNAS*, September 22, 112(38), 11899–11904. Retrieved from https://doi.org/10.1073/pnas.1502108112. https://www.pnas.org/content/112/38/11899?utm_campaign=later-linkinbio-my. mouthful&utm_content=later-2610869&utm_medium=social&utm_source= instagram.

Wolf, N. (1991). *The Beauty Myth: How Images of Beauty are Used against Women*. London: Vintage/Penguin Books.

World Bank (2019). *Population, Female (% of Total Population)*. Retrieved from https://data.worldbank.org/indicator/SP.POP.TOTL.FE.ZS.

World Bank (n.d.). *Population, Total*. Retrieved from https://data.worldbank.org/ indicator/SP.POP.TOTL?end=2019&start=1960.

WRAP (2021). *Food and Drink*. Retrieved from https://wrap.org.uk/food-drink.

WRAP (2020). *Food Surplus and Waste in the UK – Key Facts*. Updated January 2020. Retrieved from https://wrap.org.uk/sites/files/wrap/Food-surplus-and-waste-in-the-UK-key-facts-Jan-2020.pdf.

WRAP (2009). *Household Food and Drink Waste in the UK*. Retrieved from http://www.wrap.org.uk/node/13529.

WRAP (2007). *Understanding Consumer Food Management Behaviour*. Retrieved from http://www.wrap.org.uk/content/understanding-consumer-food-management-behaviour-0.

Wright, C., & Nyberg, D. (2015). *Climate Change, Capitalism and Corporations: Processes of Creative Self-Destruction*. Cambridge: Cambridge University Press.

Xanthos, D., & Walker, T. R. (2017). International policies to reduce plastic marine pollution from single-use plastics (plastic bags and microbeads): A review. *Marine Pollution Bulletin*, 118, 17–26.

Xie, J., Nozawa, W., & Managi, S. (2020). The role of women on boards in corporate environmental strategy and financial performance: A global outlook. *Corporate Social Responsibility & Environmental Management*, 27, 2044–2059.

Yoon, Y., Gurhan-Canli, Z., Schwartz, N. (2006). The effect of corporate social responsibility (CSR) activities on companies with bad reputations. *Journal of Consumer Psychology*, 16(4), 377–390.

YouGov (2021). *Do Brits Bring Their Own Bags Instead of Buying New Plastic Bags?* https://yougov.co.uk/topics/science/trackers/do-brits-bring-their-own-bags-instead-of-buying-new-plastic-bags.

YouGov (2020). *Do You Support or Oppose the Price of Plastic Bags in England Increasing from 5p to 10p?* https://yougov.co.uk/topics/politics/survey-results/daily/2020/09/02/18d46/1.

Yudina, O., & Fennell, D. (2013). Ecofeminism in the tourism context: A discussion of the use of other-than-human animals as food in tourism. *Tourism Recreation Research*, 38(1), 55–69.

Yule, G. (2006). *The Study of Language.* Cambridge: Cambridge University Press.

Yu, Y., & Choi, Y. (2016). Stakeholder pressure and CSR adoption: The mediating role of organizational culture for Chinese companies. *The Social Science Journal*, 53, 226–235.

Zacharias, U., & Arthurs, J. (2008). Introduction: Race versus gender? The framing of the Barak Obama-Hillary Clinton battle. *Feminist Media Studies*, 8(4), 425–433.

Zhang, J., & Swanson, D. (2006). Analysis of news media's representation of corporate social responsibility. *Public Relations Quarterly*, 51(2), 13–17.

Zimmer, K. (2020). *Gender Gap in Research Output Widens During Pandemic.* Retrieved from https://www.the-scientist.com/news-opinion/gender-gap-in-research-output-widens-during-pandemic-67665.

Zimmerman, M. E. (1990). Deep ecology and ecofeminism: The emerging dialogue. In Diamond, I., & Orenstein, G. (eds), *Reweaving the World: The Emergence of Ecofeminism.* San Francisco: Sierra Club Books, pp. 138–154.

Zyglidopoulos, S. C., Georgiadis, A. P., Carroll, C. E., & Siegel, D. S. (2011). Does media attention drive corporate social responsibility? *Journal of Business Research*, 65(11), 1622–1627.

Index

Note: **Bold** page numbers refer to tables; *italic* page numbers refer to figures and page numbers followed by "n" denote endnotes.

abolitionism 19
Acker, J. 49n2
"Action on Sugar" 86
Adams, C. 38, 43
Adler, D. 132
Agenda 21 168
agenda-setting 1, 16n3, 82, 87, 88, 98n7
Altmeppen 90
Alves, I. M. 55
Alvesson, M. 23
anti-capitalist movement, ecofeminism as 20–32
anti-essentialist view of ecofeminism 8
Archambault, A. 26
Asefi-Najafabady, S. 133
autonomy 18, 50n3, 83, 170

Bajželj, B. 51n8
Bandyopadhyay, S. 100
Banerjee, S. B. 4
Barclays 90
Bari, J. 47, 48, 52n11
Barry, N. 78–79
Basel Convention 125
Beauvoir, S. de 18
Beer, R. 95
Bernstein, S. 166
Billard, G. 141
Birkeland, J. 40
Blair, T. 120
Blanco, H. 41, 164–165
bloke-ification 26, 37
blokishness 2, 4, 5, 24, 94, 95
Blue Planet 144
Boero, N. 13
Bordo, S. 34–35

Borrelle, S. B. 142, 143
Boucher, J. 141
Bowd, R. 9, 62, 89
Bowen, H. 60–61
Bowie, N. E. 15n2, 64, 73, 76, 79
Brexit 10, 110, 111, 125
Bronson, D. 35
Brundtland, G. H. 59, 167
Brundtland Report (1987) 56, 165
Buhr, H. 8, 89
Business Roundtable 118

Cahan, S. F. 87
Cammaerts, B. 85–86
Campbell, J. L. 61–62
capitalism 4–6, 8, 17, 19, 22, 28, 45, 49, 50n3, 51n6, 57, 89, 91, 92, 97n2, 99, 104, 107, 109, 115, 116, 119, 122, 123, 135, 136, 139, 140, 146, 151, 152, 155, 156, 157, 161, 163–168, 170, 171; corporate social responsibility 60–65; ecofeminist critique of 3, 46, 48; Marxism's view of 31; media's view of 14; neo-liberal 55; and patriarchy 3, 9, 26–40, 47; role in environmental degradation 59; shareholder vs stakeholder orientation 66, 68–70, 74–76, 78–80
capitalist inequality 164
capitalist patriarchy 23, 28, 31, 36, 38, 40
Carlson, R. 18
Carroll, A. B. 59, 71, 72, 167
Carroll, C. E. 9, 87
Cartesian dualistic objectivism 33
Cartesian masculinity 34–35
Center, A. H. 96n1

220 Index

charitable giving 6, 89
Chen, C. 87
Chen, L. 87
China 124
Chomsky, N. 54
Ciplet, D. 123–126
Clark, C. E. 96n1
Clarke, J. P. 30
class inequality 20, 21
Cleveland, C. J. 100
climate governance approach 123
Clinton, H. R. 37, 85, 89
community development 9
conformism 43, 81, 168
Connell, R. 40–41
constructionist ecofeminism 13, 25, 28
consumerism 4, 5, 28, 43, 46, 54, 56, 63, 65, 73, 74, 76, 105, 110, 114, 115, 120, 128, 135, 136, 147, 148, 156, 157, 159, 164
Conway, E. 103
Copenhagen Climate Conference of the Parties (2009) 21
Corbyn, J. 85, 113–114
Cornia, A. 89
corporate social responsibility (CSR) 1, 3–10, 13, 15–16n2, 15n1, 16n3, 16n4, 48, 53–98; ambiguities 60–65; capitalism 60–65; definition of 60; and media 80–91; media coverage of 4–7, 12; press coverage of 116–121, **116, 117**; shareholder vs stakeholder orientation 66–80; women and 91–93
Croatia: corporate social responsibility in 97–98n6
Cross, C. L. 32–164, 163
CSR-CSI model 62
CSR *see* corporate social responsibility (CSR)
cultural ecofeminism 24, 28, 47, 50n5
cultural masculinity 2, 161
Cushion, S. 16n3
Cutlip, S. M. 96n1
cyber/ecofeminism 35

Daily, C. M. 77
Daily Mail 10, **11,** 12, 15, 164, 165; corporate social responsibility 120; economic growth 105–107, **106,** 113–116; food waste 157, 158, **158,** 160; global warming 127–128, **127,** 138–141; plastic pollution 144, **145,** 148, 151–156

Daily Mirror 85
Dalton, D. R. 77
Daly, H. 102, 133
Darwinism 27
d'Eaubonne, F. 22, 24, 45, 162–163
De Bruyn, S. M. 103, 104, 118
DeCillia, B. 85–86
deep ecology 109; vs ecofeminism 44–48
De Jong, M. D. T. 87
Delworth, T. L. 160n1
democratic socialism 66
Descartes, R. 34
Diers-Lawson, A. 54
Difference Approach 2, 23, 49n1
DMG 90
Dobson, A. 26
Dodd, M. D. 64
donations 9, 63, 76, 89, 140
Douthwaite, R. 121n1

ecofeminism 2, 3, 17–52; as anti-capitalist movement 20–32; anti-essentialist view of 8; constructionist 13, 25, 28; criticism of 44–48; cultural 24, 28, 47, 50n5; cyber/ecofeminism 35; vs deep ecology 44–48; definition of 14, 20; hierarchy of 37–44; liberal 50–51n5; material 31; materialist approach to 30; and Nature, relationship between 3, 5, 8, 12, 14, 15, 17–20, 24–38, 40, 45, 48; radical 24, 50n4; and science, relationship between 32–37; social 28; socialist 3, 24, 28, 31, 32, 38, 39, 48, 91; and technology, relationship between 32–37
ecofeminist analysis 9, 12, 27
ecofeminist theory 3, 6, 8, 12, 15, 28, 37, 43, 123, 148, 150, 163
eco gender gap 148
economic freedom 66
economic growth 5–8, 10–13, 15, 20, 21, 23, 48, 49, 54, 56, 57, 63, 96n2, 99–105, 121n1, 122, 147, 150, 155, 161, 163, 165, 166, 168, 169, 171; conditional supporter of 103; global warming and 126–128, 131, 135–137; population and 51–52n9; press coverage of 105–116, **106, 117,** 119, 120; radical supporter of 103; strong antagonists on 104; weak antagonists on 103–104
economic responsibilities 71–73

Index 221

eco-villages 30
ecowomanism 24; *see also* ecofeminism
eco zealots/eco-warriors 138
Ehrlich, P. R. 100
Eisler, R. 24, 33
Ellen MacArthur Foundation 141
emissions 43, 44, 51n8, 56, 91, 112, 119,
  123, 124, 126, 128, 129, 131–134, 139,
  142, 143, 153, 155–157
Engels, F. 57
Enron 60, 75, 97n5
environmental activism 7, 12, 30, 152
environmental damage 54, 63, 64,
  125, 165
environmental degradation 4, 5, 8, 19,
  20, 25, 42, 47, 48, 59, 61, 63, 100, 103,
  104, 122, 156, 159, 167, 169
environmental governance 125, 126, 147,
  160, 161
environmentalism 2, 4, 6, 7, 12, 18, 25,
  41, 48, 49n3, 53, 54, 99, 100, 113,
  126, 137, 138, 147–149, 153–156,
  163; market 125, 150; neoliberal 123,
  125, 126
environmental movement, anti-
  consumerism and 41
environmental protection 5, 7, 18, 19, 25,
  31, 41, 46, 48, 50n3, 57, 59, 60, 69, 71,
  91, 100, 103, 105, 107, 124, 125, 133,
  136, 159, 160, 164, 166, 167
equality 2, 10, 45, 47, 60, 66, 85, 86, 93,
  132, 133, 148; gender 22, 91; pay 92;
  policies 55, 92; of women 2, 23, 24,
  107, 114; *see also* inequality
essentialism 27, 47, 50n5
Ethical Consumer 64
ethical responsibilities 71–73
European Environment Agency 59, 168
exploitation 4, 8, 20–22, 32, 35, 40, 43,
  45, 69, 81, 97n2, 103, 112
Extinction Rebellion 113, 114, 138,
  151, 152
Eyal, C. 16n6

FareShare 157
Far Right 124, 125, 131
femininity 40–41, 149
feminism: ecofeminism (*see*
  ecofeminism); liberal 24, 47, 49–50n3,
  50n5, 85; Marxist 38–39; radical 3, 17,
  24, 42, 47, 50n3, 50n4; socialist 3, 17,
  24, 32, 38, 52n10
Fernandez-Feijoo, B. 91

Financial Times 89
Food and Agriculture Organization of
  the United Nations 51n8
food production 101, 105, 157
food waste 156–160; press coverage of
  157–160, **158**
Footprint Network 103
Foster, J. B. 57
Foster, J. M. 63
Fox, B. 47
framing 87, 88, 98n7
Frankental, P. 55
Freeman, R. E. 71, 73–76, 96n1, 116
free market system 68
Friedman, M. 1, 3, 7, 8, 15–16n2,
  61, 64, 66–70, 73, 78, 79, 89, 116;
  Capitalism and Freedom 15n2; "Social
  Responsibility of Business is to
  Increase its Profits, The" 68
"Friedman-Freeman debate" 73

Gaard, G. 23, 44, 124–125, 161
Galić, B. 29
Gallagher, M. 95
Galvin, R. 133
Gamson, W. A. 13, 88
Gan, A. 54
gay masculinity 40
Gelin, M. 149
gender 5, 11, 16n2, 21, 34, 50n4, 128,
  132, 145, 149, 158; bias 44; eco gender
  gap 148; equality 22, 91; identity
  42; inequality 133; relations 24;
  socialisation process 17, 25, 29, 93
Georgescu-Roegen, N. 100
Georgiadis, A. P. 9, 87
Ghanem, S. I. 98n7
Gilbert, A. 141, 143
Gilligan, C. 42
Gills, B. 21, 36, 56, 114–116
Global Carbon Footprint 103, *104*
Global North 17, 21, 22, 56, 109,
  124–126, 131, 132, 135, 157, 166
Global South 17, 21, 22, 43, 52n10, 102,
  103, 105, 110, 124, 125, 130, 156
global warming 43, 51n8, 110, 122–126,
  144, 150, 156, 157, 160, 160n1; press
  coverage of 127–141, **127**
Gosselt, J. F. 87
Graber, D. 95
Grafström, M. 8, 9, 89
Great Pacific Garbage Patch 142
green policies 55

222 *Index*

greenwashing 55, 61, 65, 70
Griffin, S. 14, 15, 29, 43
Grossman, G. M. 100
Grunig, J. E. 53, 96n1
Guardian's Observer 10
Guardian, The 10, **11,** 12, 15, 85, 90, 164, 165, 169; corporate social responsibility 117–120, **117**; economic growth 105–115, **106**; food waste 157–160, **158**; global warming 127–138, **127**; plastic pollution 144–151, **145,** 154, 156

habitus theory 2
Hallen, P. 44
Hamilton, J. T. 88
Haward, M. 142–143
Healy, N. 133
hegemonic masculinity 17, 31, 38, 40, 42, 161
Hofkirchner, W. 89
Holdren, J. P. 100
Holy, M 48
Houghton, J. 122–124, 160n1
Howell, R. 149
Hudson, D. 76
Hunt, T. 53, 96n1
Hutchins Commission (the Commission on the Freedom of the Press) 83, 169; "Free and Responsible Press, A" 82

ILO *see* International Labour Organisation (ILO)
India: Chipko movement 19
industrialization 100, 101, 105
inequality 8, 28, 30, 42, 46, 48, 49n2, 74, 105, 132; capitalist 164; class 20, 21; gender 133; pay 22; political 43; of women 4, 23, 39; *see also* equality
Intergovernmental Panel on Climate Change (IPCC) 59, 167; on global warming 122; Special Report on Climate Change and Land 103
International Labour Organisation (ILO) 22
IPCC *see* Intergovernmental Panel on Climate Change (IPCC)

Jackson, T. 104–105
Jensen, M. 76–78
Jimenez-Martínez, C. 85–86
job creation 8
Jones, B. 9, 62, 89

journalism 2, 3, 5, 10, 16n3, 24, 26, 88, 89, 107, 117, 120, 137; bloke-ification in 37; distinguished from media 90; masculine domination in 94; masculinisation of women in 7, 8; women in 94–95, 106
journalistic codes 83, 90, 170
Journal of Marketing and Morality 78

Kamble, B. P. 24
Keeley, B. 121n3
Kelsey, S. 51n7
Kenya: Green Belt Movement 19
Keynesian economics 20, 97n3, 132, 159, 167
Keynes, J. M. 51–52n9
Knutson, T. R. 160n1
Krueger, A. B. 100
Kunert, J. 89
Kyoto Protocol of 1997 56, 59, 126, 166, 168

Lasch, C. 84
Latapí Agudelo, M. A. 58–59, 167, 168
Latouche, S. 23
Leahy, T. 41, 164
legal responsibilities 71–73
Le Pen, M. 37
liberal ecofeminism 50–51n5
liberal feminism 24, 47, 49–50n3, 50n5, 85
liberalisation 4, 7, 9, 65, 71, 119, 171
liberalism 15n2, 16n2, 66, 67, 69, 83, 131, 169
Lippmann, W. 84
Liu, Y. 92
Lucas, C. 11
Lunenberg, K. 87

Maathai, W. 19
MacKinnon, C. 24, 29
Magalhães, J. 85–86
Magdoff, F. 57
Mail on Sunday 10
managerial capitalism 73
Mandel, E. 96–97n2
Margolis, J. D. 63
market-based approach to corporate governance 126
market environmentalism 125, 150
market freedom 63
marketisation 4, 7, 71
Markey, E. 132

Marx, K. 57, 81, 168
Marxism 31, 47
Marxist feminism 38–39
masculine habitus 24, 26
masculinity 3, 4, 6, 37–44, 125, 149, 156, 170; Cartesian 34–35; cultural 2, 161; gay 40; hegemonic 17, 31, 38, 40, 42, 161; in journalism 94; militarized 36
Mason, M. 126
mass media 8, 81
material ecofeminism 31
materialist approach to ecofeminism 30
May, T. 37
McCann, D. P. 79
McCombs, M. 16n6, 98n7
McNealy, J. E. 84
McVea, J. 74
Meadows, D. 101, 105; *Limits to Growth, The* 100, 103; *Limits to Growth – The 30-Year Update* 103
media: agenda-setting theory of 1; bias 85, 87; corporate/capitalist 4; corporate social responsibility and 80–91; coverage of CSR 4–7, 12, 49; critical political economy of 81; distinguished from journalism 90; on emissions and pollutions 43; mass 8, 81; news 5, 6, 9, 48, 87, 88; press as form of 6; sense-making analysis of 10–13
Mellor, M. 38
Merchant, C. 28, 30, 38
militarized masculinity 36
Millett, K. 54
Mill, J. S. 83, 169
Mishan, E. J. 121n1
Modigliani, A. 13
Montreal Protocol (1987) 59, 125, 167
Morgan, J. 21, 36, 51n6, 56, 102, 114–116, 133
Murdochs 90

Naess, A. 45–46
neo-capitalism 70
neoliberal(ism/ization) 4–7, 9, 10, 12, 13, 21, 22, 38, 56, 58, 97n4, 105, 108, 109, 116, 119, 120, 123, 126, 131–132, 135, 137, 140, 147, 156, 159, 161–171; economics 109, 165; environmentalism 123, 125, 126, 147; globalisation 57; policies 5, 13, 108, 110, 119, 124, 135, 147, 162; wheel of 4, 5, 7, 161, *162,* 165, 170

neoliberal system 4
New Green Deal 132, 133, 135, 136
news media 5, 6, 9, 48, 87, 88
News of the World 94
newspaper coverage analysis 10–12
News UK 90
Nguyen, N. H. 87
Nunn, A. 20–21

Obama, B. 75
Observer, The 95
Ocasio-Cortez, A. 132, 133, 149
oppression 3, 8, 15, 17, 19, 20, 25, 27–29, 33, 34, 37, 38, 42, 43, 45, 46, 50n4, 51n5, 52n10, 107, 161
Our Common Future 59, 167
Our World in Data 141
over-production 4, 86
Owens-Ibie, N. 83, 169

Panayotou, T. 100
Paris agreement 123, 125, 130
patriarchy 3, 6, 9, 13, 14, 17, 19, 20, 24, 26–40, 43, 46, 47, 50n5, 52n10, 107, 109, 120, 125, 141, 161, 163, 164, 169; capitalist 23, 28, 31, 36, 38, 40; capitalism and 3, 9, 19, 26–40; definition of 40, 50n4; masculine 23, 34, 44; oppression 20; social construction of 8
pay: equality 92; inequality 22
Pedersen, E. R. 77
Peterson, T. B. 83
Plaisance, P. L. 82
Planned Parenthood 76
plastic pollution 141–144; press coverage of 144–156, **145**
Plumwood, V.: dualisms 33, **34**
political freedom 66
political inequality 43
Pollin, R. 131, 132
polluter pays principle 125, 159
pollution 43, 51n8, 56, 59, 63, 100–102, 105, 108, 132, 133, 137, 139, 166, 167; plastic 141–156, **145**; prevention of 68, 92
Post, J. E. 96n1
poverty 62, 79, 110, 123, 155
press 6, 81, 83; agentry model 53; coverage: of corporate social responsibility 116–121, **116**, **117**; of economic growth 105–116, **106**; of environmental affairs 122–160; of

224 Index

food waste 157–160, **158**; of global warming 127–141, **127**; of plastic pollution 144–156, **145**; responsibility of the 161–171
Press Gazette 10, 80–81
Preston, L. E. 96n1
Price, S. 20–21
psychosexual schism 38
Puleo, A. H. 29–30

Quested, T. E. 157

racism 19, 43, 46, 48, 105
radical ecofeminism 24, 50n4
radical feminism 3, 17, 24, 42, 47, 50n3, 50n4
Reach 90
Reagan, R. 6, 58, 63, 116, 119, 165, 167
Reaganomics 58, 167
Responsibility to Socialise Corporations (RSC) 82, 169
Rhodes, C. J. 141
Rice, C. 37
rights of suppliers 7
Ripple, W. J. 51n8
Ritchie, H. 142
Roach, C. 25
Roberts, T. 125, 126
Roser, M. 142
Rothermeres 90
Royal Dutch Shell 131
RSC *see* Responsibility to Socialise Corporations (RSC)
Ruether, R. 18

Salleh, A. K. 3, 20, 21, 27, 29, 31, 36–38, 45, 47, 163
Sandoval, M. 4, 53, 82, 89, 90, 140, 168, 169
Schramm, W. 83
Schwartz, M. S. 72
Selden, T. M. 100
sexism 19, 20, 26, 27, 32, 48, 105
sexual harassment 26
Shafik, N. 100
shareholder vs stakeholder orientation 66–80
Shiva, V. 20, 22, 31
Shuchman, M. 86
Siebert, F. 83
Siegel, D. S. 9, 87
social ecofeminism 28
socialist ecofeminism 3, 24, 28, 31, 32, 38, 39, 48, 91

socialist feminism 3, 17, 24, 32, 38, 52n10
social responsibility (SR) 15n1, 67, 84; definition of 71
Song, D. 100
South Asia: economic growth 110
Spathi, C. 141, 143
speciesism 19, 20, 42, 48, 105, 111, 114, 115, 128, 131, 136, 141, 146, 147, 150, 163
SR *see* social responsibility (SR)
stakeholder management 54, 59, 73, 167
stakeholder vs shareholder orientation 66–80
Stiglitz, J. 125
Stone, G. C. 16n6
Stop Food Waste Day 160
sub-Saharan Africa: economic growth 110
Suffragette movement 19
Sunday Mirror 94
Sun, The 16n5, 90
sustainability 7, 8, 53, 54, 56, 63, 91, 133, 165
sustainable development 21, 56, 58, 59, 92, 123, 149, 165, 167

Tarascio, V. J. 51n9
Telegraph, The 16n5, 90
Tench, R. 9, 62, 89
Thatcher, M. 5, 37, 58, 63, 116, 119, 120, 165, 167
Thatcherism 58, 116, 120, 167
Three-Domain Model of CSR 72–73
Thunberg, G. 11, 149, 154
Thurman, N. 89
Times, The 16n5, 103
tokenism 93, 94
Trump, D. 125, 130–131
Twine, R. 48
Tyco 60, 75, 97n5
Tyndall Centre 56

UK 6; advertising industry 23; Brexit 10, 110, 111, 125; climate change 135; corporate social responsibility 54; economic growth 103; food waste 160; Government 64, 144; Great British Spring Clean (2019) 155; green policies 129; liberalisation 7; marketisation 7; media 85, 86, 90; plastic pollution 142, 144; position of women in organisations 92, 94; public polls 80; shopping behaviour 41, 51n7

Index 225

UNCED Earth Summit, Rio de Janeiro (1992) 56, 165
UNDP 22
UNFCCC *see* United Nations Framework Convention on Climate Change (UNFCCC)
United Nations (UN) 59, 130, 156, 167; Conference on the Law of the Sea 125; Environment Assembly 142
United Nations Framework Convention on Climate Change (UNFCCC) 125, 126, 168
UN *see* United Nations (UN)
US: corporate social responsibility 70; economic growth 103, 121n1, 124, 131; environmental damage 125–126; food waste 157; New Green Deal 132, 133, 135, 136; New Left 70; plastic pollution 142; scrutinisation of media 85

Value Maximization Proposition 76
Van Liedekerke, L. 81, 168
Van Sebille, E. 141, 143
veganism 42, 43
vegetarianism 42, 43
Villegas-Ortiz, L. 133
Von Werlhof, C. 39–40

Waitrose 146, 159

Walsh, J. P. 63
Ward, S. 84
Wargan, P. 132
Warren, K. J. 28
Watts, W. 100–101, 105
White, N. 33
Wilkes, M. S. 86
Wilson, E. 13–14
Windell, K. 9
Winter, J. 16n6
Wolf, N. 52n10
Woman and Nature 14
women: and corporate social responsibility 91–96; empowerment 22; equality of 2, 23, 24, 107, 114; inequality of 4, 23, 39; in journalism 94–95, 106
working rights 7
WorldCom 60, 75, 97n5
World Commission on Environment and Development 59, 167; Brundtland Report (1987) 56, 165
WRAP 144, 157

Xie, J. 92

YouGov 144

Zyglidopoulos, S. C. 9, 87